THE POLITICAL HISTORY OF ENGLAND.

Edited by the Rev. W. HUNT, D.Litt., and

REGINALD LANE POOLE, M.A., LL.D.

8vo.   12 vols.   7s. 6d. net per volume.

VOL. I. FROM THE EARLIEST TIMES TO THE NORMAN CONQUEST (to 1066). By THOMAS HODGKIN, D.C.L., Litt.D., Fellow of University College, London; Fellow of the British Academy. With 2 Maps.

VOL. II. FROM THE NORMAN CONQUEST TO THE DEATH OF JOHN (1066 to 1216). By GEORGE BURTON ADAMS, Professor of History in Yale University. With 2 Maps.

VOL. III. FROM THE ACCESSION OF HENRY III. TO THE DEATH OF EDWARD III. (1216 to 1377). By T. F. TOUT, M.A., Professor of Mediæval and Modern History in the University of Manchester, Fellow of the British Academy. With 3 Maps.

VOL. IV. FROM THE ACCESSION OF RICHARD II. TO THE DEATH OF RICHARD III. (1377 to 1485). By C. OMAN, M.A., LL.D., Chichele Professor of Modern History in the University of Oxford; Fellow of the British Academy. With 3 Maps.

VOL. V. FROM THE ACCESSION OF HENRY VII. TO THE DEATH OF HENRY VIII. (1485 to 1547). By H. A. L. FISHER, M.A., Fellow and Tutor of New College, Oxford; Fellow of the British Academy. With 2 Maps.

VOL. VI. FROM THE ACCESSION OF EDWARD VI. TO THE DEATH OF ELIZABETH (1547 to 1603). By A. F. POLLARD, M.A., Fellow of All Souls' College, Oxford; Professor of English History in the University of London. With 2 Maps.

VOL. VII. FROM THE ACCESSION OF JAMES I. TO THE RESTORATION (1603 to 1660). By F. C. MONTAGUE, M.A., Professor of History in University College, London, formerly Fellow of Oriel College, Oxford. With 3 Maps.

VOL. VIII. FROM THE RESTORATION TO THE DEATH OF WILLIAM III. (1660 to 1702). By RICHARD LODGE, M.A., LL.D., Professor of History in the University of Edinburgh; formerly Fellow of Brasenose College, Oxford. With 2 Maps.

VOL. IX. FROM THE ACCESSION OF ANNE TO THE DEATH OF GEORGE II. (1702 to 1760). By I. S. LEADAM, M.A., formerly Fellow of Brasenose College, Oxford. With 8 Maps.

VOL. X. FROM THE ACCESSION OF GEORGE III. TO THE CLOSE OF PITT'S FIRST ADMINISTRATION (1760 to 1801). By the Rev. WILLIAM HUNT, M.A., D.Litt., Trinity College, Oxford. With 3 Maps.

VOL. XI. FROM ADDINGTON'S ADMINISTRATION TO THE CLOSE OF WILLIAM IV.'s REIGN (1801 to 1837). By the Hon. GEORGE C. BRODRICK, D.C.L., late Warden of Merton College, Oxford, and J. K. FOTHERINGHAM, M.A., Magdalen College, Oxford; Lecturer in Classics at King's College, London. With 3 Maps.

VOL. XII. THE REIGN OF QUEEN VICTORIA (1837 to 1901). By SIDNEY LOW, M.A., Balliol College, Oxford; formerly Lecturer on History at King's College, London; and LLOYD C. SANDERS, B.A. With 3 Maps.

LONGMANS, GREEN AND CO., 39 Paternoster Row London;
New York, Bombay and Calcutta.

STANDARD HISTORICAL WORKS.

A HANDBOOK IN OUTLINE OF THE POLITICAL HISTORY OF ENGLAND TO 1906. Chronologically Arranged. By the Right Hon. A. H. DYKE ACLAND and CYRIL RANSOME, M.A. Crown 8vo, 6s.

ANNUAL REGISTER (THE). A Review of Public Events at Home and Abroad, for the year 1910. 8vo, 18s.

Volumes of the ANNUAL REGISTER for 1863-1909 can still be had. 18s. each.

THE HISTORY OF ENGLISH RATIONALISM IN THE NINETEENTH CENTURY. By ALFRED W. BENN. 2 vols. 8vo, 21s. net.

A HISTORY OF ENGLAND. By J. FRANCK BRIGHT, D.D. Crown 8vo.

Period I.—MEDIÆVAL MONARCHY: the Departure of the Romans to Richard III. From A.D. 449 to 1485. 4s. 6d.

Period II.—PERSONAL MONARCHY: Henry VII. to James II. From 1485 to 1688. 5s.

Period III.—CONSTITUTIONAL MONARCHY: William and Mary to William IV. From 1689 to 1837. 7s. 6d.

Period IV.—THE GROWTH OF DEMOCRACY: Victoria. From 1837 to 1880. 6s.

Period V.—IMPERIAL REACTION: Victoria. From 1880 to 1901. 4s. 6d.

HISTORY OF CIVILISATION IN ENGLAND AND FRANCE, SPAIN AND SCOTLAND. By HENRY THOMAS BUCKLE. 3 vols. Crown 8vo, 10s. 6d.

WORKS BY MANDELL CREIGHTON, D.D., LL.D.

HISTORY OF THE PAPACY FROM THE GREAT SCHISM TO THE SACK OF ROME (1378-1527). 6 vols. Crown 8vo, 5s. net each.

HISTORICAL ESSAYS AND REVIEWS. Crown 8vo, 5s. net.

HISTORICAL LECTURES AND ADDRESSES. Crown 8vo, 5s. net.

QUEEN ELIZABETH. With Portrait. Crown 8vo, 5s. net.

THE HISTORICAL GEOGRAPHY OF EUROPE. By EDWARD A. FREEMAN, D.C.L., LL.D. 8vo, 12s. 6d.

ATLAS to the above. With 65 Maps in Colour. 8vo, 6s. 6d.

WORKS BY JAMES A. FROUDE.

THE HISTORY OF ENGLAND, from the Fall of Wolsey to the Defeat of the Spanish Armada. 12 vols. Crown 8vo, 3s. 6d. each.

THE DIVORCE OF CATHERINE OF ARAGON. Crown 8vo, 3s. 6d.

THE SPANISH STORY OF THE ARMADA, and other Essays. Crown 8vo, 3s. 6d.

ENGLISH SEAMEN IN THE SIXTEENTH CENTURY. Crown 8vo, 3s. 6d. Illustrated Edition. With 5 Photogravures and 16 other Illustrations. Large crown 8vo, 6s. net.

THE ENGLISH IN IRELAND IN THE EIGHTEENTH CENTURY. 3 vols. Crown 8vo, 10s. 6d.

SHORT STUDIES ON GREAT SUBJECTS. 4 vols. Crown 8vo, 3s. 6d. each.

Pocket Edition. 5 vols. Fcp. 8vo, cloth, 2s. net each; leather, 3s. net each.

THE COUNCIL OF TRENT. Crown 8vo, 3s. 6d.

LIFE AND LETTERS OF ERASMUS. Crown 8vo, 3s. 6d.

CÆSAR: a Sketch. Crown 8vo, 3s. 6d.

LONGMANS, GREEN AND CO., 39 Paternoster Row, London;
New York, Bombay and Calcutta.

THE CONSTITUTIONAL HISTORY
OF ENGLAND

VOL. III.

THE
CONSTITUTIONAL HISTORY
OF ENGLAND

SINCE THE ACCESSION OF GEORGE III.

BY

SIR THOMAS ERSKINE MAY, K.C.B.
(LORD FARNBOROUGH)

Edited and Continued to 1911 by FRANCIS HOLLAND
In Three Volumes. 8vo
Vols. I. and II., 1760-1860. 15s. net
Vol. III., by FRANCIS HOLLAND, 1860-1911. 12s. 6d. net

LONGMANS, GREEN AND CO.
LONDON, NEW YORK, BOMBAY AND CALCUTTA

THE
CONSTITUTIONAL HISTORY
OF ENGLAND

SINCE THE ACCESSION OF GEORGE THE THIRD

BY THE RIGHT HON.
SIR THOMAS ERSKINE MAY, K.C.B., D.C.L.
(LORD FARNBOROUGH)

EDITED AND CONTINUED TO 1911 BY
FRANCIS HOLLAND

IN THREE VOLUMES
VOL. III.
BY
FRANCIS HOLLAND
1860-1911

LONGMANS, GREEN AND CO.
39 PATERNOSTER ROW, LONDON
NEW YORK, BOMBAY AND CALCUTTA
1912

All rights reserved

342.42
M451co
v.3

15 June '14
Hist.

125138

PREFACE

TO

THE THIRD VOLUME.

In writing a continuation of Sir Erskine May's history, I have thought it best to adhere to the general arrangement he adopted and, in his own words, "to deviate from a strictly chronological narrative" by devoting separate chapters to separate subjects. Some repetition is inseparable from this method. It has been my endeavour to avoid this as much as possible, not always, it is to be feared, with success. Another consequence has been that I have been obliged to leave out of its original place the supplementary chapter, containing a review of events between 1860 and 1870, which Sir Erskine May added to his later editions. But, in order to preserve as far as possible all the work of that eminent historian, the greater part of the supplementary chapter has been incorporated in the first and fourth chapters of the new volume.

My original idea was not only to adopt in the continuation the general form of Sir Erskine May's history, but also to make the successive subjects which he chose for his chapters the subjects respectively of the chapters in the new volume. But this soon appeared to be impracticable. The Crown alone is the subject of more than half of the first of his original three volumes. The reason of this is manifest. During the first half of the period which he treats, the Crown was the very centre of the constitutional struggle. Their position with regard to the Crown was the main dividing line between the two parties, at a time when the Tories, brought once more to Court by George III. after their long exile, sought with much temporary success to increase the royal power and influence, to limit which was the main object of the Whigs. But in the period under review in the third volume of this edition, there has been little or no change in the constitutional position of the Crown. There have been bold strokes of prerogative, such as the abolition of army purchase in 1871 by royal warrant, or the pressure brought to bear upon the peers to pass the Parliament Bill of 1911; but these have been made on the advice of constitutional Ministers who commanded the confidence of the House of Commons, and they were in no way associated with the personal will of the sovereign. The wise use of the influence of the Crown by Queen Victoria is admirably described by Sir Erskine May at the end of his second chapter; and her example has been followed by her successors. The position and influence of the Crown to-day remain very much what they were in 1861, when the death of the Prince Consort deprived the Queen of the councillor by whose advice and her own remarkable good sense she had impressed upon the monarchy what may prove to be its most lasting character. With regard to the House of Lords, for the sake of chronological sequence, and because the early proposals for reform were few and relatively unimportant, an account of those proposals has been combined with that of House of Commons reform in a single chapter, while in the last chapter the recent constitutional crisis has been separately treated.

To continue the work of a distinguished historian

is an arduous undertaking in which few have succeeded; but if a general sympathy with the outlook of an author were of itself a sufficient qualification for such a task, that at least, in the present instance, would not have been lacking. Sir Erskine May shared to the full the optimism conspicuous in the Whigs of his generation, and may be thought by some even to have overestimated the blessings to a nation derivable from a firm adherence to the principles of civil and religious liberty. Disliking democracy almost as much as arbitrary government, it was his fortunate lot to describe the gradual acceptance of these principles; and he ended the first edition of his history in 1861 when the Whigs were resting after their successful labours, with the aged and conservative Lord Palmerston at the helm. The enfranchised classes were then quite content with the existing social and political organisation, although ready enough that their representatives should level down any irregularities that might appear on the legal or constitutional surface. Lord Palmerston himself, as was observed by Bagehot, drove quite out of his mind all that was not immediately practicable; while whatever of the public attention was not engrossed by foreign affairs was chiefly given to theological controversy. On fundamentals there was perhaps less disagreement than in any earlier or later times. Toryism seemed practically extinct; the Whigs had "settled into office and were dumb". The death of Lord Palmerston broke up this halcyon epoch. The Reform Bill of 1867 was passed, and the winds were loosed from their bag; a new generation of statesmen arose to deal with new problems, and the era of democracy began. The vicissitudes of the constitutional struggle that ensued, with the gradual change in the political centre of gravity, it has been my endeavour in this volume to describe. There are many who, if living at the time when Sir Erskine May wrote the preface to his first volume, would have shared his cheerful outlook; but who would now regard the future with the distrust and despondency that he deprecated. Yet it can hardly be denied that the general state of the British people has been and is one of progressive improvement; and, if this be so, even pessimists must admit that the changes which they dislike have not hitherto justified their forebodings.

16th September, 1911.

CONTENTS

OF

THE THIRD VOLUME.

CHAPTER I.

Parliamentary Reform.

	PAGE
Political tranquillity under Lord Palmerston	1
Attempts to disturb the franchises of 1832	2
Dissolution of Parliament, 1865	2
Death of Lord Palmerston and revival of Parliamentary Reform	3
Earl Russell's Reform Bill	4
Resignation of the Russell Ministry	5
Hyde Park Riots	6
Mr. Disraeli's Reform resolutions	7
The Reform Bill of 1867	8
Redistribution of seats	9
Meeting in Hyde Park, 6th May, 1867	11
The Reform Bill in the Lords	12
Mr. Disraeli, Premier	13
The Scotch Reform Act, 1868	13
The Irish Reform Act, 1868	13
Election Petitions Act, 1868	14
Abolition of proxies	14
The two theories of representation	15
Change in the balance of power effected by the Reform Act of 1832	17
Parliamentary Government between 1832 and 1867	18
Effects of the Reform Act of 1867	20
The greater vicissitudes of opinion	21
The lesser vicissitudes	22
Lord Russell's Life-peerage Bill, 1869	23
Ballot Bill, 1870	25
Ballot Bill of 1871 rejected by the Lords	25
Ballot Act, 1872	26
Renewed proposals for reform in 1872	27
Mr. Trevelyan's Reform Bills and resolutions, 1873-1879	28
Movement in the country	30
Corrupt and Illegal Practices Act, 1883	31

CONTENTS

	PAGE
The Reform movement in 1883	33
The Franchise Bill of 1884	34
Franchise Bill rejected by the Lords	37
Intervention of the queen	38
The bill passed	39
Conservative character of the Act	39
The Redistribution of Seats Act, 1885	40
Reform proposals in the "Newcastle programme"	42
Registration Bill of 1894	43
Proposals for the reform of the House of Lords in 1888	44
Parliamentary Reform in abeyance, 1895-1905	45
Unionist movement for a fresh redistribution of seats	46
The proposals of 1905	47
The General Election of 1906	48
Plural Voting Bill rejected by the Lords	49
Contemplated Reform Bill postponed by constitutional crisis	50
Lord Newton's bill for the reform of the House of Lords	51
Report of the Select Committee on Reform	52
Liberal objections to the scheme	52
Liberal suggestions for re-constitution of a Second Chamber	53
Lord Rosebery's resolution	54
Electoral anomalies	55
Schemes for proportional representation	57
Women's suffrage	59
First stages of the movement	60
Proceedings in Parliament	62
Women's suffrage in the colonies	63
Progress of the movement at home	64
The Conciliation Committee and its bill	65

CHAPTER II.

PARTY.

The close of an era	67
The new leaders	67
Mr. Disraeli at Edinburgh, 1867	68
He becomes Premier, 1868	69
Parties and the Irish question	70
The General Election of 1868	72
Character of the new Parliament	73
Mr. Gladstone's first Ministry	75
Liberalism and the doctrine of *laissez-faire*	76
Growing unpopularity of the Government	79
Mr. Disraeli's speech at the Crystal Palace, 1872	80
The Conservative party and social reform	81
Mr. Disraeli refuses to take office on Mr. Gladstone's resignation in 1873	82
The last work of the Parliament of 1868	84
Unauthorised expenditure	84
The question of the vacation of Mr. Gladstone's seat on becoming Chancellor of the Exchequer, 1873	85

CONTENTS

	PAGE
The dissolution of 1874	86
Victory of the Conservatives	87
A third party	88
The Parliament of 1874	89
Whigs and Radicals	90
Mr. Chamberlain and the caucus	90
The Home Rule party in the House of Commons	92
Obstruction	94
Danger to party government	95
The case of John Mitchell	96
Victory of Liberals at election of 1880 and Mr. Gladstone's second administration	99
Weakness of the Government: its causes and significance	100
Obstruction of the Coercion Bill of 1881: debate closed by the Speaker	101
New rules of procedure in House of Commons	102
Their tendency and results	103
Rigidity of party ties increased by democracy	103
The "fourth party"	104
Lord Randolph Churchill and Tory democracy	105
Struggle for control over the party organisation	108
Change in the political centre of gravity	109
Mr. Chamberlain's independent action	109
The unauthorised programme	111
Defeat and resignation of the Government	112
Conservative relations to the Irish party in 1885	113
Open disagreement between Whigs and Radicals	113
Results of the election of 1885	114
Mr. Gladstone's conversion to Home Rule	115
His return to power: secession of the Whigs	116
The party split: adherence to Mr. Gladstone of the Liberal Associations	117
Dissolution of 1886 and Unionist victory	118
Lord Salisbury's second administration	119
Liberal policy of the Unionist Government	120
The Liberals in opposition: the Newcastle programme	121
The triumph and fall of Mr. Parnell	122
Mr. Gladstone's fourth administration	124
Action of the House of Lords: retirement of Mr. Gladstone	124
Lord Rosebery, Premier, 1894-95	125
The budget of 1894	126
Lord Salisbury's third administration	127
Depressed condition of the Liberal party	128
The Newcastle programme and the working classes	129
A period of prosperity and confidence	130
Reaction after the South African War	131
Retirement of Lord Salisbury, 1902	131
Mr. Chamberlain declares for Tariff Reform	132
Division in the Unionist party	133
Resignation of Mr. Chamberlain and of the Free Trade Ministers, September, 1903	134
Change in the character of the Conservative party	134
Resignation of Mr. Balfour, 1905	136

	PAGE
Liberal victory at election of 1906	136
Return of fifty-six Labour members	137
Origin and progress of the Labour party	137
The Trade Disputes Act, 1906	140
Legislation of the Liberal Government	140
New tendencies	141

CHAPTER III.

The Home Rule Movement.

The Fenian conspiracy and its effects	142
The Home Government Association founded	143
The Home Rule League, 1873	145
Mr. Butt's scheme of Federation	146
His action in the Parliament of 1874	147
Causes of his failure	147
The Parnellite group	148
Mr. Parnell	149
Breach between Mr. Butt and Mr. Parnell	150
Aims and methods of Mr. Parnell	151
The three movements	152
The "New Departure"	153
Foundation of the Land League, 1879	154
Mr. Parnell in the United States, 1879-1880	155
The General Election of 1880: Mr. Gladstone's address	156
Mr. Parnell chosen leader of the Home Rule party	157
The Lords reject Compensation for Disturbance Bill	158
Evictions and outrages: Habeas Corpus Act suspended	159
The Land Act of 1881	159
Arrest of Mr. Parnell	160
The Kilmainham Treaty	160
The Phœnix Park murders	161
Foundation of the National League	162
Position of Mr. Gladstone with regard to Home Rule	163
Mr. Chamberlain's scheme for a National Council	164
Defeat and resignation of the Government, 1885	165
The Conservative Government do not renew the Crimes Act	165
Moves and countermoves: Irish vote cast in favour of Conservatives	167
Results of General Election of 1885: Nationalist victories in Ireland	168
Mr. Gladstone forms a Home Rule Government	171
The Home Rule Bill of 1886	172
It is rejected on second reading by the House of Commons	175
The Land Purchase Bill	176
Unionist victory at General Election of 1886	176
Mr. Parnell's Tenants' Relief Bill rejected	176
The Land Act of 1887: revision of judicial rents	177
Crimes Act of 1887	177
The new closure rule	178
Closure by compartments	178
The Round Table Conference	179

	PAGE
"Parnellism and Crime": the forged letters	181
Report of the Special Commission	181
Death of Mr. Parnell	182
Mr. Gladstone's return to power, 1892	183
The Home Rule Bill of 1893 compared with that of 1886	183
It is passed by the Commons, but rejected by the Lords	184
Retirement of Mr. Gladstone, February, 1894	185
Irish policy of the Unionist Government of 1895	186
Report of the Financial Relations Commission	187
Irish Local Government Act, 1898	188
Establishment of Council of Agriculture, 1899	188
The United Irish League	189
Mr. Redmond elected leader of re-united Nationalist party	190
Origin of land purchase agreement	191
The Land Purchase Act, 1903	193
Devolution	194
Reports of the Irish Reform Association	195
Resignation of Mr. Wyndham	196
The Irish Councils Bill of 1907	197
Mr. Asquith's declaration at the Albert Hall	199
The Irish hold the balance in the Parliament of 1910	200

CHAPTER IV.

Religion and the State.

Relations of the State to religion	201
Modification of the idea of an Established Church	202
Church rates, 1866-68	203
Irish Church Question, 1868	204
Mr. Gladstone's resolutions	207
His Suspensory Bill rejected by the Lords	207
The dissolution of 1868	208
The Irish Church Bill, 1869	208
Question of concurrent endowment	209
The Lords' amendments: action of the queen	210
The bill passed	211
University Tests Act, 1871	212
Education of the people	213
Elementary Education Act, 1870	215
Irish University Education	217
Defeat of the Irish University Bill, 1873	218
The Endowed Schools Bill, 1874	219
The Public Worship Regulation Act, 1874	221
Mr. Bradlaugh elected member for Northampton, 1880	222
He claims to make affirmation	223
Select Committee reports against his claim	224
He is allowed neither to affirm nor take the oath	225
Subsequent proceedings	226
His re-elections and his eventual admission	226
Resolutions against him expunged, 1891	227

	PAGE
The Burials Act, 1880	228
Religious teaching in elementary schools: grievances of High Churchmen and Dissenters	229
School attendance made compulsory, 1880	229
Free education instituted, 1891	231
Education Bill of 1896	231
The Education Act of 1902	232
Nonconformist objections to the bill	233
The Education Bill of 1906	234
It is lost through a disagreement between the Houses	236
Later Education Bills proposed but not carried	237
The question of disestablishment	240
The Church in Wales	240
The Welsh Church Bill, 1909	241
Marriage with a deceased wife's sister legalised, 1907	242
Irish University Act, 1908	243
Amendment of the Royal Declaration	244

CHAPTER V.

LOCAL GOVERNMENT AFTER 1870.

State of Local Government in 1870	246
Creation of the Local Government Board, 1871	247
The Public Health Act, 1872	248
The Public Health Act, 1875	249
Quarter Sessions and County Rates	250
The Local Government Act, 1888	252
Withdrawal of the licensing clauses	253
The London County Council	254
The Local Government Act, 1894	256
Parish meetings and parish councils	258
Gradual organisation of local government	260
The London Government Act, 1899	261
The Metropolitan Water Board, 1902	262
Growth, decline, and revival of central control	262
Central control over poor law administration	264
Reports of the Poor Law Commission, 1905	266
Central control over other local bodies	266
Inspection and advice	267
Summary of results	269

CHAPTER VI.

REFORMS IN THE CIVIL SERVICE, THE ARMY, AND THE JUDICATURE

Liberalism and the doctrine of *laissez-faire*	270
Changes in the system of Civil Service appointments	271
Open competitive examinations established by Order in Council, 1870	272

CONTENTS

	PAGE
History of army purchase	273
The Government resolve to abolish the system, 1871	274
The Army Regulation Bill rejected by the Lords	275
Abolition of purchase by royal warrant	276
Mr. Cardwell's army reforms, 1870	277
Constitution of the Army Council and the Defence Committee, 1904	279
Reconstruction schemes of Mr. Brodrick and Mr. Arnold Forster	280
Mr. Haldane's reforms	280
The system of voluntary enlistment	281
Arguments for and against compulsory military service	282
The Courts of Law	283
Recommendations of the Judicature Commissioners, 1869	285
Judicature Act of 1873	286
Judicature Acts of 1875 and 1876	287
Admission of the evidence of prisoners, 1898	289
The Beck case	290
Institution of a Court of Criminal Appeal	291

CHAPTER VII.

THE SELF-GOVERNING COLONIES AFTER 1860.

Public opinion and the colonies in the mid-Victorian period	293
The three successive policies	295
Growth of the Imperial idea	296
French and English in Canada	297
Canadian federation	298
The Dominion of Canada Constitution Act, 1867	299
Movement in Nova Scotia against the Federation Act	300
Contrast between British policy with regard to Canada and to the other colonies	301
The Imperial connection in Australasia, how preserved	302
The constitutional crisis in Victoria, 1865	303
The crisis of 1878	304
The Victoria Parliament Bill, 1878	305
Despatch of Sir Michael Hicks Beach	306
Settlement of the dispute, 1881	308
Internal defence of self-governing colonies	308
Question of colonial contribution to Imperial defence	309
The first colonial conference meets, May, 1867	311
Conference at Ottawa, 1894	312
Mr. Chamberlain at the Colonial Office	312
The second Colonial Conference, 1897	313
The federation movement in Australia	315
The Commonwealth of Australia Act, 1900	316
Character of Australian federation	317
Origin of the jurisdiction of the Judicial Committee	318
Difference of opinion with regard to Appeals	320
Settlement by compromise	322
Proposed appellate tribunal for the Empire	322

xvi   CONTENTS

	PAGE
The Conference of 1902	323
The Conference of 1907	325
Proposal for an Imperial Council	326
British expansion in South Africa and its causes	328
Annexation of the Orange State and withdrawal, 1847-1854	328
Sir George Grey's policy of federation in 1858	329
Responsible government introduced into Cape Colony, 1872	329
Annexation of the Transvaal, 1877	330
The first Boer war and the Convention of Pretoria	331
Mr. Rhodes and his objects	332
The Jameson raid, the second Boer war, and the Peace of Vereeniging	333
Concession of self-government to the new colonies	334
Disappearance of early obstacles to Union of South Africa	335
Union of South Africa effected, 1909	336
The native question	338
Proposals for Imperial Federation	339
The question discussed	340

CHAPTER VIII.

THE PARLIAMENT BILL.

Action of the House of Lords during the Parliament of 1906	343
Difficulties of the Government	344
Sir Henry Campbell-Bannerman's resolution, 1907	346
Fall in land values and its consequences	350
The rival proposals for raising additional revenue	351
Claim of the Lords of a right to force a dissolution	352
Rejection of the Budget of 1909 by the House of Lords	353
Effect on finance	354
Resolution passed by the House of Commons	355
The General Election of January, 1910	355
Mr. Asquith's speech at the Albert Hall	356
Result of the General Election: questions at issue	357
Dissension among the Ministerialists in the new Parliament	359
Debate on the Address	360
Lord Rosebery's resolutions	362
Resolutions with regard to the relations between the two Houses passed by the House of Commons	362
The preamble of the Parliament Bill	364
Mr. Asquith's statement of action contemplated by Ministry	365
The Budget of 1909 agreed to by the Lords	366
Death of King Edward VII., 6th May	366
Conference of party leaders on constitutional question	366
Failure of the Conference to reach agreement	367
Ministers advise a dissolution	368
Lord Rosebery's resolution	369
Lord Lansdowne's resolutions	370
The policy of referendum adopted by the Unionist party	371
The General Election of December, 1910	372

	PAGE
The Parliament Bill passed by the Commons	372
Lord Balfour's bill for a referendum	373
Lord Lansdowne's bill for the re-constitution of the House of Lords	374
The Lords' amendments to the Parliament Bill	377
Ministers and the Opposition	378
Proposed creation of peers	379
Lord Lansdowne's advice to his followers	380
Vote of censure	381
The Commons disagree to amendments	382
The bill passed	382
Retrospect	383
Conclusion	384

CHAPTER I.[1]

PARLIAMENTARY REFORM.

THE period of Lord Palmerston's last administration was marked by unusual political tranquillity. The discussions upon Parliamentary reform in 1860 had failed to awaken any excitement, or even interest, in favour of further electoral changes. After thirty years of agitation and legislative activity the minds of men appeared to be at rest. The Crimean war and the Indian mutiny had served to divert public attention from domestic politics; and the great civil conflict in the United States engrossed the thoughts of all classes of Englishmen. *Political tranquillity under Lord Palmerston.*

Such being the sentiments and temper of the country, the venerable statesman who directed its policy, as First Minister, was little inclined to disturb them by startling experiments in legislation. No ruler was ever more impressed with the practical wisdom of the maxim "*quieta non movete*" than Lord Palmerston in the last years of his long political life. Originally an enlightened member of that party which had been opposed to change, he had developed into a member of the Liberal administration which had carried the Reform Act of 1832. Henceforward he frankly accepted the policy and shared the fortunes of the Liberal party until he became their popular leader. He had outlived some generations of his countrymen; he had borne a part in the political strifes of more than half a century; he had observed revolutions abroad and organic changes at home; and in these, his latter days, he was disposed, as well by conviction as by temperament, to favour political tranquillity. Of rare sagacity and ripe judg-

[1] The first eight pages of this chapter are in the main reproduced from the supplementary chapter which appeared in the later editions of Sir Erskine May's history. I was anxious to preserve that chapter in this edition, but it was impossible, consistently with the scheme of this volume, to retain it in the original form.

VOL. III. I

ment, it had long been his habit to regard public affairs from a practical rather than a theoretical point of view ; and the natural inertness of age could not fail to discourage an experimental policy.

The miscarriage of the Reform Bill of 1860 had demonstrated the composure of the public mind ; and Lord Palmerston perceived that in a policy of inaction he could best satisfy the present judgment of the country and his own matured opinions.

Such an attitude, if it alienated the more advanced section of his supporters, was congenial to the great body of the Whigs, and disarmed the Opposition, who were convinced that his rule would insure the maintenance of a Conservative policy.

Hence, during his life, the condition of the country may be described as one of political repose. There was no great agitation or popular movement ; no pressure from without ; while within the walls of Parliament this adroit and popular Minister contrived at once to attach his friends and conciliate his opponents.

Attempts to disturb the franchises of 1832.

The question of Parliamentary reform, now dropped by the Government, was occasionally pressed forward by other members. In 1861 Mr. Locke King sought to lower the county franchise to £10, and Mr. Baines to reduce the borough franchise to £6 ; but neither of these proposals found favour with the House of Commons. Again, in 1864, these proposals were repeated, without success, though supported by strong minorities. Meanwhile, reformers were perplexed by the utterances of statesmen. The veteran reformer, Earl Russell, had lately counselled the people of Scotland to " rest and be thankful," while Mr. Gladstone earnestly advocated the claims of working men to the suffrage.

In 1865 Mr. Baines's bill revived the discussion of Parliamentary reform. Though supported by Government it was defeated by a considerable majority. The debate was signalised by a protest against democracy by Mr. Lowe, which foreshadowed his relations to his own party and to the cause of reform at no distant period.

Dissolution of Parliament, 1865.

After this session, Parliament, which had exceeded the usual span of Parliamentary life,[1] was dissolved. The elections were

[1] Upwards of six years.

not marked by the excitements of a severe party conflict; no distinct issue was referred to the constituencies; and general confidence in Lord Palmerston was relied upon by candidates rather than any special policy; but the Liberal party gained a considerable accession of strength.

There was, however, one memorable election. Mr. Gladstone, who had represented the University of Oxford for eighteen years, lost his seat, and was returned for South Lancashire. As member for the University his career was always restrained and trammelled: as member for a great manufacturing and commercial county, he was free to become the leader of the Liberal party. *Mr. Gladstone rejected by the University of Oxford.*

At length in October, 1865, the aged Premier died, at the summit of his power and popularity; and at once a change came over the national councils. He was succeeded by Earl Russell, the acknowledged leader of the Whigs, and the statesman most associated with Parliamentary reform. He had felt deeply the loss of his own measure in 1860, and the subsequent relations of Lord Palmerston's Government to its policy. They had fought their way into office as champions of reform, and at the first check had abandoned it. For five years they had been content to rule and prosper, without doing further homage to that cause; and now Earl Russell, Mr. Gladstone, and other members of the Cabinet would no longer submit to the reproach of insincerity. Nor was a change of policy, at this time, dictated merely by a sense of honour and consistency. It rested upon a continued conviction of the necessity of such a measure, in the interests of the State, and in fulfilment of obligations which Parliament, no less than Ministers, had assumed. And further it was deemed politic, with a view to satisfy the long-deferred hopes of the more advanced members of the Liberal party who had been the chief gainers by the Liberal successes at the preceding election. Accordingly, in the autumn, Earl Russell announced that the consideration of reform would be renewed in the approaching session. *Death of Lord Palmerston. Earl Russell Premier.* *Revival of Parliamentary Reform.*

There were, however, some considerations, not sufficiently weighed at the time, which had a disastrous influence over the fate of Ministers, and of the measure to which they stood committed. Parliament had recently been dissolved, while *Considerations adverse to its settlement.*

Lord Palmerston was still Minister, and reform had been treated, upon the hustings, with little more earnestness than in the House of Commons. Hence the cause was without the impulse of a popular demand. Again, a large proportion of the members returned at the general election, sharing the sentiments of Lord Palmerston and the late Parliament, had no inclination to disturb the political calm of the past few years. But above all, in this, the first session of a new Parliament, members were invited to recast the constitution of the House of Commons, many of them to forfeit their seats, and all to return speedily to their constituents. The political situation, indeed, may be compared to a feast offered to guests who had lately dined.

Earl Russell's Reform Bill. At the first meeting of the Cabinet after Lord Palmerston's funeral, Ministers had taken means to collect ample electoral statistics:[1] and early in the session of 1866 were prepared to submit their proposals to Parliament. Warned by the obstacles which a comprehensive measure had encountered in 1860, they confined their scheme to a revision of the franchise, reserving for another session the embarrassing problem of a redistribution of seats. It was proposed to reduce the occupation franchise in counties to £14 annual value, and in boroughs to £7. The addition to the voters was estimated at 400,000, of which one-half would be working men. This measure, however moderate and cautious, was at once beset with difficulties. Though falling short of the views of Mr. Bright and the Radicals, it was supported by them as an "honest measure". But it was denounced by the Conservatives, and even by several Whigs, as democratic and revolutionary; and an alarming defection soon disclosed itself in the Ministerial ranks. Comprising about forty members, it numbered among its leaders Mr. Lowe, Mr. Horsman, Mr. Laing, Lord Elcho, Earl Grosvenor, and Lord Dunkellin. This party was humorously compared by Mr. Bright with those who had gathered in the "cave of Adullam," by which name it was henceforth familiarly known.

Earl Grosvenor's amendment. The first weak point in the scheme which was assailed was the omission of a redistribution of seats. This was

[1] Mr. Gladstone's speech on introducing the English Reform Bill, 12th March, 1866.

brought to an issue by an amendment of Earl Grosvenor, on the second reading of the bill, when Ministers, after a spirited debate of eight nights, and in a very full House, escaped defeat by five votes only.[1] Deferring to the opinion of so large a minority, Ministers promised a bill for the redistribution of seats, and reform bills for Scotland and Ireland, before they proceeded with the original measure.

On the 7th May these bills were introduced. By the Redistribution of Seats Bill, thirty boroughs having a population under 8000 lost one member, and nineteen other seats were obtained by the grouping of smaller boroughs—forty-nine seats being available for larger places. Though sharply criticised, this bill was read a second time without a division: but Ministers were obliged to agree to a proposal of Mr. Bouverie to refer it and the Franchise Bill to the same committee, with a view to their consolidation. Nor was this all; the measure was already too large to be fully discussed, when Sir R. Knightley carried an instruction to the committee by a majority of ten, to provide for the better prevention of bribery and corruption at elections. *Bills for the franchise and re-distribution of seats united.*

In committee Lord Stanley moved, without notice, the postponement of the franchise clauses; but was defeated by a majority of twenty-seven. Mr. Walpole moved that the occupation franchise in counties should be raised to £20, and his amendment was lost by fourteen votes only. Mr. Hunt proposed that the county franchise should be based on rating instead of rental and was resisted by a majority of seven; and lastly, Lord Dunkellin moved a similar amendment in regard to boroughs, which was carried against the Government by a majority of eleven. *Continued opposition to the bill.*

Ministers now perceived that the game was lost. They had declared their resolution to stand or fall by their bill; and its fate was beyond hope of recovery. They submitted their resignation to the queen, who hesitated to accept it; and a vote of confidence was about to be moved with a view to re-establish them, when they finally determined to resign.[2] Their defeat, indeed, had been sustained upon a question of second- *Resignation of Ministers.*

[1] Ayes, 318; noes, 313.
[2] Mr. Crawford, member for the City of London, was on the point of rising to give notice of a vote of confidence, when he received a letter from Earl Russell announcing his resignation.

ary importance, and might have been repaired at a later stage of the bill: but they had been sorely pressed on other occasions, their party was disorganised and broken up, it was plainly impossible to pass the bill, and they could not abandon it without discredit.

Earl of Derby Premier, 1866.
Such was the issue of this infelicitous measure. A strong Ministry was ruined; a triumphant party overthrown; and the minority again placed in power, under the Earl of Derby and Mr. Disraeli. But events of higher importance resulted from the miscarriage of this measure. For some years reformers had been indifferent and inert; when Earl Russell promised reform, they trusted him, and were calm and hopeful; but now that he had been driven from power, and supplanted by the opponents of reform, they became restless and turbulent. The spirit of democracy was again awakened, and the new Government were soon brought into collision with it. A meeting in Hyde Park had been announced by the Reform League for the 23rd of July, as a demonstration in favour of an extension of the suffrage. Ministers being advised that the Crown had power to prevent such a meeting in a Royal park,[1] and fearful of a disturbance to the public peace, instructed the police to close the gates of the park, and prevent the entrance of the multitude expected to assemble there. The gates were accordingly barred; and the leaders of the League, on being refused admittance, proceeded, according to previous arrangement, to Trafalgar Square to hold their meeting. Meanwhile, the park gates were securely held, and a considerable police force was collected inside. But the vast enclosure was without protection, and the mob, pulling down the railings, rushed through every breach, and took forcible possession of the park. Democracy had overcome the Government; and the maintenance of order was afterwards due, as much to the exertions of Mr. Beales and the Reform League, as to the police.

Popular agitation.

Hyde Park riots, 23rd July, 1866.

Impulse given to reform.
These events increased the public excitement, and en-

[1] This right had been affirmed in 1856 by an opinion of the law officers of the Crown, Sir A. Cockburn and Sir R. Bethell, and of Mr. Willes. Mr. Walpole, the Home Secretary, was of opinion that "the right thing to do was to allow the meeting to take place, and merely suppress any symptoms of disorder". But he was over-ruled by his colleagues.—See Walpole's *History of Twenty-five Years*, ii. 173.

couraged the activity of the reformers. Several important meetings and popular demonstrations were held, which stirred the public mind: while political uneasiness and discontents were aggravated by commercial distress and an indifferent harvest.

Public opinion had, at length, been aroused in favour of reform: a meeting of the Reform League was held in the Guildhall at which the Lord Mayor himself presided, while Mr. Bright, the most eloquent and popular of the Radical leaders, addressed great popular assemblies in support of residential manhood suffrage and the ballot, at Manchester, Birmingham, Leeds, Glasgow, and Dublin. But the House of Commons had lately shown its disinclination to deal with the question; and the party of which the new Ministry was composed, aided by a strong body of Whigs, had defeated Earl Russell's moderate measure, as revolutionary. Would Ministers resist reform, and count upon the support of their new allies: or venture upon another Reform Bill, and trust for success to adroit management and the divisions in the Liberal party? Position of Ministers in regard to reform.

These questions were set at rest at the opening of the session, by the announcement of a Reform Bill in the queen's speech. No position could be more embarrassing for a Government. In a minority of seventy in the House of Commons, representing a party opposed to the principles of reform, brought into power by resisting such a measure when offered by the late Government, confronted by a strong party in the House pledged to reform, and by popular agitation: in what manner could they venture to approach this perilous question? At first they invited the House no longer to treat reform as a party question, but to concert a satisfactory measure in friendly consultation; and for this purpose they offered to submit resolutions as the basis of a bill. Such a course was naturally objected to as designed to evade Ministerial responsibility; and when the resolutions appeared they proved too vague and ambiguous for effective discussion. In explaining them, indeed, Mr. Disraeli sketched the outline of the Ministerial scheme: but they were eventually withdrawn; and Ministers were forced to commit themselves to more definite proposals. And here the difficulties of their position were disclosed by the resignation of three members of the Cabinet—the Earl of Carnarvon, Lord Cranborne, and General Peel. Their reluctance had already induced the Government to sketch out a less bold scheme than their colleagues had been prepared to propose; and their retirement, otherwise a source of weakness, now enabled the Cabinet to agree upon a more extended measure.

<small>Earl of Derby's Reform Bill.</small>
At length, on the 18th March, the bill which had caused so much expectation was introduced. The franchise was granted in boroughs to every householder paying rates who had resided for two years: in counties to every occupier rated at £15; and there were added various franchises, based upon education and the payment of taxes. As a counterpoise to the extended occupation suffrage, a scheme of dual voting was proposed for voters of a higher qualification. There was to be a redistribution of thirty seats. The Conservative Ministers, guided by Mr. Disraeli, had come to the conclusion that no resting-place was possible short of household suffrage, and they hoped to combine this with the creation of other suffrages which would have left the working classes in a voting minority, and consolidated the electoral power of the middle classes. These calculations, however, were frustrated by the position in which Lord Derby and Mr. Disraeli found themselves.

<small>Surrender of the securities and compensations.</small>
When the Russell Ministry resigned in June, 1866, their successors had taken office with the fixed resolution that they would not repeat the humiliating experiences of 1852 and 1858, and merely act as a stopgap until the Liberal chiefs had had time to compose their differences and were ready to return to power. But they had failed to persuade Mr. Lowe and other dissentient Liberals to join the Cabinet, and were in a minority of nearly seventy in the House of Commons. Thus, when the bill of 1867 was introduced, and when the attempt to commit the whole House to a scheme by means of resolutions and so to carry a measure by consent had failed, power and responsibility were found to be divided. Power was in the hands of Mr. Gladstone; while responsibility rested lightly on the shoulders of Mr. Disraeli. The inconvenience of this state of things was soon apparent. Mr. Disraeli was determined to succeed where so many had failed, and to pass a Reform Bill into law. But to do this he was compelled to surrender all those "safeguards" by which he had recommended the

measure to his party, and to consent to "household suffrage pure and simple" in direct contradiction to the declaration he had made in the debate on the introduction of the bill. Of the ten demands made by Mr. Gladstone at an early stage in the discussions the only one of a Conservative tendency was to exclude the poorest class of voters—those below the £5 rating limit—from the franchise. This was defeated; but the other nine were conceded. The dual vote, a proposal to give an additional vote to payers of direct taxes of the annual amount of twenty shillings, was abandoned; the two years' qualifying residence was reduced to one; the lodger's franchise was introduced; the important distinction between the compound householder, who compounded with his landlord for the payment of rates, and whom it was originally proposed to exclude from the franchise, and the non-compounder was removed; the tax franchises and other "fancy franchises" disappeared; the occupation franchise in counties was reduced; and the voting papers were given up. However much they disapproved of the bill, Liberals felt that they could hardly resist changes sanctioned by Conservatives; and could only show their distinctive principles by sweeping away the safeguards with which their opponents had thought fit to hedge round a democratic measure. "We are about," said Mr. Lowe, in the debate on the third reading, "to enter upon a new era, when the bag which holds the winds will be untied and we shall be surrounded by a perpetual whirl of change, alteration, innovation, and revolution." By the bill in its final shape *The ultimate form of the bill.* household suffrage with a qualifying residence of one year was established in boroughs; a lodger franchise of £10 was added; and a £12 occupation franchise given to the counties, while the £10 qualification for owners and long leaseholders was reduced to £5.

The scheme for the redistribution of seats was also enlarged by the increase in the number of seats redistributed from thirty to fifty-two. On May 31st Mr. Laing had carried against the Government an amendment in committee to deprive of one member all boroughs which, at the census of 1861, had a population of less than 10,000; and this defeat obliged ministers to re-model their scheme. Twenty-five seats were added to the county representation; nine new boroughs *Re-distribution of seats.*

returned members; the great towns were given additional seats; and the Universities of London, Edinburgh, and Glasgow were also enfranchised.[1]

Every provision, indeed, which had reconciled Conservatives to the measure was struck out; every amendment urged by the Liberal party was grafted upon the bill. And thus the House of Commons found itself assenting, inch by inch, to an extended scheme of reform, which neither Conservatives nor Whigs wholly approved. Parties had been played off against one another, until a measure which gratified none but advanced reformers—probably not more than a sixth of the House of Commons—was accepted, as a necessity, by all.

While the bill was under discussion in the House of Com-

[1] Redistribution of seats by the Acts of 1867 and 1868.

ENGLAND.

Disfranchisement.

6 boroughs returning 2 members } totally disfranchised . .	17
5 ,, ,, 1 member }	
35 ,, ,, 2 members, deprived of 1 member each	35
	—52

Enfranchisement.

London University to return 1 member	1
Salford to return 2 members instead of 1	1
Leeds, Liverpool, Birmingham, Manchester, 3 members instead of 2	4
Chelsea and Hackney to return 2 each	4
9 other new boroughs to return 1 each	9
	—19
Yorkshire (West Riding) to be divided into three divisions instead of two, each returning 2 members . . .	2
Lancashire to be divided into four divisions, each returning 2 members instead of North two and South three . . .	3
10 counties to be divided into three instead of two divisions, each returning 2 members	20
	—25
	+19
	44

The 8 seats thus lost were apportioned thus:—

An additional member to Merthyr-Tydvil	1
2 new Scotch University constituencies, each 1 member . .	2
Additional members to Glasgow and Dundee	2
3 counties (Aberdeen, Ayr, Lanark) divided into two divisions, returning 1 each	3
Perthshire and Selkirkshire to return 1 member conjointly instead of 1 each	1—2
A member for the Border Burghs	1
	—8

mons the public excitement gave an impulse to the Liberal **Meeting in Hyde Park, 6th May, 1867.** party in passing every amendment favourable to extended franchises. And one remarkable episode illustrated at once the strength of popular sentiment, and the impotence of the executive Government to resist it. A great demonstration in favour of reform was announced to take place on the 6th May in Hyde Park, when Mr. Walpole, the Home Secretary, in deference to a decision of the Cabinet and against his own judgment, issued notices stating that the use of the park for the holding of such meeting was not permitted, and warning all persons to refrain from attending it.[1] But, in spite of these notices, the meeting was held, and large assemblages of people occupied the park without disorder or disturbance.

The right of the Government to prohibit the meeting was contested, not only by Mr. Beales and the Reform League, but by Mr. Bright and many other members of the Liberal party. On the other hand, the conduct of the Government in first prohibiting the meeting—for the notices issued to warn persons of the consequences of attending the meeting were interpreted as a prohibition—and then allowing it to take place, in defiance of their authority, was censured as bringing the executive into contempt. Mr. Walpole, a man of a highly-strung and vulnerable temperament, bowed to the storm; and, in spite of the friendly remonstrances of Lord Derby, to whom such sensitiveness was incomprehensible, and who was aware that his own share in the responsibility for the issue of the notices had been greater than that of the Home Secretary, persisted in resigning his office, though he consented to retain his seat in the Cabinet.

Meanwhile, the state of the law in reference to the use of **Unsatisfactory state of the law.** the parks for public meetings was so unsatisfactory that the Government had brought in a bill to prohibit, under the penalties of a misdemeanour, the holding of any meeting in the royal parks without the consent of the Crown. This bill, being violently opposed, was overtaken by the close of the session and abandoned; and the law was left uncertain and incapable of enforcement until 1872, when a bill was passed to enable the Office of Works to regulate public meetings by

[1] For the difference of opinion between Mr. Walpole and his colleagues, see *History of Twenty-five Years*, ii. 197.

rules subject to revision in Parliament. It cannot be questioned that the meetings of 1866, and 1867, should either have been allowed, or effectually prevented. The latter course could only be taken at the risk of bloody collisions with the people; and, accordingly, such meetings, having since been permitted, have been held with little resulting inconvenience, and with scarcely any influence on the action of Governments.

Proceedings in the Lords upon the Reform Bill.

In the House of Lords, where the Reform Bill, had it not been introduced by a Conservative Government, would probably have been rejected, or at least amended so drastically as to secure its withdrawal, several amendments were made; but the only one of importance agreed to by the Commons was a clause of Lord Cairns, providing, with a view to the representation of minorities, that in places returning three members no elector should vote for more than two candidates. This clause was hotly denounced by Mr. Bright and the Radicals, who held that its practical effect would be to deprive the great towns affected of two-thirds of their representative strength, since the member whom the system enabled the minority to return to Parliament would neutralise the voting power of one of the members chosen by the majority. The Liberal party were never reconciled to this experiment, and it did not survive the next Redistribution Act in 1885. One important effect it had, for it was the immediate cause of the foundation of that local Liberal Association at Birmingham, which, under the nickname of the caucus, was destined to play so prominent a part in the political history of the next generation. This was originally formed with a view so to distribute Radical votes as to secure to that party all the three seats at Birmingham. After the successful accomplishment of this result the machinery created for a single object was kept in being, improved, and employed to further the general objects of the party.

Dissolution no longer to follow the demise of the Crown.

One other constitutional change effected by the Act of 1867 remains to be noticed. Until the end of the seventeenth century the death of the sovereign of itself dissolved Parliament. By a clause in an Act passed in the reign of Queen Anne the Parliament existing at the demise of the Crown might continue for a term of six months and no longer. At the instance of Lord Stanhope, a clause was now introduced into the Reform Act to repeal this clause and to remove all limitation of the duration of Parliament connected with the demise of the Crown.

The scheme of enfranchisement was not yet complete. The settlement of the boundaries of boroughs and the divisions of counties was referred to a commission, and the consideration of the Reform Bills for Scotland and Ireland was postponed until the next session. Boundaries of boroughs and counties.

Before these measures were introduced, in 1868, the Earl of Derby was obliged by ill-health to retire, and was succeeded as Premier by Mr. Disraeli, to whose extraordinary tact, judgment, and address the passing of the English Reform Act was acknowledged to be due. Many difficult questions remained to be settled, which needed the exercise of all his abilities. The Scotch Reform Bill, founded generally upon the same principles as the English bill, proposed an increase of seven members to represent Scotland. This provision contemplated an addition to the number of the House of Commons, which was resisted; and justice to the claims of Scotland was eventually met by the disfranchisement of seven English boroughs having less than 5000 inhabitants; and in this form the bill for the representation of Scotland was passed. Resignation of Earl of Derby. Mr. Disraeli Premier. The Scotch Reform Act, 1868.

The Reform Bill for Ireland left the county franchise unaltered, reduced the borough franchise, and proposed a partial redistribution of seats, which was shortly abandoned. By an Act passed in 1850 an occupation franchise of £12 based on rating had been created for county voters in Ireland and an occupation franchise at the value of £8 had been likewise given to the boroughs. The county franchise therefore already stood at the same point at which it was fixed for England by the Act of 1867, and thus no change was needed. The franchise in boroughs was reduced from £8 to £4, that figure being chosen because in Ireland poor rates in respect of tenements valued at or below £4 were paid by the owner, and not by the occupier. To lodgers the right of voting was given on the same terms as in England. It was calculated that the effect of the bill would be to increase by about 9,313 the existing number of 30,700 borough electors in Ireland. The measure, avowedly incomplete, and unequal to the English and Scottish schemes, was nevertheless assented to, The Irish Reform Act, 1868.

as at least a present settlement of a question beset with exceptional difficulties.

The boundaries of the English boroughs and the new divisions of the counties, were still to be settled; and, after an inquiry by a select committee, the boundaries, as defined by the commissioners, were, with several modifications, agreed to.

<small>Election petitions and Corrupt Practices Act, 1868.</small> The series of measures affecting the electoral system was not even yet concluded. A measure was, after long discussions, agreed to, for transferring the cherished jurisdiction of the Commons, in matters of election, to judges of the superior courts. A Select Committee of the House of Commons had, in 1867, reported in favour of this course, recommending that the judge by whom the case was tried should be given power to decide on both the facts and the law, and should also report on the prevalence of bribery in the constituency inculpated. After much discussion and negotiation caused by objections expressed by the judges to the proposed arrangement, and after the withdrawal of several alternative schemes, an act was eventually passed under which election petitions are tried by two judges selected from a rota formed by the judges of the superior courts. The act proved very successful, and imputations of party bias in the trial of petitions have from the time of its passage almost entirely disappeared. Lastly, a bill was passed to facilitate the registration of the year, so as to insure the election of a Parliament during the autumn by the new electors.

<small>The abolition of proxies.</small> A reform in the procedure of the House of Lords of no great practical importance, but of some constitutional interest, synchronised with these great changes in the constitution of the House of Commons. Early in the session of 1868 the Lords abandoned one of their most ancient privileges—the right of voting by proxy. Historical philosophers contended that this privilege was analogous to that enjoyed by the Estate of the Commons, who, being too numerous to assemble like a Polish diet in their own persons at Westminster, were represented there by proxies. They pointed out that originally the privilege belonging to a peer of voting by proxy could only be exercised by the permission of the Crown—a permission given to meet the convenience of peers absent from the country on important public business—just as the Commons could not

choose proxies to represent them in the Lower House except on the issue of writs from the Crown in Chancery. But the royal assent had long been dispensed with; the origin of the right was forgotten; and its exercise had been restricted by orders that no peer should hold more than two proxies and that these proxies should not be used in Committees or when the House sat as a Court of Appeal. It was felt to be anomalous that a peer, perhaps in a distant country, should be able to vote by proxy on a question to the discussion of which he had not listened; although in fact a large proportion of the members of the House of Commons and a smaller proportion of those of the House of Lords do, habitually, without the aid of proxies, vote in divisions after debates from which they have been absent. Accordingly, on the recommendation of a Select Committee, a Standing Order was passed by general consent to provide: "That the practice of calling for proxies on a division be discontinued, and that two days' notice be given of any motion for the suspension of this order". Thus the privilege was not technically abandoned; but there was a common understanding that its exercise should never be revived.

The change in the balance of constitutional forces brought about by the Reform Act of 1867 was hardly less important in its results than that which followed the great measure of 1832. Since the middle of the eighteenth century there have been two conflicting theories concerning the nature of electoral power. On the one hand it has been considered as a trust conferred on certain carefully-selected categories of persons who were held to be most likely to exercise it for the common advantage. There were the freeholders of land whose interest in the prosperity of the country was deemed to be more permanent and insoluble than that of other persons, and there were the owners of other forms of property, who, being with the freeholders the principal contributors to the national revenue, were admitted to the franchise on the historic ground that representation should accompany taxation. The representatives whom they chose were not delegates, but rather plenipotentiaries, and were held to represent the Commons of England much more than the localities which returned them to Parliament. That the electors were the persons best fitted

The two theories of representation.

to choose worthy representatives of the nation was taken to be the justification of their privilege. The franchise, in this view, was regarded as a part of the constitutional machinery designed to a certain end—that end being the production of an assembly in which all national interests were adequately represented; and it was contended that it was by no means clear that this object could be better secured by extending the suffrage to persons whose circumstances rendered it unlikely that they could form any clear notions of national expediency. "The distribution of political power in the community," said Mr. Disraeli in 1874, "is an affair of convention, and not an affair of moral or abstract right, and it is only in this sense that we can deal with it."[1] Perhaps the underlying assumption in this theory is that the existing social organisation is on the whole the best possible, and that consequently to give the suffrage to those on whom it bears hardly is a dangerous policy. By the supporters of the opposite view, the member of Parliament is considered rather as a delegate of his constituents than as a national representative, and his main duty is to further their interests and enforce their views. From this standpoint the greater the grievances of a class, the more does it need representation; a position precisely the opposite to that which connects the continued prosperity of a country with the exclusive representation in the political assembly of its more prosperous citizens. Thus the suffrage appears as a natural and individual right whether it be conceded or withheld. Even in the eighteenth century this view found its advocates, and was made popular by the writings of Rousseau; but its formulation by the cruel demagogues of the French Revolution, together with the combined reasoning and rhetoric of Burke, produced a reaction, and, in England, although the leading Whig reformers advocated their cause on quite other principles, delayed the advent of reform.

Character of the franchise of 1832.

The authors of the Act of 1832 regarded that measure as a final settlement, and it was far from their intention to transfer the right to be represented from property to the individual. On the contrary, the suffrage was made to rest strictly on a property or rental qualification, and the few

[1] Selected Speeches, vol. i., p. 625.

existing electoral privileges of the working classes where they survived at Preston, Coventry, and other places, were seriously curtailed. But the excellent results of that measure, especially when contrasted with the dire prophecies of national ruin made at the time of its enactment, caused men to augur equally happy consequences from a further extension of the suffrage and qualified their faith in the theory of Burke. In 1864 Mr. Gladstone, in words that may be contrasted with those already quoted from Mr. Disraeli, said: "I venture to say that every man who is not personally incapacitated by some consideration of personal unfitness or of political danger is morally entitled to come within the pale of the constitution".[1] Yet his proposal in 1866 to lower the borough franchise from £10 to £7 householders hardly gave effect to this principle.

By the Reform Act of 1832 the powers previously exercised by an incongruously selected and very small electorate, over which the Crown exerted a paramount influence, were transferred to the middle classes. Before 1830 the confidence of the House of Commons, recognised since the Revolution of 1688 as essential to the continued existence of a Ministry, almost invariably followed the choice of the Crown, whereas since that date the choice of the Crown has followed the direction given by the House of Commons. No instance can be cited before 1830 in which the King's Ministers appealed in vain to the constituencies. Whatever the composition of the House of Commons at the time of the dissolution—even if, as in 1784, 1806, and again in 1807, a hostile majority had rendered the dissolution necessary—the king was always able to obtain for the Ministers of his choice—whether Whig or Tory —a majority at the polls. When in 1812 the Prince Regent was accused of bad faith in not dismissing his Tory ministers and bringing his old allies the Whigs into office, it was never even suggested that he would have had any difficulty in securing for them a majority in the House of Commons. This state of things was entirely changed by the Act of 1832. When William IV., who perhaps had not perceived the change that had taken place in the political centre of gravity, dismissed the Whigs in 1834, and called Sir Robert Peel into

Change in the balance of power effected by the Reform Act of 1832.

[1] Life of Gladstone, vol. ii., p. 126.

power, his Minister was left in a minority in the election which followed, and for the first time in our political history a Ministry was compelled to resign office as the direct result of a general election. Thus the principal constitutional effect of the Act of 1832 was to transfer the selection of Ministers, so far as their political character was concerned, from the Crown to the House of Commons. The first great extension of the suffrage made the electorate independent of the Crown; the next great extension was destined to bring the House of Commons under the control of the electorate.

Government of England between 1832 and 1867.

The middle classes, to whom a general political control had been transferred by the Act of 1832, made a good use of their privilege. In the opinion of Mr. Lecky the world has never seen a better constitution than England enjoyed between the Reform Act of 1832 and the Reform Act of 1867;[1] while even Mr. Gladstone, writing in 1877, in the course of an article in which he defended the policy of a yet wider extension of the suffrage against the attacks of Mr. Lowe, made the significant admission that in his judgment, "as a whole, our level of public principle and public action was at its zenith in the twenty years or so which succeeded the Reform Act of 1832, and that it has since perceptibly gone down".[2] The first Reform Act had no effect on the composition of Governments. The class of men who had governed the country before 1832 continued to govern it after that date; nor, during the whole period, can a single Cabinet be cited the composition of which was materially affected by the enlargement of the constituency. The middle classes were unorganised and sent few of their own order to represent them in Parliament. Some rich men of the middle class no doubt found their way into the House of Commons to whom it would have been difficult to find seats before 1832; but they entered it at an advanced age, they had had no political education, and they could not, therefore, aspire to office. No definite programmes of legislation were submitted to the electorate, and consequently electors had no share in the initiation of laws. The question they had to decide at a general election was whether the one of the two parties which happened to hold power at the time of the dissolution should continue in

---

[1] Democracy and Liberty, i. 21.
[2] Nineteenth Century, vol. ii., p. 554, November, 1877.

office or give place to its rival; and, with the single exception of the election of 1841, they always voted by a small majority for the Whigs. The broad general principles of the two parties they knew, or they imagined they knew, but there was scarcely any bidding for their support by engagements to legislate in their particular interests as a class on the part of the rival leaders. A House of Commons, once elected, had much more freedom of action than it has now. The Government did not regard a defeat in the House, except on very crucial matters, as a summons to resign or to dissolve, since the majority was held to have been chosen to exercise a general control over legislation and administration, and, while maintaining the general principles of the party, by no means to be bound to endorse all the actions and legislation of particular Ministries. Thus in 1850 the Russell Ministry was defeated in twelve divisions, in 1851 in thirteen; in each of the sessions of 1853 and 1854 the Aberdeen Ministry was defeated fifteen times; and Lord Palmerston, in spite of his great popularity, sustained with much cheerfulness an equal number of reverses in 1856. A political campaign conducted by Cabinet Ministers or ex-Cabinet Ministers in furtherance of some legislative project was unknown. Statesmen occasionally made speeches at banquets or in their constituencies, and at such times sometimes took the country into their confidence as to the measures they intended to produce; but, as was truly observed by Bagehot, "the mass of the 'ten-pound' householders did not really form their own opinions, and did not exact of their representatives an obedience to those opinions".[1] In 1841, the Melbourne Government was defeated in its attempt to substitute a low fixed duty on corn for the existing sliding scale; and, being defeated in the election which followed, was succeeded by that of Sir Robert Peel. But when, five years later, Sir Robert proposed and carried the repeal of the Corn Laws, he did not think it necessary previously to consult the electorate which had given him his majority; nor, when he was succeeded in office by the Whigs, did a dissolution immediately follow the change of ministry.[2]

Effective control of Government by House of Commons during that period. Its causes.

[1] English Constitution, Introduction, p. x.
[2] Sir Robert indeed was accused of betraying his party, and it was contended that he should have left the task of carrying out his policy to the Whigs with whom it had been in some measure associated; but there was no emphatic de-

Again, the result of the election of 1865 was really a vote of confidence in Lord Palmerston, who was known to be opposed to reform; but on the death of that statesman in the same year, the first measure introduced by his successor Lord Russell was a Reform Bill. In fact, although, since 1832, the Cabinet, in the happy phrasing of Prof. Lowell, made laws by and with the advice and consent of the House of Commons, the advice and consent of the electors were deemed to be quite unnecessary. We may, therefore, here take note of two important constitutional changes brought about by the extension of the suffrage to the working classes: first, the transference of a large share of control over legislation, and even in some measure of its initiation, from the House of Commons to the electorate; and, secondly, through the opening, as it were, of direct communication between the Cabinet and the country, of an increase in the power of the Cabinet with a proportionate diminution of that of the House of Commons.[1] The former tendency is less marked when a Conservative than when a Liberal Government is in office, because, owing to the action of the House of Lords, it has become practically impossible for a Liberal Government to pass into law a party measure of a controversial nature without strong popular support; whereas their rivals can carry without much difficulty any bill, whether popular or unpopular, as to the merits of which their party is agreed.[2]

Effect of Reform Act of 1867 to transfer power from the House of Commons (a) to the electorate, and (b) to the Cabinet.

The first step and the second. A contrast.

No better illustration could be found of the truth of the French proverb that it is the first step alone that is difficult, than the contrast between the spirit in which the first Reform Act was carried, and that which accompanied its no less drastic successor in 1867. The enthusiastic hopes and the

mand, as there would have been in later times, that he should dissolve Parliament and obtain a mandate from the country before proceeding to action.

[1] The outward signs of this transfer of power from the House of Commons to the Cabinet have been the gradual absorption for Government business, not without protest, but still with a general acquiescence, of most of the time of the House; their consequently exclusive power in the initiation of controversial legislation; and the invention of devices, such as closure by compartments, for pushing this legislation through. But just as the veto of the Crown fell into disuse because the Crown through influence was able to hinder the progress of bills at an earlier stage; so, although Ministers are rarely defeated in the open, a very real pressure prevents them from persisting in proposals distasteful to the majority of their supporters.

[2] The passage of the Parliament Act has now modified these conditions.

fears of national ruin alike excited by the proposals of 1831 could no longer be aroused. Experience had shown their vanity; and though the "leap into the dark," whereby the power to make laws and taxation was entrusted to the representatives of a class which paid no direct taxes and whose votes might be attracted by proposals of legislation condemned by economists as unsound, was in reality more formidable than the earlier experiment, such considerations had little weight. The Act was passed by a Conservative Government called to office by their success in defeating the much more moderate proposals of their predecessors and by a Parliament distinctly opposed to reform. A large majority of members in both Houses were dissatisfied with the bill. Even Mr. Bright, the most distinguished advocate of a democratic suffrage, considered that it went too far, and that it would have been better, by relieving the smallest occupiers from the liability to pay rates, to exclude what he described as the *residuum* from the franchise. But men were weary of the subject and longed to have done with it. Both parties were committed to reform, and when, after so many failures, a settlement appeared inevitable, few members of Parliament were willing to offend the new electors by showing themselves hostile to their claims.

The rapid oscillations of the political body since 1867 were foretold by the opponents of the Reform Act, whose prophecies on this subject have been verified by experience. It needed no extraordinary sagacity to have foreseen that this would be the case, for it is clear that the better educated a man is the more likely is he to have reasoned political convictions and principles; and, this being the case, he will in normal circumstances either vote with his party at a general election or else abstain from voting. Educated opinion changes; but it changes slowly. Certain grand periodical oscillations, recurring as the generations succeed one another, may be observed by students of history. Thus in the middle of the eighteenth century, Whig doctrines were in the ascendant; at its close, the educated classes were mainly Tory. Again, in the middle of the nineteenth century the central current of education and intelligence was Liberal; but towards the close it was becoming ever more Conservative until, almost at the end of the century, Conservatism, according to Mr. Matthew

The greater vicissitudes of opinion.

Arnold, had reached its zenith. The new generation which has grown up during the long tenure of power by the Unionists shows some signs of a contrary tendency; and these deeper changes of opinion, indicating the natural reaction of a new generation against established modes of thought, may be expected to continue.

The lesser vicissitudes.

Of a very different nature are the rapid changes of view manifested by a section of the electorate sufficiently large to bring the two parties alternately to power since 1867. Party organisers affirm that the voters who change sides at a general election belong mainly to the working classes; and this is natural enough. It is due partly to their lack of political conviction and inaptitude for abstract thought; and partly to a vague sense that they are unjustly treated by the existing organisation of society. The rival parties bid against one another for their support; promises are made to them, especially by opposition candidates; and when they have voted on the faith of these promises they are perpetually disappointed through the natural impotence of Governments to remove their troubles, and therefore continue to turn uneasily first to one side and then to the other in the hope of amelioration.

The election of 1841 was, as we have seen, the only occasion on which between 1832 and 1867 the electors returned a Conservative majority; but from 1867 until 1910 every general election, except the abnormal one of 1900 held in the middle of the South African war, has resulted in a change of Government.

Lord Russell's Life-peerage Bill.

In 1869, in the year after the re-modelled electorate, by returning the largest Liberal majority since 1833, had shown its confidence in Mr. Gladstone and his Irish policy, an attempt was made by that indefatigable reformer, Lord Russell, to strengthen the House of Lords by modifying in some degree the hereditary character of its constitution. He introduced a bill by which he proposed to authorise the Crown to create life-peerages. The limitations he suggested were that not more than twenty-eight life-peers should sit at the same time in the House nor more than four be created in a single year. He proposed to restrict the choice of the Crown to persons who had sat in the House of Commons for ten years, to judges of the Superior Courts, to ex-law officers of the Crown, persons distinguished in science, literature, or art, and finally, to persons who had held office under the Crown for not less than five years. The principle of the bill was supported on second reading by Lord Derby and by Lord Cairns as well as by Lord Salisbury, who gave it as his opinion that the House of Lords was drawn too much from the single class of landed proprietors, and would gain strength if other elements could be introduced into its composition. The second reading was accordingly carried in spite of the opposition of Lord Malmesbury; and the bill went through committee. But, before the third reading came on in July, the relations between the two Houses had become strained over the Irish Church Bill, and the indignation of the peers had been excusably roused by some injudicious menaces on the part of Mr. Bright. "Instead of doing a little childish tinkering about life-peerages," he had written in a letter intended to be read at a public meeting, "it would be well if the peers could bring themselves on a line with the opinions and necessities of our day. In harmony with the nation, they may go on for a long time ; but throwing themselves athwart its path, they may meet with accidents not pleasant for them to think of." Such language coming from a Cabinet Minister gave little encouragement to the advocates of the proposed reform. Lord Cairns, who led the opposition in the Upper House, had given a hesitating support to the bill on the second reading, while declaring it to be open to grave objections. But when the bill came on for third reading he pointed out that he had been misled by Lord Granville, the leader of the House, from whom he had understood that the Government were warmly in favour of the bill; and he contended that in view of the opinions expressed by a Cabinet Minister concerning the House of Lords it would be dangerous to send down a discussion concerning its constitution to the other House. This, he said, would be to incur a great risk for the sake of a small and doubtful benefit. These views prevailed, and Lord Malmesbury carried the rejection of the bill by 106 to 77.[1] Thus was defeated the first important

Rejected by the Lords.

---

[1] Lord Malmesbury returned from Italy in order to oppose the bill and was so gratified by his success that he inserted the whole of the speeches made by him against it in his diary. He was of opinion that it was "one of the first

proposal for the reform of the House of Lords—made in his old age by the statesman who thirty-eight years previously had introduced the great measure for the reform of the House of Commons. Had the bill passed into law there can be little doubt that its principle would soon have been extended by the repeal of the provisions limiting the number of life-peerages; the practice of making new hereditary peerages would perhaps have been gradually discontinued; and the consequent modification in the character of the House might have averted the struggle for existence with a Liberal, Government which the permanent conservatism of the large majority of the House involved in its composition was certain sooner or later to bring about. The two men mainly responsible for arresting this natural development of the House of Lords in accordance with its historic traditions were Lord Malmesbury and Mr. Bright. To Mr. Bright also the policy of limiting by statute the powers of the House of Lords as opposed to that of reforming its constitution owes its inception.

The Ballot.

After the franchise had been conferred on the working classes it became, in the opinion of most Liberals, a matter of urgency to protect them from intimidation in its exercise; and the device of the ballot, so long fruitlessly advocated by independent Liberals, at last found favour in the sight of the party leaders. This question had long divided the Liberal party. It had been the distinctive principle of advanced Liberals, but had been opposed by Lord Palmerston and by most of his Whig followers. In 1869, however, the recent extension of the representative system, disclosures at the late general election, and the altered relations of the leaders of the Liberal party to that section of their followers who favoured secret voting, brought about a change of policy in regard to that question. Ministers accordingly proposed an inquiry into the mode of conducting Parliamentary and municipal elections, with a view to limit expense, and to restrain bribery and intimidation; and it was generally understood that this inquiry was designed to prepare the way for the general adhesion of ministers and the Liberal party to the principle of secret voting.

principles of the constitution that a peerage should be hereditary".—*Memoirs of an Ex-Minister*, ii. 394.

This committee continued its investigations throughout the session, and, being reappointed in 1870, presented a report, recommending several changes in the mode of conducting elections, and the adoption of secret voting. The Government introduced a bill founded upon this report, but the education bill and other important measures interfered with its further progress. Ministers, however, and the Liberal party, now stood committed to the principle of the ballot; and this most important constitutional question, which for nearly forty years had been discussed rather as a political theory than as a practical measure, was accepted by a powerful Government, and a large majority of the House of Commons, as the policy of the State. *Ballot Bill, 1870.*

In 1871 another bill was brought in for introducing the ballot both at Parliamentary and municipal elections, and passed, after protracted discussions, by the Commons: but it was received by the Lords at so late a period of the session that they declined to consider it. This bill as originally introduced contained a clause to relieve candidates from the payment of election expenses and to charge them upon the rates. It was pointed out by Mr. Forster, the Minister in charge of the bill, that there was no case either in our colonies or in any other nation where the expenses of the returning officer were not borne by the constituency. It was contended that the existing system was wrong in principle, since public requirements should be defrayed out of public funds, and mischievous in practice because of the limitation it imposed on the choice of candidates. In boroughs these expenses had been borne by the constituencies until the Reform Act of 1832, at which time the Whig leaders, anxious concerning the results of their step in advance on the road to democracy, and not disposed to make the House of Commons too easy of access under the new conditions, transferred the burden to the candidates. It was argued by the opponents of the clause that at a time when it was admitted that the state of local taxation had reached its utmost limit, it would be wrong to shift the pecuniary burden of these elections from themselves and to place it on the ratepayers; and it was also contended that the number of candidates would be inconveniently increased if this were done. These consider- *Ballot Bill of 1871. Passed by the Commons but rejected by the Lords.*

ations prevailed, and the clause was rejected by a large majority.

Ballot Act, 1872.

Early in the session of 1872 Mr. Forster, on behalf of the Government, introduced a third bill to provide for the use of the ballot at Parliamentary and municipal elections and to abolish public nominations. The Government respected the decision to which the House had come in the previous session; and the new bill did not include any provisions for altering the incidence of election expenses. They, however, supported a clause proposed by Mr. Fawcett in committee to charge election expenses upon the localities in which the elections were held, but this proposal was none the less rejected by a majority of 92. The bill was read a third time at the end of May, and was passed by the Lords with important amendments during the month of June. Their proposal to make the ballot optional would have defeated the main purpose of the measure; and was not insisted upon when disagreed to by the Commons. But an amendment with the object of providing means for the identification of voters on a scrutiny met with a more favourable reception; and with some modifications was adopted by the Commons. It was enacted that a counterfoil of the voting paper marked with the voter's number on the register should remain with the presiding officer. By this means, whenever a scrutiny was found necessary, the voter could be identified and unauthorised votes cancelled. An amendment made by the Lords to limit the operation of the Act to eight years was also reluctantly accepted by the Commons. Consequently since 1880 the Act has been annually renewed by its inclusion in the Acts passed to continue expiring laws.

Results of the Ballot Act.

It was hoped that the system of secret voting would do away with bribery by removing the temptation to bribe; but it was found that money was still paid for votes even though there was no security that the bribed voter would fulfil his bargain. Bribery moreover in the form of " payment by results " could not be affected by the introduction of the ballot. On the other hand there can be no doubt that the ballot really shelters the dependent voter from the pressure of undue influence, especially where this is indirect; and that, with the abolition of public nominations, it has rendered elections more quiet and orderly. In Ireland where the tenant was at once less friendly to his landlord, and, owing to the fact that throughout the greater part of the country agriculture is practically the sole industry, more immediately dependent upon him for his livelihood, the protection afforded by the ballot was more marked in its effects than in England. To Mr. Parnell, then a young and unknown Irish squire living on his land in County Wicklow, whose chief interest was apparently cricket, the measure seemed, so we learn from his biographer, " of greater practical importance than either the Irish Church Act or the Land Act, for it emancipated the voters. 'Now,' he said, 'something can be done, if full advantage will be taken of this Ballot Act.'" The Irish voter, so he thought, was now a free man who could send whom he liked to Parliament. "An independent Irish party, free from the touch of English influence, was the thing wanted, and this party could be elected under the Ballot Act."[1]

The Reform Act of 1832 had been described by some of its authors as a final settlement. No one claimed finality for the Act of 1867. The suffrage was no longer regarded as a trust committed to those whom the State in its wisdom considered to be best qualified to exercise it, but rather as a right which " every man not presumably incapacitated by some consideration of personal unfitness, or of political danger" was morally entitled to enjoy. True the Conservative leaders continued gently to protest against this doctrine of abstract right and to deny that a wrong was done to any class of citizens, "if for the sake of maintaining a good, convenient, and proper electoral system they were excluded from the franchise".[2] But their own action in 1867 had weakened the force of this position and they were reluctant to alienate the affections of those from whom they foresaw that it would be impossible long to withhold the vote by denying that their enfranchisement was compatible with a good electoral system. Accordingly as early as 1872, in the very first Parliament elected under the Act of 1867, Mr. Trevelyan, the protagonist of the movement for the fresh extension of the suffrage and for many years its chief promoter, invited the House of Commons to affirm the almost indisputable proposition: "That this House would be more

Renewed proposals for reform in 1872.

[1] O'Brien's *Life of Parnell*, i. 56.   [2] Sir Stafford Northcote in 1877.

likely to devote due and adequate attention to the wants and interests of our rural population if householders outside the boundary of Parliamentary boroughs were in possession of the franchise"; with the corollary at that time more open to question that it was expedient to extend to counties the occupation and lodging franchises then in force in boroughs. In his reply to the able speech in which Mr. Trevelyan moved his resolution Mr. Gladstone based his refusal to vote for it on his favourite ground that the House of Commons ought not to pass abstract resolutions except with the intention of giving to them practical effect, and that the time had not yet come to do this. He, however, gave it as his opinion that the line of demarcation then existing between the county and borough franchise could not long continue for the reason among others that the continual mutual encroachments of urban and rural districts tended to make ever more and more remote from reality the geographical distinctions contained in the Act of 1867. The resolution was defeated in a small House by a majority of 78.

Mr. Trevelyan's County Franchise Bill, 1873.

In the following year Mr. Trevelyan embodied his proposals in a bill. This was talked out on a Wednesday afternoon, but was supported in a long speech by Mr. Forster, with whom, as he was authorised to inform the House, Mr. Gladstone concurred in the view that the extension of the household suffrage to the counties was just and politic in itself and could not long be avoided. These distinguished ministers, however, could not speak in the name of the Government, because that Government contained, in Mr. Lowe and Mr. Goschen, two of the most able and resolute opponents of the proposed reform.

Position taken on the question in 1874 by the party leaders.

The question of the county franchise was not neglected by the party chiefs during the general election of 1874. In his Greenwich manifesto Mr. Gladstone declared himself in favour of the creation of "peasant boroughs" or groups of rural villages to which the household suffrage should be given. Mr. Disraeli, in his address, while abstaining from any criticism of the rural householder as unfit for the franchise, declared that his inclusion would involve a redistribution of political power so great as to make it necessary to remodel the entire representation of the United Kingdom. "The Conservative party," he said, " will hesitate before they sanction further legislation which will inevitably involve, among other considerable changes, the disenfranchisement of at least all boroughs in the kingdom comprising less than 40,000 inhabitants."

This ingenious line of defence, by which the sympathies of the members for the boroughs threatened with disfranchisement might naturally be secured, was again adopted by Mr. Disraeli, when, in the spring of 1874, it fell to him as Prime Minister to resist the second reading of a new bill introduced by Mr. Trevelyan. Admitting that the rural householder was just as competent to exercise the franchise as the town artisan, he argued that the extension of the suffrage to 1,000,000 new voters must be accompanied by a large measure of redistribution, and must lead in time to a system of equal electoral districts. For organic changes so great as this so soon after the Act of 1867 he did not think the country was prepared. The motion for the second reading was defeated by a majority of 114.

Not discouraged by these reverses, Mr. Trevelyan reintroduced his bill in 1875. It was rejected on second reading by a majority of 102. Lord Hartington, the leader of the Opposition, in his speech on this occasion gave it as his reason for abstaining from the division that although he held that the franchise in counties ought to be equalised with the franchise established in boroughs, he could not vote for a bill which, unless accompanied by a measure for the redistribution of seats, would create the most serious anomalies in our representative system. He thought that redistribution could only be carried by a Government, and that the interest in the House and in the country which would enable a Government to carry through an adequate scheme did not at that time exist. *Bill to enfranchise rural householder reintroduced by Mr. Trevelyan in 1874 and 1875.*

In 1876 and in 1877, Mr. Trevelyan, instead of reintroducing his bill, endeavoured to meet the valid objections made by Lord Hartington by moving resolutions in favour not only of reform but also of redistribution. He moved : (1) " That, in the opinion of this House, it would be desirable to adopt an uniform Parliamentary franchise for borough and county constituencies " ; and (2) " That it would be desirable so to redistribute political power as to obtain a more complete representation of the opinion of the electoral body ". The de- *Mr. Trevelyan moves resolutions in favour of reform and redistribution. He is supported by Lord Hartington, 1876-1879.*

bate in 1876 was illustrated by speeches for and against the resolutions by Mr. Bright and Mr. Lowe, but its chief interest lay in the reply of the Prime Minister. The redistribution called for by so large an addition to the number of voters in the county constituency would, he declared, break up the existing borough constituency and destroy the variety of character derived by the House from the municipal communities. The resolutions were defeated by a majority of 99.

In moving the same resolutions in 1877 Mr. Trevelyan pointed out that during the preceding decade a large mining and manufacturing population had sprung up outside the limits of the Parliamentary boroughs, and challenged his opponents to show cause why the inhabitants, for instance, of Heywood and Accrington should be deprived of the rights enjoyed by their fellow-workmen in the older towns, or why the householders of Battersea should not share the political privileges of the householders of Southwark. On this occasion he was supported by Lord Hartington, who considered that the time had come when the county householders and the country ought to know what was the attitude of each of the great parties in the House in relation to the question. Immense though the difficulties connected with redistribution might be, it was the duty, so he now thought, of the Liberal party to face them; and whenever it should have the power to satisfy a claim, the abstract justice of which was generally admitted. This change of attitude on Lord Hartington's part produced an effect in the division lobby; for the majority by which in a full House the resolutions were now rejected was reduced to 56.

Movement in the country. In the meantime the movement in favour of reform was beginning to excite some interest in the country, and the endeavours of Mr. Joseph Arch and other perambulating agitators to create a sense of wrong in the slow mind of the agricultural labourer were not wholly without effect. The Reform League which had been dissolved in 1869 was revived in the autumn of 1876; public meetings were addressed by Mr. Bright and other orators; and an attack on the proposal for the further extension of the franchise made by Mr. Lowe in the *Fortnightly Review* called forth a vigorous reply from

Mr. Gladstone in the *Nineteenth Century*. The latter circumstance was the more significant when it was remembered that it was never the custom of Mr. Gladstone to enter into a political controversy unless with the intention of giving practical effect to his views.

Twice more before the general election of 1880 did Mr. Trevelyan in 1878 and 1879 propose his resolutions to the House of Commons. He was supported by the whole strength of the Opposition with the distinguished exceptions of Mr. Goschen and Mr. Lowe. Lord Hartington spoke on each occasion. In the course of the earlier debate he pointed out that the reformers of 1832 had not wished to abolish the old distinction between the property franchise in the counties and the occupation franchise in the boroughs, but that the Conservative amendment known as the Chandos Clause, by the enfranchisement of tenants-at-will paying £50 a year, had broken through this principle for the first time, and that the last Conservative Government by establishing a £12 occupation franchise in the counties had completely changed the character of the county constituency. There was no longer any principle underlying the distinction drawn between the urban and the rural householder, and since it had been admitted by the Conservative chief that the one was just as competent to exercise the franchise as the other, it was difficult to show cause why it should be maintained on the ground of expediency. Mr. Trevelyan's resolutions were defeated in 1878 by a majority of 52, and in 1879 by 291 votes to 226. At the general election of 1880 the assimilation of the county to the borough franchise was advocated in most of the election addresses issued by Liberal candidates; and when the new Parliament with its large Liberal majority assembled, it was understood that it would not be dissolved until this reform had been accomplished.

The next important measure relating to Parliamentary elections, however, which received the Royal Assent was the Corrupt and Illegal Practices Act of 1883. The special Commissions appointed to inquire into the conduct of a number of boroughs where there had been election petitions disclosed in their reports an extent of corruption which called aloud for a remedy. It was found necessary to disfranchise Sandwich

Corrupt and Illegal Practices Act, 1883.

and Macclesfield, in both of which boroughs half of the voters were found to be guilty of corruption. The members for Chester, Boston, Oxford, and other places were unseated. The expense of the election had been enormous. To remedy this state of things Sir Henry James, the Attorney-General, introduced in 1883 the most stringent measure yet proposed for the restraint of corrupt practices. By this Act, which was read a second time without a division on June 4th, the evil was dealt with by remedies, which, without departing from traditional methods, greatly increased their strength and efficiency. They may be considered under three heads:—

(i) The penalties for corrupt practices were greatly increased. They were made punishable by imprisonment with hard labour or by a fine of £200. The disabilities to which candidates were subject when reported to the House as guilty of corrupt practices were also increased. If the candidate were reported by an Election Court to have been knowingly guilty of treating or undue influence, or of any corrupt practice, he was excluded not only from sitting in Parliament for seven years, but for the same constituency for ever; and if found guilty of treating through his agents he was excluded from sitting for the same constituency for seven years. (ii) Certain classes of acts were newly defined and forbidden. Treating on the part of the candidate had been unlawful since the seventeenth century. It was now defined as the giving, or paying, the expense of giving, any meat, drink, entertainment, or provision with the object of corruptly influencing voters, and made an offence when committed by persons other than candidates. Undue influence was defined as the making use, or threatening to make use, of any force, violence, or restraint, or inflicting, or threatening to inflict, any temporal or spiritual injury on any person in order to influence his vote; or by duress or fraud impeding the free exercise of the franchise by any man. (iii) The total amount of the expenses of elections and the purposes to which they might be directed were limited. The personal expenses of a candidate were limited to £100. The maximum amounts to be spent by returning officers were fixed.[1] Certain practices

[1] The maximum sums fixed were as follows: for a borough of under 2000 electors, £350; of over 2000 electors, £380 with £30 more for every additional

were made illegal with a view to diminishing expenditure. The conveyance of voters to the poll in hired vehicles was prohibited.[1] It was required that the candidate should not have more than one authorised agent, through whom all legitimate disbursements were to be made; paid canvassers were prohibited by the provision that no person except those mentioned in the schedule to the Act should be employed for pay; and the number of committee rooms was regulated.

On going into committee, Mr. Broadhurst, a member who had been a working man, moved as an instruction to the committee that they should make provision for charging the expenses of returning officers upon the rates. A resolution of Mr. Ashton Dilke in favour of this course had been carried in 1882 by a majority of two. Mr. Gladstone now expressed himself in favour of the principle of the instruction; but held that its acceptance would involve a violation of the understanding under which the Opposition had agreed to the second reading. The motion was, therefore, rejected by a large majority. The bill, after a committee stage of twenty-one days, was reported on the 13th July, and, after a rapid and peaceful passage through the House of Lords, received the Royal Assent in August. It has proved perhaps the most successful of the Acts passed by the Parliament of 1880. In 1880 the election by about 3,000,000 electors cost £3,000,000. In 1885 the election by 5,670,000 electors cost only £780,000.

The question of reform was much in the minds of men in the year 1883. Mr. Chamberlain and Sir Charles Dilke, in the Cabinet, and Mr. John Morley, who supported their views in the press, stood out as the principal champions of the cause. In June, during the celebration held at Birmingham in honour of the veteran reformer, Mr. Bright, Mr. Chamberlain declared himself in favour of a suffrage from which no man who was expected to fulfil the duties of a citizen should be excluded; of equal electoral districts, in order that every vote might have an equal value; and of the payment of members, in order that

The Reform Movement in 1883.

1000: in the counties, for constituencies of under 2000 electors, in Great Britain, they were not to exceed £650, and in Ireland £500: of over 2000 electors, £710 in Great Britain and £540 in Ireland, with £60 more in Great Britain and £40 more in Ireland for every additional 1000 electors.

[1] That this was a considerable saving may be judged from the fact that in 1880 no less than £750,000 was expended in carrying voters to the poll.

no man with a capacity to serve his country might be excluded from Parliament by want of means. On the 27th September a mass meeting, estimated at 50,000 men, assembled under the presidency of Mr. Morley to pass resolutions in favour of assimilating the borough and county franchises. On the 17th October, at a reform conference at Leeds, 2500 delegates representing 500 Liberal Associations in all parts of the kingdom met together, with Mr. Morley in the chair, to suggest a programme to the Government for the next session. The chief points discussed on the platform and in the press were (1) whether the direction to be taken was to be that of equal electoral districts or of proportional representation; (2) whether redistribution should accompany or follow the extension of the franchise, and, if the latter, at what interval of time; (3) whether Ireland should be included in the bill. The majority of Liberals were found to be in favour of giving equal treatment to Ireland; of advancing in the direction of equal electoral districts; and of postponing the consideration of a scheme of redistribution until after a franchise bill had been passed. They were, however, for the most part disposed to leave the settlement of these questions to the Government, for whom Mr. Chamberlain claimed a Radicalism more advanced than that professed by the majority of their supporters in the House of Commons. Yet Lord Hartington, who represented the views of the moderate section of the cabinet, and whose speeches in the country scarcely affected to conceal the difference of view which separated him from Mr. Chamberlain, publicly questioned the wisdom of including Ireland in the new Reform Bill, and pointed out the dangerous addition of strength which that inclusion would give to the Irish malcontents.

The Franchise Bill of 1884.

On the 28th February, 1884, Mr. Gladstone introduced the Franchise Bill. By giving to the counties the household and lodger franchise he calculated that 1,300,000 new voters would be added to the English, over 200,000 to the Scotch, and over 400,000 to the Irish constituency. In all, to the existing 3,000,000 voters in the United Kingdom 2,000,000 others would be added. The strange English system of retaining all the old franchises and superadding new, which has done so much to complicate our election law, and has given so much work to lawyers and agents, was with a single exception adhered to in this bill. In the boroughs the household and lodger franchises of 1867 were retained; the £10 clear yearly value franchise was extended to land held without houses or buildings; and a new service franchise was created for inhabitants of a legal house who were neither occupiers nor tenants. In the counties the £50 franchise, created by the Chandos Clause, was abolished for the sake of uniformity—this being the sole exception to the conservative rule just referred to; the £12 occupation franchise of 1867 was reduced to £10; the service, lodger, and household franchises of the boroughs were imported; and the old property franchise of the 40s. freeholder was left untouched. No condition as to residence was imposed on the freeholder; but to prevent abuses the incorporeal hereditaments, capable of being used for the creation of fictitious votes, with the exception of tithe rent charges and hereditaments acquired by descent, marriage settlements, and wills, were disqualified.

In the course of his speech Mr. Gladstone promised a Registration Bill when the Franchise Bill had made sufficient progress, but postponed until the following session the question of Redistribution.

The introduction of the Franchise Bill gave new life to the Government and embarrassed the Opposition. The Conservatives did not venture to oppose the scheme on principle. They had themselves conferred household suffrage on the boroughs; their leaders had frequently admitted that its extension to the counties was merely a matter of time and convenience. The Lancashire Conservatives—an important section of the party—approved the measure. Lord Randolph Churchill and his small following, though criticizing its introduction as inopportune and premature, were half-hearted in their opposition from the beginning, and during the later stages of the discussions not only ceased to oppose its further progress, but even resisted amendments proposed from the Conservative benches for the exclusion of Ireland, and for the postponement of the coming into operation of the bill until after redistribution had been effected.

The Opposition and the bill.

It was, however, on these two points that the bill could

The inclusion of Ireland.

be most plausibly resisted, and that Lord Salisbury in his speech on the 16th January had intimated that it would be resisted. The inclusion of Ireland, however essential from a Liberal standpoint it may have been, did undoubtedly present grave dangers. The Irish electorate was increased from some 200,000 to about 700,000 voters; and the new voters belonged to a class more than forty per cent of whom were said to be illiterate. Unquestionably a new and most formidable weapon would be placed in the hands of Mr. Parnell, and the temptation to purchase from him by concessions the votes which the enfranchisement of the Irish peasantry shortly afterwards enabled him to command, proved to be one which neither of the two English parties was able altogether to resist.

Misunderstandings with regard to redistribution.

On the question of the production of the Redistribution Bill before the passage of the Franchise Bill both parties had a fair case; if, at least, it is admitted that the Opposition were morally entitled to accept or reject through their majority in the House of Lords the Franchise Bill by reason of their approval or disapproval of the policy pursued. For they could fairly contend that if they agreed to a Franchise Bill without seeing the Redistribution Bill they would be compelled either to accept without amendment any scheme of redistribution which the Government might be pleased to propose or else to face a general election on the new franchise, but without any change in the disposition of seats. On the other hand, Liberals feared that if the two bills were brought forward together the Conservatives might use their majority in the House of Lords to refuse their consent to the Franchise Bill until the Government had accepted their amendments to the Redistribution Bill. To meet in some sense the objections of the Opposition Mr. Gladstone had in his introductory speech given a sketch of the Redistribution Bill which he proposed to introduce in the following session, but this did not satisfy his opponents. On the second reading Lord John Manners moved an amendment on behalf of the Opposition to the effect that consent must be withheld from the Franchise Bill unless that bill were accompanied by a measure for the redistribution of seats. The Government defeated this amendment by the large majority of 130 and the division showed that the passage of the measure through the House of Commons would be attended with little difficulty.

In Committee the dissensions between the Tory democrats led by Lord Randolph Churchill and the Conservatives of the old school smoothed the way for the bill. In spite of an eloquent speech from Mr. Plunket and the former hesitation of the Whigs, Mr. Brodrick's amendment to exclude the Irish was rejected by 332 to 137 votes, and the bill was read a third time without a division at the end of June. *Franchise Bill passed by the Commons.*

In the House of Lords Lord Cairns, on behalf of the Opposition, moved a reasoned amendment to the second reading to the effect that the House, while prepared to concur in a well-considered and complete scheme of reform, did not think it right to assent to a bill having for its object a fundamental change in the electoral body, which was not accompanied by provisions for the redistribution of seats, or by any adequate security that the bill should not come into operation except on an entire scheme. This amendment was carried by 205 to 146 on the 6th of July in spite of the disapproval of *The Times*, the bishops, and, according to Mr. Gladstone, the more sober-minded of the Conservative peers. Thereupon a meeting of the Liberal party was summoned to the Foreign Office on the 10th July. An autumn session in which the Franchise Bill should be re-introduced was announced, and the contest was transferred from Parliament to the platform. Mr. Gladstone indignantly scouted the suggestion that the action of the Lords should be submitted to the country by a dissolution. They would hazard nothing, he said, while the country would be put to the expense of a general election. "If the country disapproved of the conduct of its representatives it would cashier them, but if it disapproved of the conduct of the peers it would simply have to see them resume their place of power, to employ it to the best of their ability as opportunity might serve, in thwarting the desires of the country expressed through its representatives."[1] On one issue and one issue alone was he ready to allow the House of Lords to force a dissolution, and that was on the question of organic change in their own powers or constitution. But this issue he was at that time unwilling to raise until the Lords by rejecting the Franchise *Bill rejected by the Lords.*

[1] Life of Gladstone, iii. 130.

Bill a second time had made it clear that no other alternative to surrender remained open. Nor was the cause of quarrel worthy of so serious an outcome. No point of principle was involved. The two parties mistrusted each other's intentions, and the only problem to be solved was the manner in which they could give to one another security that this mutual distrust was undeserved. Negotiations followed. Mr. Gladstone proposed that identical resolutions should be passed, declaring that each House had passed the Franchise Bill in reliance on the promise of the Government to introduce a Redistribution Bill in the next session, and that this resolution should be embodied in an address to the Crown. But this proposal naturally did not satisfy Lord Salisbury, whose doubts related less to the intention of the Government to introduce a Redistribution Bill than to the character of the bill which, the Franchise Bill once being secure, they would introduce. By

Intervention of the queen. a memorandum to the queen at the end of August Mr. Gladstone succeeded in rousing her Majesty's fears as to the results in the direction of a movement for organic change which would follow from continued resistance on the part of the Lords. In the autumn the queen wrote to Mr. Gladstone and to Lord Salisbury and urged an exchange of views between the leaders.

Negotiations. The session began on the 23rd October, and the Franchise Bill in unaltered form was read a third time in the House of Commons on the 11th November. On the 14th Mr. Gladstone had a conversation with Sir Stafford Northcote in which they discussed the principles of redistribution, and Mr. Gladstone promised the introduction of a Redistribution Bill into the House of Commons after the Franchise Bill had been read a second time in the House of Lords, provided that he was assured that the Franchise Bill should not be thereby endangered. Lord Salisbury, however, still declared that the Lords could not pass the Franchise Bill until they had received the Seats Bill from the Commons, and for a time the outlook appeared menacing.

At last, however, a device was hit upon which saved the situation. The redistribution proposals of the Government were to be privately shown to the Opposition leaders before the Franchise Bill had left the hands of the Lords; they were to be discussed by them with the representatives of the Government; and if an agreement was arrived at, the Franchise Bill could be at once made law and a Redistribution Bill on the agreed lines introduced in the succeeding year. Thus the Conservatives would be secured from the danger of a General Election on the extended franchise in the old constituencies, and the Liberals from that of being obliged as the price of the Franchise Bill to consent to objectionable alterations in their scheme of redistribution.

On the 19th November the party leaders met at the house of Mr. Gladstone. Lord Salisbury and Sir Stafford Northcote represented the Opposition, while Lord Hartington, Lord Granville, and Sir Charles Dilke were present with Mr. Gladstone at this informal conference. After all the speeches, disputes, mutual imputations, and mutual distrust of the past six months it was found that on the subject of redistribution there was no serious difference of opinion between the rival chiefs. Indeed Mr. Gladstone affected to be shocked by Lord Salisbury's readiness for change and disregard for tradition and declared himself to be the stronger Conservative of the two. Several friendly meetings resulted in a perfect understanding between the leaders; they parted on the best of terms; and to the great pleasure of the queen, whose influence had been perhaps the most important factor in bringing about a settlement, and the general relief, the bill was now passed by the Lords, and became law on the 9th December. *Agreement effected. Bill passed.*

That the Reform Act of 1884 was finally passed with the assent of both parties is not surprising. Whatever might be thought of the wisdom or unwisdom of the Act of 1867 no intelligible reason could be given for refusing to one section of the working classes the franchise which had been conceded to another. The reform was lateral and not vertical. Nor could the distinction any longer be drawn between the urban and rural householder, even if that distinction had been a sufficient reason for denying a vote to the latter, for a large proportion of the newly enfranchised voters lived in urban districts. No one was disfranchised by the bill. The property vote was retained, although constituting a violation of the uniformity of county and borough franchise aimed at by the Act; although, too, it might fairly have been contended that it was a mere *Conservative character of the Act.*

survival of the old distinction between the property franchise in the counties and the occupation franchise in the boroughs, and that since occupation had become the qualification of the great majority of voters in counties as well as in boroughs the property vote was an anachronism. No attempt was made to abolish plural voting. In order to satisfy a powerful Liberal opposition the Act of 1867, passed by a Conservative Government, went further than most Liberals desired; the same consideration, *mutatis mutandis*, caused the Act of 1884 to be drawn by a Liberal Government on Conservative lines.

The Redistribution of Seats Act, 1885.

In the first half of 1885 the Redistribution Bill which had been introduced into the House of Commons and read a second time in December, 1884, was passed by both Houses of Parliament, practically without opposition, and received the royal assent on the 25th June. By this Act all boroughs with a population of less than 15,000 were disfranchised, and merged into their counties. These counties were subdivided into single-member districts, so that the voter who had lost his vote for the borough gained a vote for the electoral district of the county in which his borough was situated. Under this provision eighty boroughs were disfranchised in England, two in Scotland, and twenty-two in Ireland. All towns with a population under 50,000 were to be represented by one member only—a provision which deprived thirty-four boroughs in England and three in Ireland of one of their members. Macclesfield and Sandwich were disfranchised for corruption. Towns with a population of over 100,000 were divided into separate constituencies and received additional members in proportion to their population. The representation of the city of London was reduced to two, but greater London returned sixty-two members. Six additional members were given to England and twelve to Scotland, by which means the total number of members was raised from 652 to 670. Preferential treatment was accorded to Ireland; for whereas her population only entitled her to ninety-one, or at most to ninety-three, members she was allowed to retain the 105 members given her by the Reform Act of 1832. It was thought that as, at the time of the Union, when her population was about half that of Great Britain, the share of representation allotted to her in the United Parliament was but one-sixth of the whole, it would be ungenerous now that her population had been so largely reduced owing to misfortunes, for the occurrence of which her powerful neighbour could not altogether disclaim responsibility, that an exactitude in the proportions between population and representation should be for the first time insisted upon. On the other hand, when it is remembered how largely the working order of the constitution depends on the assumption of the existence of two parties and the command of a steady majority in the House of Commons by the one in power; when, too, it is considered how serious a disturbance in that working order was caused by the rise of a third party unconnected with either of the English parties and hostile to the very existence of the United Parliament, it may be regretted that so fair an opportunity was not taken for reducing the number of the Irish members to a more equitable level, especially as the population of Ireland was showing a continued tendency to decrease. The common argument that Ireland had a sort of treaty right to the number of members assigned to her at the Union is not a very convincing one in view of the fact that Pitt, the author of the Union, during a debate in Committee on the resolutions introducing the Act, resisted an amendment moved by Mr. Grey on the ground that it was pernicious in tendency in its apparent implication, that it would not be open to Parliament at any time to reduce the number of the Irish members should circumstances justify such a reduction. He at the same time asserted the absolute independence of Parliament in this matter.[1] This is a better answer to the treaty argument than that generally given to the effect that the treaty of Union, if treaty there was, has already been violated by the disestablishment of the Irish Church. For that answer may be met by the obvious rejoinder that where both parties to a treaty are agreed to disregard one of its articles there is no breach of faith; and that a majority of British as well as of Irish members were in favour of disestablishment.[2]

[1] Parliamentary Register, vol. 72, 5th May, 1800.
[2] Effects of Redistribution Act of 1885.

ENGLAND.

Disfranchisement.	Seats.
13 boroughs returning 2 members merged in counties	26
66 ,, ,, 1 member ,, ,, ,,	66

Liberal pledges of reform.

In the succeeding years until 1892 little was heard of further proposals for the reform of the House of Commons. Ireland absorbed the attention of the nation; the aged Liberal chief continued in political life only with a view to the settlement of the Irish question; and gave his sanction to other projects merely with the object of gaining adherents to the cause he had at heart. On the 3rd of March, 1891, Mr. Stansfield moved a resolution in favour of the abolition of plural voting, but it was negatived by a majority of 102. The "Newcastle Programme," agreed to at the annual meeting of the Council of the National Liberal Federation in October of the same year, comprised among other reforms, the abolition of plural voting, payment of members, and the "mending or ending" of the House of Lords. Henceforward the party was pledged to deal with these subjects whenever it should have the power. The adoption of this programme hung like a weight round the neck of the Liberal Government of 1892, for while it offended and alarmed many powerful interests, it

36 boroughs returning 2 members deprived of 1 member	36
Macclesfield and Sandwich disfranchised	4
	—132
This with 6 new seats allotted to England and Wales gave 138 seats to be disposed of	138

Enfranchisement.

London, including Croydon, to return 62 members instead of 22	40
Additional members given to provincial boroughs	26
New provincial boroughs created	6
Additional members allotted to counties	66
	—138

SCOTLAND.
Disfranchisement.

2 boroughs returning 1 member each merged in counties and 12 new seats allotted to Scotland	14

Enfranchisement.

7 seats allotted to counties and 7 seats to Aberdeen, Edinburgh, and Glasgow	14

IRELAND.
Disfranchisement.

22 boroughs returning 1 member each	22
3 „ „ 2 members each lose 1	3
	—25

Enfranchisement.

21 seats allotted to counties	21
4 „ „ „ Dublin and Belfast	4
	—25

caused dissensions and irritation in the Liberal ranks owing to the impossibility in which the Government found itself of carrying it into law.

Some attempts, however, to redeem these embarrassing pledges the weak Liberal Government which succeeded with the help of the Irish vote in driving Lord Salisbury from office after the General Election of 1892 was obliged to make. At the beginning of the session of 1893, in the course of which the Home Rule Bill was passed by the House of Commons, bills were introduced for quinquennial Parliaments, for the amendment of registration, and for the limitation of each elector to a single vote. The introduction of these bills served in 1893 merely as a declaration of policy, and they were not further pressed. On the 24th of March a resolution in favour of payment of members was carried by 276 votes against 229, and again in 1895 by 176 against 158. But the rejection of the Home Rule Bill by the House of Lords combined with the retirement of Mr. Gladstone early in 1894 to weaken the influence of this House of Commons; and little importance was attached to its abstract resolutions.

In April, 1894, Lord Rosebery's Government introduced a bill to reduce the period of qualification for the franchise to three months and to provide for half-yearly registration. The bill also provided that all Parliamentary elections should be held on the same day and that no elector should vote on that day in more than one constituency. It also abolished the rating qualification. The second reading of this bill was carried by a majority of only fourteen and the Government, much occupied during this session with Sir William Harcourt's celebrated budget, did not proceed further with it. *Registration Bill of 1894.*

The frequent differences between the two Houses during the Parliament of 1880, and the rejection of the first Franchise Bill by the Upper House, caused the powers and composition of that House to be much discussed during the general election of 1885, and proposals for its "mending or ending" to be freely canvassed on Radical platforms. On the 5th of March, 1886, a resolution condemning the hereditary principle was moved by Mr. Labouchere in the House of Commons. Mr. Gladstone resisted this motion on the ground that it was inopportune. He said that he had always refused to assent *The position of the House of Lords. Mr. Labouchere's resolution.*

to an abstract resolution unless he was prepared to follow it up by action, and that the time for this had not yet come. The resolution was defeated by a majority of thirty-six.[1]

The question of the constitution of the House of Lords was again under discussion in 1888. The Conservatives were in power, but many of them thought that it would be prudent to forestall by a moderate reform the more drastic remedies now openly advocated by their opponents. On the other hand, Radicals were disposed to resist all changes involving the maintenance of the hereditary principle lest they should thereby strengthen the House of Lords.

Lord Rosebery's scheme of reform.

On the 9th of March Mr. Labouchere again moved his resolution in the House of Commons. Mr. W. H. Smith, the leader of the House, in resisting the motion, admitted that some alteration was desirable, and agreed with a previous speaker that it was by the Conservatives that such alteration ought to be effected. On the 19th of March in the same year Lord Rosebery, in the House of Lords, moved for a Select Committee to inquire into the subject. He took the opportunity to explain his own scheme of reform. While he did not desire to abolish the hereditary principle, he was of opinion that no peer outside the royal family should be a member of Parliament by right of birth alone. To representatives chosen by the peers he proposed to add other men who had achieved distinction in a public career. He attached a high importance to the existence of a second chamber. His motion was negatived by ninety-seven votes against fifty.

Lord Salisbury's proposals.

On the 26th of April Lord Dunraven withdrew a bill for the reform of the House of Lords on the promise of the Government to deal with the matter, and on the 18th of June Lord Salisbury fulfilled this pledge. He introduced a bill on that day to provide for the creation of a limited number of life-peers and for the exclusion of unworthy members from the House. Under this measure a maximum of five life-peerages in any one year might be created; but the total number was never to exceed fifty. In respect to three out of these five life-peers the choice of the Crown was restricted to judges, generals, admirals, ambassadors, privy councillors, and ex-governors of colonies. The two additional life-peers were to

[1] 202 to 166.

be appointed in regard to some special qualification to be stated in the message to the House announcing the intention of the Crown to make the appointment. Power was also to be given to the House to expel members for the period of the current Parliament by an address to the Crown praying that their writs of summons might be cancelled. The bill was read a second time on the 10th of July, but it met with a cold reception and was dropped. The only outcome of all that was said, written, and threatened in this year was that in 1889, after the report of a Select Committee appointed in 1888, the Lords made a few changes in their Standing Orders, among which the order establishing a quorum of thirty in divisions and those for the constitution of Standing Committees were the most important.[1]

An attempt to rouse the country on the question of the House of Lords was made by Lord Rosebery after his resignation in June, 1895, in view of the General Election which immediately followed. But even had this been possible in the spring of 1894 it was now too late. On the subject of Home Rule a majority in the country agreed with the House of Lords and disagreed with the House of Commons, and the operation of "ploughing the sands" which followed the rejection of the Home Rule Bill had brought Ministry and Irish-Liberal majority into disesteem. *Lord Rosebery in 1895.*

During the ten years of Unionist rule to which the elections of 1895 and 1900 gave birth the question of reform in either House of Parliament was in abeyance. The position of the House of Lords had been greatly strengthened by their successful rejection of the Home Rule Bill, and Conservative statesmen were no longer apprehensive, as they had been in 1887, that, by leaving the ancient edifice unrepaired, they might bring about its destruction at some future period by the rougher methods of their opponents. No Government Bill passed by the Conservative House of Commons was rejected by the Lords, and if the Conservative Ministers were unwilling to accept Lords' amendments these were never insisted upon. No imaginable assembly, therefore, could have been more conveniently constituted from the standpoint of a Unionist Ministry; and, except for the apprehension *Parliamentary reform in abeyance 1895-1905.*

[1] See *Encyclopædia Britannica*, 10th edition, article "Parliament".

just mentioned, there was nothing to make them desire its reform. Nor did the Opposition wish for reform. Radicals wished to curtail the powers of the House of Lords, and the more extreme among them to abolish it altogether; but they thought that to reform it would be to strengthen its powers of resistance to their own projects. The franchise reform known as "one man, one vote," and the simplification of the registration laws continued to be parts of the Liberal programme. But during the first seven years of the Unionist Ministry the Government was so strong, and the Opposition so weak and divided, that the views and proposals of the latter were not a matter of much account. Lord Rosebery began by abandoning the Newcastle Programme, and in the autumn of 1896 resigned his leadership; his successor, Sir William Harcourt, resigned in December, 1898; and in 1899 the outbreak of the South African war revealed a new fissure in the party structure almost as formidable as that which divided Whigs from Radicals in 1885.

Unionist movement for a fresh redistribution of seats.
In the later years of the Unionist Ministry when it had been weakened by the unpopularity of the Education Act of 1902, by the party split on the fiscal question, and by the resignation of some of its most powerful members in 1903, the question of a new redistribution of seats, made urgent in the view of many by the growing over-representation of Ireland, began to occupy the minds and the pens of the rank and file of the Unionist party. The answer to the Liberal demand for "one man one vote" had been that until each vote had the same value it would be irrational to abolish one electoral anomaly and to leave a greater subsisting. But although the Unionists cried out against reform without redistribution, they seem to have had no objection to redistribution without reform; and although they argued that if every man was restricted to one vote, every vote must have the same value, they saw nothing in the corresponding proposition that if every vote was given the same value, every man should be restricted to one vote.

Every Government is reluctant to deal with the question of redistribution. They are unwilling to alienate those of their supporters whose seats under an equitable scheme must be suppressed; and when in possession of a comfortable majority they are unwilling to embark on a measure, the passage of which must be followed by a dissolution. In 1905, however, in the fifth year of the Parliament of 1900, redistribution occupied the first place in the King's Speech.

The Houses were informed that the attention of Parliament would be directed to "proposals for diminishing the anomalies in the present arrangement of electoral areas". Lord Lansdowne, however, explained in his speech on the address that no bill would be introduced during that session owing to what he described as the physical impossibility of finding time. This plea was open to criticism, for not only did Parliament meet late (on the 15th of February), but in the short session of 1905 fewer bills were passed into law than in any other for a hundred years. *[margin: Introduction of the question.]*

On the 11th July notice was given of resolutions in which the plan of the Government was set forth. There were only two: the first covering the whole of the Government scheme for redistribution, the second relating to the appointment of Boundary Commissioners who were to report on changes necessary to give effect to the provisions of the first.

The first resolution declared the expediency of a revision of the existing d stribution of seats whereby the minimum population in a borough entitled to return a member was to be reduced to 18,500, while the minimum population in a county so entitled was left as high as 32,500.[1] This was not considered to be just by the Opposition, because the large majority of the smaller boroughs which would thus escape disfranchisement returned Unionists, while the disfranchisement in the counties told most severely against Ireland. *[margin: The resolutions of 1905.]*

The resolutions, however, were never debated. The Speaker, on the point being raised by the Opposition, ruled *[margin: Withdrawal of the resolutions.]*

---

[1] (a) The number of members of the House of Commons was not to be materially altered: (b) new members were to be given as follows: (i) a municipal borough or urban district with a population exceeding 65,000 was to become a separate constituency; (ii) a county or borough with a population of 65,000 was to have an additional member for every completed additional 65,000: (c) members were to be taken away as follows: (i) a borough with a population of less than 18,500 was to cease to exist as a separate constituency, and (ii) a county or borough with two members and a population of less than 65,000 multiplied by the number of its members was to have one less member for every complete 65,000 of the deficiency; (d) the county or borough was, so far as practicable, to be made coextensive with the administrative county and the municipal borough respectively.

that the resolutions ought to be divided into eight or nine separate parts, and that these should be discussed, one after another, in committee of the whole House. Thereupon Mr. Balfour withdrew the resolutions on the ground that this procedure would require more time than could be spared at that late period in the session, but promised that a bill based on the resolutions should be introduced in the following year, and that in the meantime a Boundary Commission should be issued in accordance with the terms of the second resolution. But his sudden and unprecedented resignation in December, while Parliament was not sitting, relieved him from the obligation of fulfilling this undertaking.

The General Election of 1906.
The General Election of 1906 resulted in the return of an overwhelming Liberal majority, and during their first year of office there were no signs that Sir Henry Campbell Bannerman's Government were losing ground in the country. Supporters of the Newcastle Programme, therefore, were justified in hoping that the harvest of their wishes would at last be reaped. But through their majority in the House of Lords the Unionist opposition were able in the Parliament of 1906 to prevent this consummation.

The Plural Voting Bill.
Early in the first session of this Parliament a bill for the abolition of plural voting was introduced by Mr. Harcourt, the new First Commissioner of Works. It provided for the imposition of a penalty on any Parliamentary elector, registered in more than one constituency, who should vote in any constituency except that selected for the purpose. The voter was annually to choose which of his several votes he would exercise during the subsequent year, and, unless it were cancelled, his selection would hold good for that period.

Rejected by the Lords.
The opposition to this measure, as in the case of the Registration Bill of 1894, took the traditional form of an objection that it was not accompanied by a measure of redistribution. This objection when urged against the Franchise Act of 1884 had considerable weight; but its relevancy was less obvious when brought against a bill for restricting each elector to a single vote. To have added 2,000,000 new voters to the counties without any redistribution of electoral power would have been largely to increase the already serious inequalities in the value of a vote; but the abolition of plural voting, so far

as in this respect it had any effect at all, would have tended to diminish these inequalities, since by reducing the number of out-voters it would have made representation to depend more nearly on the actual population of a constituency and less on a more or less artificial register. There was, however, a general feeling on the Unionist side that it was unfair that an anomaly which told in favour of the Conservatives should be removed, while another anomaly which favoured their opponents was suffered to remain. Mr. Chamberlain denounced the bill as "the most audacious proposal ever introduced into the House"—a view which only served to show how far he had travelled since the days when in 1884 he inveighed against the Lords for insisting on the production of a scheme for redistribution as a preliminary to their assent to the Franchise Bill. On the 14th May the Plural Voting Bill was read a second time by a majority of 403 votes to 95. In the autumn it passed through committee on allotted days prefixed by resolution of the House, and on the 3rd December it was read a third time by 333 to 104. On the 10th December it was rejected by the Lords on the second reading by a majority of 100 (143 to 43). The amendment whereby it met its fate was moved by Lord St. Aldwyn, and set forth that, while willing to consider a complete scheme, the House declined to entertain a bill imposing penalties for the exercise of the franchise by persons to whom it was entrusted by law, and leaving untouched the most glaring anomalies in the distribution of electoral power.

This summary rejection by the House of Lords of a bill passed by enormous majorities in the first session of a new House of Commons, and concerned only with the qualifications of electors of that House, was a significant illustration of the new attitude which the successful rejection of the Home Rule Bill had emboldened the permanent Conservative majority in the House of Lords to assume towards Liberal majorities, however large and however recent, in the House of Commons.

The only further attempt at electoral reform made by the ministry during this Parliament was the London Government Bill of 1909, the object of which was, by the introduction of the rule of "successive occupation" for registration purposes, to save large numbers of the rapidly-moving population of

The London Government Bill, 1909.

London from forfeiting their votes when they changed their domiciles. Plural voting is illegal in the great provincial towns of England; the bill made it illegal in London also. The Lords rejected this bill on the ground that it was incomplete.

<small>Contemplated Reform Bill postponed by constitutional crisis.</small>

It was not the fault of the Liberal Ministry that no more comprehensive scheme of reform was offered to the consideration of the Parliament of 1906, for if the Lords had not by the rejection of the Finance Bill compelled the Crown to dissolve Parliament in January, 1910, the Government had intended during that year to introduce a large measure dealing with the whole question. In May, 1908, a deputation of sixty Liberal members interested in the enfranchisement of women waited on Mr. Asquith, who had just succeeded to the post of Prime Minister, to ask him to give further facilities for the discussion of a Women's Enfranchisement Bill, which had been read a second time by a large majority, or else to promise that the Government would, before the end of the current Parliament, deal with the question themselves or allow others to do so. In his reply Mr. Asquith pleaded want of time; but he announced that it was the intention of the Government before the dissolution of the current Parliament to introduce a comprehensive Reform Bill to deal with the grosser anomalies of our electoral system, including the length of the residence necessary for qualification as an elector, and plural voting. He suggested that to this bill an amendment introducing women's suffrage might be proposed; and, the Government being themselves divided on that issue, he promised that the question should be left open by them and the fate of such an amendment decided in all freedom by the House. He attached, however, two significant conditions to this important concession; firstly, that the change should be on democratic lines; and secondly, that it should prove to be supported by an overwhelming majority of women as well as of men.

The story of the conflict between the two Houses of Parliament belongs to another chapter. The question of the powers of the House of Lords and of the relation borne by the fresh and emphatic assertion by that House of legal rights supposed to have been practically abandoned to the privileges of the House of Commons, has become to some extent interwoven with the question of the reform of the constitution of the Upper House. The subjects are, however, perfectly distinct and it is with the latter only that we are here concerned.

The reform of the House of Lords attracted, as we have seen, but little attention during the ten years of Unionist rule between 1895 and 1905. But the defeat by that House in 1906 of the Education Bill and their rejection of the Plural Voting Bill followed by the resolutions directed against this veto moved by the Prime Minister and carried by immense majorities in the spring of 1907, convinced the more prudent of the Unionist peers that the subject could no longer be safely neglected. *Reform of the House of Lords.*

On the 6th May, 1907, Lord Newton moved the second reading of a bill for the re-constitution of the House of Lords. He desired (i) to modify the hereditary element, by enacting that a peer by descent alone should have a right to sit only if he possessed certain special qualifications, or were elected as a representative peer; (ii) that representative peers should be elected for a Parliament only; (iii) that power should be given to the Crown to appoint not more than 100 life peers; (iv) that the number of bishops should be reduced in proportion to the number of hereditary peers; (v) that the system of electing representative peers for Scotland and Ireland should be assimilated to that proposed for England; and (vi) that any hereditary peer who so desired might stand as a candidate for the House of Commons, provided that by so doing he forfeited for ever his right to sit as a member of the House of Lords. *Lord Newton's bill of 1907.*

These proposals were well received; but Lord Cawdor proposed as an alternative to proceeding with the bill that a Select Committee should be appointed to consider the subject. Lord Newton agreed to this suggestion; but Lord Crewe, on behalf of the Government, protested that it was not expedient to proceed with proposals for reform until provision had been made for an effective method of settling differences with the Commons. The Government therefore declined to be represented on the Committee. Lord Rosebery, whose name had been long associated with House of Lords reform, was appointed chairman, and Lord St. Aldwyn, Lord Halsbury, Lord Selby and other distinguished men were chosen as members. *Select Committee appointed. The bill withdrawn.*

In December, 1908, the Committee reported the results of their labours. They proposed that a distinction should be *Report of the Committee.*

drawn between peers and Lords of Parliament and that, except in the case of the Royal family, a peerage alone should not entitle the holder to a seat in the House. The hereditary peers, including those of Scotland and Ireland, were to elect 200 representatives to sit in that House for each Parliament, the election being conducted by a form of cumulative voting. The bishops were to elect eight representatives; while the archbishops sat as of right. The Committee expressed its regret that it could not agree in devising a method whereby other forms of religion might be represented. They suggested that official representatives of the self-governing colonies and of India might be introduced into the House. Besides the elected peers, any hereditary peer should be entitled to sit who had been a Cabinet Minister, Viceroy of India, Governor General of Canada or of Australia, High Commissioner of South Africa, who had held any of certain Colonial Governorships or high offices, or had been Lieutenant General or Vice-Admiral on the active list, or had sat for a certain period in the Commons. This recommendation would add about 130 peers to the House. The Crown should be empowered to summon four life peers annually, so long as the total did not exceed forty. The Lords of Appeal in Ordinary would still be Lords of Parliament. This would reduce the number of members from over 600 to under 400. There had been proposals to admit elected representatives from County Councils and Municipal Corporations; but the Committee, being almost equally divided, made no recommendation.

Liberal objections to the scheme. The fatal defect in this scheme from a Liberal point of view was that while it deprived the Crown, acting on the advice of the Ministry, of its last resource in a numerous creation of peers, it seemed likely to entrench the Conservative majority more securely than ever in the House of Lords. It left the Liberal grievance untouched. For this grievance was not that obscure and irresponsible peers acting independently and contrary to the wishes of their leaders made controversial Liberal legislation an impossibility without a fresh dissolution on each controversial measure, but that this was done under the guidance of the official leaders of the Unionist party. There could be no doubt that, in spite of the cumulative vote, almost all the 200 representative peers and a large majority of the 130 hereditary official peers would under the scheme be Unionists, and that they would follow the same leaders as did the actual majority in the House of Lords. The only remedy left to a Liberal Ministry would be by new creations to "swamp" the anomalous constituency by which the elective peers were chosen and this could hardly be considered desirable. The difficulties of Liberal legislators could be in no way diminished nor the relations of Liberal Ministries with the House of Lords in any way facilitated by the adoption of the scheme; but as all the members of the Committee but three were strongly opposed to most Liberal legislation it is possible that this circumstance did not appear to them a formidable objection.

No further step was taken until after the rejection of the Finance Bill by the House of Lords in 1909. At the general election which followed in January, 1910, the powers of the House of Lords were more discussed than their constitution; but the Foreign Secretary, Sir Edward Grey, and the Secretary for War, Mr. Haldane, declared themselves in favour of a Second Chamber, elected on a democratic basis and by the same electorate as the first. They suggested that the members of this Second Chamber should be much less numerous than those of the first; that they should be elected by very large constituencies; and that half of them should be re-elected every four years. If the two Houses disagreed, they proposed that their differences should be settled in a joint session. The advantages claimed for this scheme are twofold. In the first place, the "gusts of popular opinion," by which the results of general elections are said to be often determined, would be less felt in the Second Chamber owing to the system of periodical renewals of half instead of the whole of the members; and in the second place, the great size of the constituencies would tend to secure the selection of distinguished men as candidates by the two parties.
Liberal suggestions for re-constitution of Second Chamber.

In moving on the 29th March, 1910, that the House should resolve itself into a Committee to consider the relations between the two Houses of Parliament, Mr. Asquith, the Prime Minister, was careful to make it clear that he did not consider the resolutions which he was about to move or the bill to limit the powers of the House of Lords founded upon them as a final
Mr. Asquith on the composition of the Second Chamber.

solution of the question. He intimated that a measure for the reform of the constitution of the House of Lords should follow the limitation of its powers. "The body," he said, "which is to discharge these functions (i.e. consultation, revision, and delay) consistently with the maintenance of the predominance of this House, must be a body which is relatively small in number. It must be a body, if it is to have any credentials whatever for the performance of its task, which rests upon a democratic and not a hereditary basis. It must be a body which, by virtue both of its origin and of its composition, of its atmosphere, of its constitutional attitude, is not, as the House of Lords is, governed by partisanship tempered by panic, but a body which is responsive to, representative of, and dependent upon the opinion and will of the nation." This policy was registered in the preamble of the bill brought in to give effect to the resolutions on the relations between the two Houses of Parliament, wherein the intention was formally stated "to substitute for the House of Lords as it at present exists a Second Chamber constituted on a popular instead of a hereditary basis".

Lord Rosebery's resolutions.

In the meantime Lord Rosebery was endeavouring to persuade the peers to reform themselves; or at least by solemn declarations to show that they had altogether abandoned a *non possumus* attitude with regard to a change in their constitution. On the 14th of March he moved: "That the House do resolve itself into a Committee to consider the best means of reforming its existing organisation, so as to constitute a strong and efficient Second Chamber". This motion having been agreed to, he proceeded to move three resolutions: "1. That a strong and efficient Second Chamber is not merely an integral part of the British constitution, but is necessary to the wellbeing of the State and to the balance of Parliament. 2. That such a chamber can best be obtained by the reform and reconstitution of the House of Lords. 3. That a necessary preliminary of such reform and reconstitution is the acceptance of the principle that the possession of a peerage should no longer of itself give the right to sit and vote in the House of Lords."

The first two of these resolutions were carried without a division; and the third, although not received with enthusiasm, was eventually agreed to after long debates by 175 votes against 17. Not one-third of the members of the House of Lords took part in the division, and the majority would not have been so large had it not been made clear that the terms of the resolution did not abolish the hereditary basis of the House of Lords, but only made it necessary that the hereditary right to a seat in that assembly should be accompanied by some other qualification. The death of King Edward VII. during the spring recess, and the consequent postponement of the presentation to the House of Lords of the Ministerial resolutions concerning the relations of the two Houses of Parliament already passed by the Commons, caused Lord Rosebery to postpone the production of the further resolutions on House of Lords reform which it was his intention to move, although in doing so he denied that his proposals were to be considered as a rival scheme to that of the Government, or that the two subjects were germane to one another.

The effectiveness of the existing electoral system for securing a true representation of the will of the electors has been much discussed and questioned in recent years, and there have been many suggestions for improving it. Mr. Gladstone claimed for the Act of 1885 that by its substitution of single-member constituencies for the historic two-member system it provided for the representation of separate interests and pursuits, and thus in some degree for the representation of minorities. To go further and to provide for the direct representation of minorities would, he thought, be to introduce a system novel, artificial, and beset with difficulties. When there are only two parties—as was the case in the United Kingdom in 1885—votes will be given at general elections either for or against the Government without much regard to local considerations or the personality of candidates, and with single-member districts minorities defeated in one district will be represented by the return of the party candidate in another. But the English system of election by relative majorities, under which it is not necessary for the successful candidate to obtain a majority of the total votes polled but only more votes than any one of his rivals, presupposes for its justification in reason the existence of only two contending parties. Where there are more than two parties in Parliament; and more than two candidates, each

Electoral anomalies.

of them representing a separate party, seek election in a constituency, it may often happen that the least popular of the three may be victorious. The appearance of the Labour party on the political stage—a party which, while it regards most projects of Liberal legislation as steps in the right direction and therefore generally votes with the Liberals, claims complete independence of that party and maintains a separate organisation, has convinced most men that the system of election by relative majority must be abandoned. At the General Election of 1906 there were thirty three-cornered contests, in some of which the least popular of the candidates was elected owing to the "split vote," as it is called, of his opponents. The system has been rejected by most of the great countries of Europe, and outside the United Kingdom subsists only in the United States, Denmark, Bulgaria, and Greece. There is a strong current of opinion in favour of the adoption either of the second ballot or of the newly devised system of the alternative vote to the end that this anomaly may cease.[1]

Minority representation.

The question of minority representation has grown in importance at each successive extension of the suffrage. It is feared that the numerical preponderance of a single class in nearly every constituency may eventually exclude every other

---

[1] The countries which have rejected or abandoned the relative majority system have for the most part adopted that of the second ballot. Under this system, where no candidate secures an absolute majority of the votes cast at the first election, a second is held, at which, in most cases, only those two candidates compete who have received most votes at the first ballot. This system is in force, with differences, in Austria, France, Germany, Italy, and several of the smaller European countries. But a method has been devised and adopted with success in Queensland and Western Australia, whereby the advantages of the second ballot may be secured, and success at the polls made conditional on the gain of an absolute majority, without the inconvenience and expense of a second election. This is the alternative vote—a scheme now supported by nearly all the former advocates of the second ballot. Under this system the voter arranges the candidates in the order of his preference by placing the figures 1, 2, 3 against their names on his voting paper. "At the first count only first votes are reckoned. If then no candidate is found to have obtained an absolute majority, the candidate who has received the smallest number of first votes is regarded as eliminated, and his voting papers are distributed according to the names, if any, marked 2 on them. The papers on which no second preference is marked are regarded as 'exhausted,' and their number is deducted from the total for the purpose of calculating the absolute majority at the second count. If still no candidate has received such a majority, the process is repeated as often as necessary until the desired result is obtained." The adoption of the alternative vote was recommended by the Royal Commission of 1910, and their advice was generally approved. Cd. 5163.

class from representation to the House of Commons; and a new Reform Act including the payment of members[1] and their election expenses out of public money and abolishing plural voting would greatly increase this danger.

Many schemes for the representation of minorities have been proposed, all of which presuppose multi-member constituencies, and to all of which there are formidable if not insuperable objections. The "limited vote," when the voter has fewer votes than there are seats to be filled, was tried in a few constituencies returning more than two members between 1867 and 1885, but it was not considered a success, and has now few supporters. The "cumulative vote," when the voter has as many votes as there are seats to be filled, but is allowed to distribute them as he pleases, or to accumulate them on one candidate, was in force for School Board elections between 1870 and 1902. To both these systems it has been objected with great force that they depend for their successful working on party organisation and "the implicit obedience of the elector to the directions of the party manager". And the bulk of well-wishers to minority representation are now united in support of the system known as the "transferable vote" or "proportional representation"—a development of the scheme originally proposed by Mr. Hare in 1859, and supported by John Stuart Mill.

In this system constituencies return several members, and the elector indicates the order of his preferences as in the case of the alternative vote. A qualifying number of votes is then ascertained by dividing the votes cast by the number of seats to be filled plus one, and adding one to the result. Any candidate who obtains this quota is declared elected. The surplus votes of the candidates who have obtained more than the quota are then transferred to the unelected candidates indicated by the figures 2, 3, and so on, as the next preferences of the electors whose votes are transferred. The candidates lowest on the poll are then eliminated, and their votes are transferred according to the second preferences of their supporters. *Scheme for proportional representation.*

This ingenious scheme has been advocated by Conservatives who fear an era of class legislation and by philosophical Liberals *Objections to the scheme.*

[1] In the summer session of 1911, the payment of a salary of £400 a year to non-official members of the House of Commons was approved by a resolution of the House and voted in committee of supply.

of a doctrinaire type, whose chief aim in legislation is logical completeness, and to whom the complications of a system add to its attractions. It is, however, open to many and serious objections. Although it is true that it would mitigate the exaggeration of majorities at general elections and might cause the proportions of party in the country to be more accurately mirrored in the House of Commons, it is questionable whether this would be altogether an advantage. Small majorities imply weak Governments. It has been calculated that in the Parliaments of 1895 and 1900 the Unionist majorities, warranted by the Unionist voting strength, would have been in each case two only, instead of 150 and 134 respectively, while in 1886 the Unionists would actually have been in a minority of eighteen. It would seem, therefore, that the system would tend to make Governments weaker and general elections more frequent. The difficulty of fitting by-elections into the scheme; the inconsistency of election by late preferences with our party system; the increase in the number of candidates and of members unattached to any party which might result from the change, and the resulting instability of Ministries; the loss of directness and simplicity in the mode of election; all these considerations tend to render the plan unpopular both with statesmen and the electorate, so far at least as elections for the House of Commons are concerned.

Report of the Royal Commission. A strong Royal Commission, under the presidency of Lord Richard Cavendish, was appointed in December, 1908, " to examine the various schemes which have been adopted or proposed, in order to secure a fully representative character for popularly-elected legislative bodies, and to consider whether, and how far, they, or any of them, are capable of application in this country in regard to the existing electorate ". The report of the Commission was published in 1910. The Commissioners recommended the adoption of the alternative vote in cases where more than two candidates stand for one seat. Of schemes for producing proportional representation they thought that the transferable vote would have the best chance of ultimate acceptance, but, for the reasons just referred to, they " were unable to recommend its adoption in existing circumstances for elections to the House of Commons ".[1] These

[1] Cd. 5163, p. 37.

reasons, however, would not militate against the use of the transferable vote in the election of such a Second Chamber as has been advocated by Sir Edward Grey and Mr. Haldane. It lends itself so well to their plan of large constituencies, periodical but partial re-elections, and small numbers, while the assembly elected under the system would still, in the words of the Prime Minister, be " responsive to, representative of, and dependent upon the opinion and will of the nation," that it is reasonable to suppose that proportional representation may be a part of the reform which they have in view. Such a solution has been suggested by Mr. Lecky and other writers, and favourably noticed in the report of the Royal Commission; it is not open to the objections advanced by that Commission to its applicability to the House of Commons; and would lessen the danger of the exclusive predominance of a single class which, after the passing of the next Reform Bill, may have to be confronted.

One other subject connected with Parliamentary reform remains to be noticed in this chapter. In the Middle Ages and up to the beginning of the seventeenth century the property franchise was occasionally exercised by women as well as by men. The franchise was attached not to citizenship but to property, and so long as the root idea of the House of Commons was that of the assemblage, at the bidding of the Crown, of the representatives of owners of property in order that they might, before or after the redress of their grievances as the case might be, give and grant some part of the property of those whom they represented or of their own to the Crown to be applied to public ends, there appeared to be no reason why property should be less represented when its owner was a woman than when he was a man. Accordingly we find that a certain Dame Dorothy Pakington in the reign of Elizabeth returned two members to represent her or her property in the House of Commons. But the practice of women voting had fallen into disuse even before its formal condemnation by Lord Coke, and the dictum of that great authority was for the time conclusive. *Women's suffrage.*

Little was heard of the subject during the first half of the nineteenth century. But the theory that gradually gained ground during this period that the vote is a natural right, and *Beginnings of the movement.*

that every citizen of a commonwealth who contributes, by rates or taxes, to the public revenue, or by labour to the public wealth, is entitled to a share in the management of its affairs, caused certain political philosophers like Mr. John Stuart Mill and Professor Cairnes to ask themselves in what way women failed to fulfil these conditions. The opponents of woman suffrage contended that the franchise was not a natural right, but a privilege granted to certain categories of persons with a view to good government, and that the natural distinction between the sexes justified the political distinction sanctioned by the laws of every European country. The first branch of this argument was, however, weakened by each fresh extension of the suffrage, and especially by the principles on which the last two Reform Acts were based. The issue is one of singular difficulty, for the contending parties have no common ground; their arguments are based on different assumptions; and they resemble combatants who cannot reach one another; they wave their swords furiously, and merely strike the air.

Mr. Mill's amendment. On the 7th June, 1866, shortly before the resignation of the Russell Ministry and while their Reform Bill was still under discussion, Mr. John Stuart Mill, the most distinguished champion of women's rights, presented a petition to the House of Commons praying Parliament to remove the anomaly by which some holders of property were given the right to vote while others equally qualified were excluded. In the following year on the 20th May he moved an amendment to Mr. Disraeli's Reform Bill, to substitute in respect of the franchise the word "persons" for the word "men". On this amendment the question was for the first time debated in the House of Commons. The subject, however, excited more amusement than interest, and the amendment was defeated by 196 votes against 73. In the same year the National Society for Women's Suffrage was formed, and in April, 1868, the first public meeting in support of the cause was held in the Free Trade Hall in Manchester.

Claims under the existing law. The next step taken by the promoters of the movement was to ascertain their rights under the existing law. The Reform Act of 1832 had qualified the voters with whom it dealt as "male persons," but the Act of 1867 described them merely as "men". And it had been enacted in another connection that "in all acts words importing the masculine gender shall be deemed to include the female, unless the contrary be expressly provided". Moreover these Reform Acts had not abolished the old property franchise of the forty shilling freeholder, and it was historically certain that under this franchise women had in former times recorded their votes. Four test cases, therefore, were brought on appeal before the Court of Common Pleas: (1) That of women householders of Manchester who had sent in their claims to be put on the register under the Act of 1867; (2) that of a lady in South-East Lancashire, who claimed to be registered as a forty-shilling freeholder under the statute of Henry IV.; (3) 1431 women of Salford who, having been placed on the register by the overseers, had been struck off by the revising barrister, without any one having objected to them; and (4) 857 women who had sent in their claims to be put on the register at Salford. The Court held that, as the cases had been taken in the name of women as appellants, it could not hear them, because a woman had no right to the appeal granted by the Registration Act.

In 1869 the first public meeting held in London in support of women's suffrage was addressed by Mr. John Stuart Mill, Mr. Charles Kingsley, Prof. Fawcett, Mr. John Morley, and other distinguished men. In the same year the municipal franchise was given to women by the bill for the regulation of municipal corporations. Before the passing of this Act the municipal franchise differed in different boroughs, in some of which women had the vote, and in others not. *The meeting of 1869.*

In 1870 a bill for the enfranchisement of women, introduced by Mr. Jacob Bright—who was now recognised as the Parliamentary leader of the movement—was unexpectedly read a second time, by 124 votes to 91. Thereupon Mr. Gladstone, who was opposed to the principle of the measure, intervened, with the result that a few days later the motion to go into committee was defeated by a much larger majority. By the Education Act of 1870 women were given votes for the newly-created school boards, and Miss Becker, the leading spirit among the women promoting the movement and the editor of their organ, the *Women's Suffrage Journal*, was elected a member of the board at Manchester. *Mr. Jacob Bright's bill of 1870.*

Proceedings in Parliament. In 1871, 1872, and 1873 Mr. Jacob Bright re-introduced his bill—to be defeated on second reading by majorities of 69, 80, and 67 respectively. At the General Election of 1874 he was himself defeated, and in the Conservative House then elected a Conservative member, Mr. Forsyth, succeeded him in his leadership. Mr. Disraeli, the Prime Minister, and his principal colleague, Sir Stafford Northcote, were both of them supporters, if somewhat academic supporters, of women's suffrage, and the Parliament of 1874 was not more opposed to the change than its predecessor. The subject was not regarded with much seriousness, the debates were characterised by a certain levity, and no one expected or really desired an early settlement of the question. In 1875 Mr. Forsyth's bill was rejected by a majority of only 25; in 1876, when Mr. John Bright, who had formerly supported the movement, not only voted but spoke against the bill, this majority rose to 89; it was 80 in 1878; and a resolution moved in 1879 was rejected by a still larger majority.

In the next three Parliaments the changes in procedure brought about by the Parnellite tactics of obstruction in the House of Commons made it increasingly difficult for private members to find opportunities for the discussion of their bills and resolutions. An opportunity, however, presented itself during the committee stage of the Reform Bill of 1884, when Mr. Woodall moved a new clause to provide that words importing the masculine gender should include women. To this clause Mr. Gladstone offered the "strongest opposition in his power," and declared that if it were carried he would abandon the bill. It was consequently rejected by a large majority (271-135).

In the autumn of 1884 the Trade Union Congress passed a resolution in favour of extending the franchise to women ratepayers, but the times were not propitious and the movement at this period appeared to lose ground. A great reform had just been effected in the electoral law, and the claims of women to be included in it had been emphatically rejected. It did not appear probable that the question would be reopened for the present, and there was no lack of great problems to occupy the attention of the political world. It was indeed claimed that 343 known friends to women's suffrage had been elected to the House of Commons of 1886—a clear majority; but these friends were occupied with other matters, there was a great pressure of business, and in point of fact until 1892, the last year of this Parliament, no debate took place on the subject. In that year a bill of Sir Albert Rollit for the extension of the suffrage to women came up for discussion. The second reading was negatived by 175 to 152, but received the support of Mr. Balfour, the leader of the House.[1]

In the crowded sessions of the short Parliament of 1892 no time was found for a debate on women's suffrage. Not only Mr. Gladstone but his successor in the leadership of the House, Sir William Harcourt, was an opponent of the proposal. The general movement, however, gathered force in the colonies and showed some signs of reviving vitality at home. In September, 1893, women's suffrage was established in New Zealand; in December, 1894, this example was followed by South Australia. A petition for the vote said to be signed by 248,000 women was presented to Parliament in 1894, and the Local Government Acts of 1888 and 1894 admitted women to the local franchise on equal terms with men.

Women's suffrage in the colonies.

In the next Parliament further progress was made. In 1897 Mr. Faithful Begg's Suffrage Bill was read a second time by a majority of 71 and since 1902 every bill on the subject has been approved by a majority of the House of Commons.

As time went on the methods of the suffragists increased in energy, and a section of them became of opinion that if Parliament could not be persuaded, it might at least be worried into concession. When monster petitions and great meetings in Hyde Park proved of no practical avail, war was declared on all Governments who hardened their hearts against the

New methods.

---

[1] Though the period of 1886-1892 was a period of discouragement to the supporters of women's suffrage, the activity of women in other political directions and the eagerness with which this activity was welcomed and employed by the political parties supplied the suffragists with an argument in favour of the fitness of women for political life. It was at this time that the Dames of the Primrose League played a conspicuous part, while the Women's Liberal Federation and the Women's Liberal Unionist Association did good work on behalf of their respective parties. It was illogical and ungenerous, so it was argued, to make use of the services of women in the preparations for an election, and then to deny them any weight in the actual contest on the ground that they were unfitted to pronounce on political issues.

claimants and a succession of minor outrages was the result. Proceeding on the principle which Mr. Gladstone had done so much to justify that to gain a political end it is necessary to be troublesome, a section of the claimants broke windows, interrupted speeches, and subjected Cabinet Ministers, even those who favoured their cause, to petty annoyances and in some cases to actual assault of a contemptible kind. When put into prison for short terms on refusing to be bound over to keep the peace the new martyrs embarrassed the administration by refusing to eat their dinners and by breaking in other ways the prison regulations. These tactics had at all events the effect of keeping the movement before the eyes of the public and filling the newspapers with the proceedings of its promoters; and, in a democratic country, this is not a negligible circumstance. But they also stiffened opposition and confirmed opponents in their views of the danger and folly of concession.

Non-party character of the majority in favour of Women's Suffrage Bill an obstacle to its progress.

The majorities in the House of Commons recorded in favour of women's suffrage, leading as they do to nothing, naturally exasperate the suffragists and wear the appearance of insincerity. But this is to some extent an appearance only. Under existing conditions and the increased rigidity of party all controversial legislation is the work of the Government. The time allotted to the discussion of private members' bills—more numerous now than ever before—has been limited to the morning sittings on Fridays before Whitsuntide with two other morning sittings after that date; and it is understood that in the case of contentious bills the division on second reading is an expression of opinion on the part of the House rather than of any intention to pass the measure into law. No private member's bill to which the Government refuse special facilities, if opposed by a resolute minority however numerically insignificant, has the smallest chance of passing into law. Before therefore legislation on any controversial subject is possible, a Cabinet must be found all the members of which are agreed as to its desirability, and this means that the bill must have been adopted by one of the two great parties as a party measure. A bill which fulfils this condition has a much better chance of success, though supported by a majority of only ten, than another with a majority of a hundred in its favour, but to which a section of the Cabinet is opposed.

Of the seven statesmen who have held the post of Prime Minister during the last forty years, four have been Liberals and three Conservatives; and it has so chanced that of the three Conservatives all have supported women's suffrage, while three out of four of the Liberal premiers have been opposed to it. Nevertheless there is, as might be expected, a majority in the Liberal party in favour of the change, and a majority in the Unionist party against it, while the Labour party have made the abolition of the electoral disabilities of women a part of their programme.

We have seen how in reply to a deputation of Liberal members Mr. Asquith, in 1908, pledged himself if certain conditions were complied with to leave the question of women's suffrage an open question for the House if an amendment were proposed to the Reform Bill which it was then the intention of the Government to introduce before the dissolution. In his speech at the Albert Hall in November, 1909, Mr. Asquith, at the request of the Women's Liberal Federation, declared that this pledge was still binding on the Government if they should remain in office after the election and should introduce a Reform Bill into the new Parliament.

In 1910, a committee of members of Parliament, presided over by Lord Lytton, and known as the Conciliation Committee, met in order to devise a measure which should unite in its support all sections of the adherents to the cause of women's suffrage. The result of their deliberations was the introduction on the 14th June by Mr. Shackleton, a Labour member, of a bill to extend the Parliamentary franchise to women occupiers. The bill excluded women from the ownership vote and from plural voting. The suffrage was given only to those women who already exercised it in local and municipal elections. In order that the new Parliament might have an opportunity of recording its opinion on the subject Mr. Asquith gave two days out of Government time for the second reading of the bill. The debate took place on the 11th and 12th of July, and from the seriousness with which the subject was for the first time approached by opponents as well as by supporters this discussion contrasted favourably with its predecessors. Mr. Asquith and Mr. Austen Chamberlain spoke against the bill; Mr. Balfour and Mr. Haldane in its favour. Mr. Balfour's support was

The Conciliation Committee and its bill.

not very enthusiastic ; he declared himself of opinion that the interests of women did not suffer by their exclusion from the franchise, but that no harm would be done by giving the vote to the women whom it was proposed to enfranchise, and that to do this involved no logical or practical necessity whatever for subsequently removing the remaining political disqualifications of women. Mr. Lloyd George and Mr. Churchill explained the votes they gave against the bill, while they professed to be supporters of women's suffrage, by describing it as undemocratic. The second reading was carried by 299 votes against 190 ; but the academic nature of this vote was shown by the majority of 125 by which the bill was immediately afterwards sent to a Committee of the whole House instead of to a Standing Committee. By this proceeding the bill was lost, since all the time of the House for the rest of the session was assigned under the Standing Orders to Government business, and a Government, the chief of which was a declared opponent of the measure, would naturally not be disposed to grant to it any further facilities.[1]

[1] In 1911, however, the Government promised that facilities should be given to the Conciliation Bill in the session of 1912.

CHAPTER II.

PARTY (1865-1909).

THE death of Lord Palmerston in 1865, the final resignation of Lord Russell in 1866, and the retirement of Lord Derby in 1868—statesmen who alternately or in combination had governed the country for a generation—would have marked the close of an era even if their disappearance from the political stage had not coincided with the Reform Act of 1867. The reign of the great Whig families, established by the Revolution of 1688, overthrown by George III., and resuscitated by the Reform Act of 1832, was brought to a final end. In the reformed Parliaments before 1867 there was much unreality in party distinctions, and it was possible for public men to pass from one side to the other without any loss of credit. Lord Palmerston, the Liberal chief, had been a Tory during the first half of his life, and had served in successive Tory Governments. Lord Derby, on the other hand, first became famous as a Whig Minister. They had held office together under Lord Grey, and neither they nor the parties they led were separated by any deep-seated differences of principle. Lord Derby did not share Lord Palmerston's sympathy with struggling nationalities or his hatred of oppression on the continent; and Lord Palmerston did not share Lord Derby's affection for the Church or his Protectionist convictions. But, nevertheless, a certain levity of temperament distinguished both statesmen, and they liked one another personally. They were succeeded at a critical time by two men of a different character and origin; differing from one another even more widely than they differed from their predecessors; each of them filled with ambitio and spurred by that noble infirmity to devise new ways and

The close of an era.

The new leaders.

means whereby they might win the favour of a widely extended constituency. Complete dis-sympathy amounting to dislike separated Mr. Gladstone and Mr. Disraeli, and lent a zest to their dissensions unknown to the immediately preceding generation. Like Sir Robert Peel, Mr. Gladstone took no far views. He admitted that he could not take much interest in a question until it was ripe for settlement; but when that time came he entered into it with a passionate ardour which surprised those who remembered his previous indifference, and even caused them unjustly to suspect his sincerity. Mr. Disraeli's imagination, on the other hand, loved to wander over wide tracts of the past and future; and, whatever may be thought of certain passages in his adventurous life, it must be admitted that intellectually at all events he was a man of principle. He delighted in broad generalisations, and was not satisfied until he had found in them a *rationale* of the direction he gave to his party. Thus he defended his policy of reform by references to the views of Bolingbroke and Pitt, whom, in their character of reformers, he claimed somewhat erroneously as leaders of the Tory party. To reconcile Toryism and democracy—*res olim dissociabiles*—on the basis of the maintenance of national institutions, combined with social progress, he conceived to be his mission; and the shape into which he moulded his party, together with the ideals, towards the attainment of which he endeavoured to direct its efforts, have in no small measure endured.

Mr. Disraeli at Edinburgh. In October, 1867, Mr. Disraeli went to Edinburgh and made an important speech. An extract from it may serve to show, not what the Tory party had distinctively been in the past, nor what it actually was at the time, but what under the moulding influence of a man of imagination, it was destined in some measure to become. After an ingenious, if unconvincing, defence of his consistency on the question of reform, he admitted that the new Act would give " in some degree a new character to the Constitution, and introduce some new powers and influences into its play and action," and he explained what in his view should be the position of the Tory party with respect to the " great questions " which would in consequence arise. He said: " In a progressive country change is constant; and the great question is, not whether you should resist change which is inevitable, but whether that change should be carried out in deference to the manners, the customs, the laws, and the traditions of a people, or whether it should be carried out in deference to abstract principles, and arbitrary and general doctrines. The one is a national system ; the other . . . is a philosophic system. Both have great advantages : the national party is supported by the fervour of patriotism ; the philosophical party has a singular exemption from the force of prejudice. Now, my lords and gentlemen, I have always considered that the Tory party was the national party of England. It is not formed of a combination of oligarchs and philosophers who practice on the sectarian prejudices of a portion of the people. It is formed of all classes, from the highest to the most homely, and it upholds a series of institutions that are in theory, and ought to be in practice, an embodiment of the national requirements and the security of the national rights." [1] This speech, delivered not very long before the first election under the new suffrage, is important because of the formative influence it exercised on the Conservative party. Social reform was to be opposed to the Liberal agitation for organic change, and the strong case which could undeniably be made out against certain of our ancient national institutions—as, for instance, the Church of Ireland—was to be parried by a frank appeal from philosophy to the national history.

On the 24th of February, 1868, Lord Derby was obliged by increasing ill-health to resign office. He was succeeded by Mr. Disraeli, whose indomitable courage and perseverance were thus at last rewarded by the prize which had been the object of his life-long ambition. Mr. Disraeli had declared at Edinburgh that it was his function to "educate his party" in principles which to his constructive imagination appeared the secular heritage of the Tory party, while to the practical shrewdness which he combined in a remarkable manner with dreaming detachment they seemed to offer the surest road to ultimate victory. Mr. Gladstone beheld with ill-concealed dissatisfaction the advancement of a rival, the fashion of whose mind he could not understand, whose sarcasms he resented, and the half-truth of whose epigrams and phrases appeared to him mere

Resignation of Lord Derby. Mr. Disraeli Premier.

---

[1] Kebbel's Selected Speeches of Lord Beaconsfield, vol. ii. p. 488.

magniloquent insincerity. But to eject him was more difficult than it would have been in later times. The party system was much less rigid then than now, and the mere fact that there was a Liberal majority in the House of Commons would not then of itself have been thought a sufficient reason for moving a vote of want of confidence in a Conservative Government. The differences which separated the parties under the Palmerston régime were not very marked or definite, and this House of Commons had been elected to support Lord Palmerston. It was necessary for Mr. Gladstone to find some political subject which might unite the Liberal party against the Government, which he could persuade himself was "ripe for settlement," and which would compel Conservatives to act on the defensive. He found it in Ireland.

The question of Ireland.   The Fenian movement in Ireland, as the conspiracy organised and financed by Irish settlers in America, to establish an Irish republic was called, although less really formidable to the English Government than the more national movements of later times, excited in 1867 great alarm. The trials and condemnation to death or long terms of imprisonment of the Fenian prisoners—some of whom were men of pure and disinterested character—were far more effective in kindling a hatred of English rule in the minds of the Irish of Ireland than had been all the efforts of the Fenians themselves. Both English parties admitted the existence of Irish grievances but failed correctly to diagnose the cause of Irish discontent. When in these circumstances Conservative Ministers spoke of the possibility of establishing a system of concurrent endowment of the churches and promised an inquiry into the relations between landlord and tenant, Mr. Gladstone at once outbid them and declared boldly for the disestablishment of the Irish Church. This, with legislative relief to Irish tenants, and provision for Irish education, was to restore peace to Ireland, and to accomplish this end was to be the grand mission of the Liberal party.

Parties and the Irish Church question.   The position of the Conservatives was embarrassing. They could not defend the Irish Church as it stood with all its anomalies; and, although their sagacious chief was right in his disbelief that the existence of that Church was a principal cause of Irish discontent, even the possibility that it might be so would suggest to the English electorate a pleasant way of ridding themselves of their Irish difficulties with much seeming generosity, but at no cost at all to themselves. In vain did Mr. Disraeli suggest a policy of levelling up instead of levelling down—a policy, as he explained it, of encouraging and endowing other religious agencies for good without destroying that which already existed—Mr. Gladstone's eloquence swept all such complicated notions away. The Liberal majority in the House of Commons were now more ready to follow him than they had been in the preceding year, and the Government were repeatedly defeated. Resolutions in favour of disestablishment were moved and carried, the protest of Mr. Disraeli that the House had no moral competence to deal with a question undiscussed at the time of its election without a previous appeal to the country was denounced by Mr. Gladstone as containing a doctrine ultra-democratic and anarchical, and a bill for suspending the exercise of patronage in the Irish Church was passed by the Commons, but thrown out by the Lords.[1]

These defeats on the chief question of the day compelled the Ministry to take steps to rectify its position. A Minister, according to the old constitutional view, who is in a minority in the House of Commons is entitled to advise the sovereign to dissolve Parliament if he has a reasonable prospect of victory at the polls, but not merely in order to increase the number of his supporters. In 1868 the question was complicated by the fact that the appeal if taken immediately would be to the old constituency which Parliament by its recent legislation had declared to be inadequate. Mr. Disraeli, in the Ministerial statement which followed an interview with the queen upon the subject, informed the House that he had advised her Majesty to dissolve Parliament, but that he had as an alternative tendered his resignation in case the queen should be of opinion that the question at issue could be more satisfactorily settled, or the interests of the country more advanced, by the retirement of Ministers. The queen, he said, refused to accept his resignation, and expressed her readiness to dissolve Parliament "as soon as the state of public business would permit". *Mr. Disraeli's advice to the queen.*

[1] On June 29. Mr. Disraeli's interview with the queen followed the defeat of the Government on the resolutions in the beginning of May.

Mr. Disraeli, in the course of his statement, further claimed the constitutional right of a Minister, upon taking office, to advise the dissolution of a Parliament elected under the influence of his political opponents. He hinted that although Lord Derby had waived that right, it did not therefore lapse, and that permission had been given by the Crown for its exercise whether the appeal were made to the old or to the new constituency. He eventually met the criticism which this position naturally evoked by a promise to abstain from all controversial legislation, and to dissolve Parliament in November if, as was hoped, the Boundary Bill and the two Reform Bills for Scotland and for Ireland had by then become law. The position of a Government which for more than two years had held office without a majority in the House of Commons was, even in 1868, strongly felt to be anomalous; but the contention that so long as a Ministry had not been condemned by a formal vote of want of confidence its position was not untenable, had not at that time lost all its weight. The Ministry was still held to derive its commission from a House of Commons elected largely to use its own judgment, and therefore entitled to act independently of the electorate. So long, therefore, as the confidence of the House was not entirely withdrawn from the Ministry, continuance in place if not in power was possible. In later times the commission of the Ministry has been perceived to proceed from the electorate—members are returned with the definite mandate to support one party or the other in measures with which those parties are publicly associated, and if, like the Liberal Unionists in 1886, they are compelled to withdraw their support, they must coalesce with their former opponents or disappear from public life.

The general election of 1868.

On the 11th of November, 1868, Parliament was dissolved, and the new character of the constituency to which the two parties made their appeal showed itself in some measure in the manner in which the ensuing election was conducted. In no previous instance had a leader of the Opposition gone to the country with a definite legislative programme, in virtue of which, and to give effect to which, he appealed to the electorate to dismiss the Government and to set him in their place; and there was no previous instance of a political platform campaign in the modern sense conducted by the chief of one of the two great parties. But Mr. Gladstone, in 1868, standing for the new constituency of South West Lancashire, made successful speeches at St. Helens, Warrington, Liverpool, Newton Bridge, Wigan, and Ormskirk; all of which were fully reported in the *Times*, and filled the nation with amazement. Mr. Bright, the most prominent of the Radicals, whose supposed revolutionary views and intentions had caused much perturbation on both sides of the Speaker's chair in the House of Commons, where they provided a never-ceasing theme for discussion and reprobation, had hitherto held an unquestioned supremacy on the platform. It was on the platform that he had won his fame; and it was still to popular audiences that he delivered the best of his speeches, but he was now almost eclipsed on his own ground by a rival who had held high office under the Crown. The Prime Minister, on the other hand, adhered on this occasion to the old traditions. Except for the customary speech at the Guildhall banquet and for an address which he issued to his constituents in October, he preserved a complete silence. The result of the elections caused little surprise. The Liberals made a net gain of fifteen seats from their opponents, counting thirty on a division, and could show a majority of about 120 votes. This was the largest majority secured by either party since 1833, and was a sign that the era of great majorities had begun. It was a tribute to the extraordinary popularity enjoyed at that time by Mr. Gladstone; for the chief political issue of the day was not of a nature to rouse much enthusiasm in England. Much the greater number of the new boroughs returned Liberals; in Scotland, out of fifty-three members only seven were elected as Conservatives, in Ireland thirty-seven out of 105. On the other hand, the counties as a rule supported the Government, and in Lancashire all the four county divisions chose Conservatives—Mr. Gladstone himself and Lord Hartington being among the rejected candidates. It was observed that the extension of the electorate had greatly increased the expenses of election and had improved the chances of success for rich men. "Many men," according to a writer in the *Annual Register*, " were deterred from engaging in contests which could not be carried on without a heavy cost, and there were not a few constituencies for which none

Character of the new Parliament.

but men of considerable wealth could venture to present themselves." Thus for the working class voter the choice lay only between one rich man and another; and, as Mr. Gladstone himself at a later time allowed, the chances of an entrance into Parliament for men who had nothing to rely upon but their talent and their character, diminished by the Reform Act of 1832, were at first reduced almost to zero by that of 1867. Except for this advance of the money power, the character of the new House of Commons differed little from that of its predecessors, and it was still, in the opinion of an Edinburgh reviewer, "the most aristocratical body in the world". No less than 110 of its members, according to an analysis made at the time by the *Pall Mall Gazette*, were sons or brothers of peers, there were fifty-seven baronets, and of the other members those who did not belong to the landed gentry were for the most part large manufacturers, bankers, or railway directors. The professional class is described as a small residue in the new house.

Radical disappointment. This result was profoundly disappointing to the Radical party. "The new voters," wrote the most able exponent of its views in the *Fortnightly Review*,[1] "have come into power, and they have returned the old kind of men, on the old principles." "Intellect," he declared, "had been ostracised from this chamber of mediocrity." Some justice there certainly was in this complaint. John Stuart Mill lost his seat at Westminster, and the House could no longer boast of a Radical philosopher; Mr. Horsman, Mr. Milner Gibson, Mr. Roebuck, Lord Amberley, Mr. Bernal Osborne, and other men of independent mind, little docile to the party whip, were also defeated—irregularities pared away by the levelling plane of the democratic vote. "Through England," wrote the Edinburgh reviewer already quoted, "and even in Scotland, wherever men came forward with the strongest pretensions to extreme opinions, whether as philosophers or as working men, they were rejected by the constituencies." Indeed that opinions in advance of the time should find favour with constituencies composed of great numbers of average men implies a contradiction in the terms. It was to his appreciation of this truth that Mr. Gladstone, who did not disguise his indifference to political questions until they were ready for settlement, owed

[1] Mr. John Morley.

his power, and became time and again the man of the moment. "If it is the office of law and of constitutions," he wrote in the chapter of autobiography published about this time, "to reflect the wants and wishes of the country (and its wishes must ever be a considerable element in its wants), then, as the nation passes from a stationary into a progressive period, it will justly require that the changes in its own condition and views should be represented in the professions and actions of its leading men."[1] Perhaps it was because he held the view that a statesman is entitled to adapt his professions and actions to the changing wishes as well as wants of the people that he became the most conspicuous figure in the new democracy.

When the result of the election was no longer doubtful Mr. Disraeli bowed to the verdict of the electors and resigned office without meeting Parliament. His action in so doing created a precedent which has since been generally followed. It was especially remarkable on the part of a Minister who had ruled the country for two years without the support of a majority in the House of Commons, and was the first open acknowledgment of the truth that a Ministry in reality derives its commission from the electorate.[2]

Mr. Disraeli resigns without meeting Parliament.

The Government formed by Mr. Gladstone on the resignation of Mr. Disraeli was comprehensive in its character, containing representatives of every section of the Liberal party. Mr. Bright, the chief spokesman of the Radicals, became, as President of the Board of Trade, the colleague, not only of the whig Duke of Argyll, but also of his old opponent, Mr. Lowe, whose eloquence had been the main instrument in the destruction of Mr. Gladstone's Reform Bill of 1866, but who now entered the cabinet as Chancellor of the Exchequer. Mr. Forster, the new Vice-President of the Council, was a Yorkshire manufacturer; Mr. Goschen was well known in the world of finance; Mr. Childers had been a member of an Australian legislature, while the other members of the Government were for the most part drawn from the old governing class. Mr.

The new Ministry.

---

[1] A Chapter of Autobiography, p. 11.
[2] "The growth of democracy was increasing the power of the electors, and diminishing the independence of the representatives; and the first election in which all borough householders were entitled to take part was the first election whose decision, without any Parliamentary confirmation, decided the fate of a Ministry" (Sir S. Walpole, *History of Twenty-five Years*, ii., 348).

Gladstone himself, full of energy, carried along by his own eloquence, and perhaps a little misled by the size of the majority returned to support him, was inclined to move faster than most of his colleagues, those colleagues than the majority behind them, and that majority than the electors who had returned them to Parliament. He had submitted one question and one question alone to the decision of the electorate—a fact which gave to the Government considerable freedom of action after that question had been disposed of by the passage into law of the Irish Church Act.

The Parliament of 1868-1874.

Of the crowded sessions of this famous Parliament little need here be said. The Government, in Mr. Goschen's phrase, " spent their majority like gentlemen," and much far-reaching legislation was the result. This Parliament was the last in which the two-party system might be observed in perfect working order, and it was also, with the exception of that of 1885-86, the last in which the views of a Liberal Government were in advance of those of their supporters.

Liberalism and the doctrine of laissez-faire.

The work of the Liberal party in the generation which succeeded the Reform Act of 1832 was one of clearance rather than construction, and was based on the doctrine of *laissez-faire*. The removal of obstacles to freedom of thought and movement in religion and trade respectively, was the aim of the most important legislation of that period. Equality of opportunity, abolition of privilege, restriction to its lowest point of Government interference with the liberty of the individual, the career open to talents, such had been throughout the country the objects and ideals of the Liberal party and especially of Cobden, Bright, and the Manchester school of Radicals. By the Parliament of 1868, this work was almost completed, and after its dissolution there was little left for Liberalism as understood by its chief interpreters of that generation to do. In 1868 Mr. Gladstone had succeeded in abolishing compulsory Church rates. In 1869 the Irish Church was disestablished; in 1870 appointments in the civil service were for the most part thrown open to competition, and the grave dangers of a "spoils system," or the wholesale discharge of officials on a change of Ministry, which might possibly have followed the transfer of the power of nomination to Governments chosen by a democratic electorate, were, it is to be hoped, thereby for ever averted; in 1871 the Act to abolish religious tests at the Universities of Oxford and Cambridge was at last agreed to by the Lords; and in the same year the system of purchasing commissions in the army was abolished on the advice of the Ministry by a royal warrant. Thereafter, few privileges remained, few artificial state-raised obstacles to the progress of the individual were left, to be cleared away. But the very success of the champions of *laissez-faire* contained within itself the seeds of failure. It involved the sacrifice of average to exceptional ability, while at the same time legislation founded on their principles of political equality had placed electoral predominance in the hands of the multitude. The Manchester leaders objected to all state regulation of labour, but even the mid-Victorian Parliaments had passed the Factory Acts in spite of their opposition. The practical inconsistency involved in their logically coherent political and economic views had been perceived by Mr. Lowe—one of the most clear-sighted adherents of the school—and had formed one of his chief objections to the extension of the suffrage. He shared the opinion that the chief functions of Government were to keep the peace, to enforce contracts, and to preserve to every man the liberty to dispose of himself and of his labour in the manner he thought best; but he held that of all Governments, a Government resting on a democratic suffrage was the least likely to confine itself within these limits. "Democracy," he said, "is the enemy of competition, and ever places its trust not in the increase of consumers, but in the compulsory diminution of producers." The Radicals of the Victorian era honestly believed that if all obstacles to the production of wealth were removed its distribution might be left to take care of itself, but they provided an antidote for the mischiefs that might have resulted from the acceptance of this theory by entrusting power to those who would have been the chief sufferers through its unqualified application. The confused and tumultuous protests of Carlyle against the reigning ideas were in manner too rhetorical and in suggestion too vague to have much effect upon the political thought of his day, but they were enforced with more clearness and precision and in exquisite English by his disciple John Ruskin, whose economic views, long disregarded as the speculations of an amiable visionary, have proved, whether for good or for evil, more dynamic in their effects than those of his disdainful antagonists. It was slowly becoming clear to the minds of men that the evils with which the Parliaments of the future would have to cope were not derived from the mischievous activity of the state but rather from its inactivity, and that they were incident to that very unrestricted competition which it had for so long been the object of statesmen to bring into being.

Among the first of those who had the sagacity to perceive that the era of organic change was drawing to a close and giving place to that of social reform was Mr. Disraeli. The state machine had now been in course of repair for nearly half a century and might at last be considered in fair working order. But the attention of the Liberals had so long been fixed, and rightly fixed, on its imperfections that they seemed in contemplating means to have forgotten the end, or rather they had no longer any clear conception of what that end should be. Mr. Bright indeed and the Radicals perceived religious inequality in the existence of the Church of England and political privilege in that of the House of Lords, and they were therefore anxious fundamentally to modify the powers of the latter and to sever the former from its connection with the State, but neither Mr. Gladstone nor the mass of the Liberal party sympathised with them in these objects. Liberals had not abandoned their old principle that Government is a necessary evil whose activity ought to be reduced to a minimum, and consequently their very success in abolishing privileges and redressing inequalities lost them the support of those who now looked to Government for positive rather than negative advantages. Moreover, their two chief violations of the doctrine of non-interference—the Education Act of 1870 and the Licensing Act of 1872—useful measures though they were, were hardly of a nature to convince the Government that the time had come for the State to take its part in the organisation of the national life, for the first lost them the support of the Nonconformists and the second arrayed against them the formidable liquor interest. It is significant that neither of these measures commanded the full approval of Mr. Gladstone. In the case of the Education Act—the work of Lord de Grey (afterwards Lord Ripon) and Mr. Forster—we learn that he "acquiesced rather than led," and he would personally have preferred the Scotch plan of allowing the local school boards to give what religious instruction they pleased, or as an alternative that public money should be granted in aid of secular instruction alone; while Mr. Bruce, the Home Secretary, complained that he was unable to interest Mr. Gladstone in his licensing bill—a measure dealing with the hours of closing and the adulteration of beer—and that the Premier cared for nothing but "free trade" in liquor. Not only did the Government consider schemes for the improvement of the condition of the people beyond its province, although the increase in the number of paupers in England and Wales from 920,344 in 1866 to 1,081,926 in 1869 seemed to call for State action, but in their capacity of stewards of the national revenue, they thought it right to refuse to incur expense in order to preserve Epping Forest from enclosure, and they declined to abandon certain profits for the sake of securing to the public the full enjoyment of the New Forest, or even to endow London with the land reclaimed for the construction of the Thames Embankment, although this work had been completed at the cost of the London ratepayers. On all these three questions Ministers were defeated in the House of Commons in 1871.

The new voters of the working class paid no direct taxes, and, therefore, cared little for the economy of public money, which with Mr. Gladstone was a ruling passion, and perhaps the single object from the pursuit of which throughout his career he never varied. On the other hand, they liked a spirited foreign policy, and thought that the Prime Minister was too little careful of the national honour in his acquiescence in the repudiation by Russia of the treaty of 1856, and in his submission to a foreign tribunal of the claims made by the United States for damages due from England for the escape of the *Alabama* and the other vessels employed by the Confederates. They had certainly none of the enthusiastic affection for the national institutions with which Mr. Disraeli chose to credit them, but the attacks which certain of the advanced Radicals were making at this time on the Church, the House of Lords, and the Monarchy itself, left them cold. No improvement in the conditions of their life had resulted from the legislation

Growing unpopularity of the Government.

of this Parliament, and the only two Acts which directly concerned them—the Education and Licensing Acts—they regarded with dislike. The other classes of the community beheld with alarm the ceaseless activity of the Government, and dreaded what seemed its destructive tendency. And lastly, Mr. Gladstone had declared that his mission was to pacify Ireland; he had been raised to power with that direct object in view; and he had utterly failed in its accomplishment.

Mr. Disraeli at the Crystal Palace. Such was the position of the Liberal party when Mr. Disraeli made his great speech at the Crystal Palace in June, 1872. It has been truly observed that in this speech he laid down the main principles of the Tory policy for the next thirty years or more.[1] He defined the three great objects to be sought by Toryism as "the maintenance of our institutions, the preservation of our empire, and the improvement of the condition of the people," and he accused the Liberal party of attacking the national institutions, of indifference, or rather hostility to the empire, and of neglecting the welfare of the people. He maintained that the Tory party was, and with certain degenerate intervals always had been, the national or constitutional party and the guardian of our institutions—a remarkable thesis since it can hardly be denied that the British constitution, like the British empire, is historically a Whig creation. With regard to the colonies, he admitted that the grant of self-government was just and necessary, but he accused the Whigs of having conferred it with a view to separation. He declared that it ought to have been conceded as "part of a great policy of Imperial consolidation," and to have been accompanied by provisions for an imperial tariff, a common defensive organisation of the military and naval forces of the empire, and a representative council in London. By these suggestions the orator cast a seed amid his party destined to germinate in the minds of Unionist statesmen in the future— with what result it is impossible to foresee. The third object of the Tory party, "not inferior to the maintenance of the empire, or the upholding of our institutions," was to be the elevation of the condition of the people.

The Conservative party and social reform. In this connection Mr. Disraeli was able to make a fair appeal to the later traditions of his party. Lord Shaftesbury,

[1] Lowell's Government of England, i., 539.

the chief author of the Factory Acts, was, it is true, not a party man, and he was more attached to Lord Palmerston than to any other statesman of his day, yet it is certain that he was by sympathy a Conservative, that he relied mainly on that party for support, and that his most conspicuous opponents were Radicals of the school of Manchester. The Tories indeed showed little interest in the subject until their long tenure of power had been brought to an end by the fall of the Wellington Ministry in 1830; and the House of Lords in 1816 had refused to consent to a bill to limit the hours of labour of children in factories to ten hours a day, or rather they had restricted the bill to cotton mills and extended the hours of work to twelve. But the Select Committee on child labour in factories, by whose report the appalling evils incidental to it were revealed, was appointed in 1831 at the instance of Mr. Sadler, an uncompromising Tory; and Lord Ashley abandoned the conduct of the Factory Bill of 1833 because the Whig Government, under the influence of the manufacturers, insisted on lowering the age of the children whom it protected and increasing the number of hours in the day during which they might work. In subsequent Factory Bills the proposal to restrict the labour of young persons to ten hours was, it is true, resisted by the Government of Sir Robert Peel, but it was supported by the bulk of the Tory party then in revolt against their chief, and opposed by the majority of Whigs and Radicals. It was eventually carried in 1847, chiefly by the votes of the Tory Opposition and against the resistance of Lord John Russell, the Whig Premier. Mr. Disraeli was, therefore, able with some show of justice to claim as the hereditary and traditional policy of the Tory party the policy of improving by State action the condition of the people, and he was doubtless right in his view that such a policy was more likely to be appreciated by the people " than the ineffable mysteries and all the pains and penalties of the Ballot Bill ". They would be idiots, he contended, did they not perceive that " the time had arrived when social and not political improvement is the object which they ought to pursue ". Mr. Disraeli was right, and a new generation of Radicals with principles poles asunder from those of their predecessors was beginning to agree with him; but in the meantime he was the first to occupy this new field, and he was shortly to reap the advantage of his clearness of vision through the votes of the class he had enfranchised.

The defeat of the Irish University Bill in 1873—the measure in which Mr. Gladstone addressed himself to the third and last category of Irish grievances which he had pledged himself to redress—led to the resignation of the Government. Defeats at by-elections had borne eloquent witness to their growing unpopularity, and there was scarcely a section of the community which their legislation, useful though most of it was, had not in some way offended. After accepting Mr. Gladstone's resignation, the queen sent for Mr. Disraeli and requested him to form a new Ministry. But that astute statesman declined to repeat for the fourth time his experiences of 1852, 1858, and 1866-68 by taking office in a Parliament in which his followers were in a minority. His political prospects were now too good to incline him to compromise them by placing himself in the humiliating position of a Minister on sufferance, compelled, whenever he made a proposal, to listen to lectures and to accept modifications from an imperious leader of the Opposition. He pointed out that the majority which had defeated the Government was a combination actuated by contrary motives, for that while Conservatives and Liberal dissentients opposed the bill because it sacrificed Irish education to the Roman Catholic hierarchy, the Irish Roman Catholics, on the other hand, took objection to its inadequacy. He told the queen that he had no doubt of his ability to form a Government, but that he could not undertake to carry on the affairs of the country in the present Parliament. To the suggestion that in that case he should dissolve, he objected that an immediate dissolution was impracticable—that he was unwilling to accept the estimates of his predecessors—and that he saw no reason why he should be compelled to go to the country at the head of a weak and discredited Ministry, when what was needed was that the country should pronounce judgment on the principles and policy of Mr. Gladstone and his colleagues. Mr. Gladstone, in a long letter to the queen, took grave exception on constitutional grounds to Mr. Disraeli's decision. He pointed out that the division of the House on the 11th March was a party division carrying "the well-known symbol of such divisions in the appointment of tellers of the Opposition and Government respectively," and that the vote was given after his formal declaration that the result was vital to the existence of the Ministry. By the force of a "well-established party usage," whenever in the course of the preceding half century an Opposition had in these circumstances been victorious, its leaders had always, on the resignation of the Government, formed, or endeavoured to form, a Ministry of their own, and it was the clear duty of every Opposition to take the full responsibility for their actions. In his reply Mr. Disraeli contended that Mr. Gladstone's doctrine would place an arbitrary power in the hands of a Prime Minister since it implied that "wherever a Minister is so situated that it is in his power to prevent any other Parliamentary leader from forming an administration likely to stand, he acquires thereby the right to call on Parliament to pass whatever measures he and his colleagues think fit, and is entitled to denounce as factious the resistance to such measures". Few people will now doubt that Mr. Disraeli in this controversy was in the right. The custom of making every question of importance a question of confidence which Mr. Gladstone did so much to inaugurate has immensely increased the driving power of Governments, and proportionately diminished the independence of the House of Commons. The growth of the party organisations outside Parliament, due mainly to the necessity for dealing with the exigencies of an extended electorate, by bringing pressure to bear on private members and thereby acting for the Government much as certain religious orders fought the battles of the pope, have contributed to the same result. Although the fact that the confidence of the House of Lords was not essential to the existence of a Ministry deprived the peers of all control over administration or foreign policy and rendered them powerless as a Government-making organ, yet, in their character as a part of the legislature, this very circumstance increased their power, since their amendments to bills did not bring about inconvenient resignations, or, as an alternative, render necessary an immediate account of their actions to constituents organised locally under central direction. The time was approaching when every member of the House of Commons at issue with his party on some important question was to find himself, if unwilling to retire or to be driven from public life, confronted with the alternatives either of suppressing his convictions on that question or else of changing sides and adopting bodily all the principles of his whilom antagonists.[1]

The last work of the Parliament of 1868. Shortly after Mr. Gladstone's return to office Mr. Fawcett's bill for the abolition of religious tests at Dublin University was at last passed into law with the help of the Government, and the exclusion of Roman Catholics from the honours and emoluments of Trinity College thereby removed. This Act, passed in the last year of the last Parliament wherein the traditional principles of that Liberalism whose chief aim was the abolition of privilege still held sway, cleared away from our national institutions almost the only religious disabilities still remaining, and may in some sense be said to have completed the emancipating labours of half a century. The country, disinclined for further political change and dreading the volcanic energies of the Prime Minister, was disposed to rest without being thankful; while the Government, discouraged by its recent defeat, was further embarrassed by internal dissension.

Unauthorised expenditure. In 1869 the telegraphic business of the country had been taken over by the State. Mr. Scudamore, the civil servant who had conducted the purchase on behalf of the Government, finding in 1872 that the money allotted by Parliament to defray the charge was insufficient, supplemented it without Parliamentary authority by using for the purpose no less than £800,000, partly out of the post office receipts which ought to have been paid over into the Exchequer, and partly out of the savings bank's deposits which ought to have been passed on to the National Debt Commissioners. Mr. Lowe, the Chancellor of the Exchequer, had been informed of this unauthorised expenditure, but was unaware of its extent; while Mr. Monsell, the Postmaster-General, was kept in ignorance of the whole transaction. Attention having been called to the matter in Parliament, Mr. Gladstone, by temperament disposed to condemn this kind of irregularity with an almost exaggerated earnestness, accepted a motion of Sir John

---

[1] It is a matter of surprise to foreign observers how many of our public men have adopted without reproach the latter course, and it has led them to throw doubt on the seriousness of our political differences.

Lubbock that it is the duty of the Government to take effective measures to prevent the recurrence of such a proceeding.

This incident, and the conduct of Mr. Ayrton, the First Commissioner of Works, who disclaimed responsibility for an estimate which he was obliged by his office to propose to the House, thereby eliciting from the Prime Minister a sound pronouncement on the nature and limits of Ministerial responsibility, brought about shortly after the prorogation a reconstruction of the Government. The most important of the changes was the transfer of Mr. Lowe to the Home Office and his replacement as Chancellor of the Exchequer by Mr. Gladstone himself. This arrangement involved the possibility, which the Premier had overlooked, that by accepting the seals of the Exchequer in addition to the office he already held he had legally vacated his seat. By an Act of 1708 members of the House of Commons, appointed to offices of profit under the Crown existing before 1705, were obliged to vacate their seats.[1] This Act was modified by a clause in the Reform Act of 1867, which provided that if a member after being returned to Parliament had accepted one of certain offices enumerated in the schedule, and had subsequently accepted another of those offices in lieu of and in immediate succession to the first, he should not vacate his seat. But Mr. Gladstone had accepted the Exchequer, in addition to and not in lieu of the Treasury, and consequently, according to Lord Chancellor Selborne and other legal authorities, his seat was vacated. The law officers, however, took a different view, for although they admitted that the case was not covered by the Act of 1867, they denied the applicability of the Act of Anne. They argued that the Chancellorship of the Exchequer was a branch of the Treasury, and that therefore there was no fresh assumption of office within the terms of the Act, and they cited the case of Mr. Perceval who, when in 1809 he accepted the First Lordship of the Treasury in addition to his actual office of Chancellor of the Exchequer, did not vacate his seat. The difficulty was serious, for Mr. Gladstone's seat was not a safe one, and in their present weak and disorganised state his colleagues could hardly venture to face the Opposition in his

Reconstruction of the Government. Question raised whether Mr. Gladstone had vacated his seat on becoming Chancellor of the Exchequer.

[1] This was first enacted by 7 and 8 Will. III.: the statute of Anne extended the law of the English Parliament to that of Great Britain,

absence. Moreover the budget which Mr. Gladstone was contemplating for the coming year involved large reductions in the army and navy estimates, and to these reductions neither Mr. Cardwell, the Secretary for War, nor Mr. Goschen, the First Lord of the Admiralty, would consent.

Dissolution of Parliament. Mr. Gladstone's address. In these circumstances Mr. Gladstone determined to advise a dissolution of Parliament. His decision took the country by surprise. It was first announced and defended in a long manifesto which he addressed to his Greenwich constituents in January, 1874. After rehearsing the achievements of his Ministry, he reminded his readers that the Government had resigned office in the preceding March, on the defeat of their Irish University Bill; but that Mr. Disraeli, on being sent for, had declared himself unable to replace them in the present Parliament. Since that time defeats at by-elections had indicated that the Government was losing favour with the country. Mr. Disraeli's refusal to take office had left the Crown without an alternative Government during the continuance of the present Parliament, and it was therefore desirable that that Parliament should be brought to an end, and an opportunity given to the country of making its choice between the two parties. He went on to promise that should the country continue to give him their confidence he would abolish the income tax, reduce local taxation, and give to the general consumer "some marked relief in the class of articles of popular consumption". He touched lightly on the "judicious adjustments" of existing taxes that the fulfilment of these pledges would necessitate, without specifying the nature of those adjustments.[1]

Character of his proposals. The address contained no declaration of policy or legislative proposals; the appeal to the direct pecuniary interests of the voter was doubtless considered sufficient in itself to win his support. These offers were made by Mr. Gladstone without previous consultation with his colleagues until the last moment, and they were at the time, and have been since, very generally condemned. Lord Selborne, at that time and afterwards Mr. Gladstone's Chancellor, has written that "an electioneering address from the Prime Minister, propounding by anticipation

[1] Some years later Mr. Gladstone explained that these adjustments would have taken the form of the imposition of death duties resembling those that have been in force since 1894, but there was no hint of this in the manifesto.

a popular budget, was a dangerous as well as a new thing".[1] The abolition of the income tax may not appear to be a democratic proposal, but it was the payers of income tax whom the legislation of the Government had especially alienated; they bore at that time a much greater numerical ratio to the whole of the electorate than they have borne since 1885; and had they swallowed the bait thrown out to them the Government would have been saved. Mr. Gladstone's difficulties about his seat, his recognition of the unpopularity of Ministers, and the consequent necessity of finding some proposal " large and strong and telling upon both the popular mind and the leading elements of the constituency "[2] if the fortunes of the party were to be restored, his choice of finance as such a subject, and his wish to avoid "the risks of the kind that were run in the budget of 1853," that is to say an announcement of "impositions as well as remissions of taxes," had led him inevitably, as appears from his correspondence, to the decision to dissolve. But the dissolution took place under novel circumstances, for none had ever been previously attributable to Ministerial difficulties such as these. And if the dissolution itself was unprecedented, so was the conduct of the election. Mr. Gladstone himself displayed an almost feverish activity. "It is a new thing," wrote Lord Shaftesbury in his diary, "and a very serious thing to see a Prime Minister 'on the stump'. Surely there is some little due to dignity of position."[3] But this new phenomenon of Ministers themselves conducting a political campaign in the country was a necessary result of the extension of the suffrage. Power had passed from the House of Commons to the electorate; extra-Parliamentary party associations formed on the model of the American caucus with the object of promoting party interests in the constituencies had grown up; and platform speeches had become more important than speeches in the House of Commons because, since 1867, it had become of more importance to influence electors than members.

The result of the first election held under the ballot was the return of a Conservative majority for the first time since 1841. It seems strange in the light of our subsequent experience, but it is none the less true, that in no previous instance

Victory of the Conservatives.

[1] Memorials Personal and Political, vol. i. p. 330.
[2] Letter to Lord Granville, 8th January, 1874, Life of Gladstone, vol. ii. p. 481. [3] Life of Lord Shaftesbury, vol. iii. p. 349.

had a Prime Minister in possession of the confidence of a majority of the House of Commons appealed to the country and appealed in vain.[1] The swing of the lengthened pendulum was at last becoming visible to all, and the fate of the first Ministry, which, having dissolved Parliament while still commanding the confidence of the House of Commons, suffered defeat at the polls, proved the fate of each succeeding Ministry till the end of the century.

A third party. The most remarkable result of the election, however, was the return, together with 350 Conservatives and 244 Liberals, of no less than fifty-eight Home Rulers for Irish constituencies. The electoral successes of the Home Government Association, founded in Dublin in 1870, had been rapid and continuous. Six Home Rulers were returned at by-elections during 1871 and 1872—among them Isaac Butt, the first leader of the Irish Nationalists—and at the time of the dissolution they held ten seats. The full significance of the movement dawned slowly on the minds of men, and they did not at first perceive that the entrance of this new element into political life involved the breakdown of the two-party system and all that depended on it. Yet we can now see that it was inevitable that the rise of a third party with no interest in the right working of a constitutional machinery from which its very object was to sever itself, with no preference for one Government over another save in so far as the one or the other contributed to the end it had in view, a party moreover sufficiently powerful to hold the balance unless one side or the other had an overwhelming majority, must in the end destroy a system which can only work when successive Governments have majorities large enough to carry their legislation and to resist all attacks on their administration. Before the Parliament of 1874 came to an end it was found necessary to make important alterations in the time-honoured procedure of the House of Commons in order to adapt it to the new conditions.

Resignation of Mr. Gladstone. Rather against his own judgment—for in such matters he was still a Conservative—Mr. Gladstone, yielding to the opinions of his colleagues and the exhortations of the press,

---

[1] The nearest parallel was Lord Melbourne's dissolution in 1841, but it must be remembered that that dissolution followed a vote of want of confidence in the Ministry passed by the House of Commons.

followed the example set by Mr. Disraeli in 1868 and resigned office without meeting Parliament. He still clung to the old principle that it was "Parliament and not the constituencies that ought to dismiss the Government," and thought that "the proper function of the House of Commons could not be taken from it" without some diminution of its dignity and authority. The real innovation, however, had been the dissolution itself, and the offer of a popular budget to the constituencies before it had been produced or even suggested in the House of Commons. It has now become unlikely that any Ministry, when a large and undisputed majority of its declared opponents has been returned at a general election, will ever again await a hostile vote in the new Parliament before resigning office.

The first years of the Parliament of 1874 were years of tranquillity. Mr. Disraeli, the Prime Minister, for the first time in his life held office with an obedient majority at his command, but he was thought to be less successful in this position than when he led the House in a minority. His impatience of detail combined with the carelessness induced by an assured majority to involve him on every question in minor difficulties, and the day-to-day business of Parliament was not very efficiently conducted. He had not, however, forgotten the improvement of the condition of the people which with the preservation of the empire and the maintenance of national institutions were to be the three great objects to be sought by Toryism, and some useful social legislation connected with the better housing of the working classes and with sanitary reform was the result. Such measures were laughed at by Sir William Harcourt as a "policy of sewage," and that uncompromising but belated individualist, Mr. Fawcett, declared that the working classes were able to take care of themselves and needed no State intervention on their behalf; yet few would now be found to question their utility. But whatever the shortcomings of Mr. Disraeli's leadership might be, the Opposition were in no condition to take advantage of them. Mr. Gladstone, noting the "absence of any great positive aim for which to cooperate" among Liberals, and resenting what he considered the disloyalty of a section of his followers during the last Parliament, considered that his work was at an end. He was a very irregular attendant at the House of Commons during

The Parliament of 1874.

the session of 1874, and, disregarding all protests, resigned, in 1875, his leadership into the unwilling hands of Lord Hartington, a statesman whose opinions were conspicuous for their moderation. The political activity of the Liberal party was confined to its more advanced section, and its centre was rather at Birmingham than at Westminster. There the new Liberal Association, organized on a democratic and representative basis by Mr. Chamberlain, Mr. Schnadhorst, and Mr. W. Harris, had succeeded in excluding their opponents not only from the Parliamentary representation of the city but also from all share in municipal government. Their success caused the "Birmingham plan" to be imitated in many other places, and all that remained to be done was "to link the associations together by permanent ties, and assure unity of action by a central organisation".[1]

Whigs and Radicals.

The Radicals of Birmingham disliked the Whigs even more than they disliked the Conservatives. They felt no sympathy for their individualism, and regarded them as opportunists and aristocratic office-seekers who could not be trusted to grapple with reform. Mr. Chamberlain himself had attacked the late Government in the press in their last year of office, and in a later article he attributed the defeats of 1874 to Whig ascendency and the consequent lack of sincerity and vigour in the counsels of the party. The replacement, therefore, of Mr. Gladstone by Lord Hartington in the party leadership gave deep dissatisfaction to the Radicals, and when the Eastern question drew the Liberal Achilles from his tent and engaged him in a fierce campaign against the foreign policy of the Government, the new Liberal Associations entered eagerly into the movement and denounced the lukewarmness of the Whigs. Mr. Gladstone did not hesitate to arm himself with the powerful weapon thus offered to his hand, and gave the sanction of his approval to the "National Federation of Liberal Associations" by making a great speech on the Eastern question at Birmingham on the occasion of its first meeting in 1877.

Mr. Chamberlain and the caucus.

Mr. Chamberlain had been returned to Parliament as member for Birmingham in 1876, and it is scarcely an exaggeration to say that from that date until his secession ten years later on the subject of Home Rule, he was the most

[1] Ostragorski, i. 174.

powerful man in the party. By means of the caucus—a nickname taken from American politics and given by Lord Beaconsfield to the new Liberal Associations formed on the Birmingham plan and united in the National Liberal Federation —he was able to control the Liberal electorate in most of the urban constituencies, and his power was relentlessly employed to bring pressure to bear on recalcitrant members of the party. What distinguished the caucus from former leagues and unions like the Anti-Corn Law League, the Reform Union, or the Registration Societies, was that it had no definite political aim. As Mr. Gladstone said in 1877, " a man is not bound by the Birmingham plan to subscribe to any list of political articles ".[1] He was to support the measures advocated by the chiefs who had found favour in the sight of the organisation, and his mission was to support those chiefs through good times or bad whether he approved all their measures or the reverse. For the time the hopes of the caucus centred in Mr. Gladstone. Before the end of the Parliament of 1874 Mr. Chamberlain had openly repudiated the leadership of Lord Hartington, who was reluctant on patriotic grounds to make the foreign policy of the Government the chief object of attack, and who detected exaggeration in Mr. Gladstone's philippics ; while Radicals of the old school who, like Mr. Joseph Cowen, attached importance to individual independence of thought and action in members of Parliament, and valued principles rather than power, fared no better at his hands. Mr. Chamberlain had done a great work at Birmingham, which owed to him in large measure its admirable civic order and prosperity, and he desired to do a great work for England. But he was profoundly convinced that for this an irresistible driving force was essential, and that union was the only source of strength—to obtain which it was necessary to offer the alternatives of expulsion or submission to all those Liberals who dissented in any degree from his views. Members of Parliament were to be merely tools in the hands of a Radical Government representing the democracy, and if these tools were inefficient they were to be cast aside or returned to their makers—the Liberal Associations—for repair. Candidates proposed by a local caucus were required to pledge themselves beforehand to abide by the decisions of the caucus.

[1] Speech at Nottingham, 27th September, 1877.

Mr. Forster at Bradford, on refusing in the year 1878 to give this pledge, became at once the object of a violent attack and was denounced as a traitor to Liberalism. Mr. Gladstone himself intervened to put an end to the dispute, and a compromise was arrived at by the substitution with respect to the assurance demanded of the candidate of the words "may be" for "shall be" required. Mr. Forster agreed to this, and was accordingly nominated as candidate by the Association. Old-fashioned Radicals noted with dismay that after the emancipating labours of half a century terminated by the Ballot Act the individual was once more being sacrificed to the machine, and that the assumed will of a triumphant democracy swayed and formulated by an active minority was likely to prove as little open to reason or tolerant of obstacles as had ever been that of king or oligarchy.

The Home Rule party in the House of Commons.
The return of the fifty-eight Irish members pledged to Home Rule did not materially affect political life in the early days of the Parliament of 1874. They were led by Mr. Isaac Butt, an eloquent barrister who had defended the Fenian prisoners in 1865, but who was a man of moderate views, decorous manners, and Conservative antecedents. He had founded the Home Government Association and invented the name of Home Rule, and he desired, after uniting all parties in Ireland in support of the cause, gradually, by strictly constitutional methods, and the pleadings of eloquence, to persuade the predominant partner to concede some measure of national self government on a federal basis to Ireland. With this object in view he made annual motions in the House of Commons in favour of Home Rule. His speeches were listened to with friendly interest and even admiration, but his motions were rejected by immense majorities composed of Liberals and Conservatives voting together. Nor was he more successful in his attempts at legislation. He succeeded indeed in 1874 in passing through the House of Commons a bill for assimilating in certain respects the privileges of Irish corporations to those enjoyed by English boroughs, but the House of Lords, departing for once from their usual practice, threw out a bill passed by a Conservative House of Commons and approved by a Conservative Government. Irish bills for municipal reform, for Parliamentary reform, for fiscal reform, were thrown out in

the House of Commons in the session of 1876, though supported by nearly all the Irish members. Mr. Gladstone's imprudent declaration that it was the Clerkenwell explosion and the rescue of Fenian prisoners in Manchester that had made it necessary to disestablish the Irish Church was now being supplemented by an illustration of the insufficiency of constitutional methods to procure the removal even of the lesser Irish grievances. The lesson was taken to heart, and, with the entry into Parliament of Mr. Parnell in 1875, a movement began through which avowed enemies of England were introduced into the very citadel of English political life, while it incidentally had the effect of changing fundamentally the procedure of the House of Commons and the conventions on which that procedure was based.

Charles Stewart Parnell was, in 1875, a young Protestant Irish landlord of good family, who from his Irish-American mother had inherited a detestation of England and a deep resentment of what he conceived to be the wrongs which Ireland had endured at her hands in the past. Cold, haughty, taciturn, and absolutely fearless; with few general interests or sympathies, no literary culture or gift of eloquence, but with a mind free from cant and a surprising faculty for seeing with eyes unblurred by surrounding conventions the things before him exactly as they really were and for perceiving the directest road to his goal, he did not disguise the contempt which he felt for the majority of his fellow-men and their pretences, nor was he scrupulous in the methods he employed for bending them to his objects. To the opinion formed of him in the House of Commons he was completely indifferent: its approval gave him no pleasure, its disapproval caused him no pain. He perceived that the only way to compel English members to give their attention to Irish business was to prevent them from doing their own, and that the only way in which a handful of Irishmen could accomplish this was by using their position to obstruct the working of the Parliamentary machine. His relations to Mr. Butt in this Parliament resembled in some degree those of Mr. Chamberlain to Lord Hartington. Both men had but a small body of allies in the House, and both drew their strength from extra-Parliamentary forces. But whereas Mr. Chamberlain relied on the "Liberal Parliament outside the

Character and policy of Mr. Parnell.

Imperial legislature"—to quote his own description of the Federation of which he was himself the chief author and the leading spirit—the organisation on which Mr. Parnell leant for support was of a very different character. He had enlisted the sympathies of a large section of the American Fenians, and, supported by the Irish Republican Brotherhood, he derived his driving power from the party of physical force. The failure of Mr. Butt to obtain justice for Ireland in the session of 1876 seemed to prove the inadequacy of his methods, and Mr. Parnell drove home the lesson in a speech he made at Manchester in the following year. "Did we get the abolition of tithes by the conciliation of our English tormentors?" he asked. "No; it was because we adopted different measures. Did O'Connell gain emancipation for Ireland by conciliation? . . . Catholic emancipation was gained because an English king and his Ministers feared revolution. Why was the English Church in Ireland disestablished and disendowed? . . . It was because there was an explosion at Clerkenwell, and because a lock was shot off a prison van at Manchester. We will never gain anything from England unless we tread upon her toes; we will never gain a sixpennyworth from her by conciliation."[1]

Obstruction in the House of Commons.

In the House of Commons the new tactics were inaugurated by the deliberate obstruction of the Mutiny Bill and of the South Africa Bill during the month of July, 1877. With the help of about six followers Mr. Parnell succeeded in paralysing the work of the House of Commons. All night sittings followed one another until Mr. Butt himself thought it his duty to denounce the new plan of campaign amid the cheers of Liberals and Conservatives. Mr. Parnell treated his protest with contemptuous indifference and quietly persisted in his tactics. In 1878 a committee was appointed "to consider the best means of promoting the despatch of public business". Its recommendations were of a mild character. The most important of them, strengthened and adopted early in the session of 1880, embodied in its earliest form the rule dealing with "order in debate". It provided for the suspension from the service of the House during the remainder of the sitting of members named by the chair as obstructing the rules of the House, and for their further suspension for a week or more at

[1] O'Brien's Life of Parnell, i. 130.

the pleasure of the House if found guilty of the same offence three times during the session.

It is doubtful whether the House would have consented even to this moderate restriction of discussion had it not been for the events of 1879. But in May of that year Mr. Butt, "hunted and harassed by debt and illness," died, and Mr. Parnell reigned in his stead. The new member had suspended his policy of obstruction while the committee of 1878, of which he was himself a member, was sitting, but in 1879 he renewed the struggle on the Mutiny Bills. The ground he chose was the abolition of flogging in the army, in his efforts to suppress which he was supported by Mr. Chamberlain and the Radicals, and met with no small measure of success. After a prolonged contest lasting from May into July the Government agreed to confine corporal punishment to offences punishable with death under the provisions of the Act, thus continuing it only as a milder alternative to the extreme penalty.

Mr. Parnell had undoubtedly succeeded in his object of lowering the prestige of the House of Commons. Before this Parliament was dissolved he had established therein a third party, the professed object of which was to discredit that assembly and by demonstrating its incapacity to deal with the affairs of the United Kingdom to prove the necessity of conceding Home Rule to Ireland. The two-party system was at an end, and it remained to be seen whether a constitution under which the chief executive officer was not, as in the United States, elected for a term of years, and under which the assembly itself to which he was responsible did not, as in France, practically enjoy a like fixity of tenure, could permanently repose upon other foundations. Since 1867 the Prime Minister had become the elect of the nation—the Cæsar of the democracy. But his power continued immediately to rest on the steady support of the majority of the House of Commons, so that it seemed probable that when a third party, equally independent of Liberals and Conservatives, and therefore beyond his control, should hold the balance, his credentials would disappear, while there would be none to replace him. France indeed was governed during the first three decades of the Republic by a rapid succession of ephemeral Prime Ministers; but this is scarcely possible under the English system so

Dangers to party government.

long as the two great parties divide between themselves almost equally the suffrages of Great Britain, so long as their differences are deep-seated and hard to compromise, and so long as the leader of each party is practically elected for life or until he himself chooses to retire. The British constitution, as Mr. Gladstone had remarked, "more than any other leaves open doors which lead into blind alleys; for it presumes, more boldly than any other, the good sense and good faith of those who work it". It was precisely this presumption that was now breaking down, for the Parnellite obstructors were using rules devised for the orderly furtherance of business in the House of Commons to make it an object of contempt.

The case of John Mitchell.

Other questions had offered themselves for settlement in the Parliament of 1874 owing to the appearance of a third party in the House of Commons. Mr. John Mitchell, editor of the *United Irishman*, who had been sentenced to penal servitude for his share in the rising of 1848 but had escaped from prison two years later and had since resided in America, was in 1875 elected member for Tipperary. A felon who has neither served his sentence nor received a pardon is disqualified from sitting in Parliament. Accordingly, on the motion of Mr. Disraeli, the House resolved that Mr. Mitchell was incapable of being elected and a new writ was ordered for Tipperary. It was contended, on the other side, that as Mr. Mitchell could no longer be compelled to serve out his sentence or be prosecuted for prison-breaking, he could no longer be considered as a felon, and was therefore qualified to serve. However, the view of the Government prevailed. Mr. Mitchell was at once re-elected for Tipperary. The case was brought before the Dublin court of common pleas where it was decided that he was incapable of sitting in Parliament; whereupon, the House of Commons, fortified by this decision, resolved that the name of Stephen Moore, his Conservative opponent, who had polled a minority of votes, should be substituted for that of John Mitchell in the return. A protracted struggle would probably have followed had not the death of Mr. Mitchell, which occurred almost immediately after his second election, set the question at rest.

Dissolution of the Parliament of 1874.

The Parliament of 1874 was dissolved in March, 1880. For the four preceding years the attention of the country had been concentrated on foreign affairs. It was the foreign policy of the Government in the east which had drawn Mr. Gladstone from his brief retirement, it was by its foreign policy that the Ministry was to stand or fall. Had the dissolution taken place in 1878 when Lord Beaconsfield—for by this name Mr. Disraeli had been known since his entry into the House of Lords in 1876—returned amid the applause of his countrymen bearing "peace with honour" from Berlin, the issue would almost certainly have been determined in his favour. But the last two years of his administration were less successful. Rain spoiled the harvests; while the farmer did not as of old derive from a rise in prices compensation for the poorness of the crops, because the development of wheat production in the west of America and the extension of the British commercial marine facilitated the import of food stuffs to such a degree that in 1879 "the worst harvest which the farmer had experienced for many years was accompanied by the lowest prices which the actual generation of farmers had ever known."[1] Foreign trade simultaneously declined; its value in 1874 was £667,000,000; by 1879 it had been reduced to £611,000,000. Moreover, the wars in Afghanistan and Zululand, questionable in themselves, and attended with unexpected difficulties, tended to discredit "jingoism," as the Imperial policy of Lord Beaconsfield was irreverently nicknamed. Mr. Gladstone's firm and perfectly sincere persuasion that he was warring against the powers of evil was always impressive; but, reinforced by the spectacle of two expensive and unfortunate little wars, the precise objects of which it was difficult to explain, by a contracted foreign trade, successive deficits, increased taxation, and agricultural depression, it tended to become irresistible.

The day after the announcement of the dissolution, Lord Beaconsfield published his manifesto in the form of a letter to the Duke of Marlborough, then Irish viceroy. Its subject was "the danger, in its ultimate results scarcely less disastrous than pestilence and famine" threatening Ireland on account of the new movement for Home Rule. He made a solemn appeal to all men of light and leading to "resist this destructive doctrine," and, so far as in him lay, made the Irish question the main issue to be determined at the polls.[2] Mr. Gladstone in

Manifestoes of Mr. Gladstone and of Lord Beaconsfield.

[1] History of Twenty-five Years, iv. 379.   [2] See Chapter III., p. 156.

his reply declared that the chief enemies of the Union were those who had maintained in Ireland an alien church, an unjust land law, and franchises inferior to our own, and he proceeded to make a general attack on the policy of the Ministry. On the 16th of March he started for Midlothian—the Conservative seat he had elected to contest—where his three years' oratorical campaign was at last brought to a successful conclusion. Divinely strengthened and led on as he believed himself to be,[1] the torrent of his indignant eloquence swept everything before it, and the enthusiasm he inspired was illustrated by the fact that at every place at which he spoke the Conservatives were defeated. The London press indeed was on the Ministerial side. But the power of the press had been greatly diminished by the extension of the suffrage. The mass of the working class electorate read cheap local papers, which, being numerous, and not unequally distributed between the two political parties, neutralised each others' influence; while the electoral power of readers of *The Times* and other journals appealing to a more cultivated audience had become relatively insignificant, and quite insufficient to decide the result of a general election.[2]

Composition of the new House of Commons. Mr. Parnell chosen leader of the Irish party.

The result of the voting was a great reversal of the verdict of 1874. The new House of Commons was composed of 347 Liberals, 240 Conservatives, and 65 Nationalists. Of these Nationalists, thirty-five were followers of Mr. Parnell; the remainder followed Mr. Shaw, and adhered to the moderate and constitutional views of Mr. Butt. The divergence between these sections was indicated by the position of their seats in the new House, where Mr. Parnell and his friends marked their independence by sitting on the Opposition side, while Mr. Shaw and his followers sat with the Liberals on the right hand of the Speaker. Mr. Parnell had been brought back from the United States by the announcement of the general election. His chief object in going there had been to reconcile the Irish-American Fenians to the "new departure"; that is to say, to the agrarian and Parliamentary movement.

[1] Life of Gladstone, vol. iii. 1.
[2] It is remarkable that from 1841 down to and including 1868 *The Times* was always on the winning side at general elections; though how far it influenced, or how far it merely represented, the opinions of the electorate, it is difficult to determine. Since that date its views have been more often repudiated than endorsed by the electors.

He was never weary of declaring his conviction that much could be done through the " Parliamentary machine " if only his Fenian allies would trust him, and he clearly perceived that the full sympathy of the Irish people could only be enlisted in the political issue by connecting it closely with the question of the land. To the mass of the Irish people Home Rule was a means to an agrarian end ; to the Fenians, on the contrary, the land question was a means to a political end. And that political end was the establishment of an Irish republic. At the election Mr. Parnell displayed an activity which rivalled that of Mr. Gladstone, and his endeavours were chiefly directed towards replacing the moderate Home Rulers—Whigs, as they were called—by followers of his own. His success was apparent in the ensuing May, when the whole Irish party met to choose a leader, and Mr. Parnell was chosen with twenty-three votes over eighteen given to Mr. Shaw.

When the result of the elections was known Lord Beaconsfield resigned ; and the queen, after vainly endeavouring to persuade Lord Hartington to attempt the formation of a ministry, by his advice sent for Mr. Gladstone, to whom the Liberal victory was mainly due.[1] The Ministry formed by Mr. Gladstone was for the most part of a Whig character, but the inclusion of Mr. Chamberlain as President of the Board of Trade went far to neutralise the Whig element. Mr. Chamberlain, with no previous official experience, and only four years of Parliamentary life to his credit, brought to the Government the powerful support of the organisation, in the foundation of which he had taken so leading a part, and with him the caucus may be said to have come into power. In a letter to *The Times* he claimed for the representative Liberal Associations the chief credit for the victory, and pointed out that almost every borough possessing such an association had returned the Liberal candidate. However this may have been, it seems certain that the troubled career of the Government of 1880 could not have lasted so long amid the internal dissensions in which the party was involved had it not been for

Mr. Gladstone's second administration.

---

[1] Before definitely declining to form an administration, Lord Hartington, by the queen's desire, ascertained in conversation with Mr. Gladstone, that that statesman "would not act in a Ministry except as first Minister". Life of Gladstone, vol. ii. 622.

the pressure brought to bear upon Liberal members by the action of the caucus—a pressure which probably would not have been exercised if its chief representative had not been a member of the Cabinet. Mr. Gladstone had not, in the first instance, intended to include a single representative of the new Radicalism in the Cabinet. But when he proposed to Sir Charles Dilke—then in close association with Mr. Chamberlain—that he should join the Government in a subordinate capacity, he found, to his surprise, that Sir Charles would only come in on conditions. These were, that either Mr. Chamberlain or himself were to have Cabinet office—otherwise neither would join the Government. Mr. Gladstone was indignant, but gave way; and when Mr. Chamberlain entered the cabinet Sir Charles became Under-Secretary for Foreign Affairs.

Weakness of the Government. Its causes and significance.

The action of the Government of 1880 was usually the result of compromise between men of signal ability but divergent opinions, and was consequently marked by weakness and vacillation. If Mr. Chamberlain was able almost singly to hold his own in the Cabinet against his Whig colleagues, it was owing to the support which he received on most occasions from Mr. Gladstone; and if Mr. Gladstone gave him this support, this was due less to any general agreement in outlook than to the Prime Minister's conviction that it was "the office of law and of institutions to reflect the wants and wishes of the country," and to his belief that Mr. Chamberlain was better placed than other ministers for ascertaining these wants and wishes. To Lord Rosebery Mr. Gladstone wrote in September, 1880: "What is outside Parliament seems to me to be fast mounting, nay to have already mounted, to an importance much exceeding what is inside". With this impression it is not surprising that—to quote the words of another of his colleagues—he allowed "speeches *outside* to affect opinion, and politically to commit the Cabinet in a direction which was not determined . . . by the Government as a whole, but by the audacity" of his new associate.[1] Mr. Chamberlain's original design in forming the National Liberal Federation was that a party programme should be formulated by the organisations outside Parliament; and forced "by a little gentle pressure" on the leaders within. For him it was a fortunate

[1] Letter of Duke of Argyll to Mr. Gladstone, 18th December, 1885.

circumstance that when called upon, for the first time, to take office, it was under a chief who believed in the paramount importance of these outside influences, and who held that the changes in the condition and views of the people should be represented in the professions and actions of its leading men.

The Government had not been long in office before Lord Beaconsfield's warning that dangers worse than pestilence threatened Ireland was terribly justified. There was no allusion to the Irish land question in the Queen's Speech. The announcement was made that the Peace Preservation Act would not be renewed. At the urgent request of the Irish members, however, a bill was introduced and passed through the Commons, to provide for the payment in certain cases of compensation for disturbance to evicted tenants who could convince the Land Court that they were unable to pay their rent; but this was rejected by the House of Lords. In the autumn there was distress in Ireland so great that in General Gordon's opinion the Irish were reduced to a state "worse than that of any people in the world". A furious land agitation, conducted by Mr. Parnell and his allies, accompanied this condition of affairs. During the course of the year there were 10,457 persons evicted and 2,590 agrarian outrages. Activity and energy of a sinister kind were not lacking that winter; and Mr. Parnell was right in the belief, which he had expected at Ennis in September, that the Land Bill would be proportionately strengthened.[1] At Limerick in November he explained that he did not believe in the permanence of an Irish party in the English Parliament, but that he thought it possible by great exertions and by great sacrifices to maintain the independence of the party until, after a short and sharp struggle, legislative independence should be restored to Ireland. In the same month, Mr. Parnell and his chief lieutenants of the Land League were the subjects of a Government prosecution, but when they were brought to trial in January, 1881, the jury failed to agree upon a verdict.

In these circumstances the Government decided first to restore order by the suspension of the Habeas Corpus Act, and then to redress Irish grievances by drastic land legislation. Accordingly on the 24th January, 1881, the Protection

Irish disturbances.

Obstruction of the Protection of Life and Property Bill. Debate closed by the Speaker.

[1] See below p. 159.

for Life and Property Bill was introduced and a struggle began, the most permanent constitutional effect of which was fundamentally to change the historic procedure of the House of Commons. On the 25th January Mr. Gladstone moved that the bill should have precedence. Mr. Parnell and the Irish met this motion by open obstruction, and it was only carried after a continuous sitting of twenty-two hours. On Monday, the 31st January, the Government announced their intention to carry the first reading by the end of the sitting. The Irish resolved to prevent this; and, after the House had sat for forty-one hours, the debate was only closed by Mr. Speaker Brand, who, on his own authority, and to vindicate the credit and dignity of the House, declined to allow any further speeches, and put the question on the first reading. He rightly held that there are occasions when equity and common-sense must overrule the strict letter of the law; but, as the executive officer of the House, commissioned to administer its rules, he had, before taking action, privately stipulated with Mr. Gladstone that business should be regulated for the future either by giving more authority to the House or by conferring greater power on the Chair.

New rules of procedure in House of Commons. The Speaker's conditions were complied with in the following year (1882) when no less than thirty-four nights were devoted to the discussion of new rules of procedure. These rules were designed to check the obstruction of Government business, by conferring new powers on the Speaker, and by limiting the number of questions on which private members might raise a debate. Nineteen nights were occupied by the discussion of the closure rule which, in this its earliest form, placed the initiative of declaring the sense of the House that the debate should be closed in the Chair, and required for the success of a closure motion the support of 200 members in a full House or of 100 members when less than forty divided against it. This proposal was vigorously denounced by the Conservatives; but, a few years later, when they themselves were in power, they considerably strengthened it by transferring the initiative in closing a debate from the Chair to the House and by reducing the number of necessary supporters of the closure motion from 200 to 100.[1]

---

[1] In its earlier form the closure was only twice put into operation; owing to the reluctance of successive Speakers to use so invidious a weapon.

The tendency of the new rules was to increase the amount of time available for Government business, and with it the rigidity of party ties. Almost every division was now becoming a party division, almost every question a question of confidence vital to the Government, scarce any time or place was soon to be left to private members for independent action. Each successive extension of the suffrage strengthened this development, for the size of constituencies made it difficult for a member to be personally known to the bulk of his constituents, or to derive from them a general commission based upon their confidence in his judgment; while it was impossible for him to unite his supporters in any collective views except those bound together and embodied in the party programme. *Their tendency and results.*

Those who rule, according to Bentham, will always do so, not in the interest of the governed, but in their own. The acceptance of this maxim by the old school of Radical individualists had led them to conclude with their master that the only way to secure the greatest happiness of the greatest number is to place a share of power in as many hands as possible. But they seem to have overlooked the fact that large masses of men can have no corporate will of their own except in a very general sense, and that they are therefore obliged to commit their power either to a Cæsar, or to a party, or else to a Cæsar through a party. The Peelites in mid-Victorian times, while the individual was still of importance, could maintain an independent existence and "buy themselves in after putting themselves up for auction"; but no such course was open to Liberal Unionists or Unionist Free Traders in later days. Democracy was impatient of such subtleties; and the heretics, whose only fault it was that they adhered to the former principles of their respective parties, were compelled either to pass over to the other side or to abandon public life. *Rigidity of party ties increased by democracy.*

The closure proposal caused grave searchings of heart in many an old-fashioned Liberal and Radical. Mr. Gladstone himself in the previous Parliament had declared that the House of Commons was "above all and before all a free assembly;" and that it must therefore "submit to pay for its freedom".[1] But Mr. Chamberlain was now a Cabinet Minister, and the power of the caucus was brought into action in order to over- *Liberal opposition to the closure quelled by the caucus.*

---

[1] "The Country and the Government," *Nineteenth Century*, August, 1879.

ride opposition. A circular, issued from Birmingham, urged the Federated Associations to declare to all whom it might concern that they expected the Government to be supported in their proposals by the whole of the Liberal party. The closure was stated to be indispensable in order to ensure the passage into law of the measures in which the Federation was interested.

Mr. Schnadhorst at Brighton, the constituency of Mr. Marriott, a Liberal member who had moved an amendment hostile to the principle of closure by a simple majority, went so far as to say that "when Mr. Gladstone and the Government met the House of Commons and said it was impossible for them to conduct the business with the present antiquated rules ... there was only one course open to every loyal member of the Liberal party—to sacrifice his personal convictions in order to support Mr. Gladstone". The Associations responded eagerly to the Birmingham appeal, and enjoined their members to desist from all opposition to the ministerial proposals. The Government threatened to dissolve if these proposals were rejected. A large majority of the dissidents yielded to these influences; and only five of them eventually ventured to vote in favour of Mr. Marriott's amendment.

The "fourth party". The first session of the Parliament of 1880 brought into public notice a group of four men who sat together on the Conservative side of the House below the gangway, and who were resolved that there should be no lack of energy in the business of opposition. Covertly encouraged by Lord Beaconsfield, Lord Randolph Churchill and his three friends were only too ready to act on his suggestion that "they need not be too scrupulous about obeying their leader,"[1] Sir Stafford Northcote, whose mild and conscientious disposition, unchanging fairness, and deference to Mr. Gladstone, whom he had formerly served as private secretary, unfitted him for the post of leader of opposition in difficult times. The friends first acted together during the Bradlaugh controversy, when they organised the resistance by which a powerful Ministry was defeated in the first year of power. They called themselves, half in jest and half in earnest, the fourth party, but they can hardly be said to have deserved a title of such importance. A party is

[1] Life of Lord Randolph Churchill, vol. i. p. 256.

a body of men bound by certain principles held in common and working together in order to give effect to them. The only principle which united Lord Randolph Churchill, Sir Henry Drummond Wolff, Mr. Gorst, and Mr. Arthur Balfour was the principle that the business of an opposition is to oppose and their only common end was to embarrass the Government. Mr. Gladstone had been rash enough to publish, in the article already quoted, a defence of Irish obstruction, in the course of which he wrote: " If a great party may obstruct, it is hazardous to award narrower limits to the small one; for it is precisely in the class of cases where the party is small and the conviction strong that the best instances of warrantable obstruction may be found". Propositions such as this Lord Randolph declared to be the charter of his party.[1] Accordingly, the Irish methods of obstruction were carefully imitated; under pretence of improving Government legislation or guarding the interests of the tax-payer much time was wasted; the vulnerable temper of the Prime Minister, who was always too apt to deal seriously with frivolous objections, was worked upon in a schoolboy spirit of mischief; and Sir Stafford Northcote was treated with a thinly disguised contempt. In the course of the session of 1880 it was computed that Lord Randolph, Mr. Gorst, and Sir Henry Drummond Wolff had together spoken 247 times and asked seventy-three questions. These arts had never before been practised by an English party. The aim of the Irish obstructionists was to destroy the dignity and authority of the House of Commons and thereby to prove the Union a failure: their goal was at all events a great one; and their cause, in their own view, the cause of a nation. But the aim of their English imitators was merely to embarrass an English Government; and, if in so doing, they incidentally brought contempt upon the Parliamentary system, that was to them a matter of indifference.

In April, 1881, Lord Beaconsfield died. He had exercised a restraining influence on the more ardent spirits of his party; who had come to regard him with an almost superstitious reverence. Lord Randolph Churchill, especially, had studied his speeches and writings with great assiduity, and

Lord Randolph Churchill and Tory democracy.

[1] Life of Lord Randolph Churchill, vol. i. p. 151.

from him derived the idea of Tory democracy—the wave on which he was destined to mount for a brief moment almost to the summit of his ambition. But if, as Lord Randolph thought, he had inherited the principles of Lord Beaconsfield, he had inherited them with an important difference. Both statesmen preached the doctrine of Tory democracy; but it was the Toryism that interested Lord Beaconsfield, the democracy Lord Randolph. Both were naturally adventurous, and the spirit of adventure tempts men far from home. The unknown is ever interesting. Thus the same temper which drew Lord Randolph into the *terra incognita* of democracy moved Mr. Disraeli to explore the serene heights of aristocracy. Lord Randolph adopted with enthusiasm Lord Beaconsfield's exposition of Tory aims, namely, the maintenance of our ancient institutions, together with the elevation of the condition of the people; but whereas Lord Beaconsfield cared much for the national institutions, but perceived that he could not enlist the sympathies of a democratic electorate in their preservation unless he associated them with proposals for social reform, the reverse was the case with Lord Randolph. His interest in national institutions was superficial and opportunist, though strong enough to enable him to remain in the Conservative ranks, but he was prepared to go lengths which would have startled Lord Beaconsfield in the direction of social reform. He confessed to a "sneaking admiration" for the Liberal caucus, and was ambitious to play the part of Mr. Chamberlain in the Conservative party.

Reorganisation of the National Union after the election of 1880.

The National Union of Conservative and Constitutional Associations had been founded as early as 1867—ten years before the National Liberal Federation came into being. "Its object was to strengthen the hands of local associations; while its work consisted chiefly in helping to form such associations, and in giving information."[1] Like the National Liberal Federation, it met annually in different places. It did not pretend in any way to direct the policy of the party, and its constitution was aristocratic rather than representative. The overthrow of 1880 was imputed by many Conservatives to defective party organisation, and to the superior efficiency of the Birmingham machinery. The same explanation *mutatis*

[1] Lowell's Government of England, i. 536.

mutandis had been given by Liberals of their defeat in 1874, and had led to the establishment of an organisation for which Mr. Chamberlain claimed the chief credit for the victory of 1880. The same cause led in the Conservative camp to the same effects. New rules were adopted by the council at the conference held in that year. It was provided that associations should be represented at the conference in proportion to their size, and that the aristocratic "vice-presidents" from the Consultative Committee should be excluded from the council. A change productive of more important results was the substitution on the council of twelve members chosen by that body itself for twenty members nominated by the chief associations.

In 1883 the selection of Sir Stafford Northcote to unveil the statue of Lord Beaconsfield appeared to indicate that he, rather than Lord Salisbury, was to be regarded as that statesman's successor in the leadership of the Conservative party. Thereupon Lord Randolph Churchill, in two letters to *The Times*, attacked this choice with his customary vehemence, denouncing the "pusillanimity, vacillation, and discouragement of hard-working followers" displayed by Lord Beaconsfield's former lieutenants in the House of Commons. He declared himself happy to be the scapegoat on which doomed mediocrities might lay the burden of their exposed incapacity. These letters he followed up by an article in the *Fortnightly Review*, entitled "Elijah's Mantle," in which he expounded the creed of Tory democracy, and plainly indicated that if Lord Salisbury's shoulders were not found to be broad enough to bear the weight of the prophet's mantle, the resources of Conservative civilisation were not at an end. In the summer of the same year he conceived the design of obtaining the control of the National Union of Associations, managed up to that time in concert with the party leaders, and afterwards of obtaining for the Union a power analogous to that of the Liberal Federation.

^{Elijah's mantle.}

The party funds were then in the hands of the "Central Committee," a body created in 1880 at the instance of Lord Beaconsfield, and consisting of the Whips, and certain other members appointed by the official leaders. In October, 1883, a conference was held by the National Union at Birmingham.

^{A struggle for control.}

A rider directing the Council to take such steps as might be requisite for securing to the National Union its legitimate influence in the party organisation was proposed to the annual report. In supporting this rider Lord Randolph attacked the Central Committee, and said that he "should like to see the control of the party organisation taken out of the hands of a self-elected body, and placed in the hands of an elected body". The rider was carried, and Lord Randolph subsequently succeeded, by the co-optation of twelve new members, in obtaining a steady majority of his adherents on the Council. On the resignation of Lord Percy in February, 1884, he was elected Chairman of the Council. Negotiations with regard to the funds were opened with the Central Committee, and after an angry correspondence ended with a notice to the National Union to quit the offices in London, which they had hitherto occupied jointly with the Central Committee. Finally, after much further disputation, peace was made; the Central Committee was abolished, but the control of the central organisation over the National Union was largely increased; Lord Randolph left the Council and was given office in the next Conservative Administration; while the mutinous spirit that had disturbed party discipline vanished during the defensive rally that followed the introduction of the Home Rule Bill. Lord Randolph's paradoxical attempt to govern the Conservative party from below failed, but he had shown himself a power to be reckoned with, and his admission to the Cabinet of 1885 was perhaps the chief result of the movement. Such is the indifference of the mass of men—especially of Conservatives—to political issues, that no political party can really receive its direction from below: the body cannot govern the head. Men who are associated with a single and definite cause capable of enlisting large popular support may, it is true, by organising popular forces, compel reluctant leaders to take action; and ambitious men may succeed for a time in setting up an informal Parliament outside the Imperial Legislature with more general objects. But when their success has brought them into the Cabinet, and the Imperial Legislature itself becomes an instrument to their hands, they are the first to repress insubordination on the part of outside agencies; and the associations to which they had given life tend to become either the obedient registrars of official decrees, or, like the Liberal Federation during Mr. Chamberlain's tenure of office from 1880 to 1885, a disciplined force charged with the repression of all symptoms of revolt within the party.

Yet, although the original Birmingham scheme that the people at large should have a share in the control and management of party policy might prove impracticable, the manner in which Lord Randolph Churchill and Mr. Chamberlain rose to power was none the less full of significance, and indicated a change in the old order of things. Both men had adopted in the House of Commons a defiant attitude towards the party leaders, and derived their importance from their influence with the popular party organisations. Success in the House of Commons was ceasing to be the shortest road to power; ex-Ministers had come to rely upon a political programme expounded from the platform and upon extra-Parliamentary organisation as the means most likely to restore them to office, while Ministers were beginning to trust to the same expedients to maintain themselves in power. The political centre of gravity was shifting from Parliament to the platform. Mr. Gladstone in 1866 created a precedent when as a Minister he conducted an agitation in the country in favour of his own Reform Bill, and again when as an ex-Minister he "was occupied," to use Lord Chancellor Selborne's words, "during the autumn of 1879 with his first Midlothian campaign, into which he threw himself like a gladiator in the arena, as no other statesman of similar position had ever done before". *Change in the political centre of gravity.*

But Mr. Chamberlain, in 1883, made a great democratic step in advance when in a speech at Birmingham he felt it consistent with his position as a Minister of the Crown to advocate an extensive scheme of Radical reform comprising disestablishment, manhood suffrage, equal electoral districts, and payment of members—a legislative programme to which few, if any, of his colleagues would have agreed. The queen, through Sir Henry Ponsonby, expressed to Mr. Gladstone her strong disapproval, on constitutional grounds, of this speech; and the Prime Minister himself was scarcely less emphatic in his condemnation; but Mr. Chamberlain was unrepentant. He claimed, shortly after, at a Cobden Club dinner an unlimited liberty of speech, and contended that the restrictions *Mr. Chamberlain's independent action.*

imposed by office were confined to action. The dangers of such a theory are obvious. The restraining influence of office on bold devisers of political experiments is of great utility, but if it is possible to separate in this way official speech from official action, colleagues in a Cabinet may be expected to outbid one another in their competition for that popular favour which may enable them to mount to the highest place.

Failures of the Government. The Reform Bill of 1884.

The Government of 1880 had come into power with promises of peace, retrenchment, and reform. But the continual wars into which they were driven, partly by circumstances, and partly by their own lack of foresight, made retrenchment impossible; nor, except during the Egyptian campaign of 1882, was there any military success to reconcile the nation to the increasing expenditure. The attempted conciliation of Ireland by arrangements concluded with Mr. Parnell was violently interrupted by the murder of Lord Frederick Cavendish, the ambassador of peace, and was followed by a new Coercion Act which, although, through the administration of Lord Spencer, it was successful in the repression of crime, left the Irish more discontented than ever. Defeats in South Africa and Afghanistan, failure in the Soudan, and failure in Ireland had, by 1884, discredited a Cabinet divided against itself, resting on a majority not homogeneous, and with difficulty held together by the coercive pressure of the caucus. The Government having failed to fulfil their promises of peace and retrenchment, there remained reform, and on this subject in 1884 there was a rally of the whole party to the support of their proposals. Of the Reform Bill of 1884, by which through the extension of household suffrage to the counties the numbers of the electorate were increased from three to five millions, an account has been given in another chapter. The first bill passed by large majorities through the House of Commons, receiving the support of Lord Randolph Churchill and his friends, but it was rejected by the House of Lords on the ground that it was not accompanied by a measure for the redistribution of seats. A formidable agitation against the House of Lords followed, during which Mr. Gladstone for once proved a moderating influence. He did not wish to raise the question of organic change of the House of Lords, but he was resolved that on no other question than organic change should the action of that assembly bring about a dissolution. "Never will I be a party," he said, "to dissolving in order to determine whether the Lords or the Commons were right upon the Franchise Bill. If I have anything to do with dissolution, it will be a dissolution upon organic change in the House of Lords."[1] In this instance the good sense of the leaders, powerfully aided by the "wise, gracious, and steady influence" of the queen, averted a crisis. The provisions of the proposed Redistribution Bill were privately shown to Lord Salisbury and Sir Stafford Northcote before the Lords gave their assent to the second Reform Bill. They proved satisfactory to the Conservative chiefs; the bill was passed in an autumn session; and was succeeded by an Act for the Redistribution of Seats in the following spring.

This interval of success, however, could not save the Government. Mr. Chamberlain's speeches became ever more uncompromising in their vehemence and his unauthorised programme which, in addition to payment of members, abolition of plural voting, and manhood suffrage, now included a graduated income tax and the breaking up of great estates as a first step in land reform, caused deep dissatisfaction not only to the queen but also to the right wing of the Liberal party. In the Cabinet he came forward with a scheme for the settlement of the Irish question by the establishment of a central board of local government in Dublin with wide but limited powers. This project won the approval of Mr. Gladstone, and was accepted by Mr. Parnell. But, in the Cabinet, though all the commoners except Lord Hartington were in favour of it, all the peers except Lord Granville were against it. It was determined to renew the Crimes Act in a modified form, and to accompany this renewal by a Land Purchase Bill. On this Mr. Chamberlain and Sir Charles Dilke resigned, but were persuaded to suspend their resignation. In foreign affairs, failure succeeded failure. The fall of Khartoum and the death of General Gordon provoked the openly expressed displeasure of the queen; and the Ministry only escaped a vote of censure in the House of Commons by a majority of fourteen. There followed the abandonment of the Soudan after the totally use-

Dissensions in the Ministry. The unauthorised programme.

[1] Life of Gladstone, vol. iii. p. 130.

less expenditure of thousands of lives and millions of money. The advance of Russia towards the north-west frontier of India elicited from the Prime Minister a warlike speech and a vote of credit from the House of Commons for eleven millions. The Government perhaps acted wisely in submitting the dispute to arbitration, but they laid themselves open to the taunt that their brave words had not been seconded by deeds.

Defeat and resignation of the Government.

On the 18th May Mr. Gladstone gave notice of the intention of the Government to renew the most important clauses of the Crimes Act. Five days later, Lord Randolph Churchill in a speech at the St. Stephen's Club gave his audience to understand that a Conservative Government would not renew the Act. This speech decided the attitude of Mr. Parnell and the fate of the Government. On the 8th June, to their great satisfaction they were defeated on an amendment to the Budget, and at once resigned. The queen sent for Lord Salisbury and after long negotiations, and a first refusal, he agreed to take office.

Lord Salisbury Prime Minister as Foreign Secretary.

An arrangement had been made between Lord Salisbury and Sir Stafford Northcote, that the one of them for whom the queen should send on the resignation of the Liberal Government should be Prime Minister, and that the other should serve under him. Accordingly, Lord Salisbury offered the Chancellorship of the Exchequer with the lead in the House of Commons to Sir Stafford, who accepted. But an unexpected difficulty arose. Lord Randolph Churchill, whom Lord Salisbury designed for the India Office, refused to join the Government if Sir Stafford led the House of Commons; and Sir Michael Hicks Beach, considering that no Ministry in which Lord Randolph was not included could hope to find favour with the country, thereupon declared that without him he must also refuse to serve. Finally Sir Stafford Northcote accepted a peerage as First Lord of the Treasury, Sir Michael Hicks Beach became Chancellor of the Exchequer and leader of the House of Commons, Lord Randolph took the India Office, and Lord Salisbury, although Prime Minister, the Foreign Office. Thus for the first time since 1766, when Lord Chatham formed his last administration as Privy Seal, the position of Prime Minister was separated from the office of First Lord of the Treasury.

The position of the new Ministry was one of great difficulty. Brought into power by the help of the Irish vote, and in a minority in the House of Commons, they were unable to advise an immediate dissolution, because the new register made necessary by the Reform and Redistribution Acts could not be ready for use until the autumn. Their only hope of gaining a majority at the coming General Election was by enlisting the support of the Irish, and to some of the Ministers this seemed possible of accomplishment by a policy of conciliation. The story of the moves and the counter-moves of the various party leaders at this time with respect to the Irish question will be told in another chapter. The Conservative party as a whole cannot be held responsible for the somewhat questionable endeavour of its chiefs to remain on good terms with the Irish Nationalists until after the General Election. The Crimes Act was not renewed, boycotting was publicly treated as a trivial offence by Lord Salisbury, Lord Spencer's administration was not defended. This policy was successful in securing for the Conservatives the Irish vote at the polls. When, indeed, on the eve of the election, Mr. Gladstone in Midlothian stated that it was the duty of the English Government to treat with careful attention any constitutional demand that Ireland might make, Mr. Parnell for an instant hoped that his conversion to Home Rule was completed and invited him to frame a constitution; but when Mr. Gladstone replied, in "sarcastic vein," that to do this would be to usurp the functions of Government, a manifesto was issued in which the Liberal party was vehemently denounced and the Irish exhorted to vote for their opponents.

Conservative relations to the Irish party. Crimes Act not renewed.

One effect of the resignation of the Liberal Government in June, 1885, was to bring to a head the internal differences of the Liberal party. Whigs and Radicals were now no longer bound together by the doctrine of collective responsibility, their chiefs were no longer colleagues in the same Cabinet and compelled to keep up some fiction of agreement. The principal object of Mr. Gladstone's manifesto of the 18th September was to find some common ground on which men who disagreed with one another upon almost every political subject might find themselves able to stand together. The differences between Mr. Chamberlain and Lord Hartington,

Open disagreement of Whigs and Radicals. The Hawarden manifesto.

long notorious, were now openly avowed by those statesmen in speeches upon public platforms, and they culminated in a pledge by Mr. Chamberlain that he would take office in no Government hostile to the reforms which he had advocated, and which Lord Hartington had attacked.[1] It would have been difficult for the most acute of critics to gather from the Hawarden manifesto on which side Mr. Gladstone's sympathies really were. To the Radicals he implied that on every subject he preserved an open mind, but the Whigs were consoled by the thesis that action must not be taken until questions were "ripe for settlement". If he, for instance, were twenty years younger and circumstances were ripe for taking such a matter in hand, either on the one side or the other, he was very far from saying that he would not urge his followers to give the first place in their thoughts and actions to the "gigantic question" of disestablishment—which was said to be supported by 374 Liberal candidates. But he was an old man and circumstances were not ripe, so the Whigs might rest in peace. These vague generalities had the desired effect, and both wings agreed to work together under their chief. The elections took place in November; the Conservatives gained largely in the boroughs, and it was clear that the constituents of 1880 would have given them the victory; but the Liberals, by the help of the new voters, secured a large majority in the counties.

Results of the election of 1885.
This result might perhaps have been anticipated. The electors of 1880, who had given the Liberals a majority, had been disappointed in their expectations; on the other hand, after each expansion of the suffrage, in 1833, in 1868, and again in 1885, the mass of the newly-enfranchised electors have voted for the party of change in the hope of bettering their condition. The final returns showed 335 Liberals, 249 Conservatives, and 86 Parnellites—the combined forces of Conservatives and Parnellites being thus exactly equal in

[1] It was the singular destiny of those distinguished men, whose mutual antagonism from the time of Mr. Chamberlain's entrance into Parliament in 1876 until the end of their political careers so much engaged the attention of the political world, never to find themselves in formal opposition to one another. For five years they were colleagues under a Liberal Prime Minister, and again for eight years colleagues under a Conservative Prime Minister; and their final resignations occurred on the same occasion, but for diametrically opposite reasons.

number to the Liberals. The Reform Act of 1884 had increased the numbers of the Irish electorate from 200,000 to nearly 700,000, and the risks attending this immense extension had been foretold. Not a Liberal was returned for all Ireland, and the eighty-six Nationalists were all of them followers of Mr. Parnell, and free from all taint of moderation. For the first time the balance between the two great historical parties was held by a third party antagonistic to both, and the dangers of such a situation, insisted upon by Mr. Gladstone before the election, quickly became manifest.

Events now moved rapidly. The result of the election had completed Mr. Gladstone's conversion to Home Rule. Although the wishes of the Irish people had been long well known they were now for the first time constitutionally expressed by the return to Parliament of an overwhelming majority of their representatives pledged to give effect to them. This was the result of the lowering of the franchise in Ireland, and it had been confidently anticipated. But it was a result quite conclusive to Mr. Gladstone's mind, to whom the presumed wishes of the electorate were ever of paramount importance. *Mr. Gladstone's conversion to Home Rule.*

On the Conservative party the election results had a contrary effect. Their best chance now was to break altogether with the Irish and stand boldly for the Union. Once again they represented a principle, they could oppose an idea to an idea, a policy to a policy, and were no longer reduced to performing the humble functions of a drag on a wheel, the onward progress of which was admitted to be inevitable. Lord Randolph Churchill and Sir Michael Hicks Beach, indeed, were anxious that an attempt at all events should be made to govern Ireland without coercion, and not, after having enjoyed the benefit of the Irish vote, at once to repudiate the conditions on which it was tacitly asked for and given, but the majority of their colleagues were against them and carried the Prime Minister with them. *The Conservatives stand for the Union.*

When Parliament met at the end of January, 1886, notice was given of a Bill to suppress the National League and to protect life and property in Ireland. On the same day the Government were defeated by a majority of seventy-nine on an amendment to the Address, moved on the subject of allotments by Mr. Jesse Collings. *Defeat of the Government.*

Their resignation.

The majority was composed of 257 Liberals and 74 Nationalists—the minority of 234 Conservatives and 18 Liberals including Lord Hartington, Mr. Goschen, and Sir Henry James. Seventy-six Liberals—among them Mr. Bright—were absent from the division. The Government at once resigned. Thus in the course of a single year Mr. Parnell had found himself able to eject from office both the Liberal and the Conservative Governments. The result, in the first instance, was the non-renewal of the Crimes Act; in the second, the introduction of the Home Rule Bill of 1886.

Return of Mr. Gladstone to power. The Whig leaders refuse to join the Cabinet.

After accepting the task of forming a Government Mr. Gladstone at once applied to Lord Hartington. The refusal of that statesman to join him was a sign of change in the Liberal party. As Lord Morley observes, it marked the withdrawal from that party, with a few exceptions, of the aristocratic element which had hitherto held the chief place in its official councils.[1] Mr. Gladstone had drawn up a memorandum which he read to those whom he wished to include in his Cabinet to the effect that examination and inquiry into the practicability of Home Rule was the basis on which he proposed to form his Ministry. Lord Hartington replied that he was opposed to the grant of a separate Irish legislature, and that since inquiry without a proposal would, by raising false expectations, lead to mischievous results, he must decline to commit himself to such an inquiry. He added significantly that he had already in the Government of 1880 made concessions on other subjects which might be thought to have shaken public confidence in him, and that if, for the sake of keeping the party together, he should make further concessions that confidence would be altogether withdrawn. Lord Derby, Lord Northbrook, Lord Selborne, and Mr. Goschen also declined to take office, and Sir Henry James, by a fine sacrifice of natural ambition to principle, refused the Chancellorship. Mr. Bright, from lack of confidence in the men to whom the new proposals would entrust the destinies of Ireland rather than from any abstract objection to Home Rule, also abstained. His abstention was a blow to the Government, for he was revered by the very class of men who were most under the influence of Mr. Gladstone. The secession of the Whigs

---

[1] Life of Gladstone, iii. 293.

from the Liberal party after their Radical rivals had captured the organisation, and with it the direction of policy, had been generally anticipated. The new Irish policy of the Government brought it about at an earlier moment than might otherwise have been the case, but a split sooner or later was in any case inevitable. Their secession of itself would perhaps not have sufficed to defeat Mr. Gladstone. But when Mr. Chamberlain and a section of his Radical followers also declared against the Government policy, that policy was doomed. Mr. Chamberlain, who had assisted in the overthrow of the Conservative Government, entered Mr. Gladstone's Cabinet in the first instance on the inquiry basis, though with considerable misgivings. But when the scheme was brought before the Cabinet in March he objected to it as too wide, while to the Land Bill—a comprehensive plan for buying out the Irish landlords by the use of British credit—he objected altogether; and, accompanied by Mr. Trevelyan, he withdrew from the Government. Thus the new departure was condemned by Lord Hartington, the leader of the Whigs; by Mr. Bright, the leader of the old Radicals; by Mr. Chamberlain, the leader of the new Radicals; and by the Conservatives. In the autumn of 1885 Great Britain had been divided into three political parties—the Conservatives led by Lord Salisbury, the Whigs led by Lord Hartington, and the Radicals led by Mr. Chamberlain. In the spring of 1886 Lord Hartington and Mr. Chamberlain were united with Lord Salisbury in their opposition to Home Rule, and by a strange fatality the three men were subsequently to work together for eight years as colleagues in the same Cabinet.

Resignation of Mr. Chamberlain and Mr. Trevelyan.

But though the Radical leader severed himself from Mr. Gladstone, he could not carry with him the organisation he had contributed so powerfully to found. Mr. Schnadhorst, the Secretary to the Federation, and the ablest organiser in the party, followed Mr. Gladstone. At a special meeting of the Council held in London on the 15th May, a resolution having been moved by an adherent of Mr. Chamberlain declaring the confidence of the Council in Mr. Gladstone, and approval of the policy of giving the Irish control over their own affairs, but requesting the Premier to amend his bill by admitting Irish representatives to the House of Commons, an amendment,

Adherence to Mr. Gladstone of the Liberal Associations.

expressing unqualified approval of the Home Rule Bill and assuring Mr. Gladstone of support, was moved to the resolution and carried by a large majority. Mr. Chamberlain thereupon withdrew from the Federation, and the first half of his career was at an end. Birmingham remained faithful to him, but not one local association seceded from the party. Throughout the country they purged themselves of dissentient members, and, though weakened by these losses, threw themselves with the utmost ardour into the Home Rule campaign. The offices of the Federation were removed from Birmingham to London and established in the same building with the Liberal Central Association to which Mr. Schnadhorst was appointed honorary secretary. Hitherto the Federation had been an instrument in the hands of Mr. Chamberlain, whom it had enabled, by the organisation of public opinion, and the intimidation of members by their local associations, to bring pressure upon his chief and upon his colleagues; henceforward it rendered faithful service to the party leaders generally whom it was anxious in no way to embarrass. The agenda of the General Meeting held every year was prepared by a small General Purposes Committee, and, as after 1887 amendments advocating reforms not included in the agenda were ruled out of order, these meetings could only by their resolutions express approval of measures selected by this committee, and found on inquiry to meet with the universal support of the party.

Unionist coalition. Dissolution of 1886 and Unionist victory.

The alliance between Whigs and Conservatives was inaugurated in April by a great meeting at Her Majesty's Theatre, when Lord Hartington and Lord Salisbury made speeches from the same platform. At the end of May the Chamberlain group, in number fifty-five, held a conference in which it was decided to vote against the bill. On the 7th June the bill was rejected on second reading by 343 against 313—ninety-three Liberals voting in the majority. The Government immediately dissolved Parliament. Before this division took place the Conservatives had pledged themselves, in the event of a general election following the rejection of the bill, to withdraw their candidates from constituencies represented by the dissentient Liberals, while these in their turn gave a similar promise in regard to Conservative seats. This agreement encouraged doubting Liberals to vote against the bill, since it was clear that the withdrawal of their Conservative opponents and the support of Conservative voters would in almost every instance secure to them the continued possession of their seats. On the other hand, their dependence on Conservative support caused them to lose their distinctively Liberal character and the principles of Liberal and Conservative Unionists soon became practically indistinguishable. The result of the election was the return of 316 Conservatives, 191 Gladstonian Liberals, 78 Liberal Unionists, and 85 Irish Nationalists. Mr. Gladstone at once resigned, and the queen sent for Lord Salisbury.

In accepting the queen's commission to form a Government Lord Salisbury obtained her permission to resign it to Lord Hartington, should such an arrangement prove to be possible. But Lord Hartington declined the proposal. He felt that in the circumstances such action would have involved a severance from Mr. Chamberlain and his friends, and the break up of the Liberal Unionist party. Lord Salisbury was, therefore, obliged to form a purely Conservative Ministry, dependent for its continuance on Liberal Unionist support. Sir Michael Hicks Beach, considering that the " position of leader in name but not in fact would be intolerable ; and that it was better for the party and the country that the leader in fact should be leader also in name,"[1] resisted the pressing instances not only of Lord Salisbury but also of Lord Randolph Churchill himself, that he should continue to lead the House of Commons, and gave up the leadership to Lord Randolph, who with it accepted the office of Chancellor of the Exchequer. Sir Michael himself became Chief Secretary for Ireland—that being thought for the moment the most difficult post in the Government.

Lord Salisbury's second administration. Lord Randolph Churchill leader of the House of Commons.

Throughout the six eventful years of the Government of 1886, the Liberal Unionists from their seats among the Gladstonian Liberals on the Opposition side of the House gave a steady and unvarying support to the Government. Nor was this made difficult for them. The Conservatives, some with resignation and others even with eagerness, had accepted the postulates of democracy, and their leaders claimed that their policy covered the whole ground of moderate reform. At a speech made at Dartford in October, 1886, Lord Ran-

Resignation of Lord Randolph Churchill. Mr. Goschen Chancellor of the Exchequer.

---

[1] Life of Lord Randolph Churchill, ii. 125.

dolph Churchill, on behalf of his party, sketched out a bold programme of legislative reform, especially with reference to Local Government and the land, while at the same time he promised to devote all his strength and influence to a reduction of public expenditure, and consequently of taxation. His attempt to carry out his pledges in this last respect brought about his resignation in December, when the Ministers responsible for the army and navy estimates refused to consent to the reductions which he thought necessary, and were supported in their refusal by the Prime Minister. No effort was made to retain Lord Randolph, whose outlook in other respects had been found to differ from that of his colleagues; and Lord Salisbury again approached Lord Hartington, under whom he offered to serve as Foreign Secretary. Lord Hartington, after some hesitation, on finding that the introduction of a body of Liberal Unionists into the Government would be distasteful to the Conservative party, declined the proposal, but persuaded Mr. Goschen, to whom Lord Salisbury next addressed himself, to replace Lord Randolph at the Exchequer. Lord Salisbury remained Prime Minister, but returned to the Foreign Office, the seals of which had been held during the first months of the Government by Lord Iddesleigh, and Mr. Smith became First Lord of the Treasury and leader of the House of Commons. Sir Michael Hicks Beach, who had sympathised generally with Lord Randolph's views, and had even offered to resign with him, was obliged to retire soon after on account of his eyesight, and his successor, Mr. Balfour, Lord Salisbury's nephew, with the help of a new Coercion Act, inaugurated unflinchingly the twenty years of resolute government which the Prime Minister had declared to be a necessary preliminary to the complete pacification of Ireland.

Liberal policy of the Unionist Government. The arrangement whereby the Prime Minister held the most laborious of the great departmental offices proved in some respects inconvenient, for it left him no time to exercise the general control over administration and legislation which gives unity and consistency to a Government, and this lack of direction proved a source of embarrassment to Ministers on several occasions during their six years of office. But the internal dissensions of the Unionists never took the form of a split between the Liberal and Conservative sections of what was beginning to be known as the Unionist party. The Government were dependent on the Liberal Unionists in the House of Commons, and the Liberal Unionists were dependent on the Conservatives in their constituencies, and thus neither section could dispense with the assistance of the other. The very fact that the Liberal Unionists, with the exception of Mr. Goschen, stood outside the ministry and were therefore uncommitted to the ministerial policy, served to convince the Cabinet that they must pursue a Liberal policy, and it cannot be denied that they advanced further to meet their allies and even Mr. Chamberlain, than did these to meet the Ministers. An Irish Land Bill in 1887, the main object of which was to admit leaseholders to the benefits of the Act of 1881, was strengthened, after strong representations from Liberal Unionists, by provisions to permit the re-adjustment of judicial rents fixed before 1886, although by the Act of 1881 the State had formally guaranteed these rents to the landlords for fifteen years. The Local Government Act of 1888, which entrusted the government of counties throughout England and Wales to local bodies elected on a democratic suffrage, effected a reform long urged by Mr. Chamberlain, and promised by Lord Randolph Churchill, and in the same year Mr. Goschen successfully carried out his conversion of the National Debt, the interest on which was reduced from 3 to $2\frac{3}{4}$ per cent until 1903 when it was further to fall to $2\frac{1}{2}$ per cent. In 1889, Local Government was extended to Scotland, in 1890 by the Tithe Rent Recovery Act the payment of tithe was transferred from occupier to owner, and in 1891, Free Education, long a principal article in the Radical programme and perhaps the inevitable corollary of compulsory education, was conceded by a Conservative Government.

After the secession of Lord Hartington and Mr. Chamberlain acceptance pure and simple of the views of Mr. Gladstone became the distinguishing characteristic of the Liberal party. What it lost in strength it gained to some extent in unity. Ireland was the all-absorbing subject of Mr. Gladstone's thoughts; and the victory of his Irish policy the single goal of his endeavour. All else appeared to him of subordinate interest, and he was prepared to agree to changes which in other circumstances he might have opposed if by so doing he could

The Liberal party during the Parliament of 1886-92. The Newcastle Programme.

forward the grand object of his closing years. The Liberal Federation had, until 1886, been addressed at its annual meetings by Mr. Chamberlain, by whom in large measure it had been founded, and whose influence and authority it powerfully helped to extend. After 1886 the annual meetings were attended by Mr. Gladstone, and his presence lent a new importance to the resolutions there carried. In 1891 the Federation met at Newcastle. Resolutions were passed in favour, among other reforms, of Home Rule, the disestablishment of the Church in Wales, Electoral Reform, Payment of Members, Land Reform, Local Veto, Taxation of Land Values, and the "Ending or Mending" of the House of Lords. Mr. Gladstone in his speech " took up *seriatim* the resolutions which had been passed by the Council Meetings and gave them the weight of his direct approval". Ireland blocked the way, and he seems to have believed that he could stimulate the zeal of the advocates of these various changes for the success of the cause he had at heart by persuading them that when once the Irish obstruction was removed, their desires would be fulfilled. But the official sanction thus given to these far-reaching resolutions proved a burden to the party in the near future. The policy came to be known as the Newcastle Programme, and all whom it offended were tempted to take refuge in the opposite camp. The opponents of Home Rule were, generally speaking, too sincere in their opposition to be induced to forgo their resistance in order to clear the way for some point in the Newcastle Programme which met their approval; while others, who might have become converts to Home Rule had they associated the cause with counsels of moderation, were alarmed at the seeming recklessness of its chief promoters.

The Irish question. Zenith and fall of Mr. Parnell.

The fortunes and prospects of the Liberal party during the whole of this Parliament continued to rise and sink with the fortunes and prospects of Home Rule. Tales of harsh treatment of the people by Irish landlords or police were listened to with interest, and excited a sympathy hitherto unknown in England. The wrongs of Irish tenants had become a party question. Nationalist speakers were welcomed at Liberal meetings, and Liberal politicians crossed over to Ireland to provide themselves with material for the case against the Government. The Crimes Act of 1887 was unpopular in England, and the proclamation of the National League that soon followed its passage was opposed by Mr. Chamberlain and disapproved by Lord Randolph Churchill. The bill, appointing a commission of three judges to investigate the truth of charges brought against the Irish leaders by *The Times* in the series of articles, entitled " Parnellism and Crime," and forced by the Government through the House of Commons in 1888 by a newly-devised measure of closure, had an appearance of unfairness, since its occasion was Mr. Parnell's demand for a Select Committee to inquire only into the authenticity of *fac simile* letters condoning the Phœnix Park murders, which were alleged to have been signed by him, and had been published by *The Times*. After the Commission had sat for fifty days, they approached the subject of the letters, and it then appeared that they had been forged by a man of notoriously bad character, and accepted without suspicion or inquiry, because the manager of *The Times* thought that they were the sort of letters Mr. Parnell would be likely to write. Although some of the other findings of the Commission, tending to show that Mr. Parnell and his leading associates had not exerted themselves to repress crime, might in other circumstances have been damaging to their cause, yet his triumphal acquittal on the main charge, and the exposure of the reckless methods of his opponents, now caused all else to be forgotten, and, had a General Election taken place in the summer of 1889, there is little doubt that the Liberal victory would have been complete, while it is even possible that Mr. Gladstone might have carried a Home Rule Bill into law. But the stars in their courses fought for the Government. In the autumn of 1890 the result of a divorce suit brought Mr. Parnell into collision with the puritan conscience of England ; and Mr. Gladstone, alarmed at a threatened Nonconformist defection, published a letter to Mr. Morley, in which he declared that the continuance of Mr. Parnell in the leadership would imperil the cause of Home Rule and would render his own retention of the chief place in the Liberal party " almost a nullity ". Although the Irish members had in the meantime unanimously re-elected Mr. Parnell to the chairmanship of the party, the intervention of Mr. Gladstone had the effect of causing the large majority of them to abandon him. A fierce struggle followed, in which the Fenian organisations took the side of Mr. Parnell; but the priesthood declared against him. Mr. Parnell fought with desperation, and attacked the Liberal leaders and his Irish opponents in reckless fashion, yet he was defeated in all the by-elections of the following year. The split in his party was not ended by his death, which took place in October, 1891, and the abuse which the rival factions heaped upon one another did much to discredit their cause in England.

General Election of 1892. Mr. Gladstone's fourth administration.

Parliament was dissolved in June, 1892, and in the General Election which followed 315 Unionists, 274 Liberal Home Rulers, 9 Parnellites, and 72 anti-Parnellites were returned to Parliament. Thus, though the Home Rulers held a majority of forty, the Liberals could only outnumber the Unionists by the help of the Irish. The new Parliament met in August, a vote of want of confidence in the Government was carried by a majority of forty, Lord Salisbury resigned, and Mr. Gladstone for the fourth time became Prime Minister.

Action of the House of Lords. Retirement of Mr. Gladstone.

With a leader in his eighty-third year, who had lost interest in all political subjects save one, and who retained the traditional Liberal dislike of State interference with the liberty of the individual—with a majority dependent upon the Irish vote—and with an extensive programme of organic reform calculated to alarm and offend all the most powerful interests of the country, the Government of 1892 appeared from the first inevitably doomed to failure. They succeeded, however, by the help of the guillotine,[1] and in the course of the longest session of Parliament till then recorded, in passing the Home Rule Bill of 1893 through the House of Commons. But the acquiescence with which its immediate rejection by an overwhelming majority of the House of Lords was received by the country, and the complete lack of friendly interest with which the fate of other measures introduced to fulfil the pledges made at Newcastle was regarded, made it manifest to all that the return of Mr. Gladstone to office was not a return to power. On the rejection of the Home Rule Bill, Ministers neither resigned nor dissolved, and this tame acceptance of defeat at the hands of the House of Lords greatly raised the

[1] See below p. 178.

pretensions and strengthened the position of that assembly. Mr. Gladstone held firmly to the principle that the only question on which the action of the House of Lords might constitutionally be permitted to bring about a dissolution was the question of the relations of the two Houses, and he was willing, in order to complete the case against the Upper House, to prolong the session in order to send up to them other bills, on the rejection or mutilation of which the appeal might be made to the country on this question. Accordingly, when in the following February disagreement between the two Houses concerning an amendment made by the Lords led to the withdrawal of the Employers' Liability Bill; and when they insisted on the amendments which they had made to the Parish Councils Bill; the Prime Minister proposed to his colleagues to dissolve Parliament on the constitutional question. But they declined to agree to this step; and Mr. Gladstone resigned. His sight and his hearing were failing; and he disapproved of the large naval estimates which Lord Spencer, with the support of the majority of his colleagues, thought necessary to the security of the country. But, had his men consented to follow him, he would have charged the enemy a last time, and fallen at least with harness on his back. In his last speech to the House of Commons, he shot a Parthian arrow at his victorious foe, declaring that in his judgment the existing state of things could not continue, and that the controversy between the two Houses, once raised, was a controversy which must go forward to an issue. The queen did not consult the retiring statesman as to the choice of his successor, but sent for Lord Rosebery, under whom with few changes the Ministry continued in office another year.

The Government, already weak, was now still further weakened by the lack of confidence subsisting between the new Prime Minister and the new leader of the House of Commons, Sir William Harcourt, who, twenty years older than Lord Rosebery, with different principles and of a different temperament, resented the choice of the Crown as an injury to himself. Three years before, in 1891, Lord Rosebery, as though he had foreseen his own fate, had expounded with great lucidity in his *Life* of Pitt the difficulties of this situation. "It would be too much to maintain," he then *[Lord Rosebery Premier.]*

wrote, "that all the members of a Cabinet should feel an implicit confidence in each other; humanity—least of all political humanity—could not stand so severe a test. But between a Prime Minister in the House of Lords and the leader of the House of Commons, such a confidence is indispensable. Responsibility rests so largely with the one, and articulation so greatly with the other, that unity of sentiment is the one necessary link that makes a relation, in any case difficult, in any way possible".[1] He was now in a position to verify by his own experience the justice of these observations. The decision of the Government not to dissolve Parliament might naturally have been held to involve the abandonment of the policy described on Liberal platforms as the "filling up of the cup," for unless the cup was to be presented to the victim there appeared to be no sufficient reason for filling it up, but such was not the course adopted by Ministers. A bill for reinstating, at a cost of £250,000 of public money, evicted tenants in Ireland who could satisfy three commissioners that they had been unable to pay their rents, having been passed through the House of Commons by a drastic use of the new closure by compartments and rejected by the Lords, unpopular bills for Welsh Disestablishment and Local Veto were in the next session introduced into the House of Commons, and with these and other measures Ministers continued, in Mr. Asquith's phrase, to plough the sands of the sea during the spring and early summer of 1895, until, at the end of June, being defeated in an unimportant division in supply, they gladly seized the opportunity to resign.

Weakness, defeat, and resignation of the Ministry.

The budget of 1894.

To the session of 1894 the one enduring achievement of this Government must be ascribed. In the region of finance the House of Commons was still held to be supreme, and the recognition of this supremacy by Lord Salisbury enabled Sir William Harcourt to carry through both Houses a budget more strenuously opposed and denounced than had been any of its predecessors. Graduated death duties on a high scale were raised by this budget on the whole of estates as a sort of toll preceding distribution among the legatees, and land was for the first time placed on the same footing as other kinds of property. In England, unlike most

[1] Life of Pitt, p. 24.

continental countries, an unlimited power of bequest or disposal of property after death is given to holders of property. This is no natural power, but a right conferred by the State. The budget of 1894 did not abrogate this right, but claimed for the State, as a consideration for its retention, a fraction from the corpus of the property so passing. The graduated percentages of duty were fixed with reference to the total amount of the property, real or personal, passing; and were paid by the separate legatees, irrespectively of the size of their legacies. It was in this respect that Sir William Harcourt's budget differed from that projected by Lord Randolph Churchill in 1886, for under Lord Randolph's scheme the graduation was regulated by the benefit received by the individual on succession. "What the living man got, not what the dead man left, was to be the unit of graduation."[1] The contrary system was perhaps adopted rather to satisfy the exigencies of a theory than because its practical justice is equally obvious.

The Government formed by Lord Salisbury on the resignation of Lord Rosebery was one of the strongest of modern times, having regard both to its composition and to the weakness and divisions of the Opposition. The Liberal Unionists, though retaining their separate organisation, no longer refused to take office, Lord Salisbury himself returned to the Foreign Office, his nephew, Mr. Arthur Balfour, led the House of Commons as First Lord of the Treasury, the Duke of Devonshire, the former leader of the Whigs, became President of the Council, Mr. Chamberlain, the former leader of the Radicals, became Colonial Secretary with important results to the Empire, while Sir Michael Hicks Beach, a statesman of Liberal ideas and a strong free trader, was appointed Chancellor of the Exchequer. In the election which followed 411 Unionists, 177 Liberal Home Rulers, and 82 Irish Nationalists were returned to the House of Commons.

Lord Salisbury's third administration.

Durability and concord have not as a rule characterised Ministries of "all the talents". Where there is no paramount will like that of a Walpole or a Pitt to enforce its decisions on the wills of confessedly inferior subordinates, men who have made their own reputations and are identified in the public eye with principles formerly proclaimed are unwilling on disagree-

Government by departments.

[1] Life of Lord Randolph Churchill, ii. 194.

ment to give way to one another. If the Government of 1895 proved an exception to this rule it was certainly not on account of any controlling influence exercised by its chief, but rather because the almost complete absence of such controlling influence left each Minister free to go his own way practically unchecked in the business of his own department. With an excellent judgment and a philosophical temperament, Lord Salisbury took refuge in abstractions from the bewildering complications of the concrete, and his interest in individual fellow-men was too slight to enable him ever really to become their leader. But he had in his brilliant nephew a lieutenant in whom he could repose a perfect confidence, whose conviction it was that the chief duty of a party leader was to keep the party together, whose singular personal attraction rendered him eminently fit to accomplish this end, and whose general scepticism, by causing him to undervalue the importance of political issues, disposed him at all times to acquiesce in the projects or policy of an enterprising colleague rather than risk the break up of the Cabinet.

Depressed condition of the Liberal party.

Not for a century had the fortunes of the Liberal party reached so low an ebb as during the first years succeeding the General Election of 1895. In 1886 the Whig magnates—the heads of the great houses connected by secular tradition with Liberalism—Russells, Cavendishes, Grosvenors, Campbells, had with a certain deliberate solemnity renounced the Liberal party and passed over to the other side, never, so it would seem, to return. Their example had been followed by the commercial plutocrats; captains of industry, merchants, manufacturers, and bankers, who, from jealousy of the aristocracy, from dislike of the corn-laws which had empowered the landed gentry to raise a heavy toll on the wages of the artisans, from non-conformist antecedents, or from a belief in unrestricted competition and the doctrine of *laissez-faire*, had up to that time been generally found on the Liberal side. The looting of the shops in 1886 and the spread of Socialist doctrines had alarmed the community of tradesmen and impelled them also in the same direction. Nor was this all. Not only were all the forms of wealth and influence now leagued together against the Liberal party, but the intellect and culture of the country appeared for the first time in the nineteenth century to have joined its assailants. Men like Mr. Matthew Arnold and Professor Huxley whose intellectual representatives of the preceding generation were nearly all of them strong Liberals were now in the Unionist camp.[1] The truth was that the task of the old Liberalism was accomplished, their emancipating labours were nearly concluded, such freedom of action for the individual as was possible under the postulates of the existing social organisation had been secured, and a new distinctive policy had yet to be devised.

So long, however, as Mr. Gladstone remained at the helm it was possible in some sort for the party to hold together. The prestige of his name, the magic of his eloquence, the volcanic energy he displayed, and the definiteness of his political aim caused his followers to hope, like Napoleon's soldiers in the hundred days, that their old chief might still lead them to victory. Indeed it has now been ascertained that in spite of the large majority secured by the Unionists in 1886 the actual voting strength in that election entitled the Home Rulers to a majority. The division between the parties was unhappily no longer in the main lateral but vertical. But the programme which would appeal to the lower section of this cleavage was as yet unknown to the Liberal leaders.

When Home Rule had been defeated and Mr. Gladstone had finally retired nothing was left to the Liberal party but the Newcastle Programme. And there was little in the Newcastle Programme to interest the working man. He cared as little for Welsh disestablishment as he did for Irish Self-Government, he disliked Local Option, and was indifferent to further electoral reform. The kind of legislation which interested him was the heritage rather of the Conservative than of the Liberal party and he felt that he was more likely to obtain it from a party that had no House of Lords to reckon with than from one whose intentions, however excellent, were liable to be thwarted by that assembly.

The Newcastle Programme and the working classes.

For a year after his resignation Lord Rosebery continued nominally to lead the Liberal party. But his leadership could

Retirement of Lord Rosebery.

---

[1] Mr. Charles Pearson, the author of *National Life and Character*, returning to England in 1890 after an absence of twenty years and a distinguished career in Australia, observed that what struck him most was that when he left this country everyone, roughly speaking, whom he met was a Liberal, whereas on his return he found that they had all become Conservatives.

VOL. III. 9

hardly inspire enthusiasm. He declared quite rightly that the Newcastle Programme had been a mistake, but while he scoffed at its contents as "fly-blown phylacteries" he had no definite policy to offer as an alternative nor any clear reasons to assign why the country should dismiss its actual rulers. In October 1896 he retired from the leadership on the plea that he disagreed with his party on the question of the right course to take with respect to the Armenian massacres, and was succeeded by Sir William Harcourt.

A period of prosperity and confidence. The Imperial idea.

Meanwhile the Unionist Government pursued its triumphant course—the only complaint made by Unionists being that the extreme weakness of the Opposition had a relaxing effect upon the party and that the Government would be all the stronger if its energies were called into play by more vigorous attacks. It was a time of great financial prosperity, of national self-confidence pushed almost too far, and of imperial self-consciousness diligently fostered by the apostles of Empire. The great pageant of the queen's second jubilee in 1897, in which the Colonial troops and all the Colonial Prime Ministers played their part, seized the national imagination and strengthened the party which was associated with imperialism. The imperial idea attracted the working classes, and in the same year their material interests were furthered by a Workman's Compensation Act providing that they should receive compensation for all accidents arising out of their employment, whether such accidents were caused by the fault of their employers or not. In 1898, the capture of Khartoum and the extinction of the power of the dervishes gratified the national pride, which had been deeply wounded by the events of 1884 and 1885, while the evacuation of Fashoda by the French at the summons of the British Government raised the same feeling to its highest point.

The South African War.

The first effect of the South African War of 1899-1902 was to increase the popularity of the Government and to complete the disintegration of the Opposition. The war fever ran through all classes; a large section of the Liberal party defended its justice and necessity; the early reverses were ascribed to misfortune or to the generals, and not to any fault of the Government; and when in the middle of the campaign Parliament was dissolved and the people were asked to sink all minor issues and to remember that a vote given to a Liberal candidate was a vote given to the Boers, they naturally responded to the appeal and returned an overwhelming Unionist majority.

After the peace, however, came a reaction. The splendid surpluses of the early days of the Government were replaced by deficits; the heavy war taxation, cheerfully paid so long as the war lasted, became unpopular when in great measure continued after the fighting was over; the weakness of our military organisation and the mismanagement of the War Office, suspected as the war dragged its weary length along and war correspondents made their reports, was revealed by the Report of a Royal Commission of Inquiry; there was much unemployment and distress among the poor. Overconfidence gave place to over-diffidence, continental methods were regarded with admiration, the virtues of our constitution began to be questioned, and the fiscal and political postulates of the preceding generation were analysed and found wanting. *Reaction.*

The resignation of Lord Salisbury in 1902, a statesman in whose judgment, caution, and ability the nation reposed a well-merited confidence, further weakened the Government. He was accompanied in his retirement by Sir Michael Hicks Beach, and this withdrawal seemed likely to leave the influence of Mr. Chamberlain, by much the most popular and conspicuous of the Cabinet Ministers, almost irresistible. At the time when he succeeded Lord Salisbury in the post of Prime Minister, Mr. Balfour was engaged in passing through the House of Commons an Education Bill, the chief object of which was to transfer the control of the National Schools from the School Boards formed under the Act of 1870 to the more recently constituted local authorities, but which contained provisions for throwing the voluntary schools upon the rates, while permitting them still to remain under private and denominational management. This arrangement appeared to many men, even among loyal Church people, of questionable expediency; while to Nonconformists it seemed an intolerable grievance. It was perhaps one of those bills which an impartial Second Chamber might have been expected to refer to the people, or at all events to consider in some detail; but the House of Lords, after strengthening it from a denomina- *Retirement of Lord Salisbury and of Sir Michael Hicks Beach. Mr. Balfour Premier.*

tional point of view by amendments to which the Government agreed, passed it in the course of a few days.

Revolt against Free Trade.

The modern Conservative party derives its origin from a revolt against the Free Trade proposals of a Conservative Government, and to this origin a considerable section of the party has always adhered. But their leaders renounced Protection after 1852, and their successive Chancellors of the Exchequer, Sir Stafford Northcote, Mr. Goschen, Sir Michael Hicks Beach and Mr. Ritchie, were all of them convinced Free Traders. There had been, from time to time, when trade was bad, a reopening of interest in the subject—notably in 1884 when the Fair Trade movement, as it was called, became of some importance, and the destruction completed or imminent of our industries by free imports was proclaimed by Lord Randolph Churchill with as much confidence and vehemence as it was by Mr. Chamberlain twenty years later. Protection, indeed, is the one policy that has been found equally acceptable to democracies and aristocracies, and it is therefore not surprising that it should always have been associated with Tory democracy. In the early years of this century Unionist publicists and politicians, conscious of the growing unpopularity of their party and in search of a policy which might enlist the sympathies of the electorate, began to demand a return to Protection, and to shift the responsibility for the impoverishment of the country, the decline in national credit, and bad trade from the vast expenditure incurred by the nation in the Boer War on to our obstinate adherence to an effete fiscal system rejected or abandoned by all other nations.

Mr. Chamberlain and Tariff Reform.

The man on whom the hopes of the left wing of the Unionist party now centred was Mr. Chamberlain. In 1903 that statesman returned from an expedition to South Africa with his head full of Empire and disposed to throw contempt on "parochial questions"—Education Bills, Licensing Bills, and the like—which, as he thought, occupied too much of the public attention. He bade his countrymen "think Imperially" and show themselves worthy of their Imperial heritage. In May, 1903, moved thereto by the refusal of Mr. Ritchie to use the shilling duty on corn for the purpose of granting a tariff preference to the colonies, and by his repeal of that duty, he propounded a new "unauthorized programme" of vast importance. The Empire was to be linked together by a system of preferential tariffs, involving the imposition of duties on corn and other kinds of food at home, bonds of interest being thus superadded to inadequate bonds of sentiment; and in the second place our industries were to be protected by general and by penal tariffs against the "unfair competition" of the foreigner. If the working classes paid more in taxation—which, however, they were assured would not be the case—they were to get more out of taxation for the old age pensions and other social reforms which a largely increased revenue paid mainly by the foreigner would render available. The rich were to profit by the relief to direct taxation made possible by the increase in the revenue; the poor, by more constant employment, by higher wages, by the lowering of the taxes on tea and tobacco, or by the above mentioned social reforms.

Mr. Chamberlain's proposals broke up the Unionist party just as Sir Robert Peel's conversion to Free Trade had broken up the Conservative party in 1846. There was a minority of Unionists both in the Cabinet and in the country, weak in numbers but strong in reputation and intelligence, who would have nothing to do with the new policy, and until they had been forced into submission or expelled from the party it was clear to Mr. Chamberlain that nothing could be effected. His first object, therefore, was to bring about the official adoption of Tariff Reform by the party. He calculated that, this once done, although they might be beaten at the next election, the swing of the pendulum or the blunders of their opponents must inevitably sooner or later bring them back into power with a majority, and that then, since, unlike the Home Rulers, they had no House of Lords to reckon with, they could, without difficulty, carry Tariff Reform through their budget. *Division in the Unionist party.*

In the meanwhile Mr. Balfour's chief preoccupation was to avert the disruption of his party. He declared himself to be a reasonable Free Trader who had no wish to protect native industries by raising prices, but at the same time he treated as absurd and pedantic the rigid dogmatism of orthodox Free Traders, and poured especial scorn on their doctrine that in no circumstances was the imposition of taxes except for *Mr. Balfour's view.*

revenue purposes legitimate. He expounded his views in a pamphlet which was first circulated among the Cabinet and afterwards published, in which he endeavoured to show that a country dependent upon imports might by the loss of markets for its exports be brought to its ruin. But he gave no opinion as to whether this danger was imminent in the case of England; nor, if it were so, did he suggest any practical methods by which it could be averted. The pamphlet was much admired, but was thought to be too academic for purposes of guidance.

Resignation of Mr. Chamberlain and of the Free Trade Ministers.

Shortly after Mr. Chamberlain's speech introducing his new policy, Mr. Balfour announced that the fiscal question would not be dealt with during the existing Parliament. In the autumn Mr. Chamberlain resigned in order that he might be more at liberty to spread his propaganda. At the same time the Free Trade Ministers, the Duke of Devonshire, Lord George Hamilton, Mr. Ritchie, and Lord Balfour of Burleigh also retired. Mr. Balfour was anxious to retain the Duke, and in order to do so showed him the letter in which Mr. Chamberlain announced his intention to resign. To the other Ministers, whose resignations were accepted with extreme promptitude, Mr. Chamberlain's intentions were not confided. This manœuvre, however, had but a few days' success, for the Duke soon followed his colleagues. The most significant appointment among the new Ministers was that of Mr. Austen Chamberlain who replaced Mr. Ritchie as Chancellor of the Exchequer.

Change in the character of the Conservative party.

The change wrought by Mr. Chamberlain in the character of the Conservative party has been very great. The rough and ready methods of the Birmingham caucus, which it condemned so strongly when employed by Mr. Chamberlain to its discomfiture in 1885, have become the methods of its choice. During the eighty years which intervened between the death of Lord Castlereagh in 1822 and the retirement of Lord Salisbury in 1902 there was nothing either active or reactionary in the policy of the party. Conservatives disliked change; but moved, when compelled to move, in the same direction as their adversaries. The pace was slower, but the direction was the same. Thus, in this period of eighty years, their three greatest legislative achievements were Catholic Emancipation, the Repeal of the Corn Laws, and the Reform Act of 1867—all of them Liberal measures. Moreover, when changes which they had resisted were brought about, they accepted them frankly, and often came to believe in their beneficial effect. There was point in Macaulay's famous comparison of the relation between the two parties to that between the fore and hind legs of a stag—both equally necessary and the hind legs always arriving at the place where the fore legs had been. But Mr. Chamberlain was the last man likely to be satisfied with a policy of hind legs, and Mr. Balfour was more inclined boldly to move in the opposite direction than to follow a Radical lead. Hence it came about that the Conservatives for the first time in their history found themselves under one leader engaged in a furious attack on an existing institution defended by the Liberals, and this in the presumed interests of the people; while the other, serenely reigning over the most aristocratic Government of modern times, was legislating on principles which to Liberals of the preceding decades had appeared to be abandoned. This altered state of affairs had also its bearing on the position of the House of Lords. For so long as only one party needed a check the partisan character of that assembly was of little consequence; but when licensing bills and education bills of opposite tendencies were presented to them respectively by the two parties some show of impartiality appeared desirable.

The re-constituted Government was weak and unpopular from the first. Harmony now reigned in the Cabinet. Mr. Balfour was on the pleasantest terms with his colleagues, chosen for the most part from among his intimate friends and relations; but they carried little weight in the country. The importation of indentured Chinese labourers to work the gold mines in the newly-annexed Transvaal, though held to be necessary to save the colony from bankruptcy by Lord Milner and the Rand magnates, was very unpopular with the working classes, and their indignation was enhanced by false or exaggerated tales of the harsh terms on which these labourers were engaged and the harsh treatment to which they were exposed. The judgment of the House of Lords in 1901 in the Taff Vale case, to the effect that trade unions were liable to damages for wrongful acts done by *[Weakness of the Government.]*

their officials during a strike, was bitterly resented by trade unionists, and inclined them to vote for Liberals and labour men who were ready to pledge themselves to change the law in this respect.

Nor was the success of the Tariff Reform movement of a nature to arrest the discredit into which the party was falling. Mr. Chamberlain had largely based his case on statistics supplied him by the years of depression which followed the war, and had imprudently proclaimed that the true test of a nation's prosperity was found in its exports. But the great revival of trade which followed in 1904 and the succeeding years, during which our exports increased with extraordinary rapidity, seemed to falsify his prophecies.

Resignation of Mr. Balfour.

In December, 1905, Mr. Balfour suddenly resigned during the recess. Such a course was without precedent in modern times; but that is in itself no good reason for condemning it. A series of adverse by-elections seemed to show that the Government in no way represented the country, and the principle that it was from the country, and not from a majority of the House of Commons, that Governments held their commission was now beginning to be recognised. Mr. Balfour had already subscribed to the principle of delegation by declaring that it would be unconstitutional to change our fiscal system without first submitting the question to the people, and that it would be unwise to discuss a subject on which they could not act—a doctrine once denounced by Mr. Gladstone as anarchical and ultra-democratic [1]—and he had refused either to dissolve or to resign when defeated in the House of Commons in the preceding summer, although the defeat took place but two days after he had appealed to his followers at a party meeting for steadier support.

Sir Henry Campbell-Bannerman Premier. Great Liberal victory at the election.

Sir Henry Campbell-Bannerman, who had led the Opposition since 1898, had, by an emphatic declaration in favour of Home Rule, drawn from Lord Rosebery a counter-declaration that he would not serve under that banner. If Mr. Balfour, in resigning when he did immediately after these utterances, counted on the outbreak of dissensions between Radicals and Liberal Imperialists when Sir Henry should attempt to form a Government, his hopes were doomed to disappointment. Without much difficulty the new Prime Minister formed a

[1] See above p. 71.

strong Cabinet, comprising representatives of every section of the party, and, though Lord Rosebery remained outside, his colleagues of the Liberal League—an association formed for the furtherance of Liberal Imperialism—Sir Edward Grey, Mr. Haldane, and Mr. Asquith, all agreed to serve. At the general election which followed in January an immense Liberal majority was returned. Only 158 Unionists were elected, while the Liberals numbered 372, the Irish Nationalists 84, and the Labour members 56. Mr. Balfour himself was defeated at Manchester, and most of his former colleagues lost their seats.

The most remarkable feature in these results was the return to Parliament of the fifty-six Labour members, of whom thirty had been named by the Labour Representation Committee, while the remaining twenty-six formed the Liberal Labour group. The formation of the Labour party dealt, whether for good or for evil, a blow at the root of the party system on which Parliamentary government in England has been hitherto based. A brief account may therefore be given of its origin and progress.

The Independent Labour Party was founded at a conference held at Bradford in 1893 with a view to unite for common action the various Socialist organisations in the country. A constitution was adopted in which the aim of the party was stated to be " the collective ownership and control of the means of production, distribution, and exchange," and the method whereby this object should be furthered, the representation of the people in the House of Commons " by men in favour of the object of the party and rigidly pledged to its policy ". The eight-hour day, unsectarian education, work for the unemployed, abolition of piece-work, overtime, and employment of children under fourteen, the extinction by taxation of unearned incomes, and universal disarmament were to form the programme for their earliest endeavours; and other measures, such as women's suffrage, municipal control of the drink traffic and hospitals, and triennial Parliaments were subsequently added to the list. In order to secure the support of working men who were not Socialists, the conference rejected a motion for adopting the title of the Socialist Labour Party. At first the movement had little success. At the general election of 1895 twenty-eight candidates were nominated by the party. Not one was returned, and Mr. Keir Hardie, their president, lost his seat.

In 1899, however, the foundation of the Labour Representation Committee entirely altered the aspect of affairs. The Trade Unions, or certain of them, had, ever since 1874, secured representation in the House of Commons. These early representatives were strong Liberals and had no intention of pursuing an exclusively class policy. They held that as members of Parliament they were in charge of the interests of the whole nation, from which the special interests of their own class could not be separated, and that, being themselves working-men, they were in a better position than others to explain what those special interests were, and to secure for them a sympathetic hearing. In 1888 a Labour Electoral Association was founded with the same objects in view. Its aim was described at the third annual congress at Hanley in 1890 as "a leavening of the House of Commons with men having a thorough knowledge of the wants of the masses". The numbers of the trade unionists were great, their funds were considerable; their weakness lay in a general indifference to politics except under the pressure of a positive grievance, and in a want of cohesion between the unions. Thus they were strong where the Independent Labour party was weak, and weak where the others were strong. A junction between the two was likely to be formidable to the older parties.

Congress of representatives of trade unions and of Socialist associations meets in London.

To promote this junction was the object of a trade union congress held in London in September, 1899. Its Parliamentary Committee was instructed to invite all co-operative, socialistic, trade union and working-class associations in England and Wales to unite in calling a convention to devise means for securing the election of an increased number of Labour members to the next Parliament. The convention met in London in the following February and was attended by delegates from the trade unions and from the various Socialist associations.

This congress began by rejecting a resolution proposed by the delegates of the Social Democratic Federation—an association of uncompromising Socialists—by which it was proposed to base the existence of the party upon the recognition of the class war and of socialism—a refusal which, when repeated in 1902, brought about the withdrawal of the Federation from the organisation. After this vote the congress proceeded to pass resolutions, afterwards embodied in the constitution of what was then called the Labour Representation Committee.

The name of this Committee was changed to that of the Labour party when the successes of 1906 had established its position in the House of Commons. The organisation is described in its revised constitution of that year as a Federation of trade unions, trades councils, Socialist societies, and local labour associations. Its total membership reaches nearly a million. The affiliated societies send one delegate for every thousand members to the annual conferences. The object of the Federation is "to organize and maintain a Parliamentary Labour party, with its own whips and policy," and to promote the election of candidates for whose candidature an affiliated society has made itself financially responsible.

Party discipline has in the case of the Labour party been carried to a point previously unknown in English political life. The attraction exercised by greater masses on smaller is as true in the moral as it is in the physical world, and the danger of absorption into the Liberal party was as present to the minds of the founders of the Labour party as it was to Mr. Parnell in respect of his own following. Hence the object aimed at by the caucus associations of the two great parties—namely, the subordination of the private judgment of the individual member to the collective decision of the party—has been expressly formulated and enshrined in the constitution of the Labour party. The members of that party were bound by a signed pledge so to submit their judgment, and the security for their observance of this pledge is the salary of £200 a year which each of them received out of the party funds and which alone rendered possible his continued existence in Parliament. In 1908 the Labour party and the Liberal Labour group in the House of Commons agreed to act together, to employ the same whips, to consult together under the same chairman, and to sign the same pledge. But a few of the older trade union members refused to sign any pledge, holding that to abandon all right to the free exercise of their judgment was contrary to the spirit of representative government and

Discipline of the Labour party.

a violation of their trust. These members became practically merged in the Liberal party.

The Trade Disputes Act. The Trade Disputes Act was passed in the first session of this Parliament. The decision in the Taff Vale case, by which the highest court of the realm held that damages might be recovered from trade unions for wrongful acts committed by their officials during a strike, was felt as a most serious grievance by trade unionists and had much influence on their votes during the General Election. The Government, early in the session of 1906, brought in a bill to provide that trade unions should only be liable in damages for acts which the by-laws of the Union involved authorised its officials to perform. The Labour party brought in a rival bill to provide that trade union funds should in no case be liable in damages for acts done by their officials. Although the Royal Commission appointed to inquire into the subject had unanimously reported against the latter course, and although it seemed unreasonable that the unions which may use their funds for the purpose of a strike should be exempt from all risk to those funds if wrongful acts expressly authorised by their by-laws are committed in the course of it, yet so many Liberal members had pledged themselves to the wider bill that the Government were obliged to give way and to accept it in lieu of their own. Nor did the House of Lords, although very few of the peers defended the bill, venture to reject or seriously to amend it.

Legislation of the Liberal Government. The great Liberal majority in the new Parliament set itself actively to work under the direction of the Government. Of party legislation indeed in the strict sense it could achieve little or nothing. Its attempts at educational and electoral reform, its proposals for reforming the Scottish land law and valuing Scottish land, its Licensing Bill, were all defeated in the House of Lords. Nevertheless, the volume of its legislation was much greater than had been that of the preceding Parliament and the content of far more importance. The Workmen's Compensation Act was extended so as to cover agricultural labourers and domestic servants; a Criminal Court of Appeal was set up, and prisoners in criminal cases were permitted to give evidence on their own behalf; a Catholic University was established in Ireland; the Small Holdings Act empowered local authorities to purchase, in certain cases compulsorily, small holdings for the use of applicants; an eight hours day was fixed for miners; local authorities were empowered to provide meals for school children; an excellent Act was passed to improve the law relating to children; labour exchanges and other methods were devised to reduce the evil of unemployment; and old age pensions were provided for all persons whose means were scanty and who were free from a few simple disqualifications.

The fiscal question, however, was still the chief subject of interest both in country and Parliament. A great change had taken place in the economic outlook of the nation. The production of wealth no longer appeared a sufficient object in itself, as it did to the middle class electorate enfranchised in 1832. The removal of obstacles to that production no longer seemed the whole duty of statesmen, beyond which their activity would be merely pernicious. Men of both parties were beginning to believe that the important points to determine were rather the kind of wealth that should be produced, and the manner of its distribution. To give a right direction to labour now appeared to many the chief function of a statesman. People saw that the actual amount of existing labour might be sufficient to meet the national wants were it not that a vast proportion of it is wasted on useless or superfluous objects. An immense deal of useless work is done; an immense deal of useful work is left undone. Clearly what is required is the regulation of labour. Both parties were agreed that the way to achieve this was to modify our system of taxation, and both parties implicitly abandoned the principle that taxes should never be imposed except for revenue purposes, though each party attacked the other for such abandonment. The Unionist plan was to divert the current of labour into more useful channels by manipulation of the tariff; the Liberal plan to achieve the same object, was, by a change in the incidence of taxation, to transfer the demand for labour into new hands and so to alter the character of the commodities demanded. Thus the budget of 1909 was a practical alternative to the policy of Tariff Reform. The leaders of the Tariff Reform party felt that this was so; and, declaring that its passage would mean the indefinite postponement of their policy, exhorted the House of Lords to reject it and to force a dissolution. This that House did, and seemed to stake its life on the event.

CHAPTER III.

THE HOME RULE MOVEMENT.

The Fenian conspiracy.

THE Fenian conspiracy for the overthrow of English government in Ireland and the establishment of an Irish republic, complete though its failure may have been to effect its main objects, had nevertheless results of the highest importance to Ireland. During the twenty years succeeding the famine Ireland, from a material standpoint, had been in a state of progressive improvement. Her wealth had greatly increased; shipping returns showed that her tonnage had trebled; the condition of the labouring classes had improved. The movement for repeal came to an end with the death of O'Connell, and to contemporary Whig observers famine and emigration appeared in the light of violent remedies administered by Providence to deal with conditions which human legislation was powerless to ameliorate.[1] Observation of the immediate effects of these calamities on Ireland gave some plausibility to this view. But famine and emigration had other results. The emigrants and their families who had settled in America were filled with bitter recollections of the past, and became the most irreconcilable enemies of England to be found among the Irish. They were the authors of the Fenian movement. It was a conspiracy of foreign growth; and it failed because, while relying purely on physical force, it received little active support or even sympathy from Irish farmers, or indeed from the great mass of the Irish in Ireland.

Its effects.

But to Mr. Gladstone the Fenian conspiracy appeared a national movement and a proof of the general discontent then prevailing in the country. A conviction of the "intensity of Fenianism," brought home to his mind by certain of its more violent developments, led him to believe that the time

[1] See vol. ii. p. 348.

had come for the disestablishment of the Irish Church and
the reform of the Irish land laws.[1] In like manner Mr. Isaac
Butt, an Irish barrister of distinction, who in former years had
been conspicuous as a Conservative opponent of O'Connell,
was convinced by his intercourse with the Fenian prisoners
whom he defended, that their intentions were pure, and that
their patriotism was sincere, and came to believe in self-
government as the only medicine for the "mind diseased" of
Ireland. Lastly, Mr. Charles Stewart Parnell, the young squire
of Avondale, was roused to action by his admiration for the
Fenian insurgents, by his hatred of the "English dominion,"
and by his belief that the execution of the Fenians concerned
in the rescue of prisoners at Manchester, when Sergeant Brett
lost his life, was a judicial murder.

In 1868 an Amnesty Association was formed for the pur- *The Amnesty Association of 1868.*
pose of obtaining the release of the Fenian prisoners, and Mr.
Butt was chosen as its president. The amnesty movement
spread with extraordinary rapidity. At a meeting in October,
over which Mr. Butt presided, 200,000 people are said to
have been present. Other meetings were held throughout
the country, and were attended by men of diverse opinions.
In 1869 Irish Protestant Churchmen were enraged at the disestablishment of the Irish Church, and were disposed to join
in any movement which would embarrass the Liberal Government. Moreover, betrayed as they considered themselves to
have been by the United Parliament, they were prepared to
consider with an open mind schemes for the delegation of
Irish business to an Irish assembly. Thus the amnesty movement brought together men who, while differing widely in
their political views and aspirations, were agreed in ascribing
the misfortunes of Ireland to English misgovernment, and in
the belief that the true remedy was some form of Home Rule.

The outcome of this revival of the spirit of nationality was *The Home Government Association founded.*
the establishment of the "Home Government Association of
Ireland". This body was founded at a meeting held in the
Bilton Hotel at Dublin, and attended by representatives of
all parties: by Orangemen and Ultramontanes, by Conservatives and Liberals, by Nationalist Repealers and Imperial

[1] See his answer to Mr. Gathorne Hardy in the House of Commons, 3rd
April, 1868.

Unionists, by Fenians and Loyalists.[1] Mr. Butt presided, and although both Catholics and Protestants were present in nearly equal numbers the proceedings were harmonious. The following resolution was first passed by acclamation: "That it is the opinion of this meeting that the true remedy for the evils of Ireland is the establishment of an Irish Parliament with full control over our domestic affairs".

Objects of the Association. The objects of the association were subsequently thus defined in resolutions drawn up by a Committee charged with that duty, and approved by the central body:—

" 1. This Association is formed for the purpose of obtaining for Ireland the right of self-government by means of a National Parliament.

" 2. It is hereby declared as the essential principle of this Association that the objects, and the only objects, contemplated by its organisation are:—

"To obtain for our country the right and privilege of managing our own affairs by a Parliament assembled in Ireland, composed of her Majesty the sovereign and her successors, and the Lords and Commons of Ireland;

" To secure for that Parliament, under a federal arrangement, the right of legislating for and regulating all matters relating to the internal affairs of Ireland, and control over Irish resources and expenditure, subject to the obligation of contributing our just proportion of the imperial expenditure;

" To leave to an Imperial Parliament the power of dealing with all questions affecting the Imperial Crown and Government, legislation regarding the colonies and other dependencies of the Crown, the relations of the United Empire with foreign States, and all matters appertaining to the defence and stability of the Empire at large;

" To attain such an adjustment of the relations between the two countries, without any interference of the prerogatives of the Crown, or any disturbance of the principles of the constitution.

" 3. The Association invites the co-operation of all Irishmen who are willing to join in seeking for Ireland a *federal* arrangement based upon these general principles.

" 4. The Association will endeavour to forward the object

[1] Sullivan, New Ireland, vol. ii. p. 300.

it has in view, by using all legitimate means of influencing public sentiment, both in Ireland and Great Britain; by taking all opportunities of instructing and informing public opinion; and by seeking to unite Irishmen of all creeds and classes in one national movement, in support of the great national object hereby contemplated.

"5. It is declared to be an essential principle of the Association that, while every member is understood by joining it to concur in its general object and plan of action, no person so joining is committed to any political opinion, except the advisability of seeking for Ireland the amount of self-government contemplated in the objects of the Association."

In spite of the early opposition of the Catholic Church, then under the influence of gratitude to Mr. Gladstone for his policy of disestablishment, and of the *Freeman's Journal*, the movement greatly prospered. Four Home Rulers, including Mr. Butt himself, were returned at Irish by-elections during 1871, and two more in the following year.

In November, 1873, at a conference held in the Rotunda at Dublin the name of "Home Rule League" was adopted by the association. Nine hundred delegates, from every county in the kingdom, attended this conference, and the requisition by which it was summoned received 25,000 signatures. After a re-assertion of the claim to the right of domestic legislation in all Irish affairs by an Irish Parliament the conference further resolved: "That in claiming these rights and privileges for our country we adopt the principle of federal arrangement which would secure to the Irish Parliament the right of legislating for and regulating all matters relating to the internal affairs of Ireland; while leaving to the Imperial Parliament the power of dealing with all questions affecting the Imperial Crown and Government, legislation regarding the colonies and other dependencies of the Crown, the relations of the Empire with foreign States, and all matters appertaining to the defence and stability of the Empire at large, as well as the power of granting and providing the supplies necessary for Imperial purposes"; and further, "That to secure to the Irish people the advantages of constitutional government it is essential that there should be in Ireland an administration of Irish affairs, controlled according to constitutional principles by

The Home Rule League.

the Irish Parliament, and conducted by the ministers constitutionally responsible to that Parliament". The Roman Catholic Church in Ireland now gave in its adhesion to the movement.

In the speech in which he expounded his plan to the conference Mr. Butt treated lightly what subsequently proved to be the grand difficulty in the way of Home Rule projects. " If I am asked," he said, " do I wish Irish members to take any part in the management of English affairs, I say for the sake of Ireland, emphatically, No. But to exclude them from this requires no violent disturbance of the whole Parliamentary system. It would be easy to hold two sessions of the Parliament at Westminster in each year, to one of which Irish members might be summoned, and in which alone Imperial measures might be discussed. . . . The absence of Irish members from the session in which English matters could be disposed of would be an improvement, and, I cannot help thinking, a relief. Their presence when Imperial matters were submitted would leave the Imperial Parliament for all Imperial purposes exactly the same as it is now."

This plan would have confined the federation to England and Ireland without affecting Scotland. But subsequently in a pamphlet called " Irish Federation " Mr. Butt explained his full policy thus :—

<small>Mr. Butt's scheme of Federation.</small>

" I intend to propose a system under which England, Scotland, and Ireland, united as they are under one sovereign, should have a common Executive and a common National Council for all purposes necessary to constitute them, to other nations, as a State ; while each of them should have its own domestic administration, and its own domestic Parliament for its internal affairs. I say ' each of them ' because, although my immediate concern is only with Ireland, I do not suppose that, if Irishmen obtain the separate management of Irish affairs, it is at all likely that Englishmen and Scotchmen would consent to the management of their domestic concerns by a Parliament in which Irish members had a voice." This scheme, though at the time it commended itself to no Englishman of political importance, and though it was subsequently abandoned by some of its friends in Ireland in favour of more extreme projects, and by others as in itself

THE HOME RULE MOVEMENT

dangerous and impracticable, was destined in a later generation to find advocates among men of all parties and to be looked to as a means of escape from a system under which the large majority of Irish representatives has no controlling voice in the determination of purely Irish issues, while they may enable English domestic legislation to be shaped by a minority of English members.

At the General Election of 1874 fifty-eight Irish members pledged to Home Rule were returned to Parliament. Mr. Butt without loss of time attempted to convert the House of Commons to his views. But outside his own party he found no support, and his motions were rejected by enormous majorities. Nor were his efforts to carry remedial legislation for Ireland attended with much better success. Part of his policy was, as Mr. A. Sullivan has described it, "to offer a bridge to the opposing forces of Irish demand and English refusal. Apart from the question of Home Rule, which he knew would require much time, he resolved to lay before the House of Commons several schemes of practical legislation, the merits of which could hardly be contested and the success of which might fairly be expected. The concession of these would, on the one hand, lead the English people gradually to look into the nature of Irish claims, and, on the other hand, lead the Irish people to place more confidence in constitutional effort." [1] Here at all events was an opportunity for Englishmen to prove that whatever rational reforms the Irish might hope to secure through an Irish Parliament they could equally well obtain from the assembly at Westminster. But, by their neglect of Irish legislation and their refusal of all Irish demands, the English Government and Parliament of 1874 effectively discouraged the moderate Home Rulers, and strengthened the conviction of the more advanced section that constitutional agitation was fruitless.

Mr. Butt had no driving force behind him. The two great forces in Ireland were Fenianism and the Catholic Church. Fenians disbelieved in Parliamentary methods; and the ill success of Mr. Butt was to them an additional proof of their futility: the Church had come late into the Home Rule movement and was out of touch with Mr. Butt who was a

Fifty-eight Home Rulers returned to the Parliament of 1874. Mr. Butt's Parliamentary action.

Causes of his failure.

[1] Sullivan, New Ireland, vol. ii. p. 404.

Protestant. The Irish people were chiefly interested in the agrarian question; they believed the land of Ireland to be their own, and that they had been dispossessed of it by men of an alien race and religion, and they were encouraged in these notions by the priests. England, on the other hand, had never been accustomed to make concessions to Ireland in quiet times; she considered that she had already made noble efforts to effect "the political and social regeneration of Ireland" and to redress all her legitimate grievances;[1] and she was not in the least likely to embark on a great constitutional change in deference to considerations of abstract justice set forth with courteous eloquence by Mr. Butt. It was quite certain that England would never agree to a "federal arrangement" until persuaded that she would thereby consult her own interest and convenience. And Mr. Butt, proud to be a member of the oldest and most illustrious representative assembly in the world, believing in constitutional methods and the power of argument, endowed with inexhaustible patience, a lover of order, and of a genial temperament, was not at all inclined to encourage the use of those practical Irish arguments which had carried Catholic Emancipation, abolished tithes, disestablished the Irish Church, and reformed the land laws. The bulk of his followers agreed with him. The first Home Rule movement was started by moderate men who did not believe in a policy of exasperation, was promoted by constitutional methods, and was laughed out of court. "The present circumstances of Ireland," wrote the Dublin correspondent of *The Times* in 1875, "may be briefly summed up in the statement that at no period of her history did she appear more tranquil, more free from serious crime, more prosperous and contented. . . . Home Rule still keeps a little cauldron simmering, but there is no fear that it will ever become formidable." And Mr. Gladstone long afterwards stated that he could not have supported Mr. Butt because there was no evidence that Ireland was behind his movement.

The Parnellite group.

To supply this evidence in the manner which had brought conviction home to the minds of English statesmen in the past became the object of Mr. Parnell and a group of four Irish members who agreed with him. The Irish bills proposed by

[1] See *ante*, vol. ii. p. 348.

Mr. Butt were not allowed to pass; Irish members, so they thought, should retaliate by taking an "intelligent interest" in English bills. The right method to convince liberal-minded Englishmen that the only way to give a good government to Ireland was to allow the Irish to manage their own affairs was, Mr. Butt contended, to bring forward every grievance of Ireland and to press the British House of Commons for their redress. This might be so, Mr. Parnell replied, if the House of Commons were composed of fair-minded Englishmen, but that was not the case. "If Englishmen insisted on the artificial maintenance of an antiquated institution which could only perform a portion of its functions by the connivance of those intrusted with its working," that connivance must be withheld. In other words, no concession must be made to the "understandings" essential to the working of the existing Parliamentary procedure.

The Home Rule pledge bound the Irish members to act together and to submit their individual judgment to the judgment of the party on Irish matters; but they had been expressly exempted, after the point had been discussed, from the necessity of sacrificing their individual liberty of action when Imperial or English concerns were the subject of debate. To trouble the harmony of Parliamentary convention, to break up the historic order of procedure, to destroy by the presence of a foreign element the health of the English political body, such were the aims of the new policy of obstruction which Mr. Parnell and his followers pursued during this Parliament with startling success. *Aims of the obstructionists.*

Mr. Parnell entered Parliament as member for Meath in 1875. His character was a striking contrast to that of Mr. Butt. Mr. Butt was genial and expansive; Mr. Parnell was taciturn and reserved. Mr. Butt admitted no force but argument; Mr. Parnell believed in no argument but force. Mr. Butt was a master of moving and swift-flowing eloquence; Mr. Parnell hated speeches, but all that he said was full of significance. Even in his maiden speech, stammered out as it was with difficulty, he expressed in a single sentence the root difference in the standpoint from which the Irish question was regarded by Englishmen and Irishmen respectively. A little before Mr. Lowe had spoken of Ireland as a geographical *Mr. Parnell.*

fragment of England. "Ireland," Mr. Parnell replied, "is not a geographical fragment; she is a nation." In the following year his interruption of the Chief Secretary to deny that any murder had been committed by the Fenians in Manchester drew upon him the attention of their powerful organisation. From that time, said one of them, "we never lost sight of him, and I think he never lost sight of us".[1]

Home Rule Confederation of Great Britain founded by Fenians.

Unlike the Home Rule League, the Home Rule Confederation of Great Britain was founded in 1873 at the suggestion and by the secret agency of Fenians. Mr. Butt, however, consented to become its president, and the Confederation did effective work in organising the Irish vote in England. A pledge was submitted to every candidate who stood in a constituency where the Irish vote was strong to vote for an inquiry into the "motive, extent, and the grounds of the demand made by a large proportion of the Irish people for the restoration to Ireland of an Irish Parliament with power to control the internal affairs of the country". This pledge was taken by several successful candidates for English constituencies. After the session of 1877 the failure of Mr. Butt's conciliatory tactics to produce any practical results was clear to all, whereas the obstruction by Mr. Parnell and his friends of the South Africa Bill and of the Mutiny Bill had had at least the effect of discrediting the Imperial Parliament as a working machine. It was in this session, during the prolonged debate on the Mutiny Bill, that the differences between the two Irish leaders came to a head. Amid the ringing cheers of Conservatives and Liberals Mr. Butt denounced the obstructive proceedings of the member for Meath and disclaimed all responsibility for him and for them. By this action Mr. Butt earned the applause of Englishmen and of the House of Commons but forfeited the confidence of his fellow-countrymen.

Breach between Mr. Butt and Mr. Parnell.

The definite breach with Mr. Butt stirred Mr. Parnell to a new activity. Mr. Butt was still followed by a large majority of Home Rulers in Parliament, and as a counterpoise to this it was necessary to Mr. Parnell to show that he was supported in the country. He was now in close communication with the Fenians, and a succession of meetings was organised for him by a member of the Supreme Council. "We are only at

[1] O'Brien's Life of Parnell, vol. i. p. 98.

the beginning of an active forward policy," he said to this gentleman, "but it must be pushed to extremes. A few men in the House of Commons can do nothing unless they are well supported in the country. Something striking must be done." Something striking was done accordingly. In September the Home Rule Confederation of Great Britain held their annual meeting in Liverpool. Their president, annually re-elected, was still Mr. Butt, but the Fenians, who had never lost their control over the Confederation, now resolved to replace him by Mr. Parnell. This was done. Mr. Parnell was elected president by acclamation and thereafter became the real leader of the Irish party. *Mr. Parnell elected President of the Home Rule Confederation in place of Mr. Butt.*

The grand object of Mr. Parnell was the overthrow of British dominion in Ireland. Deep fixed in his mind was the thought that the English despised the Irish, and by this notion his proud spirit was galled. He endeavoured to bring into line all the forces in Ireland that made for nationality, and to do this it was necessary that he himself should preserve an attitude of detachment with respect to each of them. Thus he refused to join the Fenians while keeping closely in touch with them, and expressing full sympathy with their aims. He told them that he could be of more use in the open movement, and that he was sure that he could " do something with the Parliamentary machine ". " His policy," his biographer tells us, " was to keep Parliamentarianism well in front and to mass the revolutionists behind it; the Fenians were to be his reserve."[1] Again, although not only a Protestant but a Protestant who disliked and mistrusted the Catholic Church, he was careful never to offend the Catholic priesthood or laity. In 1879, on the question of a Roman Catholic University, when moderate Roman Catholics were in favour of accepting the compromise proposed by the Government in the establishment of the Royal University—an examining body granting degrees to all who passed their examinations wherever educated—Mr. Parnell joined with the extremists in demanding a purely Catholic University. Moreover, the Government had announced that they would not deal at all with the question in that session, and it was only in order " to buy off Parnell's opposition to their measures generally " that they finally introduced and *Mr. Parnell's policy.*

[1] Life of Parnell, vol. i. p. 169.

passed the Royal University Bill. So much more effective even with regard to ordinary Irish legislation were the methods of Mr. Parnell than those of Mr. Butt.

The three movements.

There were three movements with which Mr. Parnell had to deal, and which he resolved to control. There was, in the first place, the Fenian movement, or the secret conspiracy for the establishment by physical force of an Irish Republic, organised originally from America by Irish-Americans, where the association was known as the Clan-na-Gael, and established in Ireland as the Irish Republican Brotherhood. This movement, when account was taken of the increasing population in England and the decreasing population in Ireland, seemed clearly doomed to failure, nor of itself did it ever take root in the imaginations or ambitions of the Irish people. There was, in the second place, the open Home Rule movement, which the large majority of Irishmen supported with different degrees of enthusiasm and understood in various senses—from that contained in Mr. Butt's moderate federation proposals to that involved in the almost complete independence of the self-governing colonies. And lastly, there was the agrarian movement, soon to overshadow the other two, and about to appear to the Irish leaders as the only agency by which they could enlist the enthusiastic support of the masses of the Irish people in the furtherance of their own ulterior political objects. Fenianism had been defeated in 1867; Home Rule was discredited in the Parliament of 1874; the Land League shaped the Irish question for the Parliament of 1880.

Division among the Fenians. Condemnation of the Parliamentary movement by the Supreme Council.

The interest taken by the rank and file among the Fenians, and even by certain of the chiefs, in the Parliamentary proceedings of Mr. Parnell and his band of followers caused grave misgivings to the more uncompromising of the Fenian leaders. These men regarded Parliamentarianism as bound sooner or later to destroy the separatist spirit; they thought the House of Commons an anglicising influence, and contact with Parliamentarians demoralising, and held that it was impossible for an honest man who had taken the Fenian oath to swear allegiance to the British sovereign in the manner required of members of Parliament. But the new methods adopted by Mr. Parnell went far to meet these objections in the eyes of many Fenians. So far from being anglicised by his Parliamentary life he had made himself detested by the English. He had taken every opportunity to thwart the English Government without in any degree becoming associated with the English Opposition. He had asked the Fenians for a fair trial and many of them thought that he ought to be given it. This, however, was not the opinion of Mr. Kickham—the most important member of the Supreme Council of the I.R.B.—who, early in 1878, carried by a majority of one a resolution pledging the Council to sever all connection with the Parliamentary party. Several of the minority on the Council who had voted against the resolution thereupon resigned; Mr. Biggar, Mr. Parnell's chief associate in the House of Commons, and others were expelled. Nevertheless, Mr. Parnell retained the confidence and received the support of the mass of Fenians, and was shortly to receive the active assistance of the Clan-na-Gael.

This famous association was, as we have seen, the American branch of the Fenian organisation, and an important section of it arrived in this same year at a conclusion contrary to that contained in the resolution of the I.R.B. This section was led by Mr. John Devoy and Mr. Michael Davitt, and attributed the failure of Fenianism in the past to neglect of the questions which interested the Irish people. Fenians had been occupied in the collection of arms, while the farmers who should have used them held aloof from the movement. From the public life of the country, from all employment of the existing constitutional machinery for the attainment of objects desired by the people, from the agrarian movement, the Fenian leaders had hitherto on principle abstained. And this, according to the new teachers, was the main cause of their failure. Michael Davitt, the son of evicted Irish emigrants, was indeed a Fenian, but his soul was in the land question; Devoy, on the other hand, aimed above all at the overthrow of British rule in Ireland, but was convinced that this could only be accomplished by using agrarian revolution and Parliamentary action as stepping-stones. Before the citadel could be entered it was necessary to disarm the garrison, and this could best be done in his view by the expulsion of the landlords. The outcome of these ideas was what was

The "New Departure".

called the "New Departure"; a name given to the policy of uniting Constitutionalists and Revolutionaries for the common purpose of securing self-government for Ireland. Both sections might understand the term "self-government" in their own sense; their goals might be different, but their roads lying up to a certain point in the same direction, it was obviously expedient that they should work together until that point had been reached. In the words of Mr. Davitt, "the land of Ireland was to be made the basis of Irish nationality". The "new departure" was not accepted by the Supreme Council of the I.R.B., but an important concession was made at a meeting in Paris in the permission there given to the officers of the organisation to take part in the open movement on their own responsibility if they felt so disposed.

Agrarian distress in Ireland. Foundation of the Land League.

In 1877 a period of severe agricultural depression in Ireland had set in. During that and the two succeeding years prices continually fell, there was great distress among the tenantry, landlords in many instances refused reductions of rent, and a formidable land agitation of quite independent origin was the result. In 1879 Mr. Davitt and the Fenians who shared his views threw themselves with vigour into this agitation and gave it direction. "When I was in prison," he afterwards wrote, "I spent my time thinking of what plan could be proposed which would unite all Irishmen upon some one common ground. I saw that the movements for independence of Ireland had failed for two reasons: first, that there had never been one in which the people were united; second, because the movements had been wholly sentimental. I saw that for Irishmen to succeed they must be united, and that they must have a practical issue to put before Englishmen, and the world at large. Sentiment cannot be relied upon to move neighbouring nations, and when changes of great political importance, involving an alteration in the policy of a country like England, conservative, and somewhat slow to move, are to be brought about, there must be something practical in the issue brought forward. I saw all this, and I made up my mind that the only issue upon which Home Rulers, Nationalists, Obstructionists, and each and every shade of opinion existing in Ireland, could be united, was the land question." Mr. James Lowther, who had succeeded Sir

Michael Hicks Beach as Chief Secretary, was not alive to the critical nature of the situation. In May, 1879, he replied with an air of indifference to a question put to him in the House of Commons that he was "glad to think that depression, though undoubted, was neither so prevalent nor so acute as the depression existing in other parts of the kingdom". In point of fact it was far worse. According to the report of the Registrar-General for 1879 there had been a falling off in the principal crops from the yield of the previous year to the value of £10,000,000. The value of the potato crop was more than £6,000,000 below the average. In the same year the number of persons evicted rose to 6239, from 2177 in 1877; and of agrarian outrages to 863, from 236 in 1877. In June Mr. Parnell, himself a landlord, and entering with some reluctance into the agitation, made the memorable speech at Westport, at a land meeting organised by Mr. Davitt, in which he counselled his hearers to keep a firm grip on their homesteads and lands. In October the Land League with its Central Committee in Dublin and its local branches was founded by Mr. Davitt. Mr. Parnell, being resolved in his own words "to unite all shades of political opinion in the country" in the cause of national independence, consented to become its president. At the meeting of the 21st of October, when it was inaugurated, the objects of the League were stated to be: first, to bring about a reduction of rack-rents, and secondly, to facilitate the obtaining of the ownership of the soil by the occupiers of the soil. On the motion of Mr. Parnell a resolution was agreed to: "That the objects of the League can be best attained by promoting organisation among the tenant-farmers, by defending those who may be threatened with eviction for refusing to pay unjust rents; by facilitating the working of the Bright clauses of the Land Act during the winter; and by obtaining such reform in the laws relating to land as will enable every tenant to become the owner of his holding by paying a fair rent for a limited number of years". It was reserved for a Unionist Government to give effect to the only reform in the laws originally proposed by the Land League.

In December, Mr. Parnell, in pursuance of a resolution of the Land League, set out for America for the purpose of there obtaining assistance for the objects of the League from the

Mr. Parnell in the United States 1879-1880.

Irish emigrants and other sympathisers. He was received with great enthusiasm; public honours were showered upon him wherever he went; and he was allowed to address Congress at Washington. The proposition which he endeavoured to establish in his speeches was that the landlord system in Ireland was the foundation on which English misgovernment rested and that its overthrow would make Ireland once more a nation. "The feudal tenure and the rule of the minority," he said at Cincinnati, "have been the cornerstone of English misrule. Pull out that corner-stone, break it up, destroy it, and you undermine English misgovernment. When we have undermined English misgovernment we have paved the way for Ireland to take her place among the nations of the earth. And let us not forget that that is the ultimate goal at which all we Irishmen aim. None of us, whether we be in America or in Ireland, or wherever we may be, will be satisfied until we have destroyed the last link which keeps Ireland bound to England."

The General Election of 1880. Mr. Gladstone's address.

The General Election of 1880 recalled Mr. Parnell from America. The dissolution was announced to the country by Lord Beaconsfield in a published letter addressed to the Irish Viceroy, the Duke of Marlborough. In this letter the Prime Minister took his stand on the defence of the Union and endeavoured to make that the chief issue of the election. The severance of the constitutional tie which united Great Britain to Ireland "in that bond which has favoured the power and prosperity of both" was the danger to which he drew the attention of the country. In his electoral address Mr. Gladstone denied the existence of this danger. But he added, "Let me say that in my opinion these two great subjects of local government and the land laws ought now to occupy a foremost place in the thoughts of every man who aspires to be a legislator. In the matter of local government there may lie a solution of some national and even Imperial difficulties. It will not be in my power to enter largely upon the important question of the condition of Ireland; but you know well how unhappily the action of Parliament has been impeded and disorganised, from considerations, no doubt, conscientiously entertained by a part of the Irish representatives, and from their desire to establish what they term Home Rule. If you ask me what

I think of Home Rule, I must tell you that I will only answer you when you tell me how Home Rule is related to local government. I am friendly to large local privileges and powers. I desire, I may almost say, I intensely desire, to see Parliament relieved of some portion of its duties. I see the efficiency of Parliament interfered with, not only by obstruction from Irish members, but even more gravely by the enormous weight that is placed upon the time and the minds of those whom you send to represent you. We have got an overweighted Parliament, and if Ireland or any other portion of the country is desirous and able so to arrange its affairs that by taking the local part of its transactions off the hands of Parliament it can liberate and strengthen Parliament for Imperial concerns, I say, I will not only accord a reluctant assent, but I will give a zealous support to any such scheme. One limit, *one limit only*, I know to the extension of local government. It is this; nothing can be done, in my opinion, by any wise statesman, or right-minded Briton, to weaken or compromise the authority of the Imperial Parliament, because the Imperial Parliament must be supreme in these three kingdoms. . . . But, subject to that limitation, if we can make arrangements under which Ireland, Scotland, Wales, portions of England, can deal with questions of local and special interest to themselves more efficiently than Parliament now can, that, I say, will be the attainment of a great national good."

On his return to Ireland Mr. Parnell threw himself with great energy into the election. His chief object was to drive from their seats the moderate Home Rulers who, after the death of Mr. Butt in 1879, were led by Mr. Shaw, and to replace them by followers of his own. He was opposed on opposite grounds by the bishops and by the Fenian leaders; he was supported by the priests and by the rank and file among the Fenians. The bishops gave their support to the moderate Home Rulers; the Fenian leaders were opposed to all constitutional action. The Supreme Council of the Irish Republican Brotherhood rescinded the resolution which they had passed a year before to allow officers of the organisation to take part in the open movement, and their emissaries at first endeavoured to break up Mr. Parnell's meetings. But his resolution and energy won the day. The majority of the sixty

Mr. Parnell chosen leader of the Home Rule party.

Home Rulers returned in Ireland were his nominees, and when after the election the party met to choose a leader, he was elected by twenty-three votes against eighteen given to Mr. Shaw.

Compensation for Disturbance Bill, 1880, rejected by the Lords.

In the new Parliament Mr. Parnell and his followers signified their independence of English parties by taking their seats on the Opposition side of the House while Mr. Shaw and his adherents sat with the Liberals on the Ministerial benches. The first Irish measure of the Government was a Compensation for Disturbance Bill to provide that in cases where a tenant evicted for non-payment of rent could satisfy the Land Court (1) that he was unable to pay, and that this inability was due not to his own idleness but to the agricultural depression of the current or the two preceding years; (2) that he was willing to continue the tenancy on reasonable terms; and (3) that such reasonable terms had been refused by the landlord, he should be entitled to compensation for disturbance. This bill was rejected by the House of Lords, and its rejection was the signal for most formidable disturbances in Ireland.

Agrarian agitation.

The policy of the new departure was now from a Nationalist standpoint amply justified. If farmers and priests had shown indifference or even antipathy to the political movement of the preceding decade they showed no indifference now. Lord Cowper, the Irish Viceroy, afterwards observed that "there was very little said about Home Rule at that time. It was all agrarianism, with separation in the background, and Parnell was the centre of everything." He thought that Mr. Parnell "used agrarian discontent for separatist purposes".

Mr. Parnell and the Land League.

But whatever his real views on the land question may have been, Mr. Parnell during this autumn flung himself into the work of the Land League with extraordinary energy. Unlike some of his successors, he was never of opinion that Home Rule could be killed by kindness or that it was a mistake to accept boons falling short of that ideal. "Irish nationality," he said, "must be very thin if it is to be given up for grand committees or anything else. *My opinion is that everything they give us makes for Home Rule, and we should take everything.* The better off the people are the better Nationalists they will be. The starving man is not a good Nationalist." He never forgot Mr. Gladstone's imprudent statement as to the connection between the Fenian outrages and Irish disestablishment, and the famous speech at Ennis, in which he opened the campaign, showed clearly that it was present to his mind. "He would strongly recommend public men not to waste their breath in discussing how the land question is to be settled, but rather to encourage the people in making it ripe for settlement." And again in the same speech: "Depend upon it that the measure of the Land Bill next session will be the measure of your activity and energy this winter. It will be the measure of your determination not to pay unjust rents; it will be the measure of your determination to keep a firm grip on your homesteads." How accurate was Mr. Parnell's diagnosis of the situation may be gathered from Mr. Gladstone's subsequent admission " that without the Land League the Act of 1881 would not now be on the statute-book ".[1]

The Land League was now the chief power in Ireland. Evictions and outrages simultaneously increased in numbers, and the "universal sympathy of the population with the criminals" was reported to Mr. Gladstone by Lord Cowper. The Viceroy and Mr. Forster, the Chief Secretary, were assured by the police and the officials that the suspension of the Habeas Corpus Act would suffice to restore order, and they pressed this course on the Cabinet. Mr. Gladstone declined to call Parliament together in the autumn, and a State prosecution of the leaders was first attempted. But when this had failed and disorder continually increased, a bill for the suspension of the Habeas Corpus Act was introduced in the ensuing January and only carried, after unprecedented obstruction, by the device of entrusting the Speaker with a temporary dictatorship in the matter of procedure. *Evictions and outrages. Habeas Corpus Act suspended.*

The Land Act of the same session established, in accordance with the report of the Bessborough Commission,[2] a tribunal to fix fair rents on application made, and gave fixity of tenure to tenants who paid those rents, with the right to sell their interest in their holdings. This system of fair rents, fixity of tenure, and free sale had been advocated in the preceding Parliament by Mr. Butt and his supporters, but the bills *The three F's.*

---

[1] House of Commons, 21st April, 1893.
[2] This Commission was appointed by Mr. Gladstone in 1880 and presided over by Lord Bessborough. It reported in 1881.

and motions that embodied it had been rejected by immense majorities composed of both the English parties.[1]

Failure of the Coercion Act. The Irish policy of the Government in 1881 appeared at first a disastrous failure. Hundreds of suspects, including Mr. Parnell himself, were arrested and imprisoned under the Coercion Act, and the Land League was suppressed by proclamation. But the only effect of these measures was largely to increase agrarian crime in Ireland and to strengthen the malign influence of the instigators to violence who had to some real extent been held in check by the imprisoned leaders. On the other hand, the Land Act, extorted as it appeared to be and as it really was from a reluctant Government by the fierce agitation of the preceding autumn, conciliated nobody. While it established a Land Court, with authority to cut down excessive rents, it made no provision for dealing with accumulated arrears. Thus the Court might pronounce a rent in a high degree excessive and cause it to be cut down accordingly; but if, owing to that very excess, the tenant had been unable to pay the rent in the past and had fallen into arrears he remained at the mercy of his landlord and the decision of the Court might be frustrated. For this and other reasons the bill was coldly received by Mr. Parnell, who with his party abstained from voting on the second reading, although true to his policy of always accepting what he could get, he was careful to come to the rescue of the Government whenever the bill seemed in danger. After it was passed, he dissuaded the tenants from crowding into the Land Court, and drew up test cases for submission to that Court. On the fate of these cases his advice to the mass of tenants would, he said, depend. This scheme was interrupted by his imprisonment; which, in its turn, was followed by the issue of a no rent manifesto.

Test cases submitted to the Land Court. Arrest of Mr. Parnell.

The Kilmainham Treaty. In May, 1882, as the result of the negotiations known as the Kilmainham Treaty the Irish leaders were released.[2] " Parnell and his friends," wrote Mr. Gladstone to the Viceroy, " are ready to abandon no rent formally, and to declare against outrage energetically, intimidation included, if and when the

---

[1] Jeremy Bentham might have found a fresh illustration of his axiom that a governed majority can only secure concessions from a ruling minority by causing them uneasiness in the history of the Land Act of 1881.

[2] The agreement was arrived at during Mr. Parnell's detention in Kilmainham prison. Hence the name.

Government announce a satisfactory plan for dealing with arrears." Mr. Parnell, in a letter to Captain O'Shea, declared his confidence that he could stop outrages and intimidation if the arrears question was settled. He added that if leaseholders were admitted to the benefit of the Act, and the purchase clauses were extended, the land question would in his opinion be regarded by the country as practically settled, and the Irish members be enabled to co-operate cordially with Liberals in forwarding Liberal principles. The truth was that Mr. Parnell was alarmed at the tendencies shown by the agrarian movement while beyond his control; he was anxious to be free that he might resume direction; and he felt no sympathy with Mr. Davitt's policy of land nationalisation. He had been interested in the land movement chiefly as a means to a political end; it had served its purpose, and had incidentally secured great and, in his view, just concessions for the tenants, and now he was convinced that the cause of self-government might be better promoted by other agencies.

The resignation of Lord Cowper and Mr. Forster followed the release of the Irish leaders. They were succeeded by Lord Spencer and Lord Frederick Cavendish, and for the moment a brighter future seemed in store for Ireland. These hopes were dashed to the ground by the terrible crime in the Phœnix Park where the noble-minded Chief Secretary and Mr. Burke, the Under Secretary, were stabbed to death on the day of Lord Frederick's arrival in Ireland. The blow was aimed by the irreconcilables as much at Mr. Parnell as at the Government, and for the time suspended his energy and took all heart out of the constitutional movement. The murderers were denounced by Mr. Davitt as "assassins of the people's cause," and Mr. Parnell even offered Mr. Gladstone to retire from the leadership. *The Phœnix Park murders.*

A new Crimes Act much more suited to the circumstances of Ireland than the Act of 1881 was passed in 1882. Instead of merely giving to the Government by suspension of Habeas Corpus the power of detaining suspects, it strengthened the powers of the executive to obtain criminal convictions by substituting in certain cases trial by judges or magistrates for trial by jury, and by enabling the executive to carry on secret inquiries and to summon witnesses when no person was in *The Crimes Act of 1882.*

custody charged with an offence. In the same year an Arrears Act was passed, drawn on the lines arranged in the treaty with Mr. Parnell, who now, at the expense of a disagreement with his chief colleagues, Mr. Davitt and Mr. Dillon, resolved to "slow down" the land agitation. The combined result of these conditions with the firm administration of Lord Spencer was that order was at last restored to Ireland; and from 1883 to 1887 crime of all kinds was abnormally low in that country.

Foundation of the National League. The suppression of the Land League had left the Nationalist movement without organisation in Ireland. To supply this defect a National Conference was summoned to Dublin in October, 1882, by Mr. Parnell and his principal colleagues, where the following resolutions were passed:—

That an Association be formed to attain for the Irish people the following objects:—

1. National Self-Government.
2. Land Law Reform.
3. Local Self-Government.
4. Extension of the Parliamentary and Municipal Franchise.
5. The development and encouragement of the labour and industrial interests of Ireland.

That this Association be called "The Irish National League".

The first object was defined as "the restitution to the Irish people of the right to manage their own affairs in a Parliament elected by the people of Ireland"—a definition which would enable the most moderate advocates of a federal arrangement to combine in its support with men who looked to separation. The chief aim of the proposed land law reform was to be the creation of an occupying ownership by an extension of the purchase clauses of the Act of 1881—a change to a large extent carried out by Purchase Acts subsequently passed. The programme of social and political reform advocated by the National League was intended to unite on the same platform the various movements promoted by Irish Nationalists; and its ultimate object was "gradually to transfer all local power and patronage from privileged strangers into the hands of the people, and so fortify them for the work of National self-government".

For the two years that preceded the General Election of 1885 Mr. Parnell showed little activity except on isolated occasions, and appeared to have abandoned his former policy of exasperation. He drew no nearer to any English party, and warned the Irish people not to rely on the English democracy, but he made no inflammatory speeches, and showed himself little either in Parliament or on the platform. Certain of the Liberal leaders were clearly beginning to abandon the *non-possumus* attitude with respect to Irish self-government, and this circumstance may have helped to persuade the Irish leader that moderation was then necessary for the interests of his cause. In 1883, speaking on a motion made in the House of Commons for the revival of an Irish Parliament, Mr. Gladstone advanced further in the direction of conceding the Irish claim than he had previously done, and made it clear that his resistance was based not on principle but on the practical difficulties attached both to the presence in or absence from an Imperial Parliament of Irish members when Ireland had a Parliament of her own. "I will not undertake," he said, "to say at what decision this House might arrive provided a plan were before it under which the local affairs of Ireland could be, by some clear and definite line, separated from the Imperial affairs of Ireland; but I must remind these honourable gentlemen that when they say they object to having any laws made for Ireland except by a Parliament sitting in that country, they also say that laws affecting Imperial interests are to be made here, and that these laws affecting Imperial interests would be laws for Ireland just as much as laws touching only their local affairs. . . . Until they lay before the House a plan in which they go to the very bottom of the subject, and give us to understand in what manner that division of jurisdiction is to be accomplished, a practical consideration of this subject cannot be arrived at, and for my own part, I know not how any effective judgment upon it can be pronounced". This indeed was the chief rock upon which the bills of 1886 and 1893 were wrecked, and it remains an apparently insoluble difficulty for those who would give Home Rule to Ireland without at the same time establishing a federal system for the whole of the United Kingdom.

Mr. Childers, again the Chancellor of the Exchequer, had

View of Mr. Childers.

been asking himself "whether time for discussing at Westminster the often neglected affairs of the Empire might not be better obtained by relegating to inferior legislative bodies the purely local affairs of each of the three kingdoms, than by artificial restraints on the liberty of debate, always distasteful to Englishmen," and had been wondering why it was "that our race in the great Republic and in the greatest of our colonies, requires and fully occupies between forty and fifty legislative bodies, most of them with two chambers each, while we imagine that we can adequately transact the business of England, Scotland, and Ireland, and the Imperial affairs of the whole Empire, with one Parliament only." These reflections brought him to the conclusion that "in a plan of federal Home Rule lay the salvation of Ireland".[1]

Mr. Chamberlain's scheme of a National Council.

But the statesman who at this time seemed inclined to go furthest in the direction of Irish self-government was Mr. Chamberlain. He had played the chief part in arranging the Kilmainham Treaty, and he had always endeavoured to keep in touch with the Irish members. In the spring of 1885 he submitted to his colleagues in the Cabinet a scheme of self-government for Ireland, which, though far short of Home Rule, was equally far in advance of any that had till then been proposed by a responsible English statesman. His plan was to establish a Central Board in Dublin to be chosen by representative county boards. This Central Board or National Council was to take over education, poor-law, and sanitary administration, and to have power to make by-laws, raise funds, and within specified limits pledge public credit. It was also to be empowered to pass bills which, if sanctioned by the Imperial Parliament, might become law. This scheme had been submitted to Mr. Parnell and to the Irish bishops, and had received their approval. It was warmly supported in the Cabinet by Mr. Gladstone, who regarded it "as invaluable itself, and as the only hopeful means of securing Crown and State from an ignominious surrender in the next Parliament after a mischievous and painful struggle," but the peers in the Cabinet, together with Lord Hartington, were opposed to it, and it was consequently abandoned.

The Crimes Act of 1882 was dated to expire in August,

[1] Life of Childers, vol. ii. p. 230.

1885. On the question of its renewal the Cabinet was nearly broken up. Mr. Chamberlain and Sir Charles Dilke objected to the continuance of the Act unless this was accompanied by the adoption of the proposal for a National Council; but the representations of Lord Spencer eventually prevailed, and an Irish programme comprising land purchase, an extension of local government, and a modified renewal of the Crimes Act was agreed upon. On the 15th May, the decision of the Government was announced to the House of Commons by Mr. Gladstone; on the 14th June, their budget was defeated on second reading by the combined forces of Conservatives and Irish. The Government at once resigned, and the first Ministry of Lord Salisbury came into power.

Renewal of the Crimes Act. Defeat and resignation of the Government.

The Redistribution Bill had only just become law, so that it was impossible for the new Ministry to dissolve Parliament until the autumn. Until that date it seemed essential to the party managers that there should be no quarrel with the Irish, and this could only be secured by abandoning the powers which had appeared to the retiring Viceroy to be necessary for the preservation of the peace. Lord Randolph Churchill, who, by refusing to enter the Cabinet on other terms, had succeeded in relegating Sir Stafford Northcote to the House of Lords, and of whose influence and popularity Lord Salisbury entertained perhaps an exaggerated notion, largely shaped at this time the policy of the party. He was on friendly terms with Mr. Parnell; he had affected to be much shocked when Mr. Gladstone announced his decision to renew the Crimes Act; and he had carefully dissociated his party from any responsibility for the continuance of exceptional law in Ireland. Mr. Parnell would have preferred the conversion to his views of the Conservative to that of the Liberal party, because of the control exercised by a Conservative Government over the House of Lords, and at this moment such a contingency appeared within the bounds of possibility.

Conservative Government do not renew the Crimes Act.

Lord Carnarvon, the chief author of Canadian federation, a statesman whose leanings towards Home Rule were no secret, was not only appointed Lord-Lieutenant of Ireland but in that capacity was chosen to make a statement in the House of Lords concerning the Irish policy of the Government—a duty. His

Lord Carnarvon, the new Viceroy, declares the Irish policy of the Government.

interview with Mr. Parnell. which would naturally have fallen to the Prime Minister. He announced that the Government did not intend to renew the Crimes Act in any form, and, after a significant reference to the prosperity of our self-governing colonies across the sea, expressed the hope that with good-will on both sides it might be possible to find "some satisfactory solution for this terrible question". He added that he believed these to be the opinions and the views of his colleagues. In the House of Commons, on a motion made by Mr. Parnell to call attention to the maladministration of the criminal law by Lord Spencer, Sir Michael Hicks Beach and Lord Randolph Churchill, although they opposed the motion, were so far from defending Lord Spencer that they expressed their lack of confidence in his administration, gave hopes that Lord Carnarvon would consent to an inquiry into the particular case referred to, and emphatically disclaimed all responsibility for the acts of the late Government. In July a further step was taken. At the instance of his friend, Sir Charles Gavan Duffy, an historical article by whom in favour of a moderate scheme of Home Rule, entitled "An Appeal to the Conservatives," Lord Carnarvon had himself in February sent to the *National Review*, the Lord Lieutenant invited Mr. Parnell to a secret meeting in London. This interview took place with the full knowledge and consent of Lord Salisbury, but without the cognisance of the rest of the Cabinet. Lord Carnarvon informed Mr. Parnell that he was acting of himself alone, and that his object in seeking the interview was to ascertain Mr. Parnell's desires and intentions. Although no pledges were given or promises made this interview had important effects, for it induced in Mr. Parnell's mind a belief that the two English parties had begun to bid against one another for his support, and that he could, therefore, safely raise his demands. The scheme for a National Council now appeared to him inadequate, and speaking at Dublin on the 24th August he declared that the one and only "plank" for the Irish at the coming election should be national independence. Three speeches followed that of Mr. Parnell. The first came from Lord Hartington, who in unambiguous language expressed his conviction that all England would unite to oppose this "fatal and mischievous proposal". A few days afterwards Lord Randolph Churchill spoke at Sheffield and made no allusion to Home Rule. Lastly, on the 8th September, Mr. Chamberlain at Warrington said : " Speaking for myself, I say that if these and these alone are the terms on which Mr. Parnell's support is to be obtained I will not enter into competition for it ".

On the 18th September Mr. Gladstone issued his election address from Hawarden. Subject to necessary securities for the supremacy of the Crown, the unity of the Empire, and the authority of Parliament, he expressed therein his approval of the grant to portions of the country of enlarged powers for the management of their own affairs. A counter move was made by Lord Salisbury in his speech at Newport on the 7th October. His language towards the Irish was conciliatory. He declared indeed against Home Rule, but in language less unambiguous than that used by Lord Hartington and Mr. Chamberlain ; he spoke of boycotting as a trivial matter ; and he said that to have renewed the Crimes Act immediately after having showed confidence in the Irish people by the lowering of the franchise would have been an inconsistency. On the 9th November Mr. Gladstone in Midlothian declared it to be the duty of an English Government to treat with careful attention any constitutional demand that Ireland might make—an announcement described by Mr. Parnell in Liverpool the next day as the most important ever yet delivered upon the Irish national question by any English Minister. He proceeded to invite Mr. Gladstone to advance a step further and to " frame a plan for giving to Ireland, without prejudice to Imperial unity and interests, the management of her own affairs ". But this Mr. Gladstone declined to do, declaring in a speech made shortly afterwards that it was not for him to usurp the functions of Government. His chief reason for reserve, as he explained it in a letter to Lord Rosebery, was that in his opinion the production of a plan at that moment would have made certain the opposition of the whole Tory party, and would, therefore, have been fatal to its success. He thought, too, that the only " leverage " which could carry Home Rule was to be found in " mature consideration of what is due to the fixed desire of a nation, clearly and constitutionally expressed," and that the approaching election would show whether this fixed desire existed in Ireland. Mr. Parnell now reverted to his former

Moves and counter-moves. Irish vote cast in favour of Conservatives.

attitude of hostility. With his assent a manifesto was published by the National League of Great Britain calling on the Irish to vote against the Liberal party, which had " coerced Ireland, deluged Egypt with blood, menaced religious liberty in the schools, the freedom of speech in Parliament, and promise to the country generally a repetition of the crimes and follies of the last Liberal administration ". At the general election which followed the Irish vote was cast in favour of the Conservatives.

<small>Results of the General Election of 1885. Nationalist victories in Ireland.</small>
It is probable that neither Lord Salisbury nor Lord Randolph Churchill nor Sir Michael Hicks Beach had ever any intention of making an advance in the direction of Home Rule, but when the appointment of Lord Carnarvon, the non-renewal of the Crimes Act, their carefully-guarded language, their refusal to defend Lord Spencer, and, in the case of Lord Salisbury, his assent to Lord Carnarvon's interview with Mr. Parnell are considered, they cannot be acquitted of too anxious a desire to remain at peace with the Irish until after the General Election, or even of that " faint kind of policy or wisdom " known as dissimulation. If the constitutional expression of the fixed desire of a nation had really given leverage sufficient to obtain its accomplishment, the General Election of 1885 would have carried Home Rule. The Reform Act of 1884, completing the work of Catholic emancipation and the ballot, enabled the Irish people for the first time to secure a true representation at Westminster. There was a theory much in vogue at this time that the Irish peasantry had no real sympathy with the Nationalist movement and that their enfranchisement would result in Conservative victories. Under the influence of this delusion many Tory candidates came forward. But the only effect of their candidature was to demonstrate the overwhelming strength of the Nationalists. In Munster, Leinster, and Connaught Parnellites captured every seat, and by immense majorities—even in Ulster eighteen were returned, as against seventeen Conservatives. Liberals and Moderate Home Rulers were annihilated. Mr. Parnell returned to Parliament with eighty-six followers, and since the majority of Liberals over Conservatives was also eighty-six, he now held the balance.

It is strange that so much surprise should have been caused

by Mr. Gladstone's formal conversion to the policy of Home Rule after the election of 1885. Since his speech at Aberdeen in 1871 he had never attacked the principle of this policy, and on the other hand he had long held that representative government was based on the doctrine that the will of the people as expressed by their representatives in Parliament ought to prevail. The real question was whether Ireland was to be considered as a "geographical fragment" of Great Britain, as Mr. Lowe thought, or as a nation. "I could not," Mr. Gladstone afterwards explained, "support Butt's movement, because it was not a national movement. I had no evidence that Ireland was behind it. Parnell's movement was different. It came to this: we granted a fuller franchise to Ireland in 1884, and Ireland then sent eighty-five members to the Imperial Parliament. That settled the question. When the people express their determination in that decisive way, you must give them what they ask."[1] This point of view was one consistently held by Mr. Gladstone throughout his career. Seventeen years before, he had written that it was "the office of law and of institutions to reflect the wants and wishes of the country," and he added that its wishes must ever be a considerable element in its wants. This was with reference to the disestablishment of the Irish Church, as to the imperative necessity of which he had been convinced according to his own remarkable confession by the evidence of Irish feeling conveyed in the Fenian outrages at Manchester and Clerkenwell. There is, therefore, no reason to doubt his sincerity on this occasion, or to believe, as Lord Salisbury thought, that he was "mad for office," and prepared to sacrifice the interests of his country and his own conviction for the sake of the Irish vote. His first idea was that just as Catholic emancipation and the repeal of the Corn Laws had been carried by Conservative Governments with Liberal support—though in each instance at the price of the disruption of the party—Lord Salisbury's Government might now carry through a settlement of the Irish question on a basis of moderate Home Rule, in spite of the opposition of extremists on both sides. To such a scheme he proffered his support by an informal communication to Lord Salisbury, and he appears really to have thought—mis-

[1] Life of Parnell, ii. 365.

led, perhaps, by the known views of Lord Carnarvon and the ambiguous language or silence of Ministers before the election—that this proposal had a good chance of acceptance. He was soon undeceived. Lord Salisbury coldly replied that a communication of the views of the Government would at this stage be at variance with usage, and the matter was at an end. The Conservative leaders indeed were so far from contemplating a measure of Home Rule that, urged by the mass of their supporters and no longer in need of the Irish vote, they already meditated a return to coercion. Lord Randolph Churchill and Sir Michael Hicks Beach were opposed to this course. They thought that by a bold and liberal programme of legislation they might conciliate a section of the Whigs; while by concessions to Ireland on educational questions and by an extension of land purchase they might attract the support of Irish Catholics, and so, by producing a cleavage between Clericals and Fenians, bring about the disintegration of Mr. Parnell's party. Lord Salisbury, however, after much dubitation, decided in favour of coercion, though whether his decision was based on conviction or expediency was not clear even to those who were most in his confidence. Thereupon Lord Carnarvon and Sir William Hart Dyke, the Chief Secretary, resigned. Parliament met for the business of the session on the 21st January. On the 24th Mr. W. H. Smith, the new Chief Secretary, arrived in Dublin in order to make inquiries, as Sir Michael Hicks Beach informed the House of Commons, concerning the state of the country and the necessity or otherwise of exceptional powers. On the 28th he started on his return to London. Before his arrival notice had been given in his name of a bill to suppress the National League, and to protect life and property in Ireland, while another had been announced for the extension of the system of land purchase. On the same day the Government were defeated by a majority of seventy-nine, on an amendment to the address moved by Mr. Jesse Collings on the subject of allotments. The Government resigned, and Mr. Gladstone at once accepted the queen's commission to form a new Ministry.

A new Coercion Bill announced. Resignation of Lord Carnarvon and Sir W. Hart Dyke. Defeat and resignation of the Government.

In a memorandum which he sent to those whom he asked to join him Mr. Gladstone explained the basis on which he proposed to form his third Ministry. This was an inquiry into the question whether it was or was not practicable "to comply with the desire widely prevalent in Ireland, and testified by the return of eighty-five out of 103 representatives, for the establishment by statute of a legislative body to sit in Dublin, and to deal with Irish as distinguished from Imperial affairs; in such a manner as would be just to each of the three kingdoms, equitable with reference to every class of the people of Ireland, conducive to the social order and harmony of that country, and calculated to support and consolidate the unity of the Empire on the continued basis of Imperial authority and mutual attachment". Lord Hartington refused to take office on the ground that inquiry and examination undertaken by a Cabinet could not and ought not to stop short of action, and that he was definitely opposed to the establishment of a separate legislature for Ireland. Mr. Chamberlain took a different view. He thought the conditions for the security and integrity of the Empire, the protection of minorities, and the protection of the just interests of the three kingdoms adequately recognised in the memorandum, "but," he added in his letter to Mr. Gladstone, "I have already thought it due to you to say that, according to my present judgment, it will not be found possible to conciliate those conditions with the establishment of a National legislative body sitting in Dublin; and I have explained my own preference for an attempt to come to terms with the Irish members on the basis of a more limited scheme of Local Government coupled with proposals for a settlement of the land and, perhaps also, of the education question." He, however, consented to enter the Cabinet on the understanding that he should retain unlimited liberty of judgment and rejection with regard to any scheme that might be proposed by the Prime Minister. *Mr. Gladstone's memorandum. Lord Hartington's refusal to enter the Cabinet. Mr. Chamberlain's hesitating accession.*

The new Cabinet had been formed on a basis of inquiry and examination, but it soon appeared that the business of inquiry was to be left exclusively to its chief. Mr. Gladstone at once set to work upon his scheme, planned it out by himself, and consulted no colleague who was likely to be critical. Lord Salisbury's Government were defeated on the 26th January. Not until the 13th March did Mr. Gladstone explain his plan to the Cabinet. Mr. Chamberlain was in favour of a scheme for delegating specified powers to a central body *Production to the Cabinet of Mr. Gladstone's scheme. Resignation of Mr. Chamberlain and Mr. Trevelyan.*

in Dublin while retaining Irish representatives in the Imperial Parliament and reserving for that Parliament or the British Ministry full control not only over all Imperial matters but over the customs, the judicature, and the police. He was opposed to Mr. Gladstone's proposals which in their first shape allowed the new Irish authorities "to arrange their own customs tariff, to have entire control of the civil forces of the country, and even, if they thought fit, to establish a volunteer army". Coupled with the exclusion of the Irish members from Westminster these proposals seemed to Mr. Chamberlain tantamount to a proposal for separation, and on the 26th March, accompanied by Mr. Trevelyan, he resigned.

The Home Rule Bill of 1886.

On the 8th April, Mr. Gladstone introduced his first Home Rule Bill. He proposed to establish an Irish Legislature in Dublin, for purely Irish purposes, with an executive responsible to it. To the Imperial Parliament, in which no Irish representatives were to sit, he reserved the following Imperial subjects: the Crown; peace or war; army; navy; volunteers; defence; foreign and colonial relations; dignities; treason; trade; post office; coinage. In Irish matters too the power of the Irish Parliament was subjected to important limitations. It was not to make laws relating to the endowment of religion, or in restraint of educational freedom, or to raise money from customs or excise. The police were to be eventually handed over to the new Irish authorities; but the Dublin metropolitan police were to remain for two years under Imperial control; and the Royal Irish Constabulary for an unspecified period. The Legislature was to be composed of two orders sitting together and voting together unless a separate vote was demanded. The first order was to consist of 103 members[1] elected by constituents with an occupation franchise of twenty-five pounds; and the second order of 206 members elected as at present. If the two orders disagreed the matter was to be vetoed for three years. If it was again carried by the second order at the end of that time it was to be decided by a majority of the two orders sitting together. Constitutional questions respecting the powers of the Irish Legislature were to be

[1] The twenty-eight existing representative peers of Ireland were during their lifetime to be members of this first order but no new representative peers were to be elected.

submitted to the Judicial Committee of the English Privy Council. Ireland was to pay one-fifteenth of the whole as her contribution to Imperial charges.

It will be observed that important modifications had been made in the original scheme. It was no longer proposed that the Irish Parliament should be empowered to arrange a customs tariff or to raise a volunteer army. But in meeting Mr. Chamberlain's objections on these points without conceding his simultaneous claim that Ireland should continue to send representatives to the Imperial Parliament, Mr. Gladstone accentuated the character of the most formidable objection to his proposals. This was that Ireland under the scheme would be shut out from all part in the Imperial policy of the country, and would, in very important matters, be subject to the legislation of a Parliament in which she was not represented, while, at the same time, she would be called upon to make a large contribution for Imperial purposes. This position was in itself sufficiently humiliating, and unlike that of any self-governing colony; but the proposal to separate taxation from representation, by empowering an external Parliament from which Irish members were excluded to levy and alter customs duties for Ireland, made it still less defensible. Not only was Ireland to have no voice in the application of money which she was compelled to contribute, but also, in virtue of the change in the scheme hastily adopted in the short interval between the resignation of Mr. Chamberlain and the introduction of the bill, she was to have no voice as to the ways and means for raising this money. There could be no finality in such an arrangement, and yet it was only the hope that in Home Rule would be found a final solution of the Irish question and a means of terminating the ancient quarrel between England and Ireland that could reconcile men's minds to so daring an experiment.

Difficulties connected with Irish representation in Imperial Parliament.

In the debate on the first reading of the bill Mr. Chamberlain admitted that its introduction had changed the situation, and that a wider measure than his scheme for a National Council had now become necessary. When it was first suggested Mr. Parnell had been disposed to accept that scheme for what it was worth, and had agreed that Mr. Chamberlain should go to Ireland and lay his proposals before the people; but after

Mr. Chamberlain declares for Federation.

his interview with Lord Carnarvon he suddenly changed his mind, rejected the scheme, and would no longer consent to the proposed missionary visit to Ireland. Mr. Chamberlain from that time abandoned it; and now, in the debates on the Home Rule Bill, declared himself in favour of a scheme of federation closely resembling that proposed by Mr. Butt in the opening days of the movement. "The action of such a scheme," he said, "is centripetal and not centrifugal, and it is in the direction of federation that the democratic movement has made most advances in the present century."[1] He added in the same speech, "In my view, the solution of this question should be sought in some form of federation which should really maintain the Imperial unity, and which would at the same time conciliate the desire for a national local government which is felt so strongly by the constituents of Irish members". In the debate on the second reading of the bill he was still more explicit, and declared himself in favour of a federal Home Rule arrangement for Great Britain and Ireland resembling that of the constitution of Canada "in the relations *inter se* of the provinces of Canada and the Dominion Parliament. Those are the relations," he added, "which I, for one, am perfectly prepared to establish to-morrow between this country and Ireland."[2] Mr. Gladstone in his reply contended that Mr. Chamberlain's Home Rule was more revolutionary than his own, and Mr. Gladstone's distinguished biographer endorses that view with even greater emphasis.[3] Can it, however, be denied that the powers of a Provincial Legislature in Canada are much smaller than those which Mr. Gladstone proposed to entrust to the Parliament in Dublin? In Mr. Chamberlain's words, "there is absolute and effective supremacy of the Dominion Parliament over the Provincial Legislatures. There is a veto which can be, and is, used; there is a right of concurrent legislation which can be, and is, used; and the Provincial Parliaments are subordinate bodies with distinctly defined rights of legislation expressly given to them by statute."

The Home Rule Bill excited more bitterness of party feeling than had been caused by any other question since the

[1] 9th April, 1886. [2] Hans. 306, p. 697.
[3] Life of Gladstone, vol. iii. p. 317.

repeal of the Corn Laws. Old friendships were broken up and the Liberal party was rent in sunder. The Ulster Protestants threatened resistance by arms; and their threats were approved and encouraged by leading Conservative statesmen. The Government began to make concessions. A meeting of the party was summoned to the Foreign Office on the 27th May, where the Prime Minister assured them that a vote for the second reading would pledge no man to more than a bare approval of the principle; that after the second reading the bill might be hung up until the autumn, or that Parliament might be prorogued and a new amended bill introduced in October. These considerations had some effect on the minds of waverers, and the bill might possibly have secured a second reading had not the taunts of the Opposition on the following day drawn from the Prime Minister a declaration that the bill would not be altered in essentials. On the 31st May there was a meeting held at the invitation of Mr. Chamberlain of members "who, being in favour of some sort of autonomy for Ireland, disapproved of the Government bills in their present shape". This was attended by fifty-five members, and its result decided the fate of the Home Rule Bill. A letter was read from Mr. Bright announcing his determination to vote against the bill, and the meeting resolved to follow his example. The bill was rejected on the 8th June by a majority of thirty including ninety-three Liberals.[1]

Deep feeling excited by the Home Rule Bill. It is rejected on second reading by the House of Commons.

Mr. Gladstone's Irish proposals had included a Land Bill framed with a view to protecting the interests of the landlords under the new settlement, and in order to establish a peasant proprietary in Ireland. By this it was proposed that the State should buy out the Irish landlords at twenty years' purchase of the judicial rents and re-sell the land to the tenants. The tenants were to become freeholders, subject to the payment to the State of a terminable annuity for forty-nine years equal to four per cent on the capitalised value of the former rent. The British Treasury were to advance for these purposes a sum not exceeding £50,000,000 up to March, 1890, and a Receiver-General was to be appointed through whose hands the money was to pass. These proposals failed to reconcile the landlords to Home Rule; and were disliked by the Radicals. They met

The Land Purchase Bill. Its general unpopularity.

[1] 343 against 313.

indeed with almost general condemnation, and were practically withdrawn before the defeat of the Home Rule Bill; and yet, to a later generation which, by the use of British credit to an amount double that proposed to be pledged in 1886, has attempted to effect the same objects in much the same way, they may well seem the soundest part of the Government programme.

Unionist victory at General Election of 1886.

At the General Election which followed the rejection of the Home Rule Bill, Liberals who had voted against the bill were not opposed by Conservative candidates, with the result that seventy-eight of them, out of a total of ninety-three, retained their seats. The Conservatives, who numbered 316 in the new Parliament, were dependent for their majority on the Liberal Unionists, but as these, on the other hand, owed their seats mainly to Conservative votes, each wing of the Unionist party was necessary to the other. The new Chief Secretary, Sir Michael Hicks Beach, was liberal and fair-minded; the new leader of the House of Commons, Lord Randolph Churchill, was a bold reformer, quite untrammelled by any prejudice in favour of the existing order of things. These were the men to whom for a brief period fell the difficult task of reconciling to representative institutions and equitable practice the government of a people against its consent.

Tenants Relief Bill rejected.

There was menace of fresh disturbance in Ireland. Prices were again falling; and the judicial rents, fair when imposed, were again becoming rack rents; news came once more of evictions and outrages. Since the conversion of the Liberal party to Home Rule, Mr. Parnell was anxious that the movement should be national, and not agrarian. A reversion to the land war of 1881 would, he thought, alienate their new friends, without changing Unionist convictions. The Tenants Relief Bill, which he introduced in August, was an honest attempt to prevent the rise of a fever which it might later prove difficult to cure. It provided for the admission of leaseholders to the benefits of the Act of 1881 and for the abatement of rents fixed before 1885 if the tenants could prove that they were unable to pay. The bill was rejected by a majority of 95.

Royal Commissions. The Plan of Campaign.

In the meantime Lord Randolph Churchill had announced the Government policy for Ireland. Two Royal Commissions were appointed, one to inquire into the working of the Land

Acts and another into the resources of the country. Sir Redvers Buller was at the same time sent to restore order in the west. In spite of an appeal made by Sir Michael Hicks Beach, and supported by Sir Redvers Buller, the landlords refused to stay evictions or to reduce their rent: in spite of the disapproval of Mr. Parnell, at that time very ill, the so-called "Plan of Campaign" was started as a counter-move. Under this system, when the tenant had offered a fair rent and the landlord had refused it, the money was entrusted to a managing committee and used for the purpose of resisting evictions and supporting evicted tenants. These managing committees were elected for every district, and were to deal with the landlords. The "Plan" was, on the whole, successful in effecting its objects and numerous reductions of rent were extorted.

The Commission appointed by the Government reported in February, 1887, in favour of the principles of Mr. Parnell's bill. They recommended the revision of the judicial rents and the admission of leaseholders. Such revision certainly involved a breach of the contract made by the State with Irish landlords in 1881, and it was not included in the Land Bill which the Government introduced in March. But there were tenants in Ulster as well as in the three other provinces, and they too had suffered from the great fall in agricultural values. For them too, in many instances, the judicial rents had become rack rents, and they resented the refusal of revision. This changed the situation. Ulster must not be lost to the Union. Before the close of the session, the Government had passed a bill, not only to admit leaseholders to the benefits of the Land Act of 1881, but also to revise judicial rents fixed before 1886—thus taking action denounced a little earlier by Mr. Balfour, the new Chief Secretary, as folly and madness, and by the Prime Minister as not only inexpedient but dishonest. *The Land Act of 1887. Revision of judicial rents.*

The resignation of Lord Randolph Churchill at the end of 1886, and the retirement shortly afterwards of Sir Michael Hicks Beach, cleared the way for a reversion to the old-fashioned methods of governing Ireland. An Act to strengthen the criminal law in that country was passed giving coercive powers to resident magistrates in proclaimed districts. Power was given to the Lord-Lieutenant in Council to proclaim dis- *Crimes Act of 1887.*

turbed districts, and also to proclaim and suppress any association that he deemed to be dangerous. The peculiarity of the Act was that it was perpetual, whereas the operation of all previous coercion Acts had been limited to a fixed period of time. Thenceforward criminal law was to vary in different parts of Ireland at the discretion of the Executive.

The new closure rule.

In order to pass this bill the Government were obliged to resort to expedients, which, then and thereafter, imposed grave restrictions on the liberty of debate in the House of Commons. Mr. Gladstone's closure rule of 1882 had proved a failure. It had been directed against a small minority, and had placed on the Chair the initiative in bringing it into operation. Only when it appeared to the Speaker or Chairman to be the "evident sense of the House" that the question should be put was he so to inform the House, and even then the closure was not in ordinary cases to be applied unless supported by at least 200 members. As a consequence of these restrictions the closure rule of 1882 was only twice applied during the five years of its existence, and in 1887, before proceeding with the Prevention of Crimes Bill, the Conservative Government resolved materially to strengthen it. The Irish party was twice as numerous as in the Parliament of 1880, and was now reinforced by the whole of the regular Opposition. Accordingly a new closure rule, passed after a debate extending over fourteen sittings, transferred the initiative from the Chair to the House by dispensing with the necessity of a declaration from the Chair of the sense of the House before the closure could be moved. In the following year the number of members voting for the closure before it could be carried was reduced from 200 to 100.

Closure by compartments. The effects of its introduction.

But a still greater innovation in procedure was thought necessary in order to carry the bill. Unhappily, neither of the two great English parties when in Opposition have proved superior to the temptation to imitate the Irish tactics of obstruction or the disposition, as Mr. Gladstone expressed it, "to resist the prevailing will of the House otherwise than by argument". This abuse of liberty resulted, as is generally the case, in loss of liberty; and when, after a discussion of sixteen days on the Crimes Bill, only four out of the twenty clauses had passed through Committee, the Government moved that at a certain hour on the 17th June, being the end of the following week, the Chairman should, without further debate, put all questions necessary to bring the Committee stage to an end. This was the first application of the process, afterwards nicknamed the "guillotine," and destined to be used with increasing frequency in later years. When used as an exceptional measure of necessity its application was irrational in practice, because the amount of time given to the discussion of clauses in bills varied with the order in which they were printed, without reference to their importance; and essential matters, such as the power given by the bill of 1887 to the Irish Executive to proclaim an association as unlawful, were undiscussed; but when the system was methodised and the compartments into which bills were divided for the purposes of closure were carefully selected with the object of securing that no important point should escape the attention of the House, it became much less open to objection. It is, nevertheless, clear that the very circumstances which seemed to be destroying the legislative powers of the Government have, by the changes which they rendered necessary, largely increased those powers at the expense of the House as a whole; and that the blows aimed by the Irish obstructionists at the working machinery of the House of Commons have had the effect of placing a new and powerful machinery at the service of the Government. As Lord Morley observes: "If it had really been one of the objects of Irish members for ten years past to work a revolution in the Parliament where they were forced against their will to sit, they had at least, be such a revolution good or bad, succeeded in their design".[1] The House of Commons had long since lost all initiative in controversial legislation; but it still preserved some control over its form. Of this control it was, for the time at least, in large measure deprived by the guillotine.

Early in 1887 an attempt was made to reunite the left wing of the Liberal Unionist party to the main body of Liberals. Even Lord Hartington at this time admitted that there was strong ground for recommending some change in the direction of Irish self-government. "That ground," he said at New- The Round Table Conference.

[1] *Life of Gladstone*, vol. iii. p. 377.

castle in February, "is the growing incapacity of Parliament to deal with the wants and requirements not only of Ireland, but of the whole of the United Kingdom. I believe that the idea of Mr. Chamberlain is to extend to Ireland, and not only to Ireland, but to other parts of the United Kingdom, if they desire it, on a larger scale, and over larger areas, something in the nature of the municipal government which our great cities already enjoy." But Mr. Chamberlain went further. In 1885 he had declared that the time had come "to reform altogether the absurd and irritating anachronism which is known as Dublin Castle—to sweep away altogether these alien boards of foreign officials, and to substitute for them a genuine Irish administration for purely Irish business". Nor had the events of 1886 really changed his views. Soon after the resignation of Lord Randolph Churchill he made a speech so conciliatory in tone that Sir William Harcourt, imagining agreement to be possible, invited Mr. Chamberlain and Sir George Trevelyan to confer with this object at his house with Mr. Morley, Lord Herschell, and himself. This was the "Round Table Conference"—the only attempt ever made to reunite the Liberal party. The Gladstonians conceded the important point of the retention of Irish members at Westminster, and Mr. Chamberlain agreed to the establishment of some kind of legislature at Dublin with an Executive responsible to it. Differences appear to have arisen on the extent of the powers to be delegated to the Irish Parliament, and the conference broke up. Its only important result was the return of Sir George Trevelyan to his old party, but he returned by himself. Mr. Chamberlain afterwards said that he had revived at this conference his idea of a National Council; that this had been submitted to Mr. Parnell by the Gladstonians, and by him rejected; and that this made an end in the matter. He explained to his constituents in March the conditions on which, and on which alone, he would be willing to concede a Parliament to Ireland. The chief of these were that Ireland was to be represented in the Imperial Parliament; that the Irish Parliament was to be subordinate, not co-ordinate; that the subordinate powers were to be strictly defined and limited; that the maintenance of law and order was to remain under Imperial control; that Ulster was to be treated separately; and that British credit was not to be pledged for the benefit of Irish landlords.

The Crimes Act was vigorously administered by Mr. Balfour, the new Chief Secretary. Eighteen counties were proclaimed in July; the National League in August. Many Irish members were arrested and sentenced to short terms of imprisonment by the resident magistrates. Order was restored and the country was governed as well as unhappy conditions would permit by a small and unpopular minority. On the assumption that Ireland was a geographical fragment of Great Britain all was well; but, on the assumption that her people enjoyed the blessings of representative Government, the circumstance that, in 1889, twenty-five of their chosen representatives were in prison seemed to indicate a position of unstable equilibrium unlikely to endure. *Resolute Government.*

In these years (1886-1890) Mr. Parnell preserved an attitude of moderation. He condemned the Plan of Campaign, which he thought would have a bad effect on the general political situation, and there was less indignation at the action of the Government in the few speeches which he made than was to be found in those of Mr. Gladstone. But this moderation did not abate the hostility of his antagonists. In April, 1887, *The Times*, which had been publishing a succession of articles with the object of proving the connection between Parnellism and Crime, printed a letter in facsimile over what purported to be his signature, in which the Phœnix Park murders were condoned. Mr. Parnell, yielding, perhaps imprudently, to the advice of his English allies, who feared that an English jury might be prejudiced against him, did not bring an action for libel, and in the autumn more letters were published. Mr. Parnell now asked that a Select Committee might be appointed to investigate the case. The Government refused; but offered, as an alternative, a Special Commission of three judges to examine into and report upon the truth of all the allegations contained in the articles entitled "Parnellism and Crime". A bill for the creation of this Commission was in July, 1888, rapidly forced through Parliament by the guillotine; and the Commission met. Their report, issued in 1889, acquitted Mr. Parnell and the other respondents of insincerity in their denunciation of the Phœnix Park murders and pronounced *"Parnellism and Crime." The forged letters.*

Report of the Special Commission.

the incriminating letters to be forgeries. On the other hand, they found that the respondents did not denounce the system of intimidation which led to crime, but persisted in it with knowledge of its effects, although without directly inciting persons to the commission of crime other than intimidation.

<small>Split in the Irish party. Struggle for leadership. Death of Mr. Parnell.</small>

Such interest as was felt in England in the proceedings of the Special Commission was generally concentrated on the question of the facsimile letters. The effect therefore of the report was on the whole favourable to Home Rule. But in 1890, a verdict in a divorce case was given against the Irish leader and the tide turned. Mr. Gladstone became convinced that Mr. Parnell's retirement from leadership was necessary in the interest of Home Rule; but the notion that he should retire at the bidding of an Englishman, immediately after having received an almost unanimous vote of confidence from his own party, was abhorrent to him and contrary to that principle of independence on English parties through adhesion to which he conceived that his success had been obtained. The majority of his followers, however, deserted him, led, as in other famous historical instances, by those very men who had been foremost in their professions of loyalty, and a split in the Nationalist ranks ensued that destroyed their hopes of success for a generation. Harassed and ill, Mr. Parnell fought a losing battle with feverish energy for nearly a year, and then died in October, 1891. On the same day died Mr. W. H. Smith, the greatly respected leader of the House of Commons, and was succeeded in that leadership by Mr. Balfour, the Chief Secretary.

<small>General Election of 1892. Fall of the Government.</small>

In 1892 the Government introduced a bill of a carefully guarded character to give some measure of local government to Ireland. The bill was liked by nobody and was withdrawn, and on the 28th June Parliament was dissolved. In the General Election which followed 315 Conservative and Liberal Unionists were returned, eighty-one Nationalists, and 274 Home Rule Liberals; so that there was a Home Rule majority of forty. It was accordingly by a majority of forty that a vote of want of confidence in Lord Salisbury's Government was carried in August with the result that Mr. Gladstone for the fourth time became Prime Minister.

Mr. Gladstone had remained in public life with the single

object of prosecuting the cause of Irish Home Rule, but the character of the majority which he had now secured augured ill for his success. Great Britain had returned a majority of Unionist members, and so long as the predominant partner was faithful to the Union it was unlikely that the House of Lords would suffer that Union to be dissolved. Warned by his experiences in 1886, Mr. Gladstone took counsel with others in preparing his scheme. The preparation of the new bill, we are told by his biographer, "was carefully and elaborately worked by Mr. Gladstone through an excellent committee of the Cabinet."[1] It was introduced on the 13th February, 1893.

Mr. Gladstone's return to power.

The chief point of difference between the bill of 1886 and the bill of 1893 was the provision in the latter measure that eighty Irish representatives should have seats in the Imperial Parliament. The Government at first attempted to meet the obvious objection that this arrangement would allow the Irish to interfere, perhaps with decisive effect, in purely British matters, while British members would have no corresponding influence on purely Irish affairs, by providing that the Irish members at Westminster were not to vote on matters exclusively British. But the inconveniences incident to this "in-and-out" system, as it was called, appeared to the House of Commons even more intolerable. Under it the Irish, when holding the balance, would have retained the power to secure the defeat on an Imperial question of a Government which commanded a steady majority on British questions; and their vote might even be dictated by a desire to displace a Ministry, of whose policy on some exclusively English question, such as education, they disapproved. These considerations prevailed; and the bill was altered in Committee so as to allow the eighty Irish members to vote on all subjects. Another novelty in the bill of 1893 was the substitution of a Legislative Council for the "first order" of 1886. This Council was to be composed of forty-eight councillors, elected for eight years for single-member constituencies, by voters who were owners or occupiers of land to the rateable value of £20. The other branch of the proposed legislature, the Legislative Assembly, was to sit separately, and to be composed of 103

The Home Rule Bill of 1893 compared with that of 1886.

[1] Consisting of Mr. Gladstone, Lord Spencer, Lord Herschell, Mr. John Morley, Mr. Campbell-Bannerman, and Mr. Bryce.

members elected by the existing constituencies. In other respects the new proposals closely resembled the old. Customs and excise were to be levied by the Imperial Government and to be looked upon as equivalent to an Irish contribution for Imperial purposes.

Bill passed by the House of Commons. The bill was read a second time on the 21st April by a majority of 43. It was discussed during sixty-three sittings in Committee, and at last carried through the House of Commons by a drastic employment of the form of closure invented by the preceding Government for the purposes of the Crimes Bill. The new clause to provide for the retention of Irish members at Westminster for all purposes was agreed to by a majority of 27, and the third reading was carried by 301 votes against 267.

Faults of the bill. It is rejected by the Lords. It was, however, the general opinion that the House of Commons would not have passed the bill had not its rejection by the House of Lords been a foregone conclusion. A system, under which the Irish representatives would not only be empowered to vote on purely British affairs, but would also share in the appointment and dismissal of British ministries, while English and Scottish representatives would be shut out from all part in Irish legislation or choice of Irish Governments, was unjustifiable in theory, and seemed to many likely to prove disastrous in practice. A wide door was opened to intrigue. The Irish members, it was contended, would use for Irish purposes their right to interfere in British concerns. The injustice was admitted even by leading Irish members. "I look forward," said Mr. Redmond, "to the day when the federal idea may be applied to England, Scotland and Wales, as well as to Ireland. Then the character of the so-called Imperial Parliament would be changed. It would be then only an Imperial Parliament, and all the kingdoms having their own national Parliaments might be represented in it. But if Ireland alone has a Parliament of her own, you must allow Irishmen who had sole control of Irish affairs to interfere in and probably decide English and Scotch affairs—an obvious injustice." On the 8th September, seven days after the bill had left the House of Commons where it had been discussed during eighty-two sittings, it was rejected by the House of Lords after four days' debate by a majority of 378.[1]

[1] 419 to 41.

The rejection of the bill was received by the country with satisfaction, and strengthened the position of the Upper House. Parliament, having adjourned for a short holiday, met again in the autumn, and proceeded with English bills, the Prime Minister hoping that the treatment of these bills by the peers would enable him to appeal to the country for a mandate to effect an organic change in their powers. The House of Lords so far fulfilled his expectations that they amended the Employers' Liability Bill in such a manner as to convince the Government that its withdrawal was necessary, while they did not altogether spare the Parish Councils Bill. This was in February, 1894, but, although Mr. Gladstone now thought the case against the House of Lords complete and was anxious to dissolve Parliament on that issue, his colleagues did not agree with him, and were, moreover, unable to consent to his proposed reduction of the Navy estimates. Therefore, after a last speech, in which he declared in quiet but significant words that the controversy between the two Houses was a question which, if once raised, must go forward to an issue, and seemed to leave the settlement of that issue as a legacy to his followers, in his eighty-fifth year, with sight and hearing half gone, defeated in Parliament, outvoted in the Cabinet; but with courage unbroken, with intellect unclouded, and with his interest in the war of words as keen as ever, the veteran statesman retired, and with him the question of Irish Home Rule seemed to have vanished from the political scene. His successor, Lord Rosebery, at all events, was clearly prepared to suffer its disappearance with fortitude.

The general election of 1895 found both the Liberal and the Irish parties in a state of complete disorganisation, and a great Unionist victory was the natural result. Not only was there no reconciliation between the main body of Nationalists and the Parnellite group, but that main body itself was disunited. In 1896, Mr. M'Carthy resigned the leadership, and Mr. Dillon, against the opposition of Mr. Healy, at the head of a minority, was chosen to fill his place. The mutinous activity of Mr. Healy, which had already brought about Mr. M'Carthy's resignation, culminated, after Mr. Dillon's election, in open revolt, and a third Irish Nationalist party under his leadership, with its separate association and its separate journal, came into being. Meantime the Irish people were weary and indifferent. Two good harvests and reduced rents had allayed their dissatisfaction with the existing system of administration, and the new Government appeared anxious to consult their interests and to redress their grievances. To the English, the Irish internal dissensions were unintelligible, and brought additional discredit on the cause of Home Rule. The Liberal leaders had done their best to avoid the subject at the general election, and among them the late Prime Minister had never concealed his lack of enthusiasm with regard to it. The Parliamentary movement, according to Mr. Redmond, was apparently dying in disgrace.

Killing Home Rule with kindness.
But the debates of 1893 had not been fruitless. A main Unionist position had been, that whatever reforms the Irish might hope to gain under a system of Home Rule they could equally well obtain under the Union, and Mr. Gerald Balfour, the new Chief Secretary, now resolved to translate this theory into practice, and, according to a phrase then in vogue, to kill Home Rule with kindness. Therefore, against all precedent, he determined that Irish grievances should be redressed and her just wants satisfied by a paternal Government, in spite of the fact that Ireland was then enjoying an interval of prosperity, and that she was free from agitation. His first essay in this direction was the Land Act of 1896—a measure designed to introduce an automatic system for adjusting rents; and containing clauses intended to encourage and assist the purchase of land by occupiers from the owners. The bill was welcomed with cordiality by Mr. Redmond and Mr. Healy, accepted in a grudging spirit by Mr. Dillon, and strongly resented by the landlord party.

The Dublin convention of 1896.
In the same year, a convention, summoned by Mr. M'Carthy, of about 2000 delegates, representing the Irish race in every quarter of the world, met in Dublin, and passed resolutions in favour of self-government. But the refusal of Mr. Redmond, of Mr. Healy, and also of the Bishops to countenance this assemblage detracted from its significance, and made what was intended to be a spectacle of Irish unity, yet another manifestation of Irish disunion.

The failure of the convention was counterbalanced in the autumn by a new development, which, for the moment, seemed to unite all sections of Irishmen in a common grievance against the British Government. This was the publication of the report of the Royal Commission appointed to inquire into the financial relations between Great Britain and Ireland. The Commission was presided over by Mr. Childers, and included among its members, besides Mr. Redmond and Mr. Sexton to represent Ireland, financial experts such as Lord Welby, Lord Farrer, Mr. Bertram Currie, and Sir David Barbour. Among the conclusions of the report, signed by all the commissioners but two, the following were the most remarkable : (1) That the Act of Union imposed upon Ireland a much too heavy burden, as the history of their financial relations proves ; (2) That the increase of taxation laid upon Ireland between 1853 and 1860 was unjustifiable ; (3) That an identical rate of taxation does not necessarily involve equality of burden ; (4) That the actual tax-revenue of Ireland is at present one-eleventh of that of Great Britain, and ought not to be more than one-twentieth.

Report of the Financial Relations Commission.

The grievance is perhaps, in reality, a grievance of the indirect taxpayer wherever he lives, since the sum levied on the individual in indirect taxation does not, like the sum which he pays in direct taxation, increase in proportion to his increase in wealth or taxable capacity ; but Ireland had a special claim for consideration under the terms of her bargain with England. The landlords were angry with the Government, because they considered that they had been unjustly treated under the provisions of the new Land Act. Like their predecessors in 1870, who joined in the original Home Rule movement out of disgust at the disestablishment of their Church, they combined with Nationalists to hold meetings to protest against the over-taxation of Ireland. And although the Government denied the justice of their complaints, and the enthusiasm of the landlords in the cause was short-lived, the movement was not without its effect in bringing together a section of the landlord class and a section of the Nationalists, who were some years afterwards again to combine with better success for other objects.

Both parties in Ireland join to protest against alleged over-taxation.

In 1897, a bill for establishing a new Agricultural Board for Ireland, independent of the Castle and the Irish Office, and enjoying a fixed annual grant of £150,000, was introduced. The Board was to take over the duties relating to the encouragement of agriculture exercised by other departments, and was also to superintend and organise Irish fisheries and cottage industries. The money needed to enable it to do its work was to be raised by special rates imposed by the grand juries. These bodies, however, seemed on further reflection ill-fitted to give the popular and national impetus to the scheme so essential to its successful working, and it was resolved to postpone the bill until new and representative authorities should have been constituted. Accordingly, Mr. Balfour announced the withdrawal of the bill; and at the same time, stated to the House the intention of the Government to introduce in the next session a bill to grant a full measure of local government to Ireland. This new departure was welcomed in every quarter of the House, and applauded by the country.

Irish Local Government Bill of 1898.

In 1898, the Irish Local Government Bill was passed. County councils and district councils were constituted as in England. They were to be elected every four years on a democratic franchise. No alderman or minister of religion was to serve on the councils, and each council was to co-opt three members of grand juries. The Poor Law was to be administered by boards of guardians. A sum of £730,000 was to be paid to Ireland out of the Imperial Exchequer as an equivalent to the relief afforded by Parliament to English agricultural land by the Rates Act; and other financial benefits were secured to her. The councils were to take over the fiscal and administrative duties of the grand juries. This Act was the most important advance towards Irish self-government that had yet been made. It initiated the overthrow of the supremacy of the Protestant aristocracy; afterwards to be completed by Mr. Wyndham's Land Purchase Act of 1903. The representatives of all sections of Irishmen were pleased by the Act; and promised to do their best to make it work smoothly.

Establishment of Council of Agriculture, 1899.

In 1899, the scheme for the establishment of the new Agricultural Council in Ireland was proceeded with. By the Irish Agricultural and Technical Instruction Act of that year, a representative Council of Agriculture was constituted consisting of two persons appointed by the county council of each county in each of the four Irish provinces, and of a number of persons, equal to the number of counties in each province, nominated for each province by the Agricultural Department. A separate council to deal with industrial matters, composed partly of representatives of the urban districts and partly of nominated members, was also established. An annual income of £170,000 from various sources was allotted to the new department, portions of which were appropriated by the Act to particular purposes, and the surplus to agriculture and other rural industries or sea fisheries. Lord Hartington, in 1886, had admitted that some co-ordination of local authorities for general purposes would probably in the future be found expedient both in Ireland and in the other parts of the United Kingdom; but such a result would, he thought, be the outgrowth of institutions not yet created. The Act of 1899 contained the beginnings of such a co-ordination; and was rendered possible by the concession of local government in the preceding year.

In the meantime, a new league was acquiring importance in the west of Ireland. This was the United Irish League, founded in 1897 by Mr. William O'Brien, partly with the object of securing an increase in the number of peasant proprietors by dividing up among them the large grass farms. The juxtaposition of tenants who had purchased their holdings under the Land Purchase Acts, and others, less fortunate, to whom their landlords refused to sell, and whose rents were in some cases greater in amount than the terminable annuities paid by their neighbours, was also a source of discontent, for which the league advocated the remedy of compulsory sale. The new association grew rapidly in strength and numbers. It was based on the democratic principle of making the people of each constituency self-governing within their bounds, and avoided the over-centralisation which prejudiced the popularity of the older organisations. Farmers were deterred by intimidation from taking the large grazing farms, and the Government incurred the anger of the landlord class for what was thought to be their remissness in not taking action against the league under the Crimes Act. In 1899, a constitution of the league for the province of Connaught was drawn up; and its political character was defined in the first article, which declared "the largest measure of national self-government" to be the chief object of its foundation.

The United Irish League.

Mr. Redmond elected leader of the reunited Nationalist party.

In February, 1899, Mr. Dillon resigned the chairmanship of the party with a view to reunion; and, later in the same year, the outbreak of the Boer war, and the reverses to British arms which marked its early stages, seemed to the Nationalist leaders to offer opportunities for concerted action which it would be foolish, through domestic dissensions, to neglect. The outcome of these circumstances was that, at the beginning of the session of 1900, the Nationalist members held a meeting at Westminster, and having by resolution made peace among themselves, Mr. Redmond was elected leader of the reunited party. At the General Election in October the machinery of the United Irish League was placed at the service of Mr. Redmond, and almost all the Nationalist members were returned as his supporters. Mr. Healy with a few adherents persisted in his heresy; but, though he himself retained his seat, he returned almost alone to the House of Commons. A National Convention was held at Dublin in December; when the reunion was registered and confirmed, and Mr. Healy was expelled from the party.

The Irish now entered upon a course of opposition in the House of Commons, and of agitation in Ireland, with a vigour unknown since 1890. In England, the Home Rule movement had almost disappeared. An undiminished Unionist majority was returned at the war election of 1900; the Liberal chiefs were divided among themselves; and some of them appeared to have lost all wish for or belief in Home Rule; while a declaration of sympathy with the Boers made by the new leader of the Irish party increased the disrepute into which his cause had fallen. In Ireland the power of the United Irish League grew continually; and intimidation was practised in order to compel farmers to evacuate the large grazing farms, which it was desired to break up and to secure for small proprietors. Mr. Gerald Balfour had been succeeded as Chief Secretary by Mr. Wyndham; and the business of repression was resumed with energy.

Mr. Wyndham's policy. Outbreak of lawlessness in Ireland.

But Mr. Wyndham had higher ambitions than the restoration, by physical force, of order in Ireland. Of the two grand aims of the Irish movement—the establishment of a peasant proprietary and the restoration of an Irish Legislature—the mass of Irishmen in Ireland had always cared more for the former than for the latter. To satisfy this desire by the abolition of the dual ownership through State encouragement of land purchase was a policy which, if feasible, was entirely in accord with Unionist traditions, and Mr. Wyndham had not been long in office before he set himself to carry it out on a generous scale. The omens were at first unfavourable. His first Land Purchase Bill, which was designed to quicken the rate of purchase under previous Acts, and contained no provision for the evicted tenants, gave no content to the Irish, and was withdrawn. The repudiation of this bill by the National directory of the United Irish League was accompanied by a fiery summons to the people through their county conventions to rise against the landlords and the "grazing monopolists". The familiar history repeated itself. Popular lawlessness was met by proclamations and arrests. The greater part of Ireland was proclaimed under the Crimes Act; ten Irish members were imprisoned. A Land Trust, with a capital of £100,000, was organised to prosecute Mr. William O'Brien, Mr. Redmond, and Mr. Davitt, for conspiracy. The Irish leaders replied by the collection of a defence fund, and Mr. Redmond, Mr. Davitt, and Mr. Dillon went to the United States to collect subscriptions. But men were weary of the perpetually recurring struggle; and, just at the moment when the land war appeared to be breaking out in all its old fury, the land question was in reality on the eve of a final solution. The difficulties, which English statesmen had signally failed to overcome, were to be settled by an agreement arrived at by Irishmen among themselves.

In September, 1902, Captain Shawe-Taylor, in a letter to the Irish papers, proposed a conference between representatives of landlords and tenants, to which he said that a suggestion would be submitted satisfactory to both parties. This letter was followed by a communication from the Chief Secretary of a striking nature. "No Government," he said, "can settle the Irish land question. It must be settled by the parties interested. The extent of useful action, on the part of any Government, is limited to providing facilities, in so far as that may be possible, for giving effect to any settlement arrived at by the parties." He added that any conference was a step in

Captain Shawe-Taylor's letter.

the right direction. This was an invitation to Irishmen to settle the most important of their difficulties among themselves, and so far an admission of the virtues of self-government.

Appointment of Sir Antony Macdonnell as Under-Secretary.

In October, Mr. Wyndham, at the suggestion of Lord Lansdowne, offered the post of Under-Secretary for Ireland to Sir Antony Macdonnell. Sir Antony was a strong Liberal, an Irishman, a Roman Catholic, and the brother of a Nationalist member of Parliament. He had had a distinguished career in India, and was about to become a member of the Indian Council in London with the prospect of an Indian governorship, when the appeal was made to him to sacrifice the natural objects of his ambition in order to assist in the regeneration of his native country. Mr. Wyndham asked for his help "rather as a colleague than as a subordinate," and to his representations that he was a Liberal in politics opposed to a policy of coercion, and could only take office with a view to the solution in a broadly national sense of the agrarian, educational, and political questions in Ireland, replied in effect that his views on these topics were largely shared by the Government, and would have fair opportunities given to them. It was also understood that Sir Antony was to be acceptable to " persons of many kinds and descriptions " not usually found in relations with the officials of Dublin Castle; and that he was to be given greater initiative and freedom of action than is generally allowed to Under-Secretaries. On these understandings Sir Antony accepted the post, and placed himself in communication with the Irish Nationalist leaders as well as with representatives of the Irish landlords.

Conference of representatives of landlords and tenants arrives at an agreement.

The result of these events and proceedings was that in December, 1902, a conference of representatives of landlords and tenants met in Dublin, and after six sittings, to the general surprise, succeeded in agreeing on a unanimous report. They accepted the abolition of the dual system of land tenure as the end to be aimed at, and were of opinion that the State should advance purchase money to the tenants as the means to that end. They agreed that the landlord might fairly expect to secure as income what was left of his rental after the second judicial reduction, and that the farmers might fairly object to pay annuities more than equal to what their rental would be after the third reduction. How to bridge over this difference was the difficulty, and it is perhaps not surprising that they finally agreed that the Imperial Parliament should be invited to bridge it over by a bonus or free grant.

When Parliament met in February, 1903, Mr. Redmond moved an amendment to the Address, declaring that it was essential for the Government to take advantage of an unexampled opportunity; and, by giving full effect to the unanimous report of the Land Conference, to terminate agrarian troubles in Ireland. This amendment was accepted by the House, and on the 25th March Mr. Wyndham introduced his memorable Land Purchase Bill.

The conclusions of the report formed the basis of the bill. Advances were to be made to tenants by the State to enable them to purchase their holdings from landlords. These advances, the money for which was to be raised by the creation of stock up to a sum of £100,000,000, were to be obtained by the tenant purchasers at an interest of 2¾ per cent., with a sinking fund of ½ per cent whereby their debt would eventually be extinguished and property in their holdings become absolute.[1] In addition to this a bonus of £12,000,000 was granted to encourage landlords to sell and to help tenants to buy, and provision was made for the evicted tenants. The National Convention met in Dublin, on the 16th April, and accepted the measure subject to amendments. These amendments, according to the report of the National Directory of the United Irish League, were conceded in committee "to an extent to which no great Government measure in relation to Ireland has ever before been modified in deference to the demands of Irish public opinion". And the Act was described by Mr. Redmond as "the most substantial victory gained for centuries by the Irish race for the reconquest of the soil of Ireland by the people". The representatives of the landlords were equally well satisfied. Over 200,000 occupying tenants were enabled to buy their holdings under this Act and £77,000,000 worth of property has changed hands "on terms" wrote Lord Dunraven, "recommended as fair by representatives of tenants and landlords at the Land Conference, accepted as

The Land Purchase Bill of 1903.

---

[1] It was at first proposed that the State should retain a lien of one-eighth of the purchase money but this proposal was regarded with suspicion as a step towards the nationalisation of the land and was abandoned.

fair by the whole Irish people through their representatives in Parliament, their National Convention, their local bodies, and by every means through which the opinion of the community can be made articulate, and endorsed as fair by all parties in both branches of the Imperial legislature." For the first time since the Union, Irishmen, representing conflicting interests, had met together in order to attempt to settle agrarian differences which had proved incapable of settlement by English statesmen. After six meetings they had agreed upon a scheme which, adopted by Parliament and passed into law, has proved a greater boon to Ireland than any of the numerous reforms devised by the ingenuity of English statesmen in times of emergency to accompany as palliatives their measures of coercion.

The land question had now been settled by agreement and one of the objects of Sir Antony Macdonnell had been successfully accomplished. But there were other subjects to which, when Sir Antony accepted office, it was understood between him and the Chief Secretary that their efforts should be directed; and among them was "the co-ordination of the many detached and semi-detached forms into which the Government of Ireland is at present subdivided".[1] This was the policy which came to be known as Devolution and to be associated with the name of Lord Dunraven.

Devolution.

It was difficult to dispute that some reform was needed in this direction. A system under which sixty-seven disconnected departments costing over £3,000,000 a year maintain 100,000 officials who receive in pay half the amount spent on the Government of the country appears to be indefensible on its merits. The first important step in the direction of reform was a meeting in Dublin on the 25th August of the Landlords' Land Conference Committee, numbering some 300 Irish country gentlemen; when they adopted the name of the Irish Reform Association, and chose Lord Dunraven for their president. Their first act was to publish a manifesto in which they declared their object to be by means of "a union of all moderate and progressive opinion irrespective of creed or class animosities" to promote, "the devolution to Ireland of a large measure of self-government" without disturbing the Parlia-

Report of the Irish Reform Association.

[1] Lord Lansdowne in the House of Lords, February, 1905.

mentary union. The first report of the new association was issued in August and contained the following statement of opinion :—"While firmly maintaining that the Parliamentary union between Great Britain and Ireland is essential to the political stability of the Empire and to the prosperity of the two islands, we believe that such union is compatible with the devolution to Ireland of a larger measure of self-government than she now possesses. We consider that this devolution, while avoiding matters of Imperial concern, and subjects of common interest to the kingdom as a whole, would be beneficial to Ireland and would relieve the Imperial Parliament of a mass of business with which it cannot deal satisfactorily. In particular, we consider the subject of financial administration to be wasteful, and inappropriate to the needs of the country."

This report, in spite of loud protests from *The Times* and the Orange minority, met with no expression of disapproval from the Viceroy, Lord Dudley, or from the Chief Secretary, and the Association continued its labours through the succeeding month with the encouragement of Sir Antony Macdonnell. Their second report was issued on the 26th September, and contained a detailed scheme for devolution. The proposals had been prepared with the help of Sir Antony Macdonnell, and by him discussed with the Lord Lieutenant. Mr. Wyndham, on the other hand, was abroad and took no part in these discussions.

The second report of the Association recommended, in the first place, that a new body should be created to be known as the Irish Financial Council. Of this council the Lord-Lieutenant was to be president, the Chief Secretary vice-president, twelve members were to be elected by local bodies, voting in groups, and by Parliamentary constituencies, and eleven members were to be nominated by the Crown. This council was to be given control over purely Irish expenditure, amounting to about £6,000,000 a year, and its decisions were only to be reversible in the House of Commons by not less than a one-fourth majority of votes. One-third of the members were to retire in rotation at the end of every third year. Secondly, that a mass of Irish business with which Parliament had no time properly to deal should be delegated to an assembly composed

Second Report of the Association.

of Irish representative peers, members of Parliament, and past and present members of the Financial Council. This assembly might promote Irish bills; and other business might be delegated to it by Parliament. Thirdly, the reform of Irish Private Bill Procedure.

<small>Anger of the Orange party.</small> The publication of the report aroused the anger of the Ultra-Unionists in Ireland. This party had regarded with suspicion and discontent the appointment of Sir Antony Macdonnell, and now it seemed that their worst fears were to be justified. Devolution, they said, was worse than Home Rule. In the Ministry itself, Sir Edward Carson, the Solicitor-General, and Lord Londonderry, did not disguise their dissatisfaction. The Government, once so strong, was now, weakened by the resignation of the ablest of the Ministers on the fiscal question, at the height of its unpopularity, and could hardly have survived the revolt of another section of its supporters. Mr. Wyndham repudiated the report in strong terms and reaffirmed the integrity of his Unionist principles; but Sir Antony Macdonnell remained at his post, and during the autumn the tide of Orange discontent continued to rise. Nor was the Orange opposition the only one which the new proposals encountered. A large section of the Nationalists, led by Mr. Dillon, denounced them as a plot of the landlords and of the Government to break up the Nationalist party. This section had regarded the Land Purchase Act in the same unfavourable light, and had defeated the efforts of Mr. William O'Brien's section to guide the Irish tenants in making their bargains under the Act, taking the view that the terms suggested were too favourable to the landlords. Mr. Redmond for a while wavered, but finally threw in his lot with the Dillon party; and Mr. O'Brien for a time retired from political life.

<small>Resignation of Mr. Wyndham.</small> When Parliament met in 1905, the attacks of Irish Unionists were met somewhat lamely by Mr. Wyndham, who said that in his opinion the conduct of Sir Antony Macdonnell, though perfectly honourable, had been indefensible. In the House of Lords, Sir Antony was loyally defended by Lord Lansdowne, to whose suggestion he had originally owed his appointment. The explanations, such as they were, were followed by the resignation, not of the Under-Secretary,

whose conduct had been described as indefensible; not of the Viceroy, by whom that conduct had been approved; but of the Chief Secretary himself, discouraged by the suspicion with which, however unjustly, he had come alike by Orangemen and by Nationalists to be regarded. His tenure of office, however, had left a mark on Irish history which subsequent failure might for the moment eclipse but could not efface.

At the General Election of 1906 Home Rule was not only left out of the Liberal programme, but a pledge was given by several of the Liberal leaders that, if their party obtained a majority, they would not introduce a Home Rule Bill in the ensuing Parliament. Mr. Balfour's sudden resignation during the recess was, it is true, probably hastened by a reaffirmation on the part of Sir Henry Campbell-Bannerman of his Home Rule faith, and the instant retort of Lord Rosebery that under that banner he would never serve; but Sir Henry's declaration was regarded as academic, and great numbers of Unionists voted on the Liberal side. Sir Antony Macdonnell remained in office, and it was generally anticipated that the Liberal Government would, with his help, make proposals for devolution of a kind resembling those suggested by the Irish Reform Association in 1904. In September, 1906, Mr. Redmond declared that any proposals the Government might make, so long as they were not inconsistent with the larger policy to which the Nationalists were unalterably pledged, would be submitted to a National Convention by whose verdict the Irish party would abide. On the other hand, the Government was embarrassed by a fresh outbreak of lawlessness in the west of Ireland, where a systematic attempt was being made to force the tenants of large grazing farms to quit by driving off their cattle, in order that the vacated grazing farms might be divided up and sold to peasant proprietors. Unionists clamoured for the proclamation of the disturbed districts; but the Government were reluctant to put in force an Act to the existence of which they objected on principle; and moreover they denied the effectiveness of the proposed remedy.

The Liberals and Home Rule.

On the 7th May, 1907, Mr. Birrell, who had succeeded Mr. Bryce as Chief Secretary early in the year, introduced his Irish Councils Bill. Before its introduction he had been in communication with the Irish leaders and, as the Prime

The Irish Councils Bill of 1907.

Minister afterwards declared, "had good reason to believe that the Bill would receive the most favourable reception". The Bill, he explained, was purely administrative in character, although its success would imply a capacity for self-government in the Irish which would make an excellent argument for Home Rule, and was designed to associate the sentiment of the Irish people with the legislation directing the conduct of purely Irish affairs. He proposed that eight out of forty-five administrative boards in Ireland, including the Commissioners of National Education and the Intermediate Education Board, should be placed under the control of a central council, consisting of eighty-two members elected by the local government electors, and twenty-four members nominated by the Lord-Lieutenant. The council was to work through committees, and to sit for three years. The Lord-Lieutenant might confirm or annul, or remit for further consideration, the resolutions agreed to. A new Education Department was to be constituted in lieu of the existing Commissioners. In the matter of finance a separate "Irish Fund" was to be constituted, and an Irish Treasury established by Order in Council. In addition to the cost of the departments, amounting to about £2,000,000, which it had to administer, an annual income of £600,000 to spend on the development of Irish resources was allotted to the Council.

It is condemned by the Irish National Convention and withdrawn. These proposals found no favour in the sight of that extreme section of the Nationalist party who, unlike Mr. Parnell, were afraid that acceptance of inadequate concessions might prove fatal to their larger aims. The opposition, however, of the extremists might not of itself have sufficed to destroy the bill had they not been supported from the opposite wing of the party by the priests, who were alarmed by the clause in the bill which gave a control over Irish education to a committee of the proposed council. They felt that their ascendency was threatened, and decided on resistance. Hence it was that when the Irish National Convention met on the 21st May Mr. Redmond, whose utterances had been guarded but who was supposed to have assented to the general principles of the bill, felt himself compelled to move a condemnatory resolution to the effect that, although the Irish party were willing to consider any scheme leading up to the larger settlement of complete control over their domestic affairs, which alone could satisfy Irish aspirations, the Irish Councils Bill was inadequate in scope and unsatisfactory in detail and could not be accepted. The Government thought it useless to persevere in a measure of conciliation which the Irish themselves rejected; and the bill was withdrawn.

The end of the year was marked by an attempt at the reunion to the main body of the Irish party of that section of the Nationalists who were anxious to continue the methods adopted with so much success in the Land Conference, and to work in unison with progressive landlords and Ulstermen for Irish ends. It was agreed that Nationalists should support every measure for Irish amelioration by whatever party offered; and that, whether in or out of Parliament, they should be bound by the party pledge to support the decision of the majority of their members. But the reunion soon broke down. Mr. William O'Brien, who had been a leading member of the Land Conference, and to whom the success of that conference was largely due, was of opinion that the devolution scheme offered by the Government should have been accepted for what it was worth, and that it would have paved the way to Home Rule. His views were shared by Mr. Healy and by a few other Nationalist members. He had nevertheless drawn up the terms of reunion which were agreed to; but differences of opinion concerning the policy to be pursued with regard to the Land Purchase Act brought the treaty to an end, and warfare was resumed with additional energy. Mr. Healy joined the Unionists in their attacks on the Budget of 1909 on account of the whisky tax therein imposed, and when the general election of 1910 took place, after the rejection of that Budget by the House of Lords, the dissentients were victorious in ten constituencies.

Failure of attempt at Nationalist Reunion.

Shortly before the general election Mr. Asquith made an important declaration relating to Home Rule in a speech made at the Albert Hall. He said: "Speaking on behalf of the Government, in March of last year, a week before my accession to the office of Prime Minister, I described Ireland as the one undeniable failure of British statesmanship. I repeat here to-night what I said then, speaking on behalf of my colleagues, and I believe of my party, that the solution of the

Mr. Asquith's declaration at the Albert Hall.

problem can be found only in one way, by a policy which, while explicitly safeguarding the supremacy and indefeasible authority of the Imperial Parliament, will set up a system of full self-government in regard to purely Irish affairs. There is not, and there cannot be, any question of separation; there is not, and there cannot be, any question of rival or competing supremacies, but, subject to those conditions, that is the Liberal policy."

The Irish hold the balance in the Parliament of 1910. At the general election the Irish vote was cast for the Government, and when the polls were completed they were found to hold the balance between the parties.[1] It had so chanced that the majorities elected after the dissolutions of 1895, 1900, and 1906 were exceptionally large, and gave first to the Unionist and afterwards to the Liberal Government a majority independent of support from outside the ranks of their own adherents. Thus it came about that for fifteen years our Parliamentary system, based as it is on the presumption that a steady support will be given to each Government by a majority whose opinions it shares, and from whom it derives its commission to legislate, continued to work without difficulty, in spite of the presence in the House of Commons of eighty members who owed no allegiance to either party. It was clear, however, to reflecting minds that whenever the era of great majorities should come to an end and the Nationalist party, whose chief reason for existence was to prove that the system was unworkable, should hold the balance, that system must break down. In 1910 this contingency occurred.

[1] The numbers were 315 Liberal and Labour members, 82 Nationalists, and 273 Unionists.

CHAPTER IV.

RELIGION AND THE STATE.

THE relations of the State—or the community organised for collective action—to religion, with which English history in the sixteenth and seventeenth centuries was so much concerned, continued to play therein a lesser but still an important part in later times. That the State should profess a definite form of religion was a proposition generally admitted until the middle of the nineteenth century; and, even then, the Whig statesmen and philosophers who questioned its abstract soundness had no wish to destroy the existing connection between Church and State.[1] To protect men's souls from lawless assaults appeared to our ancestors as clearly the duty of the Government as to protect their bodies or their property, and therefore those who preached doctrines inconsistent with the established religion or observed other forms of worship were punished for their contumacy. But this system was abandoned after the Revolution of 1688 except in the case of Roman Catholics, and in their case the exception to the new rule of toleration was defended on political not on religious grounds. Thereafter, the constitutional convention that every citizen was a member of the Established Church could no longer be maintained even in theory, and the meaning attached to the term establishment had accordingly to be modified. The State, however, still claimed that all those whom it employed or to whom it assigned any share of political power should conform to the established religion; and many generations of Englishmen were yet to pass away before it was perceived that the

Relations of the State to religion.

---

[1] Macaulay, for instance, while declaring that the end of government was the protection of the persons and property of the governed, not the propagation of a creed, and that to speak of an essentially Christian State was as irrational as to speak of essentially Christian horsemanship, denied that this position implied any desire to disestablish the Church.

system of attaching worldly disadvantages and civil disabilities to the profession of dissent was not the best way to promote a genuine conformity.

Incidence of the cost of maintaining the National Church.

When after a long struggle those disabilities were at last removed, there came a further question. The Church of England was established; the State, that is to say, professed a certain form of religion; was it or was it not entitled to call upon all citizens irrespectively of their creed to contribute to the maintenance of that form of religion? Here logic and justice appeared to part company. National institutions, it was contended, are properly maintained at the public expense; the Church is established and is therefore a national institution; consequently the dissenter is no more entitled to complain when called upon to pay rates for the maintenance of the fabric of churches than the Quaker when required to contribute towards the support of the army, the very existence of which his soul abhors. The answer could only be that the practical injustice of compelling a man to support a form of religion not his own is sufficiently clear; and that to free the establishment from the reproach of all reasonable grievances is to strengthen it.

Modification of the idea of an Established Church.

Nevertheless, the idea of an establishment was largely altered by these successive concessions. The State, having in the first place abandoned the attempt to produce religious uniformity by coercion; having in the second place ceased to make conformity a condition of State employment and of a share in political power; having in the third place refused to permit the Established Church to be supported like other national institutions out of public money without regard to the creed of taxpayer or ratepayer, the notion of an establishment was gradually being reduced to a formal official recognition by the State of the creed preferred by the majority of citizens. Every further sign of preference shown by the State for the religion it continued to profess, every special mark of favour or encouragement, was coming to be generally regarded as inequitable, and a violation of that perfect religious neutrality which was still held to be consistent with the existence of an establishment. In England offices and institutions often survive in name long after they have perished in reality; and, on the other hand, they exist in reality long before their formal recognition. Thus the Cabinet Council is still unknown to the constitution; Sir Henry Campbell-Bannerman was, technically, the first of our Prime Ministers; while the Lords Spiritual are still the first estate of the realm, the Privy Council is still the body by whose advice the Crown directs its policy, and every minister is appointed or dismissed by the King at his own free discretion. So far as her temporal power is concerned, this might have been the history of the Established Church. By the gradual levelling up of other forms of religion through State recognition, her pre-eminence might grow continually less conspicuous and finally disappear were not the question complicated by the existence of her endowments. These endowments may and have been regarded in three different lights: first, as the possession of the Church of England, in the same sense as their lands are the possession of the landlords of England; secondly, as a national heritage used for the present for the maintenance of a certain form of religion, but which the nation is entitled to employ in any other way which to its discretion may appear expedient; thirdly, as a fund set apart for the maintenance of religion, bequeathed to that end, and therefore not justly to be diverted to secular uses, yet a fund which may be properly employed to endow any form of religion which, by the numbers of its adherents, can claim recognition from the State. It was on these points rather than on the more abstract question of establishment that the debates on the Irish Church in 1868 and 1869 mainly turned.

The question of Church rates had been under the consideration of Parliament for thirty-five years when in 1868 it was finally settled by an Act passed at the instance of Mr. Gladstone. The Parliament of 1859 had proved less favourable to the abolition of Church rates than its predecessor, and Sir John Trelawny's annual bill for that purpose had been rejected by small majorities in 1862 and 1863. In 1866 a compromise, first suggested by Mr. Waldegrave-Leslie, was viewed favourably by Mr. Gladstone. It was to abolish compulsory Church rates and to facilitate the raising of voluntary Church rates. In 1867 Mr. Hardcastle succeeded in passing a bill through the Commons to give effect to this arrangement; but it was rejected by the Lords upon the second reading. *Church rates, 1866-68.*

At length, in 1868, Mr. Gladstone introduced a bill founded upon the same principle. The Conservatives were still in *The Act of 1868.*

office, but the majority of the House of Commons was Liberal and followed Mr. Gladstone's lead. This was a combination of circumstances favourable to the prospects of the bill, for the Government being weak was inclined to compromise, while the House of Lords will never embarrass a Conservative Ministry by resisting its wishes. By this bill it was enacted that no suit should be instituted for the recovery of Church rates, except in cases of rates already made, or where money had been borrowed on the security of the rates. Thus the bill commended itself to Dissenters as giving up the principle of compulsion; and to Churchmen as affording a legal recognition of voluntary Church rates, and providing machinery for their assessment and collection. The Church had already been practically reduced to a voluntary system of Church rates; and this bill, if it surrendered her theoretical claims, at least saved her from further litigation and obloquy. It was approved by the Commons, and was even accepted by the Lords, after consideration by a select committee, and the addition of several amendments. And thus, at length, this long-standing controversy between Churchmen and Dissenters was brought to a close. If the Church failed in securing all her legal rights the present settlement was founded upon the practical result of a long contention in the Courts and in Parliament, and was a compromise which all parties were contented to accept.

The Irish Church.

By the census of 1861 it appeared that out of a total population of 5,800,000 in Ireland only 693,000 were members of the Established Church. So remarkable a disparity induced Mr. Dillwyn, a Liberal member, to bring forward in 1864 and 1865 motions for inquiry into the Irish Ecclesiastical Establishment. In 1865, he asked the House of Commons to affirm that the position of that Establishment was unsatisfactory and called for the early attention of the Government. Sir George Grey, Lord Palmerston's Home Secretary, resisted these motions on the ground that it was unwise to reopen troublesome issues which had disorganised Ireland in a preceding generation, especially since the grievance was theoretical and not practical, and that by any attempt to redress it a great shock would be given to our laws and institutions.

Mr. Dillwyn's motions for inquiry.

Mr. Gladstone, however, then Chancellor of the Exchequer, took a different line. Two propositions were, he said, involved in Mr. Dillwyn's resolution: (1) that the present position of the Irish Church was unsatisfactory; and (2) that it called for the early attention of the Government. To the first of these propositions he could not refuse his assent, but he based his refusal to vote for the motion on his denial of the second. The time had not yet come, he argued, for dealing with the question; and, therefore, it would be wrong for the Government to agree to an abstract resolution on which they did not propose to take action. Mr. Gladstone at that time still represented the University of Oxford; and this speech caused searchings of heart to not a few of his constituents. In the summer of the same year (1865), however, he endeavoured to reassure them by a published letter to a correspondent, in which he wrote that the question was "remote and apparently out of all bearing on the practical politics of the day".[1]

Mr. Gladstone's treatment of the question in 1865.

In 1867, when the Conservative Government was in office, and he had ceased to represent the University, Mr. Gladstone, speaking on a motion for a Committee to consider the temporalities and privileges of the Irish Church, made a long step in advance by declaring that the time could not be far distant when Parliament would have to look the position of that Church fully and fairly in the face.

A step in advance.

The question of Ireland had indeed become, as Lord Stanley, the Foreign Secretary, said, the question of the day. The Fenian conspiracy for the establishment by armed force of an Irish Republic had its origin in America, and drew its chief hopes from the energies of those Irish-Americans who had fought in the civil war, lately brought to an end in that country. The rescue of Fenian prisoners at Manchester in September, followed by the explosion at Clerkenwell prison in December, produced, in the opinion of Mr. Gladstone, an attitude of "attention and preparedness" on the part of the English people "which qualified them to embrace, in a manner foreign to their habits in other times, the vast importance of the Irish controversy".[2] In other words, these outrages had convinced Mr. Gladstone that there was now an excellent chance of persuading his countrymen to deal with a question which three years before had appeared to him remote and out of all bearing on the practical politics of the day. At Southport, in

Mr. Gladstone's Irish programme.

[1] Letter to Dr. Hannah, 8th June, 1865.   [2] Hansard, 31st May, 1869.

December, he declared for a policy of reform which should pacify Ireland—reform ecclesiastical, agrarian, and educational.

Conservative proposals.

In the few days of the following session that preceded the retirement of Lord Derby, it was found necessary to carry rapidly through Parliament a bill to renew the suspension of the Habeas Corpus Act in Ireland, for the third year in succession. The Government had, in 1867, appointed a Commission to inquire into the nature and amount of the property and revenues of the Irish Church. They had also adumbrated a policy of concurrent endowment, together with the institution of a new Catholic university, and had promised an inquiry into the relations of landlord and tenant.

Mr. Gladstone's declaration.

On the 5th March, 1868, Mr. Disraeli took his seat in the House of Commons as First Lord of the Treasury and Prime Minister. On the 10th, a motion was made by Mr. Maguire to draw attention to the state of Ireland. Speaking on this motion, Mr. Gladstone declared himself openly and decisively. The Government were inquiring through their Commission into the revenues of the Irish Church. They now promised legislation for the provision of Irish railways, a Roman Catholic University, and compensation to Irish tenants for their improvements. But Mr. Gladstone declared that the time had come for more drastic measures—that justice delayed was justice denied—and that what was necessary was to terminate the existence of the Church in Ireland as a State Church, to redress the grievances of the Irish tenantry, and to provide adequately for Irish education. These were the three branches of the Irish upas-tree which it had become necessary, in Mr. Gladstone's view, to prune; and to this task he now addressed himself with the concentrated energy which always characterised him when a definite goal was in sight. In his answer Mr. Disraeli, after bewailing the unhappy fate which made the commencement of his own ministerial career coincide with the imperative necessity of immediately settling an account seven centuries old, denied the moral competence of the House to deal with a question undiscussed at the time of its election without a previous appeal to the country. This objection raised an important constitutional issue; and by a singular inversion of parts Mr. Disraeli now appeared as the champion of the democratic theory of the mandate, while Mr. Gladstone, perceiving an obstacle in his path and eager to overthrow it, maintained, with his customary passionate eagerness, the uncontrolled right of Parliament to deal with what subjects it pleased.

On the 30th March, Mr. Gladstone moved that the House should resolve itself into a Committee to consider certain resolutions in which he had embodied the first instalment of his new Irish policy. The Government met this motion by an amendment, moved by Lord Stanley, to the effect that the House, "while admitting that considerable modifications in the temporalities of the Irish Church might, after the pending inquiry, appear to be expedient, was of opinion that any proposition tending to the disestablishment and disendowment of that Church ought to be reserved for the decision of a new Parliament". Though the principle involved in this amendment, that a Parliament is morally disqualified from dealing with a great question which has never been brought before the country, has been accepted by a later generation, it was denounced at the time in unmeasured terms by Mr. Gladstone, who, although he expressed his regret that it was beyond his power to exhibit in its true colours the atrocity of the doctrine, certainly succeeded in making his disapproval sufficiently clear. Nor would it be just to doubt his sincerity when we remember that in 1886 he proposed a still greater change, never yet brought before the electorate though a General Election had just taken place. The amendment was rejected by a majority of sixty.[1] *Mr. Gladstone's resolutions.* *Lord Stanley's amendment.*

On the 30th April, after the Easter adjournment, the first of Mr. Gladstone's resolutions was carried by a majority of sixty-five.[2] It affirmed: "That it is necessary that the Established Church of Ireland should cease to exist as an establishment; due regard being had to all personal interests and to all individual rights of property". This resolution having been carried, Mr. Gladstone moved and carried a second and third consequential upon it, and followed them up by the introduction of a bill to suspend the creation of new interests in the Irish Church. This bill was passed by the Commons, against the opposition of the Government; but rejected by a large majority in the Lords. *Suspensory Bill rejected by the Lords.*

[1] 330 to 270.   [2] 330 to 265.

The dissolution of 1868.

At the General Election which followed in the autumn the main issue was the policy of disestablishing the Irish Church; the second was the confidence to be reposed, by the majority of the electors, in one or other of the great political parties, whose policy, character, and conduct had recently been displayed in the contentions of the three last eventful years.

Its decisive results.

The result of the election was decisive of these issues. All the conditions of success were on the side of the Liberal party. The policy of disestablishing the Irish Church united English dissenters, Scottish Presbyterians, and Irish Roman Catholics with Liberal politicians of every shade, who had long regarded that institution as theoretically indefensible. There was accordingly sent to Parliament a majority of about 120, pledged to support Mr. Gladstone and to vote for the disestablishment of the Irish Church. The new administration formed by Mr. Gladstone united Peelites, Whigs, and advanced Liberals: it embraced Mr. Bright and Mr. Lowe.

Church Bill, 1869.

Then was witnessed the extraordinary power of a Government representing the popular will, under an extended franchise. Mr. Gladstone had committed himself to the boldest measure of modern times. Thirty years before, the House of Lords and the Conservative party had successfully resisted the theoretical assertion of the right of the State to appropriate the surplus revenues of the Irish Church; and now it was proposed to disestablish and disendow that Church, and, after the satisfaction of existing interests, to apply the bulk of its revenues to secular purposes. Founded upon the principle of religious equality, it was a masterly measure—thorough in its application of that principle—and complete in all its details. Given the principle,—which the verdict of the electors had endorsed—its legislative workmanship was consummate. The Church was severed from the state, and its bishops deprived of their seats in Parliament. At the same time, the annual grants to Presbyterian ministers, in the form of *regium donum*, and to the Roman Catholic College of Maynooth, were commuted.

Its scope and character.

The Irish Church bill which Mr. Gladstone introduced and explained in perhaps the greatest speech he ever made, passed rapidly and with little alteration through the House of Commons. Mr. Gladstone had received from the country a commission to deal with the question, and there was nothing in the machinery of the bill to offend those who were pledged to its principle. Existing interests were dealt with in a generous spirit. A governing body was established to represent the Church and to hold its property; and to the charge of this body were committed the fabrics of all the churches with the churchyards, while it was enabled to acquire the glebe houses on easy terms. More than half of the total property of the Church was given back to the Church. It was on the disposal of the surplus of seven or eight millions which remained after this had been done that the last stand of the opponents of the measure was made.

Eight years before, in an address on the position of the Church of England, Mr. Disraeli had advanced the general proposition that the most powerful principle which governs man is the religious principle, and had drawn from it the conclusion that a wise Government would seek to include such an element in its means of influencing man. Otherwise, he added, "it would leave in society a principle stronger than itself, which in due season may assert its supremacy, and even, perhaps, in a destructive manner".[1] It was for this reason that he now maintained the position that the disestablishment of the Protestant Church in Ireland should be accompanied by a distribution of its surplus funds among the other religious communities in that country. In this there would be, in his opinion, a double gain. In the first place, the principle of property would not be violated, because those funds would be devoted to the purposes for which they had been granted or bequeathed; and, in the second place, the Roman Catholic priests would be brought into direct relations with the Government, which would then hold some security for their good conduct. This policy of "concurrent endowment" had been advocated by statesmen and philosophers since early in the eighteenth century; it was an essential part of the policy of Pitt at the time of the union; and would have been then carried out by him had he not been thwarted by the disastrous scruples of a half-insane king. The *regium donum* to the Presbyterians and the Maynooth College were experiments in the same direction, but now, through the opposition of the Nonconformists, who thought that any State

[1] Kebbel, Selected Speeches of Lord Beaconsfield, vol. ii. p. 562.

provision for Roman Catholics was State encouragement of deadly error, a fair opportunity was once more lost. It is not probable that the memory of George III. is held in much esteem by Nonconformists, yet it must be confessed that on this occasion they inherited and continued the policy of that monarch.

The Lords accept principle of bill.

The question of the disposal of the surplus fund was the last to be settled; and on it the bill was nearly wrecked. But before it could be raised in the House of Lords the assent of that assembly to the principle of the measure on the second reading had to be secured; and to many it seemed probable that it would be refused. The queen disliked the bill; but, perceiving with her customary good sense that after the nation had pronounced judgment on the question further resistance was inevitably doomed to ultimate failure and might involve danger to the constitution, she exerted her influence to effect a compromise. She brought Mr. Gladstone into communication with the Archbishop of Canterbury, and so far prevailed that the Archbishop recommended to the Lords that the bill should be read a second time with a view to amending it in Committee and saving for the Church from the wreck as much as might be possible. The bill was probably saved by her Majesty's intervention; and was read a second time in the Lords on the 18th June by a majority of thirty-three.[1]

The disposal of the surplus fund.

By the bill as it left the Commons, the surplus fund of the Irish Church had been devoted to the relief of the suffering and the insane. But the support of these unhappy people was then, as now, a charge on the rates, so that the proposal was open to the objection that the allocation of this great sum for their maintenance would be in effect a bonus to owners of real property, while the sum being much greater than was needed for economical administration, there would be danger of extravagance. The Lords then were well justified in reserving by their amendments for the future consideration of Parliament the manner in which the surplus property of the Church should be dealt with. Having done this, they proceeded to introduce the principle of concurrent endowment by empowering the Commissioners, charged with the administration of the fund, to provide suitable residences where they were required for the clergy of the disestablished Church, for Roman Catholic priests,

[1] 179 to 146.

and for Presbyterian ministers. This amendment was carried by a majority of only seven on the motion of Lord Stanhope.[1] The voting was not strictly on party lines, for the amendment was supported by Lord Russell and opposed by Lord Derby and Lord Cairns.

When the bill was returned to the Commons the Lords' amendments were treated with little respect by the Government and their obedient majority. By these amendments the provision made for the disestablished Church had been increased by some four millions; the date at which the Act was to come into operation had been postponed for a year; and the principle of concurrent endowment had been introduced in respect of a part of the surplus fund by Lord Stanhope's amendment, while its application to the whole of it was reserved for the future consideration of Parliament by an alteration in the words of the preamble. The Government agreed to make some further pecuniary concessions to the Church, amounting in all to about £700,000, but they refused to agree to the postponement of disestablishment or to the amendments relating to the surplus fund. The final struggle took place over the words of the preamble. The Lords at first insisted on the retention of the words which they had inserted, and those words the Government refused to accept. The queen once more endeavoured through the Archbishop of Canterbury to effect a compromise; but this time without success. Eventually Lord Cairns—who had himself voted against Lord Stanhope's amendment—arranged a compromise with Lord Granville to which the Lords agreed. It was settled that the surplus fund should be appropriated to the relief of unavoidable suffering in the manner Parliament should hereafter provide. This compromise, while it precluded the employment of the fund for religious purposes, and thus satisfied the minds of those who held that the State should have nothing to do with religion, gave more freedom of action to future Governments in its application than had been originally proposed. The bill, unchanged in every essential point, was then passed into law.

[2] Other questions affecting the interests of churchmen, dis-

_{The Commons disagree with the chief amendments of the Lords. The bill passed.}

---

[1] 121 to 114.
[2] This, and the succeeding five paragraphs are reproduced from Sir Erskine May's supplementary chapter.

212 THE CONSTITUTIONAL HISTORY OF ENGLAND

University tests.

senters, and Roman Catholics were also pressing for a settlement at this time. Foremost of these was that of religious tests at the universities by which dissenters were denied their share in the privileges and endowments of those national seats of learning for which churchmen alone were qualified.

The injustice of this exclusion had been repeatedly discussed: but it was not until 1866 that the entire Liberal party were determined to redress it. In that year a bill, introduced by Mr. Coleridge, was passed by the Commons and rejected by the Lords. Again, in 1868, the second reading of a bill with the same objects, introduced by Mr. Coleridge, was agreed to after full discussion and by a large majority,[1] but was prevented, by the pressure of other measures, from being further proceeded with in that session.

University Tests Bills of 1869 and 1870.

In 1869 a similar bill was passed by the Commons and again rejected by the Lords. Again, in 1870, the University Tests Bill was passed by the Commons, and referred by the Lords to a select committee, whose deliberations deferred the bill to another session. But, at length, in 1871, the same bill, having again been sent up to the Lords, was ultimately agreed to.

University Tests Act, 1871.

This Act, stating that the benefits of these Universities "shall be freely accessible to the nation," enacted that persons taking lay academical degrees or holding lay academical or collegiate offices in the Universities of Oxford, Cambridge, or Durham shall not be required to subscribe any religious test or formulary. But as it did not open to dissenters the headships of colleges, or professorships of divinity, or offices required to be held by persons in holy orders or by churchmen, some dissatisfaction was still expressed at this settlement. Otherwise another controversy was, at length, closed; and one of the last grievances of dissenters redressed.

Ecclesiastical Titles Act, 1871.

Another religious controversy was in the same year settled by Parliament. The celebrated Ecclesiastical Titles Act was an offence to Roman Catholics, while it was wholly inoperative as a protection against the Church of Rome. After an inquiry into its operation by a Committee of the House of Lords, in 1868, and discussion in both Houses concerning the form in which the law should be expressed rather than its

[1] By 198 against 140.

policy, the Act was eventually repealed, with the general acquiescence of all parties. The law and the queen's prerogative in regard to ecclesiastical titles and jurisdiction were again asserted by Parliament, but the original Act with its penalties, which had never been enforced, was removed from the statute book.

Of all social questions none can be compared in importance with that of the education of the people. Not only is it essential to their moral, intellectual, and material welfare, but at a time when large masses of the community had recently been invested with political power, it was obviously the duty of the State to apply itself earnestly to the task of popular enlightenment; and this task was undertaken immediately after the new scheme of representation had been completed. *Education.*

The view, however, that the education of the people was an essential part of the duties of the State was of late origin. During the long period of Tory ascendency before 1830 the ruling party was inclined to regard Church and State as two aspects of the same "person"—the Church being the community organised for religious purposes just as the State was the same community organised for political purposes. The only kind of education for the people thought to be important or even desirable was religious education, and to supply this was clearly the duty of the Church. In every parish was a parish clergyman, whose duty it was to see that every child within his jurisdiction was taught its catechism. Provision then was already made for the education of the people, and the State had nothing more to do with the matter. *Education of the people. Original Tory view of the subject.*

The Whigs, who succeeded to office in 1830, and who maintained their predominance with a single interruption for nearly half a century, took a different view. To them the secular education of the people appeared a matter of great importance, and their traditions were unfriendly to the Church. But their political philosophy had been deeply affected by Benthamism, and from Bentham they learnt that State interference should in every direction be restricted within the narrowest limits, and that the best results are always obtained from voluntary effort under the pressure of competition. Therefore, to encourage the voluntary efforts that had been made by the Church, and in a less degree by other religious bodies, and *Whig policy with regard to education.*

by these alone, for the education of the people, appeared to them the right policy. This they did by Parliamentary grants in aid, which increased in amount until in 1861 the sum reached was £813,442. The great cause of increase had been the capitation grant paid to the managers of schools under a certificated teacher for each child who had attended school for a certain number of days in the year. By his revised code,[1] in 1861, Mr. Lowe supplemented this arrangement by requiring that the child, before he could earn the capitation grant, should not only have attended school on the stated number of days but should satisfy examiners that he had learned how to write, read, and cipher. The effect of this change was to reduce by 1865 the annual Parliamentary grant to £636,000. This was increased by the Conservative Ministry in 1867; and by 1870 had again reached its former highest level.

The Revised Code of 1861.

Of the 4,300,000 poor children in need of education in England in 1869 it was calculated that 2,000,000 were not at school at all; that 1,300,000 were in State-aided schools; and that 1,000,000 were in other schools, which, since they submitted to no standard and received no grant, might fairly be presumed to be inefficient. The state-aided schools cost £1,600,000 a year, of which it was estimated that about one-third was provided by the State, one-third by the fees of the children, and the remaining third by the voluntary subscriptions of 200,000 persons. It had thus become clear that with whatever zeal and fidelity and pecuniary sacrifice the Church and other religious bodies had endeavoured to fulfil the task committed or left to them by the State they no longer had the strength to cope with it, and that, if it were the duty of the Government to secure to every child the benefits of elementary education, the time for legislative action had arrived.

Educational statistics in 1869.

Great advances indeed had been made in England since 1834. But as the system was entirely founded upon local and voluntary efforts, it too often happened that the places which most needed the civilising agency of the schoolmaster were left destitute. All parties admitted the necessity of providing more effectual means for the general education of the people; but the old "religious difficulty" caused the widest divergence

Divergent aims.

---

[1] The minutes of the Committee of Council on Education were codified in 1860, from which time the yearly issue was known as the Code.

of opinions concerning the principles upon which education should be conducted. The Church party naturally desired to retain the teaching of the Church catechism, with a liberal conscience clause for the satisfaction of dissenters. Another party, known as Secularists, advocated secular education only in the schools, leaving religious instruction to be sought elsewhere. Another party, again, insisted upon religious instruction in the schools, while they objected to the Church catechism and formularies.

In 1870 Mr. Gladstone's Government were prepared with a scheme for a settlement of this great social question. The bill which embodied it was introduced by Mr. Forster, the Vice-President of the Council. Although it was proposed that the Legislature should for the first time recognise its responsibilities with regard to the education of the people, the bill did not supplant but supplemented the existing system. Mr. Forster proposed to divide the country into educational districts, and to make each district responsible to the central government for the education of the children within its borders. Where the existing provision for elementary education was adequate no change was to be made, provided that the school was open to all, and that a conscience clause exempted from attendance during the hours of religious instruction the children of parents who objected to it. Where, on the other hand, there was no adequate school accommodation the local authorities were to appoint School Boards. These boards were to have power to levy rates, either to assist the existing voluntary schools or to establish new schools where they were needed. In the latter case they were in each separate instance to decide the character of the religious instruction to be given. The school boards were further permitted to make by-laws compelling parents to send their children to school.

Mr. Forster's proposals in 1870.

These proposals encountered the strongest objections, not only from the Nonconformists but from the whole of the left wing of the Liberal party, and in order to pass their bill the Government had to remodel it completely. In the first place they agreed that the boards, instead of being nominated by the town councils in the towns and by vestries in the country, should be elected by the ratepayers and that the elections should be by ballot. Provision was made for the representation

Elementary Education Act, 1870.

of minorities on the boards by the adoption of the cumulative vote. Next, as a concession to the Liberal principle that rate-supported institutions should be under the control of the ratepayers, the school boards were precluded from levying rates for the assistance of voluntary schools, although to make up for this loss the State grant was increased; thirdly, the Government agreed that the form of religious instruction to be given in board schools should not be left to the discretion of local authorities, but should be governed by the rule, first suggested by Mr. Cowper-Temple, that "no catechism, or religious formulary, which is distinctive of any particular denomination should be taught"; and, fourthly, that any district which applied for a school board might have it, whether or not the existing school accommodation were adequate. The more militant Nonconformists were not satisfied by these concessions. They objected to any State aid being given to the voluntary schools, by far the greater number of which were in the hands of the Church of England; and they complained that the bill did not make the education of children as a general rule compulsory, or abolish the payment of fees. But the mass of the people were content. They desired that religious instruction should be continued in the schools, and religious instruction was retained. On the other hand, they objected to dogmatic teaching in schools supported by the rates, and the Cowper-Temple compromise satisfied them in this respect also. It was a sign of the times that any wish to give special facilities to the form of religion professed by the State, any intention to propagate the established faith, was eagerly disclaimed by both parties. The retention of the voluntary schools was defended on quite other grounds. Sudden and violent changes of system were deemed to be contrary to the genius of the English people; to their slow growth and gradual development our institutions were thought to owe their strength; the voluntary system was in accord with the reigning doctrines of *laissez-faire;* it was approved in principle; and it was thought that all that was needed to perfect it was a more complete organisation and extended means.

In 1873 Mr. Gladstone addressed himself to the remaining branch of that upas-tree of Protestant ascendency in Ireland which he had undertaken to hew down. Religious equality of a negative kind had been secured by the disestablishment of the Irish Church; the relations between landlord and tenant had been readjusted in the interests of the latter by the Land Act of 1870; there remained the question of education. *Question of Irish University education.*

Roman Catholics had been admitted to degrees at Trinity College—the college which of itself constituted the University of Dublin—since 1793; and for half a century after that date had freely availed themselves of the privilege. But the University was governed by a senate, and the senate was composed of the Provost and seven senior Fellows of Trinity College, who were obliged to be members of the Established Church. When, in 1845, the unsectarian Queen's University was founded and endowed by the Government of Sir Robert Peel, the opposition to the "godless colleges" came at first rather from Tory Churchmen than from Roman Catholics. But soon after that date a strong movement towards centralisation made itself felt in the Roman Church. Under Pius IX. the Jesuits acquired great influence, the spiritual pretensions of Rome increased as her temporal power diminished, and the theory that for the right education of Roman Catholics a purely Roman Catholic atmosphere and exclusively Roman Catholic teachers were essential came to prevail. So it came about that not only were the Queen's Colleges denounced as pernicious to faith and morals, but Trinity College itself was proscribed, and the Roman Catholic youth of Ireland were excluded by the new principles of their directors from university training and degrees. *Position of Trinity College.*

However unreasonable this self-denying ordinance on the part of the Irish Roman Catholics might appear, the fact remained that there was no University in Ireland to which Roman Catholic fathers thought it permissible to send their sons. In 1866, Lord Russell's Government endeavoured to meet the difficulty by amending the charter of the Queen's University so as to permit that body to grant degrees to students other than those who had passed through a course of study at one of the three existing unsectarian colleges. But the courts held that such an amendment would require legislation and that the supplementary charter was invalid.

Proposals of Lord Mayo in 1868 and of Mr. Fawcett in 1870.

In 1868, Lord Mayo, Chief Secretary under the Conservative Government, proposed to establish a new university under Roman Catholic management, without interfering with Trinity College or the Queen's Colleges. This was an extension of the principle of concurrent endowment; and the opponents of that principle had no difficulty in securing its rejection. In 1870, and in the two following years, Mr. Fawcett, with the support of Trinity College itself, attempted to remove what in his view was the only real grievance of Irish Roman Catholics by abolishing the tests which excluded them from the senate and from fellowships in the University of Dublin. The Government resisted or evaded his proposals on the plea that they themselves had undertaken to deal with the matter and could not abandon their initiative. In 1873, they endeavoured to carry out their pledge. By the bill which he introduced in that year—the passing of which he declared to be vital to the Government—Mr. Gladstone proposed to create a new University of Dublin with endowments derived from Trinity College, from the Church surplus, and from the Consolidation Fund. This University was to be governed by a Council which was to appoint its officers and to be given power to affiliate to the central body colleges throughout Ireland, whether denominational or undenominational. Trinity College and the Queen's Colleges were to form part of the new University; but the faculty of theology at Trinity was to be transferred to the disestablished Irish Church. At the new University, neither theology nor moral philosophy nor modern history were to be taught; and any professor who by his language, written or spoken, should offend against the religious convictions of any student was to be liable to suspension or removal from his office. On the other hand, the forbidden subjects might be freely treated in the affiliated colleges. This bill was defeated on the second reading. The "gagging clauses," as they were called, were generally unpopular; the Irish Protestants thought that the effect of the bill might be to enable the Roman Catholics to secure a majority on the council and thereby to control University education in Ireland; while the Roman Catholics complained that no endowments were provided by the bill for their proposed colleges to counterbalance those already enjoyed by

Irish University Bill, 1873.

Its defeat on second reading.

Trinity and the Queen's Colleges. Later in the session, Mr. Fawcett, who had helped to defeat the Government bill, carried, with the acquiescence of Ministers, his own measure for abolishing tests at Trinity College. This act of justice, however, was of small practical importance, since it did not enable Roman Catholics to whom a Protestant "atmosphere" was an insurmountable barrier to secure for their sons University training or degrees, and so the problem was left over for a later generation to solve.

When the Conservatives succeeded to office in 1874, they made one vain attempt to restore some of her lost power to the Church of England. The endowed schools of England—schools enjoying in the aggregate an income of £592,000 a year—had been in 1867 the subject of an inquiry by a Royal Commission. The Commission had reported that a large proportion of them were "in a feeble and decaying condition" with a decreasing number of scholars and defective instruction. In 1869, Mr. Forster, who had been a member of the Commission, carried through Parliament a measure to deal with these evils. By this Act an executive body called the Endowed Schools Commissioners was appointed for three years with powers to frame new schemes for educational endowments. Under these schemes no one was to be disqualified for the governing body of a school, or for a mastership therein, by reason of his religious opinions; unless it had been the evident intention of the founder that the school should belong to a particular denomination. By their interpretation of this provision the Commissioners were able to open the doors of endowed schools to many children who had hitherto been shut out through the Nonconformity of their parents, but their action in so doing caused much dissatisfaction among Churchmen. *The Endowed Schools Act, 1869.*

The Commission was continued, after the expiration of their three years, until the 15th of August, 1874, and before that day arrived the Conservatives had replaced the Liberals in office. The new Ministry determined to continue the work of the Commission; but to transfer it to the Charity Commissioners. The bill which they introduced to effect this transfer contained a proposal which, had it been carried, would have restored to the Church of England the exclusive possession of the great majority of endowed schools. They proposed that whenever *The Endowed Schools Bill, 1874.*

the founders of a school had required that the scholars should attend the church of a particular denomination, or that the school regulations should be submitted to an officer of that denomination, the school must be presumed to belong to that church. Since, however, the large majority of the schools concerned had been founded at a time when no form of religion except that of the Church of England was permitted to be officially taught, and since in those days all parties were agreed that religious instruction was an indispensable element in education, it was natural that the founders of most of the schools, having to choose between the established religion and none, should have made arrangements for the attendance at church of the scholars or the submission for approval of the school regulations to the bishop of the diocese. Thirty-five of these schools had been founded, before the Reformation, when the Church of England was still in communion with Rome; forty-four of them during the Commonwealth when Presbyterianism was established by Parliamentary ordinance; but whether Anglican, Roman, or Presbyterian, the Church of England was in theory the Church of the whole nation; and the founders of schools who desired to make any arrangements for religious instruction or observances in the schools they founded could only do so within the limits of the national religion. The school endowments, therefore, might reasonably be considered as a national heritage, whereas the effect of the Government proposals would have been to confine by a religious test the benefits of the greater part of those endowments to a single denomination. Such a measure, at a time when religious tests at the Universities had recently been abolished, was plainly contrary to the spirit of the age, and the Government was obliged to abandon it. These difficulties had arisen because Conservatives had not yet quite perceived that the Church establishment in the sense attached to that term by their ancestors had long since disappeared. Time is the great disestablisher; and it is the business of man to adjust endowments to time-altered circumstances. Formerly the fact of the establishment implied that the State claimed to be in possession of religious truth. The Church was the State ecclesiastically considered. Whether the established religion were Roman, Anglican, or Presbyterian, the State could not countenance the formal propagation of error. The first great measure of disestablishment was the Toleration Act of 1689; the second, the relief of dissenting schoolmasters in 1779 from subscription to the Thirty-nine Articles.

If, however, in 1874 the Conservative Government failed to secure for the Church of England certain advantages to be derived from her connection with the State, it was more successful in bringing home to an important section of Churchmen some of the disadvantages attaching to that connection. The Public Worship Regulation Bill was not indeed a Government measure, but it could never have been passed into law without the assistance of the Prime Minister. The object of the bill was to simplify the procedure by which the illegal practices of ritualistic clergymen might be restrained. Introduced into the House of Lords by the Archbishop of Canterbury, it was radically changed in committee at the instance of Lord Shaftesbury; and provided, in its final form, for the appointment of a new lay judge by the two Archbishops before whom complaints of illegal practices might be brought against a clergyman with the consent of his diocesan. If the complainants succeeded in proving their case the judge was to issue a monition for the discontinuance of the practices impugned. Mr. Disraeli, perhaps inaccurately, described an Act which was concerned only with methods of procedure as a bill "to put down ritualism". In any case, if the suppression of ritualism was the object of the new law, it proved a complete failure. Some of the most devoted and hard-working of the clergy were to be found among the ritualists; and men whose consciences enabled them to endure without flinching the unpopularity and contempt, which the novelty of their symbolical innovations or restitutions brought upon them amid a conservative people, were not likely to be intimidated at the prospect of a monition from a lay judge. Mr. Gladstone returned to the House of Commons to oppose the bill; but the only effect of his opposition was to secure for it the support of Mr. Disraeli, and thus to enable it to pass. The debates, however, and the measure itself weakened the attachment of Mr. Gladstone and other High Churchmen to the cause of establishment.

The Public Worship Regulation Act, 1874.

In the same session, an Act to transfer lay patronage in the

Patronage in the Scottish Church. Scottish Church from the patrons to the male communicants of each kirk was also passed, in spite of the opposition of Mr. Gladstone, who now perceived in the House of Commons a tendency to become "a debased copy of an ecclesiastical council".[1] Ecclesiastical questions, however, were not much to the fore during the remainder of this Parliament. The new Court established by the Public Worship Regulation Act met under Lord Penzance in February, 1876, but its activities did little to check ritualistic illegality, and only elicited from the Church Union a denial of the authority of any secular court in matters spiritual.

The Parliamentary oath. In the succeeding Parliament the question of religious tests reappeared in an unexpected form. It had been thought that the controversy concerning Parliamentary oaths had been finally settled by an Act of 1866, which substituted for the various oaths in force another, to which no man whose religion admitted the legitimacy of any kind of oath, could object. It was true that the concluding adjuration "so help me God" would be meaningless to an atheist; but the fact that Mr. John Stuart Mill had sworn (1865) according to the older form, "on the true faith of a Christian," was sufficient to prove that a man, whose high principles were beyond dispute, would not scruple to make use of the formula prescribed by law in order to register an engagement by which he held himself to be bound, even though its terms were in part not applicable to himself. Yet the words, "on the true faith of a Christian," do involve a formal profession of faith, whereas the words of adjuration merely reinforce a declaration by a sanction which to the unbeliever has no efficacy.

Mr. Bradlaugh elected member for Northampton, 1880. At the general election of 1880, Mr. Charles Bradlaugh was returned to Parliament as junior member for Northampton. His life had been a hard struggle. Self-educated, but well-educated, he had been a private soldier and a solicitor's clerk—a training useful to him in after life when his extraordinary forensic ability was never hampered by any unwillingness to engage in a fight. Honest, combative, and courageous, a most effective platform speaker, and sustained by a consciousness of his own good faith, he had spent his life in attacking received opinions in religion and politics. He had assailed Christianity

---

[1] Life of Gladstone, vol. ii. p. 502.

with the zeal of a Christian martyr, and if fortitude in the endurance of hardships and obloquy may be considered a proof of sincerity and disinterestedness he could produce before the end of his career a record seldom in modern times exceeded. He was not only a militant atheist but a militant republican, who had published an " Impeachment of the House of Brunswick," and his attacks were rendered the more formidable by the fact that the man was no vulgar demagogue, but a master of clear and incisive English, who, while indulging his joy in combat, believed that he was furthering the best interests of his countrymen. By accepting responsibility for the publication of an American pamphlet concerning the evils of over-population and their remedies, Mr. Bradlaugh exposed himself in 1877 to a criminal prosecution as a purveyor of obscene literature, and only escaped imprisonment by a technical flaw in the indictment. This incident gave to his opponents an excuse for attacking his character and morals with which a minute scrutiny of his career would not otherwise have provided them.[1]

The first business of a new Parliament, after the election of a Speaker, is the swearing in of members. Mr. Bradlaugh had no conscientious objections to taking the oath, but thought that he was entitled under the existing law to make affirmation in lieu thereof. Being supported in this view by the late law officers of the Liberal Government, he privately communicated to Mr. Speaker Brand his wish to affirm. Afterwards, at the Speaker's invitation, he submitted to the Chair his claim to make affirmation under the Parliamentary Oaths Act, 1866. This Act gave the right to affirm to every person for the time being permitted to make affirmation. Mr. Bradlaugh contended that he was such a person, because under the Evidence Amendment Acts, 1869 and 1870, he had repeatedly made affirmation, instead of taking the oath, in courts of justice. The weak point in this position clearly was that the Act of 1866 gave the right to affirm only to persons then entitled to make affirmation; whereas Mr. Bradlaugh's affirmations in courts of law had been made by virtue of later Acts. Mr. Bradlaugh did

He claims to make affirmation instead of taking the oath.

---

[1] It is only fair to add that the pamphlet had been on sale in England for forty years, and had been presented to the London University by Mr. Grote, the historian.

not refuse to take the oath; but, wrongly imagining that an alternative course was open to him, claimed, in the first instance, to be permitted to make affirmation.

Select Committee reports against his claim.

This claim the Speaker referred to the House; and a Select Committee was appointed to inquire whether persons entitled to affirm under the Evidence Amendment Acts were, under the Parliamentary Oaths Act, 1866, also entitled to affirm as members of Parliament. The Committee, by the casting vote of its Chairman, reported that they were not so entitled. Thereupon Mr. Bradlaugh published a statement of his position, in which he announced his intention to take the oath; and, while regretting that he should be obliged to use words which would be to him but a "meaningless addendum" to the promise he was about to make, said clearly that he should none the less regard himself as bound by the spirit of that promise.

A second Select Committee.

Accordingly, on the 21st May, Mr. Bradlaugh presented himself at the table to take the oath. Thereupon, Sir Henry Wolff objected to its administration; and the Speaker admitted his intervention. Mr. Bradlaugh, having withdrawn, Sir Henry explained the reasons of his objection. These were that Mr. Bradlaugh, having implicitly admitted, by his claim to make affirmation under the Evidence Amendment Acts, that an oath was not binding on his conscience, and having avowed his disloyalty in his "Impeachment of the House of Brunswick," he was at once the type of man whom the oath was especially designed to bind, and one whom by his own confession it was totally incapable of binding. The Government, having been informed by their Whip that the feeling in the House against Mr. Bradlaugh was uncontrollable and that their majority was not to be relied upon, proposed and carried a motion to refer the question to a second Select Committee.

They report that Mr. Bradlaugh cannot legally take the oath.

Although Mr. Bradlaugh explicitly stated to this Committee that he should regard any oath that he took as binding on his conscience to the fullest degree, and that he would take no oath or go through any form unless he meant it to be so binding, they reported that an oath taken by him would not be an oath "within the true meaning of the statutes," because he had brought to the notice of the House that he was a person whom the judges had allowed to make affirmation after having satisfied themselves on his own declaration that an oath was "not binding on his conscience". But they suggested that he should be allowed to make affirmation in order that his right so to do might be tested by action at law.

Mr. Labouchere, in accordance with the recommendation of the Committee, moved (June 21) that Mr. Bradlaugh should be allowed to affirm instead of taking the oath. His resolution was supported by the Government; but was defeated on a division by a majority of forty-five.[1] Mr. Bradlaugh was thus allowed neither to swear nor to affirm. A duly elected member, who was ready to make his declaration of allegiance in any form that statute or the orders of the House might prescribe, was prevented from taking his seat without being expelled; and Northampton, by a resolution of the House, was deprived for the rest of the Parliament of half of its representation. *He is allowed neither to affirm nor take the oath.*

On the following day, Mr. Bradlaugh was allowed to plead his cause at the bar of the House. With an ability, dignity, and self-restraint, which surprised an audience to whom in the preceding debate he had been represented as a vulgar demagogue, and who had laughed in derision when Mr. Bright spoke of his "honour and conscience," he defended his own rights and those of his constituents. After further discussion, he was then called to the table, and ordered to withdraw. This he declined to do; whereupon, on the motion of Sir Stafford Northcote—Mr. Gladstone having declined to offer any guidance to the House after the rejection of his own solution of the difficulty—he was committed to the Clock Tower, from which on the next day he was, by a fresh resolution of the House, unconditionally released. Subsequently (1st July) Mr. Gladstone moved, as a standing order, that members elect should be allowed, subject to any liability by statute, to affirm at their choice; and in this more general form he succeeded in persuading a majority of the House to give effect to the recommendation of the Select Committee. *Mr. Bradlaugh at the bar of the House. He declines to withdraw and is imprisoned in the Clock Tower.*

Mr. Bradlaugh now made affirmation and took his seat; but he had no sooner given his first vote than he was served with a writ suing for penalty. In the litigation which followed judgment was given for the plaintiff, both by the Court of *Under a new Standing Order he makes affirmation and takes his seat. Litigation.*

[1] 275 to 230.

Queen's Bench (11th March, 1881) and by the Court of Appeal (31st March); the judges holding that the Parliamentary Oaths Act, 1866, was intended to apply to persons who, like Quakers, were at the time it was passed permitted by law to make affirmation in all cases, and not to those who, by subsequent legislation, should be so permitted on particular occasions and for particular purposes. The judgment of the Court of Appeal vacated Mr. Bradlaugh's seat, but he was again returned to Parliament by the electors of Northampton.

Subsequent proceedings 1882-85.
During the three following years the struggle continued. Again and again Mr. Bradlaugh presented himself to be sworn; again and again the House refused him permission to swear. On one occasion he refused to withdraw and was ejected by force. In February, 1882, he came to the table, administered the oath to himself, and, when this action was followed by a motion for his expulsion, he voted in the division by which it was carried. Expelled from the House, he was promptly re-elected by his constituents. In 1884 he again administered the oath to himself, and again voted in a division. Excluded, in consequence, by resolution from the precincts of the House, he applied for the Chiltern Hundreds; and was again, by a larger majority than before, re-elected member for Northampton. The Government having brought an action against him for illegally taking the oath, it was decided by the courts that he was incapable of taking it. Lord Coleridge defined an oath as an "adjuration made by one believing in the Deity adjured," and held that in this sense Mr. Bradlaugh was legally incapable of taking it. Against this judgment Mr. Bradlaugh gave notice of appeal to the House of Lords; but further proceedings were subsequently stopped by a writ of *stet processus* issued by the Unionist Government of 1886.

Mr. Bradlaugh permitted to take the oath by Mr. Speaker Peel in the new Parliament, 1886.
At the General Election of 1885, Mr. Bradlaugh was again elected for Northampton. Attempts once more were made to prevent him from taking the oath, but, in a new Parliament, the Speaker refused to allow intervention. "It is the right," he said, "the legal statutable obligation of members, when returned to this House, to come to the table and take the oath prescribed by statute. I have no authority, I have no right, original or delegated, to stand between an honourable member and his taking of the oath. . . . I am bound and the House is

bound by the forms of this House, and by the legal obligations and rights of members. If a member comes to this table and offers to take the oath, I know of no right whatever to intervene between him and the form of legal and statutable obligation."

From this time until his death in January, 1891, Mr. Bradlaugh continued to represent Northampton in the House of Commons; where he won general esteem by his industry, courtesy, moderation, and straightforwardness. That his exclusion had been the result rather of personal prejudice than of any general principle was attested by the circumstance that when a closer acquaintance had gained him, not only respect, but popularity on the Conservative side of the House, his former adversaries were found ready to make a change in the law to which the highest eloquence of Mr. Gladstone had failed to persuade a Liberal House of Commons to assent. In 1883, an Affirmation Bill introduced by that statesman had been rejected on second reading by a majority of four. In 1888, another Affirmation Bill, introduced by Mr. Bradlaugh himself, was passed by large majorities through the House of Commons; and, the Unionists being in office, was agreed to without amendment by the House of Lords. Finally in January, 1891, while Mr. Bradlaugh was on his deathbed, the House of Commons by a unanimous vote expunged from their journals the resolutions by which he had been excluded in former years.

His later years. Resolutions against him expunged from the journals, 1891.

Thus ended a memorable controversy. The most violent and abusive of Mr. Bradlaugh's antagonists had been men to whom party advantage is the supreme good, or to whom it is easier to satisfy themselves and others of their zeal for Christianity by their abhorrence of its theoretical opponents, than by obedience to the ethical precepts of its Divine Founder. But he was also opposed by others, who were unconsciously biassed by the belief that his character was as infamous as they held his opinions to be, and who failed to perceive that, since no man is infallible, the only safe rule to be observed in public life is to distribute even-handed justice to all, and to let the consequences take care of themselves. In one respect the course taken by the House of Commons of 1880 was even more unconstitutional than that of its eighteenth

End of the controversy. Its character.

15 *

century predecessor in the case of Wilkes. For the House of 1880 acknowledged the right of Northampton to elect Mr. Bradlaugh as their representative, although, by refusing to allow him to take his seat, it prevented him from performing his duties in that capacity. The House of 1769 showed in theory more consideration for the rights of constituencies; for, having declared Mr. Wilkes incapable of being elected, it treated the votes given to him by the electors of Middlesex as void, and seated his opponent.

The Burials Act, 1880. A long-standing controversy between the Church and Dissent of no great intrinsic importance, but productive in the past of much bitterness of feeling, was settled by legislation in the first session of the Liberal Parliament of 1880. The right at common law of every dissenting parishioner to bury his dead in the parish churchyard had been, as we have seen,[1] accompanied by an obligation to accept the ministration of the incumbent and the rites of the Church of England for that purpose. This obligation had long been felt as a grievance by dissenters, and was now removed by a bill introduced into the House of Lords by Lord Chancellor Selborne, himself a zealous High Churchman. By this Act power was given to the person in charge of a funeral to choose the religious rites to be used at the grave, and to select the officiating minister, or to have no religious service at all.

Education. The religious neutrality of the State was now almost complete. The Church, while subject to the State, and not allowed to vary her doctrines or her ritual without statutory permission, was losing, one by one, the privileges which had accompanied her subjection. In the field of popular elementary education, however, she still reaped the fruit of her admirable efforts in the past. She still retained control over the schools which she had founded. But after the State had recognised its responsibilities in the matter of education and had accepted the principle of compulsion, the question arose whether such compulsion were compatible with denominational teaching in schools which the children of dissenters were obliged to attend, even though they were exempted by the conscience clause from the religious instruction to which their parents objected. The compromise of 1870, although cheerfully accepted by

[1] See vol. ii. cxiv.

the community at large, gave little satisfaction to the partisans on either side. High Churchmen disapproved of the undenominational teaching given in the board schools, and thought it unjust that they should be rated to support religious instruction which they regarded as worthless or even misleading, while their own public elementary schools were largely maintained by their own subscriptions. Dissenters, on the other hand, held that a Government grant to privately managed schools could not be justified; they denied that Christians believed so little in common that it was impossible to give Christian teaching which did not carry with it the distinctive tenets of particular sects; and many of them thought that, if this were really so, it would be better that the teaching provided out of public money should be purely secular, while facilities might be given to voluntary agencies to supplement it by religious instruction. To these arguments it was replied that the majority of Church schools had been founded by the enterprise of the Church National Society, chiefly at the expense of private individuals whose main object had been the provision of denominational religious teaching, and that, although it was true that they could not subsist without help from public funds, to replace them by new schools on any grounds except lack of efficiency at a time when the large majority of parents did not object to the religious instruction given, would be a waste of public money. *Religious teaching in the schools. Grievances of High Churchmen and Dissenters.*

The recognition that it was the duty of the State to provide for the education of the people involved the recognition that it was also its duty to see that no children were shut out from the benefits of that provision by the neglect of their parents. The Act of 1870 empowered school boards to compel attendance at school, but did not oblige them to make by-laws with this object, and in districts where there were no school boards no duty to attend could be imposed. An advance was made in 1876, when an Act was passed requiring borough councils and rural boards of guardians, where there was no school board, to appoint school attendance committees with powers to adopt by-laws for compulsory attendance at school. But since this Act did not compel the school attendance committees to adopt the by-laws, it did not secure universal education. This was finally done by a further Act passed in 1880 which required *School attendance made compulsory, 1880.*

the local authorities throughout England and Wales to adopt by-laws for compulsory attendance. Thus education was at last compulsory, but it was as yet neither free nor unsectarian.

Board schools and voluntary schools.

The Act of 1870 had been intended to oblige localities, which had neglected that duty, to make provision for elementary education, without further interfering with districts in which such provision had already been made than by making a certain standard of efficiency a condition of State recognition. So much was this the case that by a clause in the Act the voluntary societies were given a year of grace in which to build schools with the usual aid grant from the Treasury in districts where the supply was insufficient. At first, therefore, and for some years after 1870, a much greater number of English children were taught in voluntary than in board schools. But the contest was unequal between schools supported by subscriptions and schools relying on the rates, especially when subscribers had also to pay school rates. Moreover, it was provided by the Act of 1870 that "the Parliamentary grant should not exceed the income derived from other sources," and thus the supply of money from rates enabled the board schools to earn larger grants than their rivals. The system, too, of payment by results, inaugurated by Mr. Lowe in 1861, had been largely extended and was becoming very complicated. In 1868, the Education Department offered grants for each child who had passed an examination in what were called "specific subjects," such as history and geography; in 1875, grammar, geography, history, and needlework were made "class subjects," and a grant was made to the school on average attendance if the class as a whole satisfied examiners of their progress in these studies; by later revisions of the code other kinds of grants were introduced. The voluntary schools, having less resources than the board schools, were unable to attract equally efficient teachers, and were therefore less successful in the earning of grants. Thus their poverty tended to produce inefficiency, and their inefficiency tended to increase their poverty. It was not, therefore, surprising that the board schools continually gained upon them, or that, in the name of religious education, they appealed to the legislature for relief from an "intolerable strain".

The "intolerable strain".

Fortunately for the voluntary schools they had, during the

period of their greatest distress, friends at court. For seventeen of the twenty years which followed the resignation of Mr. Gladstone in 1885 the Conservatives were in power, and the Conservative leaders were resolved that denominational instruction should not cease to be given in public elementary schools through lack of State support. By the codes of 1890 and 1900 the system of payment by results was abolished, and a single "block grant" of either twenty-one or twenty-two shillings a head, according to the efficiency of the school, was substituted. In 1891, payment of fees was abolished in most of the public elementary schools by means of a fee grant of ten shillings a head, paid annually on the average attendance of scholars between ten and fifteen years of age. Education thus became free, except by special permission of the Department, in all schools where the rate of fees charged was less than ten shillings a head. Where the rate was higher, the excess only could be charged; but, after September, 1892, the Education Department was required to see that free education was provided for all those asking for it. The drifting of children to the board schools, however, continued; and, in 1895, the Archbishop's Committee reported to Convocation that a quarter of a million pounds was needed to bring their buildings up to the standard of those in use by their rivals.

Relief measures of Conservative Governments. Payment by results abolished. Free education instituted.

In 1896, the Unionist Government brought in a bill to meet the difficulty. They proposed to increase the State subsidy to voluntary schools; to give facilities in all public elementary schools for the denominational religious teaching of the children of parents a reasonable number of whom desired it; and to constitute new educational authorities, consisting of committees of the county councils, for the administration of existing Parliamentary grants. The bill met with great opposition, and was finally withdrawn. In the following year the additional subsidy to voluntary schools was carried in a separate bill. By this Act the Education Department was authorised to distribute to these schools, in proportion to their needs, a special aid grant at the rate of five shillings a scholar; the limit to Parliamentary grants imposed by the Act of 1876 was abolished; and voluntary school buildings were exempted from the payment of rates. In the same session an Act was passed for the relief of necessitous board schools.

Education Bill of 1896. The Act of 1897.

The relief given to voluntary schools by the Act of 1897 was considerable, amounting to about £616,000 a year, but it was not nearly sufficient to place them on a financial equality with the board schools.[1] It appeared therefore that if their separate existence was to be continued they must be given rate aid, and this in 1902 the Unionist Government resolved that they should have.

The Education Act of 1902.

By the Education Act of 1902 school boards and school attendance committees were abolished and the county and borough councils working through education committees became the local education authorities in their place. The public elementary schools were divided into two classes, corresponding to the former board and voluntary schools; (1) schools provided, controlled, and maintained by the local education authorities; and (2) schools maintained, but neither provided nor effectively controlled by those bodies. The second class consisted of the old voluntary schools which were now, like the board schools, to be supported out of rates as well as out of taxes. In these schools four out of six of the managers were to be appointed according to the original trust deed, the remaining two being named by the local authorities. The local education authority was given a general control over the secular instruction and a veto on the appointment of teachers; but this veto was not to be exercised on religious grounds. The only financial burden imposed upon non-provided schools in return for the privilege of remaining outside the national system in respect of management and religious instruction, while they were brought within it in respect of maintenance, was the obligation to provide the school buildings and to keep them in repair. Even this obligation was modified by an amendment inserted by the House of Lords, and agreed to by the Commons, which transferred the cost of repairs due to wear and tear from the managers to the rates. Provision was also made in the Act for the co-ordination of all forms of education. To this end, and for the encouragement of higher education, the proceeds of beer and spirit duties, known as "whisky money," allocated under the Local Taxation Act, 1890, to local authorities for the purposes of technical and manual

[1] In 1900 the expenditure per child in voluntary schools was £2 6s. 4½d. as against £2 17s. 7½d. in the board schools (Com. Papers, 1901, xix. 1, p. 480).

instruction, were to be used by these authorities for the establishment and support of secondary schools, and they were empowered to supplement this fund when necessary by a two-penny rate.

The bill was strenuously opposed and in order to pass it the Government were obliged, after nineteen days of Committee, to revert to the practice of closure by compartments. This procedure had fallen into discredit during the Parliament of 1892 and, strongly denounced by the Conservative Opposition, it had contributed to the unpopularity of the Liberal Government. Since their fall in 1895 it had not been revived, but from this time onward its simplicity and efficacy offered to an impatient majority temptations too great to be resisted; and for the following seven years not a session passed without its employment. The House of Lords received the bill in December, and agreed to it after a very short discussion. *Bill passed by a renewed use of closure by compartments.*

The main objections urged by dissenters to this Act are: (i) that they are rated to support privately-managed schools; (ii) that in districts where there is no board school and in which therefore they are obliged to send their children to non-provided schools the only religious instruction offered is of a kind they disapprove, but which they are none the less obliged to share in maintaining; and (iii) that dissenting teachers by reason of their religion are shut out from all probability of finding employment in half the elementary schools in the kingdom. So deeply were these grievances felt by some of the dissenters, that certain of them, known as "passive resisters," refused to pay a part of their rates and suffered distraint of goods and even imprisonment in consequence. In Wales, certain of the local authorities refused to put the Act into operation and the Government were obliged in 1904 to pass an Act to compel them to do so. The Liberal party, as a whole, adhering to the principle that institutions supported by the rates should be under the control of the ratepayers, endorsed these objections; and the Liberal leaders pledged themselves to change the new law as soon as they should have the opportunity. *Nonconformist objections to the Act.*

There can be little doubt that the large majority of parents desire that their children should receive in the schools the religious instruction which they have not the time or the ability or the inclination to give to them at home. Assuming then *The two sides of the question.*

the desirability of religious instruction in the schools, the issue seems to lie between logical system, on the one part, and practical convenience on the other. When the State compels a man to send his children to school it certainly seems to be anomalous that in many cases it should oblige him to send them to privately-managed establishments where the only form of religion taught is one in which he disbelieves, and where teachers of his own faith are practically disqualified for appointment. On the other hand, the greatest enemy of the Church of England could hardly deny that in the matter of the education of the people her achievements have been great and her sacrifices considerable. When, therefore, the State was forced into a tardy recognition of its educational responsibilities, its action was governed by the consideration that to make no use of these achievements would be unthrifty and unwise, while to disregard these sacrifices would be dishonest. If these reasons made the support of denominational schools by Parliamentary grants legitimate, they also, it was contended, were sufficient to justify the use of rates for the same object.

The Education Bill of 1906. After an overwhelming Liberal majority had been returned to Parliament at the general election of 1906, the first great bill introduced by the new Liberal Government was a bill to reverse the policy of their predecessors in the matter of elementary education. The provision in the first clause, that no school thereafter should be recognised as a public elementary school, unless it was provided by the local education authority, contained the root principle of the measure. All elementary schools maintained by public funds were placed under public management, and teachers were freed from religious tests by being forbidden to give any religious teaching except that permitted by the Cowper-Temple clause in the Act of 1870. An undenominational school was thus placed within the reach of every child. The managers of non-provided schools were allowed to transfer them to the local authorities, and, if these authorities agreed to the transfer, to make the following conditions: (1) that on two mornings in the week an arrangement should be made that the children of parents who so desired it might receive denominational instruction in the school, provided that such instruction was not paid for out of public money or given by the regular teachers; (2) that they should have the use of the school building out of school hours, without cost of repair. These privileges were described as the "ordinary facilities". Further, as a concession to strictly denominational schools, to which from their situation no parent was obliged to send his child, power was given to the local authority to allow denominational teaching to be given by the regular teachers in transferred schools, situated in any urban district of more than 5000 inhabitants, if the parents of four-fifths of the scholars desired it, and if there was an undenominational school within reach. These "extended facilities," as they were called, provoked the opposition of Nonconformists without conciliating the High Churchmen, who complained that a privilege was thus conferred on Roman Catholics and on Jews to which they were just as much entitled, but from the benefits of which, owing to the situation of the greater number of their schools, they were unjustly excluded. Even the Roman Catholics were not satisfied, because the clause placed no compulsion on the local authorities to grant these extended facilities, even when the necessary conditions were satisfied. To meet in some degree these objections, the Government, by an amendment to the bill, empowered the Education Department in cases in which the local authorities had refused to grant extended facilities to replace the schools concerned in the position they were in before 1902. These schools were to receive a Government grant, but no assistance from the rates. They were in fact to be allowed to contract out of the bill. With regard to the other non-provided schools, when the local authority and the owners of the school failed to come to an agreement, if the school was privately owned or held on trusts admitting a non-educational use, it might be kept open without assistance from public funds, or closed. But if the trust was educational and came under the law affecting charities the school was to be kept open or to be appropriated to such uses as the law might decide. A Commission of three persons was to be appointed to settle the schemes under which such schools would be dealt with. There was to be a Central Educational Council for Wales.

The Lords read the bill a second time and agreed that all the elementary schools should be placed under public management, and that denominational religious instruction should be *The Lords' amendments.*

paid for in most cases by the denominations. But in other respects they transformed the controversial clauses of the bill in a manner inconsistent with its character and objects. Local authorities were compelled to take over voluntary schools, if the managers desired it, on the terms of granting ordinary facilities for denominational teaching, instead of being permitted to do so, as the Government had proposed. Extended facilities, from being the exception, became the rule. They were to be granted throughout the country, in districts rural as well as urban, when the parents of two-thirds of the children demanded them. Local authorities were required to grant them in single school districts; but, in such cases, provision was to be made for the religious instruction of dissenting children, either in the school-house or elsewhere. In these schools the regular teachers were not only permitted to give denominational teaching, but the local authorities were required to see that they were qualified to give it. Since the abolition of religious tests for teachers had been one of the main objects of the bill, this was a proposal which it would have been impossible for the House of Commons without stultifying themselves to have accepted.

They are disagreed to by the Commons and the bill is lost.

To discuss the Lords' amendments in detail would have been to enter on a new Committee stage of the bill—a course which so late in the year (10th December) was impracticable. The Government, therefore, determined to reject them *en bloc*, with a view to giving an opportunity to the Lords to reconsider their position. The motion for rejection was carried by the extraordinary majority of 309 (416 to 107)—the Irish voting with the Government on the understanding that further concessions were to be made to the denominations. Negotiations followed; and there were concessions on both sides, but more especially on the part of the Government; until the differences were said to have been narrowed down to the single issue whether head teachers in transferred schools should or should not be allowed to give religious instruction. But it is probable that there was no real anxiety on the part of the Unionist leaders to come to an agreement, for here the negotiations broke down; and, in spite of the protest and the adverse vote of the Duke of Devonshire, the Lords resolved by a large majority to insist on their amendments. They thus defeated a bill introduced in the first session of a new Parliament to give effect to the pledges made by the victorious party at the General Election, and passed through the House of Commons by enormous majorities. Yet their action was applauded by one of the great political parties, and was regarded with indifference by the country as a whole.

Though the proposals of the Government had been defeated, the existence of the religious difficulty was recognised on all sides, and no one professed to regard the settlement of 1902 as final. Speaking in January, 1907, the Archbishop of Canterbury admitted that the voluntary schools could not go on as they were, and that changes in the direction of accepting popular control and freeing teachers from denominational tests must be made. Early in the session, Mr. McKenna, the new Minister for Education, brought in a bill to transfer from the local educational authorities to the managers the cost of denominational religious education in non-provided schools. But, later in the session, the Prime Minister announced that the Government did not intend to proceed with the bill because they proposed to deal with the whole question in the following year, and because they were unwilling to give Parliamentary sanction to the idea that a denomination was entitled to purchase the privilege of teaching its particular tenets "to nearly half the children in the elementary schools in the country". *The bill of 1907.*

In 1908 the Government introduced their third Education Bill. The schools receiving rates and grants were to become provided schools, but it was now proposed that the voluntary schools, except in single school parishes, should be allowed to contract out of the bill, provided that they could show average attendances of at least thirty children. They were to receive grants but no rate aid, and they might charge fees not exceeding ninepence per week. Every educational area was to receive from four to five shillings per child more than it then received, but no area would receive more than 75 per cent. of the whole cost of elementary education. In single school districts the voluntary schools might be transferred to the local authorities; and might claim the same facilities for special religious instruction as were given in ordinary cases under the bill of 1906. *The bill of 1908.*

Compromise proposed by Bishop of St. Asaph.

Before the bill reached the second reading the Bishop of St. Asaph's had introduced into the House of Lords a measure of which both the Archbishop of Canterbury and the Government were able to express a qualified approval. The great danger to the bishop's mind was lest the Church, in her anxiety to retain control over the schools which she had founded, might not only lose this, but might lose with it the opportunity of giving special religious instruction in any of the elementary schools in the country. He proposed, therefore, that all elementary schools should be brought under public management, and that teachers should not be subjected to religious tests though they might volunteer to give simple Christian or denominational teaching. Cowper-Temple teaching was to be given in all elementary schools. Schools held by trustees might be transferred to the local education authority, the use being reserved for trustees on Saturdays and Sundays, and on not less than two other days in the week out of school hours. In return for these concessions, the right of entry was to be given for denominational instruction to children whose parents desired it in all elementary schools.

The fourth Education Bill.

Land was now in sight; the Government proceeded no further with their own bill after the second reading; and during the summer and autumn conferences were held with a view to the settlement of the question by agreement. The result was the introduction, towards the end of the autumn session, of a fourth Education Bill to which, not only the Archbishop of Canterbury, but the leading Nonconformists, were understood to have assented. By this bill rate aid was to be confined to provided schools; in which there were to be no religious tests for teachers, or obligation for them to give religious instruction. Cowper-Temple teaching was to be given during the first three-quarters of an hour of the day's work, and twice a week denominational teaching might be substituted for it for the children of parents who desired it, but not at the public cost. Assistant teachers might volunteer to give this denominational teaching, and the vexed question of the head teacher, on which the bill of 1906 had finally broken down, was settled by a compromise providing that existing head teachers might give this instruction during their tenure of office in the schools over which they then presided, or, for the next five years, if they moved to other schools. Non-provided schools might be recognised and receive the Parliamentary grant, if they were not the only school in the parish; if they contained thirty children; and if they satisfied the requirements of the code. Grants to such schools were to range from 55s. per child in the smaller schools to 46s. 6d. in schools of over 1300 children.

But against this compromise a formidable opposition arose from extremists on either side. Lord Halifax, Lord Hugh Cecil, and Dean Wace of Canterbury had previously drawn up a protest against the proposed settlement which was backed by 114,000 signatures, including those of 2000 rectors and vicars; the Roman Catholics were dissatisfied by the financial provision for the non-provided schools; and now the Representative Church Council declared against the bill. The only hope of passing the bill was by agreement, and the Government was reluctantly compelled to withdraw it. *Opposed by the extremists and withdrawn.*

Thus was destroyed the fairest chance of a peaceful solution of the religious difficulty that has hitherto been suggested. The opportunity of securing a right of entry into the County Council schools was rejected by the Church Council; and the trend of events shows ever more distinctly that, in rejecting it, they were parting with the means of influencing an increasing majority, for the sake of preserving an exclusive control over a decreasing minority of the children of the country. Between 1903 and 1909, the number of Church of England voluntary schools which were closed in consequence of failure to comply with requirements of the Education Department was 372, and the number transferred during the same period was 298. Thus in these six years the Church of England has lost 670 of her schools. No one would now dispute the right of every parent to educate his child in his own religion. But to go further and to say that every parent has an inalienable right to call upon the State to educate his child in the religion he himself professes is a proposition more open to question. Yet this right was freely claimed during the recent controversies, and on this claim were largely based the amendments of the House of Lords to the bill of 1906. The claim is of very recent origin; and was so far from being recognised by the Act of 1902, that, under the provisions of that Act, a dissenter in a single school *An opportunity lost.*

district who wished his child to receive religious instruction at school had to choose between Church of England teaching and none. Nevertheless in the admission of this right seems to lie the best hope of a solution; and the compromise of 1908, under which denominational as well as undenominational religious instruction would have been brought within the reach of almost all the children whose parents desired the one or the other, was directed to that end.

The question of disestablishment. The agitation for the disestablishment and disendowment of the Church of England reached its climax under the influence of Mr. Chamberlain during the political campaign which preceded the election of 1885. The Church, however, was never unpopular; among her clergy were to be found many devoted men who gave up their lives to the service of the poor; and the people, so far as they were at all conscious of her activities, found in that consciousness no argument for her disestablishment. Moreover, the Liberal split on the subject of Home Rule and above all the alliance formed by Mr. Chamberlain with the Conservative party placed the Church for the time altogether out of danger. In later years the attention of Radicals was diverted from political to social reform, while they adopted new views concerning the functions of the State. Abstract and sentimental grievances relating to religious inequality came to appear to them of small importance when compared with economic and other problems affecting the condition of the people which called for legislative solution. Hence the attention which the question of disestablishment attracted in 1885 has been transferred to other objects; such popularity as the cause ever possessed has very sensibly declined; and for the present at all events the measure is not likely to form a part of the overburdened Liberal programme.

The Church in Wales. The Church in Wales was in a different position. There the Nonconformists were in a majority of three to one; and there in former times the clergy of the Established Church had grievously neglected their duties. Englishmen without knowledge of the Welsh language had been in the eighteenth century habitually appointed to Welsh bishoprics and livings. For months together no sermon was preached in many a parish church, and when the silence of the pulpit was broken it was often by a learned discourse in English, addressed to a congregation who understood no language but Welsh. Naturally, therefore, the Methodist revival was more successful in Wales than in any other part of the United Kingdom, and the number of Nonconformist congregations rose from 105 in 1742 to nearly 3000 in 1861.

Although in more modern times the Church in Wales has made amends by her zeal and activity for remissness in the past, and in point of numbers is in a better position than she has been since the great Methodist secession took place, yet there has been no slackening in the demand for disestablishment on the part of the Welsh Nonconformists. Welsh disestablishment formed part of the Newcastle Programme of 1891, accepted by Mr. Gladstone; and the short-lived Government of 1892 were engaged in passing through the House of Commons a bill to disestablish and disendow the Church in Wales when they were interrupted by the defeat in supply which brought about their resignation in 1895. *Movement for Welsh Disestablishment.*

At the General Election of 1906 all the Welsh members returned were pledged to disestablishment; and in April, 1909, Mr. Asquith introduced another bill with that object. This measure provided that disestablishment should take place on the 1st January, 1911. All ecclesiastical corporations in Wales, sole or aggregate, were then to be dissolved; Welsh bishops were no longer to sit in the House of Lords; and Church of England rules would operate in Wales by agreement only. With regard to disendowment, three bodies were to be created: the Welsh Commissioners, whose appointment was to expire in 1915; the Council of Wales, representing local bodies; and the Church representative body. The Welsh Commissioners were to take over Welsh Church property. The representative body would take over Church plate and furniture, and receive from the Commissioners all Church buildings and ecclesiastical residences, together with all benefactions made since 1662. The Commissioners would transfer to existing incumbents, during their incumbency, the glebes and the open burial-grounds; but, after the termination of their incumbency, these were to vest in the parish or borough councils; the tithe rent charge on land in the county was to vest in the county council, while that on land outside would be disposed of as the Commissioners should determine. Parish property was to be *The Welsh Church Bill, 1909.*

applied to charitable and educational purposes, subject to one-tenth to be paid over to the Council of Wales. But in the session of 1909 there was no time for controversial legislation unrelated to the Budget, and the bill was withdrawn after it had been read a second time.

Marriage with a deceased wife's sister legalised in 1907.

Marriages with a deceased wife's sister were made legal in 1907, and an ancient controversy was thus at last brought to a close. There had been for several years majorities in both Houses in favour of this reform; but until a Cabinet was found, all the members of which supported it, there was, under latter-day Parliamentary conditions, no possibility of its enactment. Before 1880, when it was still possible for controversial bills introduced by private members to reach a third reading without help from the Government, bills for legalising these marriages had been several times passed by the Commons, but rejected by the Lords. In 1896 a bill with the same object was introduced into and passed by the House of Lords, but its further progress was successfully obstructed by a minority in the House of Commons. During the ten following years the House of Commons, whenever given an opportunity, recorded by large majorities its approval of the principle of the reform, but found itself, in the absence of assistance from the Government, unable to do more. At last in 1907, when a bill introduced by a private member had made some progress, the Government provided the requisite facilities out of the time at their disposal; and its passage was thus secured. The Act then passed legalised such marriages, past and future, so far as the civil law was concerned, but permitted clergymen to refuse to solemnise them, and did not even protect from ecclesiastical censure those who agreed to do so. The position of the modern High Churchman in England with regard to these marriages differs from that of either Catholics or Protestants in any other country in the world, and differs moreover from that of the Anglican High Church doctors of the seventeenth century. Unlike the majority of Protestants, who consider that these marriages were only unlawful because they were forbidden by the civil law, and who therefore find no difficulty in recognising them now that the law has been altered; unlike Roman Catholics who believe that they are unlawful only because they are forbidden by the ecclesiastical law, dispensations from which are almost always granted to those who wish for them by Rome; unlike the orthodox of the Greek Church whose view is the same as the Roman, the High Churchman holds that such marriages are incestuous and contrary to the law of God. This view has led to some inconvenience, because certain of the High Church clergy think it their duty to refuse the Sacrament to Churchmen who have contracted these marriages; although their right to do so has been contested in the courts and decided against them. The change in the law was opposed in language of surprising vehemence, but the disastrous results foretold by its opponents have not as yet become visible.

The only religious disabilities still subsisting with regard to offices under the Crown held by laymen are those which exclude Roman Catholics from the posts of Lord Chancellor and Lord-Lieutenant of Ireland. To remove these disabilities was the object of a bill introduced by Mr. Gladstone when leader of the Opposition in 1891. But the bill was rejected on second reading by a majority of 33, and these disabilities still remain on the statute-book. Religious Disabilities Removal Bill, 1891.

The question of a Roman Catholic University—the subject of so much contention in the past—was settled, practically by agreement, in the Parliament of 1906. In 1879, the Queen's University, which gave degrees after examination to students who had attended the unsectarian colleges of Cork, Galway, and Belfast, was replaced by the Royal University. This was, like its predecessor, a purely examining body, without professors or teachers; but it gave degrees to all who passed its examinations, whether they had studied at the Queen's Colleges or at private establishments. One effect of this change was largely to diminish the number of students at the well-endowed Queen's Colleges, and thus, though degrees were thrown open to all, the Roman Catholic grievance with respect to endowments was accentuated. Various suggestions were made for the removal of this difficulty. Mr. Bryce, Chief Secretary in 1906, wished to combine all the existing colleges in Ireland into one great University, under a scheme of federation, but this plan was generally unpopular. Another proposal was to add a second college to the University of Dublin, which should be Roman Catholic in the sense that Trinity College was Protestant. But this was opposed by Trinity, whose Irish University Act passed, 1908.

wishes the Government were anxious to consult, and whose traditions they desired to preserve intact.

Finally, in 1908, Mr. Birrell, who had succeeded Mr. Bryce as Chief Secretary, presented a bill to deal with the subject which met with general approval, and was passed without difficulty through both Houses. By this Act the Royal University was dissolved, and two new Universities were founded by Royal Charter. Of these one was to be in Dublin and to consist of the Cork and Galway Colleges, together with a new College acceptable to Roman Catholics; the other, in Belfast, would consist of the Queen's College already there. Both were given limited powers of affiliation. In neither were there to be any religious tests or declarations from professors. The Senates, by which the Universities were to be governed, were for five years to be nominated and afterwards to be academically elected. The professors at the new Dublin College were to be appointed by a statutory commission. The Exchequer charge for Irish University education was raised from £36,880 to £80,000 a year, and the income of £20,000 paid out of the Irish Church Fund to the Royal University was divided between the two new Universities.

Amendment of the royal declaration, 1910.

One other measure, framed in a conciliatory spirit and indicative of the decline of ancient religious animosities, remains to be noticed. When, after the revolution of 1688, Roman Catholics were excluded from the throne by the Bill of Rights, such was the distrust at that time felt for the adherents of the older form of Christianity that the authors of the measure thought the statutory exclusion insufficient unless the monarch was subjected to a test by which his Protestantism might be ascertained beyond question. They, therefore, enacted that each new sovereign of these islands should make the declaration already obligatory on persons holding office under the Crown and on members of Parliament, in which the central doctrine of the Roman Catholic Church was described as "superstitious and idolatrous". This declaration was no longer exacted from office holders and members of Parliament after the emancipating legislation of 1828 and 1829; and in 1910, at the beginning of a new reign, although there was no wish to reverse the policy of the Bill of Rights with respect to the exclusion of Roman Catholics from the throne, it was felt that this exclusion might be secured without obliging the king to use language needlessly offensive to great numbers of his subjects, and naturally distasteful to himself. Accordingly, by an Act passed without serious opposition in the session of 1910, a new short form of declaration was substituted for the old one. The sovereign is now required to declare "that he is a faithful Protestant and that he will according to the true intent of the enactments which secure the Protestant succession to the Throne of the Realm, uphold and maintain the said enactments to the best of his power according to law".

CHAPTER V.

LOCAL GOVERNMENT AFTER 1870.

State of local government in 1870. IN 1870 local government, or that part of administration which the State has thought right to delegate or to leave to local authorities, was in England conspicuously lacking in system. There was, in the words of Mr. Goschen, "a chaos as regards authorities, a chaos as regards rates, and a worse chaos than all as regards areas".[1] As each fresh need made itself felt, the Legislature had been accustomed to create a special machinery to deal with that need. The relief of the poor, public health, the provision of highways and other such necessary public accommodations, are with public safety the main subjects of local administration; and to these came to be added the education of the people. To meet these needs new districts were formed and new authorities were constituted, but no attempt was made to fit in the new districts with ancient geographical areas or with the districts into which the country had been for other purposes divided. Poor-law unions—as groups of parishes brought together for poor-law purposes were called—and single parishes themselves were partly in one county and partly in another. Highway districts, school board districts, and burial board districts overlapped each other. There were eighteen different kinds of rates. The inhabitants of a single borough might enjoy the administration of five different authorities: the municipal council, the vestry, the school board, the poor-law guardians, and the quarter sessions. The inhabitants of local board districts—that is, of districts in which a local board of health had been appointed under the Public Health Act, 1848—might live in four different areas—the local board district, the parish, the union, the county. These various authorities were chosen by various modes of

[1] Hansard, vol. ccv. p. 1116.

election. Town councils were elected by ballot, each ratepayer having a single vote; local boards by voting papers, left at the houses of voters and collected after three days, on a system of plural voting under which the number of votes allotted to each owner or occupier varied with the rateable value of his property; boards of guardians by voting papers and plural voting; school boards by ballot and cumulative vote, and so forth. To substitute for the special authorities for special districts created for special purposes a uniform and intelligible national system has been a main object in legislation relating to local government during the past generation.

A first step was taken in 1871 by the consolidation of the central authority in the Local Government Board. Before that year central supervision had been divided among various Government departments. The reform of the poor law in 1834 had involved the appointment of Commissioners, who were afterwards organised as the Poor-law Board, under the presidency of a Minister generally in the Cabinet. The second great function of local administration—the care of public health—much neglected until 1848, was placed by an Act of that year under the control of a general board of health nominated by the Crown. This board lasted until 1858, when its powers relating to the prevention of disease were transferred to the Privy Council, while its general control over local government passed to the Home Office. A Royal Sanitary Commission, appointed in 1869, recommended, among other reforms, the constitution of one central authority with adequate powers. To give effect to this recommendation an Act was passed in 1871. The object of the Act, as stated in the preamble, was "to concentrate in one Department of the Government the suspervision of the laws relating to public health, the relief of the poor, and local government". In order to do this, the Local Government Board was created, consisting nominally, in accordance with a favourite fiction of English law, of a president and *ex-officio* members holding high offices of State, but in reality of the President, the Parliamentary Secretary, and a department with five permanent Assistant Secretaries. In this board were vested the powers and duties: (*a*) of the Poor-Law Board; (*b*) of the Privy Council, relating to vaccination and the prevention of disease;

<small>Creation of the Local Government Board, 1871.</small>

(*c*) of the Home Office, with regard to public health, sanitation, wash-houses, public improvements, housing of the working classes, and local government. Many and important powers have been added by subsequent statutes.

Reforms recommended by the Royal Sanitary Commission.

The creation of the Local Government Board was only one of the reforms recommended by the Royal Sanitary Commission. The Commissioners advised, in the first place, that all the laws relating to sanitary matters and to local government, which had been passed piecemeal since 1848, should be consolidated into one statute; secondly, that the number of authorities should be lessened by enabling the same authority to deal with different subject-matters through separate departments; thirdly, that the kingdom should be divided into sanitary districts, and that the authority in each district should be compelled to adopt and carry out the sanitary laws; and, fourthly, that the confusion caused by the overlapping of local government areas should be rectified. That the consolidation of authorities and the simplification of areas were reforms of essential importance if the local government of the country was to be made efficient, was generally admitted in 1871; and Mr. Goschen, President of the Poor Law Board, in Mr. Gladstone's Government, introduced a bill during the session of that year to further these objects. Although pressure of other business compelled the withdrawal of the bill, Mr. Goschen laid his proposals before the House in a speech which directed public attention to the existing confusion, and convinced both parties in the House of Commons that the state of affairs which he described called for reform.

The Public Health Act, 1872.

The next step forward towards the organisation of local government was made in the following year, when under the provisions of the Public Health Act, 1872, the whole country was divided into urban and rural sanitary districts. The application of the sanitary laws, which had been largely permissive, was made obligatory on the newly-constituted local sanitary authorities; and effect was given to the recommendation of the Commissioners that there should everywhere be one sanitary authority for all sanitary purposes in one place. The urban sanitary authorities were the town councillors in boroughs, improvement commissioners in Improvement Act districts, and local boards of health in local board districts.

The rural sanitary districts were made, so far as was possible, to coincide with the poor-law unions, or with the parts of unions not included in an urban district, and the authorities were the boards of guardians. The poor-law unions had been hitherto the only local government areas created by statute which covered the whole land. It was natural, therefore, now that sanitary districts were also to be made universal and that the expediency of simplification was recognised, to entrust, in the rural districts where sanitary authorities had been practically non-existent,[1] to authorities already constituted in areas already defined the duties and responsibilities created by the new Act.

The law relating to public health was codified, in accordance with the recommendation of the Sanitary Commissioners, by the Public Health Act of 1875.[2] The multiplicity of enactments, sometimes in conflict one with another, relating to public health had caused great difficulties in sanitary administration; and the repeal of these Acts, together with their re-enactment in orderly and harmonious form, saved much needless labour and expense. Progress was made in the process of consolidating authorities by a clause in the Act which provided that in all urban sanitary districts the urban sanitary authority should be the highway authority. By a later Act in 1878 an attempt was made to extend this principle to rural districts by permitting a rural sanitary authority whenever the area of a highway district coincided with that of a rural district to apply to the justices in quarter sessions to have the control of highways transferred to them. But the guardians were seldom inclined to take over additional work; and in only forty-one cases was this transfer effected.

The Public Health Act, 1875.

In the year 1877, the management of prisons was transferred, by statute, from the local authority to the Home Office. This step was thought to be necessary in order to secure uniformity in criminal justice, since the effect of sentences intended to be the same varied in actual severity according to the manner

Transfer of prisons to Home Office, 1877.

---

[1] The right to make sewers and other sanitary powers had been in many cases conferred on vestries, and these were transferred by the Act of 1872 to the boards of guardians.

[2] Mr. Disraeli, when in Opposition, had declared that public attention ought to be concentrated on sanitary legislation; and this Act, perhaps the most important of his six years tenure of office, was evidence of his sincerity.

in which they were carried out by independent local authorities.

Quarter Sessions.

While these Acts did much to organise and to improve local government in England, they left untouched one great anomaly to which attention had been for half a century continually directed. Administrative duties of high importance in the counties had been entrusted by Parliament to justices of the peace appointed by the Crown on the recommendation of the lords-lieutenant; and, in order to perform these duties, they were empowered when assembled in quarter sessions to impose a county rate.

County rates.

As early as 1836 a Commission appointed to inquire into the subject used the following language in its report: "The principle of the county rate seems open to serious objection upon the ground that the charge is imposed by persons not chosen by the ratepayers; no such tax of such magnitude is laid upon the subject except by his representatives. It is impossible not to admit that the persons who contribute to the county rate have little control over its expenditure. The administration of this fund is the exercise of an irresponsible power entrusted to a fluctuating body." To remove this anomaly it was proposed that control over the assessment and the expenditure of county rates should be transferred to county financial boards consisting in half of ratepayers elected by the different boards of guardians and in half of justices of the peace elected by justices; but although this proposal was the subject of many bills and resolutions, nothing was done. It was allowed, on the one hand, that the existing system was anomalous; it was admitted on the other that the justices discharged their administrative functions with purity, efficiency, and economy. In the matter of poor relief the ratepayers, through elected boards of guardians, possessed the right of supervision and control; and the same bodies became after 1872 the rural sanitary authorities. Highways, burial grounds, and elementary education were controlled by *ad hoc* authorities specially elected for the purpose. The duties of justices were originally almost exclusively judicial; their administrative obligations were with very few exceptions imposed upon them, as occasion arose, by the Parliaments of the nineteenth century. Thus, their control over lunatic asylums dated from 1808; their control over the police from the creation of the police force in 1829; their control over reformatory and industrial schools from 1853. Lord Salisbury, in his speech on the second reading of the Local Government Bill of 1888, declared that not one of the numerous powers transferred by the bill from quarter sessions to the new county councils, except the power over county bridges, was older than the nineteenth century. It was less an abstract objection to the existence of taxation without representation than a sense that the justices in quarter sessions could not be expected to bear the strain of the increased duties which a continually expanding perception of the requirements of local government was putting upon them that impelled the friendly Conservative Government of 1888 to transfer their administrative functions to representative bodies.

The Reform Act of 1832, which "wrested from the corporations their exclusive electoral privileges," was followed as a necessary consequence by the Municipal Reform Act of 1835 which restored to the ratepayers their control over the corporations. In like manner the Reform Act of 1884, which enfranchised the agricultural labourer, was followed by the Local Government Act of 1888 which gave him a share in the management of his local affairs. It was felt that after the political franchise had been made equal in counties and boroughs, and an identity of political rights had been secured to the counties, their admission to identical municipal privileges could not in fairness be delayed. It was irrational, as Lord Salisbury said, to give men a voting power on all the most important questions of the Empire, and to expect them to acquiesce in the doctrine that they were not fit to manage their own affairs. In 1886, Mr. Chamberlain occupied the few weeks during which he presided at the Local Government Board in the preparation of a bill for the transfer of county administration to representative bodies elected on a democratic franchise. Owing to his resignation on the Home Rule question, and the subsequent fall of the Government, the bill was never submitted to Parliament; but the Conservative Government of 1886 was dependent for its majority on Liberal Unionist support, and Mr. Chamberlain intimated to them through Lord Randolph Churchill, who shared his views on the subject, "that while prepared to give the Government policy a generous consideration, whether on foreign affairs or on the necessity for coercion, he could not support anything that he considered reactionary in local government ".[1] Lord Randolph himself, during his brief leadership of the House of Commons, had pledged the Conservative party to a genuinely popular system of local government in all the four countries which form the United Kingdom, and the failure of the Conservative Government to fulfil this pledge in respect of Ireland was the occasion of one of the few attacks which he made on his former colleagues after his hasty resignation.

The Local Government Act, 1888.

The main object of the Local Government Bill introduced by Mr. Ritchie on the 19th March, 1888, was to extend to the counties the privileges conferred on the boroughs by the Municipal Corporations Act of 1835. The administrative duties which belonged to justices of the peace in quarter sessions were transferred to county councils elected by the ratepayers in sixty-two administrative counties created by the Act. The judicial powers of quarter sessions were left untouched; and the police, since the work connected with their management is partly administrative and partly judicial, were placed under the control of a joint committee of quarter sessions and the county council. The councils were to consist of councillors elected by a direct vote for three years; and of aldermen, in number one-third of the whole council, elected for six years by the councillors, and half of them retiring at the end of each period of three years. No one might vote by virtue of ownership; but the owner of property in a county might be elected a councillor though not residing within the area of the district to whose council he was elected. Except that clergymen and ministers of religion were qualified to sit as councillors the municipal precedent as to franchise and eligibility was followed.

Powers and duties of the county councils.

The powers and duties assigned to the county councils may be classified according to the source from which they were derived. They were (1) the administrative and financial powers transferred from the quarter sessions. Such were all powers connected with county bridges, county asylums, reformatory and industrial schools, main roads, and other county property; such also were the raising, borrowing, and expenditure of money; (2) powers transferred from the justices out of sessions;

[1] Life of Lord Randolph Churchill, vol. ii. p. 221.

such as the licensing of places for the public performance of plays, and powers under the Explosive Acts; and (3) new powers, among them the power to purchase bridges, the appointment of coroners, and the power to aid emigration. The administration of the poor law was left outside the bill—a sin of omission in the opinion of some critics. In lieu of the grants-in-aid from the Imperial Exchequer to local bodies there was to be a transference from Imperial to county funds for purposes defined in the Act of the proceeds of certain license duties—including those for the sale of wine, spirits, and tobacco. Four tenths of the Probate Duty together with the revenue from the Van and Wheel Tax were also to be contributed by the Exchequer, bringing the estimated total to £5,626,000.[1]

Further progress was made in the simplification of areas. Urban sanitary districts extending over more than one county were assigned to the county to which the larger proportion of the population belonged; rural sanitary districts in the same circumstances were divided and each part was merged in the county to which it properly belonged. The bill, as introduced, transferred the issue of licences for the sale of alcoholic liquor to the county councils; and authorised them to refuse the renewal of the annual licences on giving compensation to the licence holders. This part of the bill was strongly contested by the Opposition on the ground that it gave to the licence holder a new vested interest in his licence. Sir Edward Clarke, indeed, the Solicitor-General, held that such a vested interest already existed; but this view was afterwards by the highest Court of Appeal declared to be erroneous. To facilitate the progress of the bill the Government withdrew the licensing clauses, and the law remained unaltered in this respect until 1904. The ancient and unreformed corporation of the City of London was left untouched by the Act.

Other provisions. Withdrawal of the licensing clauses.

London was made a county of itself with a separate Lord-Lieutenant and Commission of the Peace, as well as with a council, chairman, and aldermen. The aldermen were to be one-sixth of the whole council instead of one-third as in other counties. The Parliamentary divisions of the metropolis

The London County Council.

---

[1] Owing, however, to the discontinuance of the grants-in-aid which amounted to £2,600,000 the net gain to the ratepayer was £3,026,000. See Hansard, cccxxiv. p. 291.

were taken as the electoral divisions for the council; each division returning two councillors.

Until the year 1855, London outside the city had been governed by the inhabitants of the different parishes assembled in vestries, except where select vestries had under Hobhouse's Act been elected by the ratepayers. Town management was undertaken by a large number of irresponsible commissioners, appointed under no less than 250 local Acts. By the Metropolis Management Act of 1855 vestries elected by the ratepayers were established for each parish. In the twenty-two larger parishes vestries so elected were constituted local authorities; while the fifty-six smaller parishes were grouped together in fifteen districts, each under a district board, the members of which were elected by vestries of the constituent parishes. At the same time the Metropolitan Board of Works was established, the members of which were elected by the Common Council of the city, the vestries, and the district boards. To this Board was entrusted the construction of main sewers, the improvement and regulation of bridges and streets, and other analogous functions. By the Act of 1888 the Board was abolished, and its duties transferred to the London County Council. The moment was opportune; for rumours of jobs and other scandals had resulted in the appointment of a Commission to inquire into the proceedings of the Board; and, though the Commissioners acquitted the Board of the graver charges brought against them, no regret was felt at their disappearance. By its inheritance of the powers and duties of the Board of Works the London County Council was invested with a larger authority than that allotted to the other councils created by the Act. It was, however, given no powers over the metropolitan police; who, except within the precincts of the City, were left under the control of the Home Secretary.

Moderates and Progressives.

The only institution created by the Act which excited general interest was the London County Council. It gave to the inhabitants of the metropolis a new sense of corporate unity, and stirred the civic spirit within them. The first chairman elected was Lord Rosebery, a former Prime Minister, and an eloquent exponent of large ideas. Although the work of the council is administrative, party distinctions asserted themselves from the first—issue being taken on questions as to the right scope and limits of municipal activity. The Progressives, as the Liberal party in the council were called, were desirous to extend these limits; the Moderates, as their Conservative opponents were first named, to restrict them in the interests of economy. Except in 1895, when an equal number of Progressives and Moderates were elected, the Moderates suffered uninterrupted defeat at the successive triennial elections until 1907, although during the same period until 1906 the majority of the same constituencies were represented by Unionists in the House of Commons. And the Parliamentary election of 1906, at which for the first time for a generation a majority of Liberal members was returned for the London constituencies, was followed by the municipal election of 1907, at which the Conservatives, under the new name of Municipal Reformers, gained their first majority on the London County Council. The reason of this apparent inconsistency may perhaps be traced to the somewhat exalted and imperialistic spirit which animated the country, and especially London, during the closing years of the nineteenth century, with the heavy expenditure, local and national, which was its consequence, and the renewed interest in retrenchment which arose when the burden involved in that expenditure began to make itself felt. For, just as in national concerns, the Unionist party sought to captivate the imagination of the electors by the vision of a vast and world-controlling Empire, in promoting the interests of which it was held that no cost should be counted, while the Liberals in Parliament protested against the increasing expenditure and what they considered too ready an assumption of fresh Imperial responsibilities; so in the London County Council the positions were exactly reversed. There the Progressives were the party of action and enterprise; they were inclined to enter upon undertakings beseeming the largest city in the world, and to magnify the functions and position of the representative body in which they held the majority. The Moderates, on the other hand, attacked Progressive enterprise as socialistic, and stood forth as the champions of economy. The same impatience under burdens which must be borne when Imperial thinking is translated into action caused the London taxpayer to return a Liberal majority to Parliament in 1906, and impelled him in his character as ratepayer to give their opponents a first majority on the London County Council in 1907.

The provincial county councils. The provincial county councils have fulfilled the expectations of their authors. The country gentlemen, whose administrative work in quarter sessions had been admittedly honest and efficient, were ready to serve on the new bodies, and their services were generally welcomed by the electors. The elections to most of these councils are not on party lines. In the absence of party rivalry contests are few and the interest taken by the electors in the composition of the councils slight.[1] The councils work through committees; and are only obliged by the Act to meet four times in the year. The committees on finance, on education, and the visiting committee on asylums are prescribed by law; but each council has other committees for the rest of its business. No order for the payment of money can be made except on the recommendation of the Finance Committee. The Chairman, whose re-election has become customary on most county councils, is placed by the standing orders on every committee—a rule which, together with his habitual permanence of tenure, sometimes gives him great influence.

Local Government Act, 1894. The policy which found expression in the introduction of the Local Government Act of 1888 by a Conservative Government was continued and completed by their Liberal successors in the Act of 1894. This important measure was introduced by Mr. Fowler in March, 1893, and became law at the close of the longest of recorded sessions in the same month of the following year. District councils and parish councils were created by the Act; and, together with the county councils instituted in 1888, formed the basis of a complete hierarchy of local government in the rural parts of England and Wales. The parish became the administrative unit of local government; and the endeavour was made that the whole of every parish should be in the same district, and the whole of every rural district in the same county.

Rural sanitary districts were, as we have seen, first created by the Public Health Act of 1872, and the authorities in these districts were the guardians of the poor. Before 1894, the rural sanitary district embraced the area of the poor law union

[1] In 1901, out of 3349 seats in England and Wales only 433 were contested.

exclusive of any urban sanitary district within it. The magistrates of the district were guardians *ex-officio*, and the other guardians on the board were elected by the owners and occupiers of the district on a system of plural voting. The number of votes to which an owner or occupier was entitled increased with the rateable value of his house up to a maximum of six when that rateable value amounted to £250; and as he was allowed to vote in both capacities an owner who occupied his house might have as many as twelve votes. There was, moreover, a property qualification of £5 a year for the elective guardians. The sanitary areas, defined by the Public Health Act of 1872, were adopted with some re-arrangement as the areas to be committed to the care of the new district councils, chiefly because, unlike poor law unions, school board districts, and other areas defined for special purposes, regard had been had to the ancient county boundaries when they were mapped out.

The connection between poor law and sanitary administration, established by the Public Health Act of 1872, was continued by the Local Government Act of 1894. If the group of parishes forming the poor law union extended into more than one county, it was divided into two rural districts; or if not large enough to be so divided the smaller part was merged into the adjacent rural district. The sanitary powers of the guardians were transferred by the Act to the rural district councils; but since the councillors were in rural districts to act as guardians, who were no longer to be elected as such, the change was rather nominal than actual. The only change effected by the Act with regard to poor law administration was an alteration in the mode of election of the guardians. District councillors, both urban and rural, are under the Act elected by ballot for three years by the parochial electors; one-third retire in each year unless an order is made to the contrary; and there are no aldermen. In urban districts where guardians continued to be elected separately they were henceforward to be elected in the same manner; in rural districts every district councillor was commissioned to represent his parish on the board of guardians for the union comprising the district. *Ex-officio* guardians disappeared; the property qualification was abolished; no elector was allowed more than

Poor law and sanitary administration. Change in manner of electing guardians.

a single vote; and the ballot replaced the system of voting papers.

The sanitary powers exercised in urban districts by local boards were transferred to the urban district councils, and these boards were abolished. Except with regard to main roads and county bridges, which remained under the control of the county councils, the district council, whether urban or rural, also became the highway authority and the highway boards came to an end. The election to London vestries was placed on the same footing as that to urban district councils.

Parish meetings and parish councils. The consolidation of the poor law, sanitary, and highway authorities, the simplification of areas, and the institution of a uniform mode of election, in the case of all local authorities, except the school boards, were the most important changes effected by the Act of 1894. But the only part of the Act which attracted much public attention were the clauses under which parish meetings were revived and parish councils established in rural parishes. Up to 1894, the parish vestry, whether open or select, presided over by the incumbent and served by its churchwardens and overseers, was the only parochial authority. It had been deprived in the course of time of all the more important of its powers. The management of poor relief was transferred by the Poor Law Amendment Act of 1834 to the board of guardians, elected by the union comprising the parish, although the duty of assessing and levying the rate imposed by the union was left to the parish overseers and, with that of making up the parochial register of voters for Parliamentary and local government elections, now constitutes their principal function. To the guardians were also transferred in 1872 the sanitary powers, few in number and insufficiently exercised, which had belonged to the vestries. The remaining powers of urban vestries were equally insignificant; and might, it was thought, be conveniently left to them, while such other functions as in rural districts were committed to the new parish councils would in towns be better placed in the hands of the urban district councils than in any smaller bodies. Urban parishes were therefore left untouched by the Act of 1894 and it became necessary clearly to distinguish them from rural parishes. It was accordingly enacted that where a parish lay partly in an urban and partly in a rural sanitary district it should be divided into two, and that each part should become a separate parish. There are civil parishes and ecclesiastical parishes; but for the purposes of the Act a rural parish is any place which is not within an urban district, and for which a separate poor rate can be made or a separate overseer appointed.

In such parishes, a parish meeting is held at least once a year under the Act, where there is a council, and at least twice a year where there is none, which all the inhabitants on either the Parliamentary or the local government register have a right to attend.[1] In every parish with a population of over 300 there is also a parish council elected at a meeting by the parochial electors. When the population of a parish is above 100 but under 300 it may have a council if the parish meeting so resolves, and even when the population is below 100 if the county council decides to establish one and the parish meeting consents. The parish meeting may adopt such permissive acts as Parliament has passed for lighting and watching the parish or supplying it with baths, burial-grounds, recreation grounds, and libraries; and where there is no parish council the meeting has certain of its powers, including those transferred from the vestry and the appointment of overseers. It may levy a rate not exceeding sixpence in the pound. The parish council is elected for one year only. All the powers, disconnected with the Church, of the vestry were transferred to it. It appoints the overseers, may acquire and manage land for allotments, utilise wells and springs for water supply, acquire by agreement rights of way, provide buildings for public purposes, and acquire land for such buildings. It may not incur expenditure involving a rate of more than threepence in the pound without the consent of the parish meeting, and in no case of more than sixpence in the pound.

The institution of parish councils has had little effect either for good or for evil on life in country districts. The areas concerned are small; the powers of the new bodies governed by the rate limit are not extensive; and the interest of the apathetic and occupied rural population in the change, to them more nominal than real, of an administration with which they had no previous

[1] That is to say owners as well as occupiers. The vestry meetings were open only to ratepayers.

quarrel is so slight that neither the hopes of the promoters nor the fears of the opposers of the new settlement can be said to have been justified by experience.

<small>Gradual organisation of local government.</small> The Education Act of 1902 abolished school boards and transferred their powers to the county and borough councils to be exercised by those bodies through committees. The confusion of areas, rates, modes of election, and authorities reached its climax with the Education Act of 1870 under which school boards elected by a novel franchise and administering new areas for a special purpose were instituted; from that time forward a new policy had been adopted, and the task of co-ordinating the various organs of local government and evolving order out of chaos through the committal of miscellaneous powers to single bodies in lieu of the creation of miscellaneous bodies for the exercise of single powers was at length almost completed in the Education Act of 1902. The country is now divided into administrative counties and county boroughs; subdivided into districts, urban and rural, and boroughs; and again subdivided into parishes. In all these divisions and subdivisions, there are councils elected on nearly the same franchise. The only remaining local government authorities of importance acting in their own areas for a specific purpose are the guardians of the poor, and only in urban districts are these separately elected. The rural district councils and the boards of guardians are, it is true, distinct bodies; but every rural district councillor is *ex-officio* a guardian. If the union of which he is an officer happens to extend into more than one county he will serve with one set of colleagues on the board and with another on the council.

<small>London government within and without the City.</small> London was left outside the Local Government Act of 1894. The ancient City, with its Lord Mayor, its court of aldermen elected for life, its charters and privileges, its freedom from external control, its separate courts and police force, its banquets and its pageantry, was left almost untouched by the Municipal Reform Act of 1835, and all subsequent local government legislation, and stands out not only as an interesting monument of the past, but, it is said, as a model of efficient administration. The villages surrounding the cities of London and Westminster, after they had been swallowed up by the advancing tide of houses and, merged into one vast town, had

become indistinguishable one from another, retained their old names; and their inhabitants, though in number increased a thousandfold, continued to manage their own affairs assembled in their vestries. The existence of London outside the City was at last officially recognised by the creation in 1829 of Sir Robert Peel's metropolitan police force, and further progress was made in the process of adapting administrative machinery to new requirements by the reorganisation of vestries and district boards on a uniform electoral basis in 1855; by the creation in the same year of a central authority for certain public purposes in the Metropolitan Board of Works; and above all by the foundation in 1888 of the London County Council to deal with matters in which all parts of the metropolis were alike interested.

After 1894 the position of the London vestries and district boards was clearly anomalous. Alone among the vestries of England they were still the sanitary authorities for their respective areas. Woolwich still preserved a Local Board of Health. Commissioners appointed under local Acts exercised powers in respect of baths and wash-houses, libraries, and burial arrangements. Some of the vestries petitioned that their parishes might be converted into boroughs. The transference to urban district councils of the secular powers of the vestries was another course suggested. Eventually in 1899 action was taken by the Unionist Government, and the London Government Act was the principal measure of that year. This Act substituted for the existing vestries and administrative boards twenty-eight boroughs with identical powers and organisation. Seventeen of these boroughs were co-extensive with the larger parishes or districts, six were measured by the boundaries of Parliamentary constituencies, and the others were made up of combinations of the smaller parishes. No area was made a separate municipality that had not a population above 100,000 or below 400,000, or a rateable value exceeding £500,000. The powers entrusted to the new authorities included not only those which had been exercised by the vestries and district boards, but others previously committed to baths and washhouses commissioners, libraries commissioners, and burial boards. They were also empowered to promote and oppose local bills in Parliament, and to levy a single comprehensive

The London Government Act, 1899.

rate. Women, who had been eligible to the London vestries, were not at first given the same privilege in respect of the new borough councils; and, as they were also excluded from the county councils, to which bodies the functions of the school boards were transferred by the Act of 1902, the effect of the legislation of 1899 and 1902 was to deprive them of opportunities of public usefulness which many of them valued. Their privileges, however, were restored by an Act passed in 1907 which made them eligible to all borough and county councils.

Establishment of the Metropolitan Water Board, 1902.

The main sewers of London were under the control of the county council, but the water supply, a matter of equal importance to every Londoner, remained until 1902 in the hands of eight private companies. There was a general agreement that a need so universal should be supplied by a single representative public authority, but there was a difference of opinion as to the constitution of this authority. Liberals, who then commanded a majority in the county council, and were anxious to extend the powers of that body, claimed that the water supply of London should be entrusted to the council, but it was fairly objected that the area to be supplied was larger than that comprised in the county of London, and that any body appointed to administer the water supply must be representative of the whole of that area. Accordingly the Unionist Government passed a bill by which a Metropolitan Water Board was created. The board consists of sixty-seven representatives, chosen by the sanitary authorities over the whole of the water area. Fourteen are named by the London County Council, one each by the metropolitan boroughs, and the rest by the various county, borough, and district authorities within the area of supply. A member of the board must be a member of the council that appoints him. Power is given to the Local Government Board to vary the constitution of the board by Provisional Order. The establishment of a new authority to deal with a particular need was a departure in some degree from the policy which had prevailed since 1871.

Growth, decline, and revival of central control.

The reorganisation of local government in England has been accompanied and set in motion by a great revival of central control. The anarchy and confusion into which England was plunged by the internecine struggles of the old feudal nobility under the last kings of the Plantagenet line were brought to an end by the strong central government established by the Tudors. The authority of the King's Council was strengthened. To a committee of that council, known from the room in which it met as the Star Chamber, important powers were given, that they might be enabled to reach and repress the insolency of those great offenders "who being far from the king and the seat of justice . . . made their force their law, binding themselves, with their tenants and servants, to do or revenge an injury one against another as they listed".[1] The centralisation of power under the Tudors was accepted by the English people as a boon; but the extension of this principle by the first two Stuart kings, their over-government, their interference with trade and with the minutiæ of daily life caused a general irritation which was a leading cause of the Great Rebellion. The proclamations of Charles I., so far as their subject-matter is concerned, resemble the regulations and directions issued by the Local Government Board. Some contained regulations intended to prevent the spread of epidemical disease; others prescribed the use of bricks instead of wood for building houses in London; others, of a more questionable nature, regulated the charges at inns and the price of articles of food. Trade and manufactures were subjected to numerous regulations; by the *Book of Sports* the people were permitted and encouraged to amuse themselves with various games after evening service on Sunday; church attendance itself was compulsory. The first work of the Long Parliament, after its meeting in 1640, was to overthrow this system in the name of liberty, and to destroy the machinery by which it was worked. Star Chamber, Court of High Commission, Council of the North, and other such instruments of central government were swept away; while Laud and Strafford, the inventors of the policy of "Thorough," lost their heads. Thereafter an era of local self-government and freedom from central control began which, fortified by the Revolution of 1688, reached its fullest development during the eighteenth century. The Whig Parliaments, jealous by principle and tradition of the encroachments of the Crown, entrusted necessary or unnecessary powers to individuals and to

[1] Sir Thomas Smith, Commonwealth of England, iii. 4.

local authorities by innumerable special Acts. The squires and the vestries in the country; the close corporations in the boroughs were allowed to administer their respective areas practically uncontrolled. If self-government consists in freedom from external control, the century and a half that followed the Revolution of 1688 must be reckoned as the period since the Conquest in which that privilege has been the most fully enjoyed by separate districts in England. Local government was completely decentralised, for the reason among others that the Central Government itself depended upon the support of members of Parliament belonging to the class of country gentlemen in whom, as justices of the peace, the local administration of the country was vested, and who would be likely to resent any interference with their liberty of action.

Central control over poor law administration.

When, after the Reform Act of 1832, the Government became more representative of the country as a whole, jealousy of State interference became proportionately less, and was indeed replaced by a demand for State activity. The Poor Law Amendment Act of 1834 grouped parishes into unions, confined relief to destitution, and gave power to Commissioners to prohibit the grant of outdoor relief to the able-bodied. Poor Law Commissioners were appointed with extensive authority to supervise the working of the new system, and through their agency the first great experiment in central control since the seventeenth century was made. In 1847 the Commissioners, who had incurred much unpopularity, were organised on a permanent basis, with a Minister at their head, as the Poor Law Board, and in 1871 reached their final development by amalgamation with other central authorities as the Local Government Board. The control of the Local Government Board is more complete in respect of poor law administration than in respect of any other branch of local government. Strengthened since its creation by a long succession of statutes, it possesses large semi-legislative powers. These are exercised by general or special orders—general orders binding on all the unions to which they are issued,[1] special orders on individual unions only.

[1] Such was the Outdoor Relief Prohibitory Order issued in 1844, which prohibited, save in certain specified cases, the giving of outdoor relief to able-bodied persons, and such again the Outdoor Relief Regulation Order of 1852,

The Board can modify at its discretion the boundaries of unions, create new unions, or dissolve existing unions. No union officer can be appointed or dismissed by the guardians without the sanction of the Board, though any union officer may be dismissed by the Board without the consent of the guardians. Government inspectors have a right to attend and speak at meetings of the guardians. The e inspectors make a careful survey of the general local administration existing in their respective areas and report the results of their inquiries to the central authority. Most important of all is the financial control. The accounts of all boards of guardians are subjected to a half-yearly audit by the district auditor,[1] to whose investigations those concerned are bound to give every facility. The auditor hears and examines objections made by individual ratepayers, he disallows improper items of expenditure and reduces exorbitant payments and charges, and he surcharges guardians who have authorised irregular expenditure with the sums they have thus misapplied. Finally, no loan may be contracted without the sanction of the Local Government Board. But however comprehensive the control of the central authority over poor law administration may appear to be, combining as it does an interest in the details of daily life in the workhouse with the power of ordering almost any act to be done except the giving of relief in a particular case, the system does not work in a satisfactory manner. This is not because too little self-government is entrusted to the unions, but, on the contrary, because too much remains to them. The guardians, within the discretion allowed to them by statutes and orders, can and do administer the poor law very variously. There is a general demand for increased guidance on the part of the central authority, and complaint is made that the policy of the

which permitted outdoor relief subject to conditions as to setting the recipient to work in labour yards. A third order, called the Labour Test Order, was afterwards issued by the Board, having been necessitated by the inapplicability of the Prohibitory Order in unions where workhouses were overcrowded in times of industrial depression. In 1910 of 644 unions 274 were under the Prohibitory Order alone, 254 under the Prohibitory and Labour Tests Orders combined, and 116 under the Regulation Order.

[1] The country, not including the metropolis, is divided for audit purposes into thirty-three districts, under the Districts Auditors Act, 1879, and the Local Government Board appoints district auditors, who audit on the spot the accounts of all local authorities.

poor law is not at present defined with sufficient clearness. Little interest is taken in the election of guardians. In the rural districts the majority are tenant farmers, whose principal thought in poor law administration is to keep down the rates; in boroughs, on the contrary, the guardians, chiefly tradesmen, are said to regard the board as a practising ground for the Town Council, and in order to be elected are inclined to make promises of liberal relief. Thus the Local Government Board finds itself obliged to check extravagance in London and the boroughs, and parsimony in the country.

Reports of the Poor Law Commission, 1905. Both the majority and minority reports of the Commission appointed in December, 1905, to inquire into the working of the poor law, recommended that boards of guardians should be abolished. The majority of the Commissioners desired to substitute for the board in every county or county borough a Public Assistance Authority, consisting in half of persons chosen from their own body by the county or county borough council, and in half of persons appointed by the council from outside. Under this authority there should be a Public Assistance Committee in each union area. The minority proposed more simply to adopt the course taken with regard to education in 1902, and to transfer the functions of boards of guardians to county and county borough councils to be exercised through their committees.

Central control over other local bodies. The control of the central authority over other branches of local administration is less regular and direct than that which it exercises in respect of the poor law, and there is no general power of legislating by order. There is little direct power of enforcing action, even when that action is prescribed by law, and the Department can only, as a rule, compel a recalcitrant local authority to do its statutory duty by applying to the High Court for a writ of *mandamus*. Even with regard to such important matters as unadulterated food, pure water, and uncontaminated air, although numerous Acts make it the business of the Department to oblige local bodies to carry out the sanitary laws, it can only, as a rule, do this through the medium of the High Court. The Local Government Board, indeed, may make rules under various statutes relating to certain special subjects, such as the prevention of disease and accommodation on canal boats; it has large discretionary powers in case of epidemics; it can make regulations about vaccination, and may rearrange parish boundaries under the Divided Parishes Acts. Again, the Board of Agriculture, a new Central Department constituted by an Act of 1889, has the power of issuing general orders to local authorities for the suppression of disease among animals; and a wise, though at the same time unpopular, exercise of this power by an order for the temporary muzzling of dogs has earned for Mr. Long the gratitude of his countrymen by the extinction it effected of rabies in Great Britain. But these are exceptional instances provided for by the Legislature and not to be compared with the volume of general orders by which the Local Government Board directs in detail the action of poor law guardians. If, however, the central authority has little direct power of making rules or commanding particular things to be done, its authority in restraint of action is much more considerable. By Provisional Orders requiring a confirmation by Parliament, which is seldom refused, the Local Government Board may amend or repeal local sanitary Acts. Further, it may amend or disallow bylaws made by any local authority under the Public Health Act, 1875, or the Highways Act of 1878, and its sanction is required for the purchase of waterworks and in other such matters.

It is not, however, by direct administrative control, whether *Inspection and advice.* of a general or a particular kind, that the power of the central government makes itself principally felt over local bodies other than Boards of Guardians. The power of inspection and the right to advise are the main sources of its authority, and to this authority financial assistance given by the State for local purposes, and the dependence of local authorities thereon, give an irresistible sanction. There are general inspectors, who survey and report upon local administration as a whole in the districts assigned to them, and may attend the meetings of the local authorities; engineering inspectors, who are concerned with buildings and public works; medical inspectors, whose office it is to see that the local authorities are properly carrying out the sanitary laws, and that analysts of food are appointed for every district; school inspectors; and district auditors. These experts report to the central department, which is guided in its action by the facts disclosed. The information thus obtained, together with that derived from the statistical returns which the department is by statute empowered to demand from the officials of the various local bodies, enables the Board to give efficient advice to the local authorities, by whom it is consulted, and to suggest not only the principles on which they should act but the manner in which in particular cases those principles should be applied. The permanent officials employed by the local authorities, by whom in reality the local work is done under the general, and often deferential, supervision of the various committees of the councils, are in constant communication with the experts who represent the central department, and draw largely from the reservoir of central knowledge and experience. An annual report is issued by the Local Government Board to give to Parliament an account of its stewardship. This report covers the whole field of local government, and imparts the information which the Board has derived from the reports of its inspectors.

Financial supervision and support. Thus it is mainly by inspection and advice that the central authorities exert their influence on subordinate bodies. But their chief means of direct control lie in the financial support which it is in their power to give or to withhold. Not only must every loan contracted by a local body receive the sanction of the central department, not only can its auditors refuse to allow any illegal expenditure, but in carrying out some of their most important duties, such as those relating to education and the police, the local authorities are dependent to a large degree on the financial assistance of the State. And this assistance is not granted unconditionally. The Public Health Act of 1875 provides that where part of the salary of a local officer is paid out of money voted by Parliament his qualifications, conditions of appointment, duties, salary, and tenure of office may be regulated by the Local Government Board. The effect of this provision is to bring most of the medical officers of health appointed by local authorities under the direct control of the Board. In the case of the county police half the cost of their pay and clothing is defrayed out of the Exchequer Contribution Account, with the ingenious stipulation that should the police force in any county or county borough prove inefficient a fine to that amount shall be levied on the local authority, or, in other words, that the whole cost of maintenance shall be transferred to the rates. The central control secured by the education grant is of even higher importance, since non-provided schools, though maintained by the local authority, remain under private management.

The institution of three grades of local authorities—county councils, district councils, and parish councils—among which, with one exception, all functions of local government have been distributed; and their co-ordination under the supervision and control of the central authority, have been the main results of the legislation described in this chapter. The boards of guardians in urban districts, elected to perform special functions and unrelated to the other local authorities, still stand outside this system; but it is probable that whenever the poor law is reformed these small and self-contained bodies will be brought to an end, and the modern principle that a single representative body in each district should execute all the various functions of local government through separate departments will be adopted in a complete form. The real effect of these changes has been to transfer the local administration of affairs from local magnates to trained officials. The more widely the functions of government are conceived the more they tend to pass into the hands of an expert bureaucracy. The greater the complexity of administration, the larger will be the power attaching to knowledge. And since it is the nature of officials to gravitate to a centre and to refer difficult questions to a higher authority, whereas the magnate whose administrative power is an accident of his position is rather inclined to follow his own judgment and to resent external interference, this transfer of power to officials has led to a great increase in central bureaucratic authority. The growing importance of the Local Government Board and of the Board of Trade was recognised by Parliament in 1909, when the salaries of the presidents were placed on an equality with those of the Secretaries of State.

Summary of results.

CHAPTER VI.

REFORMS IN THE CIVIL SERVICE, THE ARMY, AND THE JUDICATURE.

<small>Liberalism and the doctrine of *laissez-faire*.</small> THE aim of Whigs and of Liberals of the old school was to restrict the sphere of Government activity within the narrowest possible limits, and, with that end in view, to abolish all those privileges which, based on State interference, hampered the free play of competition in the community. They wished to open an unshackled career to talents; to make the game of life a game purely of skill, and not one of skill and chance commingled. The reason why Liberals wished thus to confine the collective activity of the community to the few necessary functions of protecting persons and property, of enforcing contracts, of deciding differences by arbitration, and of organising the nation for defence against external violence was that at a time when the direction of this collective activity was concentrated in a few hands they thought that its further developments were likely to be employed, not to the general advantage, but in the interests of the directors and their class. Down to 1832, so strong was the influence of the Crown that it could always by a dissolution secure a majority in the House of Commons for the Ministers of its choice; and even in the generation that succeeded the first Reform Act the Government continued to be very aristocratic. In more recent times, when the depositaries of power had become through successive extensions of the suffrage more directly representative of the people, jealousy of Government interference and patronage ceased almost entirely to be felt by the party with which it had been especially associated, and survived only among a section of their opponents.

It was fortunate that before the Liberal party, changing its point of view, came to regard the State as the community organised for action, whose intervention, so far from being dreaded, was at every point to be invited and encouraged, a Liberal Government had arrived at the conclusion that the bulk of the patronage hitherto exercised by the Ministry with regard to appointments in the Civil Service should cease to be so exercised, and that these appointments should be made by open competitive examination.

This important reform was brought about by degrees. In 1853 Sir Charles Trevelyan and Sir Stafford Northcote had been commissioned by Mr. Gladstone, at that time Chancellor of the Exchequer, to inquire into the organisation of the Civil Service, and had reported in favour of a system of appointment by open competitive examination. In 1855, an Order in Council was issued under which three Civil Service Commissioners were appointed, whose office it was to test by examination the capacity of all candidates for the junior posts in the Civil Service. The next step was the introduction of a system of limited competition, according to which, when a vacancy occurred in any department, the Minister nominated three candidates who competed for the place. This was an arrangement likely to commend itself to Ministers, whose patronage was increased while their responsibility was diminished; and so, although a Select Committee in 1860, presided over by Lord Stanley, declared the system to be a fertile source of abuse, nothing further was done to change it until 1870. In that year Mr. Gladstone, who had long wished to abolish the privilege of nomination, was Prime Minister, and Mr. Lowe was his Chancellor of the Exchequer. No statesman of his time had so profound a distrust of democracy as Mr. Lowe—a distrust based on his experience and observation of political life in democratic communities. He knew that patronage was valued at least as much by a democracy as by an aristocracy, and was used with even less scruple for party purposes. The origin of the "spoils" system in the United States—that is of a system under which civil servants are dismissed on political grounds when one party replaces another in power—has been traced by American writers to the article in the Declaration of Rights of the Constitution of Massachusetts adopted in 1780, which contains the claim that "the people have the right at such periods and in such manner as they shall establish by their frame of government, to cause their public officers to return to private life; and to fill up vacant places by certain and regular elections and appointments". That system had never taken root in England, though we had a taste of it in 1763, but Mr. Lowe was convinced that all the abuses he had observed in other democracies were inseparable from popular government, and he was earnest in his endeavours not only "to educate our masters" but also to withdraw the Civil Service from their control. He it was who had been, when Secretary to the Board of Control, the chief author of the less necessary measure which opened the Civil Service of India to competition in 1853, and he was now successful in persuading his colleagues to agree to the adoption of the same system for the Home Civil Service.

Open competitive examinations established by Order in Council, 1870.

No legislation was needed. On the 4th of June, 1870, after the opposition of certain members of the Cabinet had been disarmed by the concession that the approval of the Minister at the head of a department should be a condition of its inclusion in the new system, an Order in Council was issued establishing the principle of open competitive examinations for filling ordinary junior posts in the Civil Service. The Order directed that from the following 31st of August all entrance appointments to all situations in the civil departments of the State, except to the Foreign Office and to posts requiring professional knowledge or peculiar qualifications, should be filled by open competition. Certain posts at the top and at the bottom of the service were also exempted from the Order, and the power of dismissal was vested in the chiefs of departments. There was also a provision that a successful candidate should pass through a six months' period of probation in order that his actual efficiency might be tested before his appointment was confirmed.

Importance of the reform.

It is difficult to exaggerate the importance of this reform. With the growth of democracy the functions of government increase in number and complexity, and the work of administration is thrown more and more into the hands of the permanent servants of the Crown. Ministers change rapidly from office to office; they are too much occupied with legislative projects and general party issues to have time to master or effectively to control the administrative business of their separate departments. Their very responsibility for what is done inclines them to follow the advice and to trust to the experience of professional administrators. The Civil Service was placed beyond the reach of party. Supporters of the Government were no longer obliged either to offend influential constituents by refusing to recommend their sons and nephews to the Patronage Secretary for appointments; or else to make such recommendations without any regard to the interests of the public service. The Patronage Secretary was no longer tempted to reward party loyalty by misusing his patronage with that object. And thus the impartiality and efficiency of civil servants were effectually secured just at the time when the growth of their power and the expansion of their functions rendered their possession of those qualities of essential importance to the nation.

In the year succeeding that in which the Civil Service had been thrown open to public competition by a Ministerial employment of the power of the Crown, another reform of the same character relating to the army was carried through by the same agency. The purchase of commissions in the army had been a practice officially recognised ever since in 1683 a royal warrant was issued ordering the payment of one shilling in the pound, on the surrender of a commission, to the person surrendering, by him to whom the surrender was made. Prohibited by William III., it was again formally authorised by Queen Anne in 1711 whenever sanctioned by the royal approbation under sign-manual and after twenty years service. In 1765, in accordance with the recommendation of a Royal Commission, purchase prices were fixed by authority from that of an ensigncy at £400 to that of the command of a regiment at £3500; and the payment of over-regulation sums was made penal in 1798. From the operation of an Act passed in 1809 "for the prevention of the sale and brokerage of offices"—purchases and sales of commissions at regulation prices were expressly excepted. While, however, this Act empowered the sovereign to sanction the sale of commissions at regulation prices it did not oblige him so to do, or in any way debar him from withdrawing that sanction at his discretion. In spite of the penalties attached to the transaction, prices much higher than those fixed by the regulations continued to be paid for commissions, nor was any serious

History of Army Purchase.

effort made to enforce the law. An officer, who had paid an over-regulation price for his promotion, held his commission as an estate in pledge with which he could not be expected to part without adequate indemnification. The system was defended on the ground that by encouraging early retirement it ensured rapid promotion, and it had been upheld by the Duke of Wellington, at a time when the possession of money was more generally associated with gentle birth than it has since become, for the reasons that made him in other respects a Tory. But it worked unjustly. The poor officer who, like Havelock, could not afford to purchase promotion saw himself passed by others in no wise his superiors in any qualification except wealth, while it was necessary to promote to the command of regiments and companies not those officers who best deserved such promotion but those who could afford to pay high prices to the men whom they replaced.

Mr. Cardwell at the War Office.

In 1871, as a result of the Franco-Prussian war, England was suffering from one of those periodical fits of extreme discomfort about herself and her defences which give to the practical reformer his opportunity. Happily such a reformer in the person of Mr. Cardwell was at that time at the head of the War Office. Mr. Cardwell had been occupied with his scheme of army reconstruction, of which a brief account will presently be given, and had found the web of vested interests incident to the purchase system an insuperable obstacle in his way. It was impossible, as he said, for our army, militia, and volunteers to be amalgamated and made interchangeable if the officers of one portion were under the Crown and a purchase system, while the others were under the lords-lieutenant, and on a footing of non-purchase.[1]

The Government determine to abolish the purchase system, 1871.

The substitution of promotion by selection for promotion by purchase and "the reconveyance of the army from the officers to the nation"[2] were conditions essential to the success of Mr. Cardwell's new scheme. Accordingly in 1871 the Government decided to bring the purchase system to an end. In giving effect to this decision two courses were open to the Government. They might, with or without the formal approval of the House of Commons, advise the sovereign to abolish purchase by royal warrant, or they might proceed by bill. The purchase

[1] Hansard, vol. cciv. p. 338.   [2] Mr. Goschen's description of the project.

system had been, if not created, at least authorised and regulated by royal warrant, and the discretionary power of the sovereign had been recognised and confirmed by the Act of 1809. On the other hand the army could not justly be reconveyed from the officers to the nation without the repayment to the officers of the expenses to which, with the assent or connivance of the authorities, they had been subjected; and this repayment involved an Act of Parliament. The Government, therefore, thought it best not to separate the means from the end, but to include both, together with other reforms, in the Army Regulation Bill which Mr. Cardwell introduced early in the session of 1871.

The purchase clauses of the Army Regulation Bill provided that after a certain day no pecuniary interest should be taken by any one in any new commission. At the same time no officer was to suffer loss by the change, for over-regulation prices as well as regulation prices were to be fully repaid. Mr. Cardwell estimated that the sum thus payable by way of compensation would amount to about £8,000,000. The progress of the bill through the House of Commons was obstructed with a persistency of which there had been few previous examples, with the consequence that not only was a great part of the session devoted to its discussion, and other bills announced in the Queen's Speech abandoned, but the whole of the bill itself had to be dropped, except the purchase clauses and the transfer of power over the militia and volunteers from the lords-lieutenant to the Crown. *The Army Regulation Bill, 1871.*

The growing unpopularity of the Government, whose conduct of foreign policy humiliated the national pride, and the rough handling which their bill had received in the House of Commons, encouraged the House of Lords to make an effort at resistance. The Lords had already in the spring passed the bill for the abolition of religious tests at the universities—a measure which they had long resisted—and perhaps they thought they had made concessions enough for a single session. However that may be, when the Army Regulation Bill came before them for second reading, an amendment was moved by the Duke of Richmond, and carried, to the effect that the peers were unwilling to assent to the principle of the measure until they had before them a complete and comprehensive scheme *Resistance of the Lords.*

for the appointment, promotion, and retirement of officers, and for placing the military system of the country on a sound and efficient basis.

<small>Abolition of purchase by royal warrant.</small> The defeat of their bill in the Upper House placed the Government in a difficult position. The session had proved a failure and their followers were discontented. Bills of importance—Mr. Goschen's Local Government Bill and Mr. Bruce's Licensing Bill—had been introduced only to be withdrawn, in order to make time for the Army Bill and an Irish Coercion Bill. To acquiesce in the loss of a measure for which so much had been sacrificed would have been a confession of impotence which Mr. Gladstone was, of all men, the least likely to make except under the pressure of overmastering necessity. However indefinite and ambiguous his speech, like that of Cromwell, may habitually have been, there was nothing indirect about his action when his imperious will was thwarted or his vulnerable temper wounded. Opposition to a Government measure by the Lords, indissoluble as they are and directly responsible to none but themselves, can only in the end be overcome by the employment of the royal prerogative. That was the consideration urged by Lord Grey in defence of the threatened creation of peers in 1832. And it was a consideration entitled to some weight in defence of the milder exercise of the prerogative to which the sovereign, on the advice of Mr. Gladstone, now resorted. Moreover, the law was habitually being violated with the acquiescence of the authorities by the purchase and sale of commissions at over-regulation prices, and it was clear that this practice could not be terminated except by the extinction of purchase as a system. These considerations prevailed; and on the 20th July Mr. Gladstone was able to acquaint an astonished House of Commons that the purchase system had ceased to exist, inasmuch as the queen, on the advice of her Ministers, had revoked the royal warrant by which it was authorised, and had issued another for its abolition.

<small>Criticisms of this proceeding.</small> This bold step was loudly condemned by the opponents of the Ministry, and met with hostile criticism on the part of some of the most influential of their supporters. The queen herself, in spite of rumours to the contrary, seems to have acquiesced without much difficulty in the course of action

proposed to her by her constitutional advisers, only submitting that since it was "a strong exercise of her power in apparent opposition to the House of Lords, she should like to have some more formal expression of the advice of the Cabinet than was contained in an ordinary letter from the Prime Minister"—a reasonable condition that was at once complied with by the embodiment of the advice in a Cabinet minute.[1] But the general opinion was, that in proceeding by bill, instead of advising the sovereign in the first instance to use the discretion confirmed to her by the Act of 1809, the Government had admitted the right of the House of Lords to a voice in the matter, and that, after having implicitly made this admission, to fall back on the royal prerogative to overrule their decision was a course of action not only insulting to the Lords but in itself unconstitutional. It was pointed out that the Act of 1809, though it recognised, did not create the purchase system or the royal power with regard to it, and that other important matters, such as the distribution of Parliamentary seats, though in former ages left by the constitution to the royal discretion, could not in modern times be varied but by Act of Parliament.[2] Advanced Liberals, like Mr. Fawcett, had not yet come to recognise the royal power as the most powerful weapon in the Liberal armoury, and still regarded its exercise with peculiar jealousy. The end, however, was gained; Mr. Gladstone had caused his will to prevail; and the Lords were obliged to pass the bill in order to secure to the officers the necessary compensation. But before doing so, they resolved that "the interposition of the Executive during the progress of a measure submitted to Parliament by her Majesty, in order to attain by the exercise of the prerogative, and without the aid of Parliament, the principal object included in that measure, is calculated to depreciate and neutralise the independent action of the Legislature".

The abolition of purchase was only one of the reforms by which Mr. Cardwell's War Secretaryship was distinguished. The Prussian victory at Sadowa in 1866, by which after a war of seven weeks, Austria, to the amazement of Europe, was com-

Institution of a short service system and a reserve, 1870.

[1] Life of Gladstone, ii. 363.
[2] See Lord Salisbury's speech, Hansard, ccviii. p. 477.

pelled to sue for peace, directed attention in England to the excellence of military organisation in Prussia and to the defects in our own. Since 1847 enlistment in the regular army had been for twelve years, and men were encouraged to re-engage at the end of that term for another nine years. Soldiers who had served the full term of twenty-one years were entitled to a pension. It was natural that after a service of twelve years soldiers should think it too late to learn a new trade, and should prefer to secure their pensions by serving for the further period, and this was usually the case. The consequence was that men were often retained in the army after they had ceased to be fully qualified for active service or had anything further to learn, and that the nation was put to a great expense in pensioning old soldiers. For this costly and wasteful system Mr. Cardwell in 1870 substituted one of short service and a reserve imitated from that which had proved so successful in Prussia. A standing army in time of peace ought, he contended, to be a manufactory for making soldiers rather than either a costly receptacle for veterans or a collection of the perfectly trained. He retained the twelve years' enlistment; but the men were to serve only seven years with the colours, and the remaining five years with the reserve. So long as the engagement was for life, as it was before 1847, or for a long term of years as it was before 1870, recruiting was difficult, and utterly unjustifiable methods were employed. Men were tempted by large bounties to join the service. They were often recruited in the public-house, and when they had enlisted were marched off under escort to the depôt. The less serious nature of the engagement men were invited to make under the short service system made it easier to find recruits, and enabled Mr. Cardwell to terminate these grave abuses. Bounties and escorts were abolished; recruiting in public-houses was discouraged; and men who enlisted under the influence of drink were released from their engagement while the recruiting officers who enlisted them were ordered to be punished. The success of this reform may be measured by the statement made thirty years afterwards by Mr. Brodrick, as Secretary for War, in the House of Commons that "Lord Cardwell's system, with but small modification, gave us during the Boer War 80,000 reservists, of whom 96 or 97 per cent.

were found efficient, and has enabled us to keep an army of 150,000 regulars in the field for fifteen months".[1]

Another reform of Mr. Cardwell of an importance scarcely less than the establishment of short service was the combination of standing army, militia, and volunteers into a complete whole on the basis of localisation. The old national force of militia, in theory raised by conscription, though in practice by voluntary enlistment, still remained to a large extent under the control of the lords-lieutenant of counties. The powers of the lords-lieutenant were now transferred to the Crown, and the auxiliary forces placed directly under the command of the generals commanding the districts. At the same time the infantry of the line were re-formed into two-battalion regiments bearing territorial titles with corresponding battalions of militia and volunteers attached to each. The battalion abroad was recruited from the battalion at home, which in its turn was to serve for recruiting and training. *Army localisation and linked battalions.*

Another of Mr. Cardwell's objects was the concentration of force. At the time of his accession to office 49,000 men, out of a total of 137,000, not including the Indian army, were dispersed among the colonies where their services, except in military posts such as Malta and Gibraltar, were little needed. By 1870 Mr. Cardwell had reduced the numbers of men thus employed from 49,000 to 20,941, and the number of troops in British pay by 11,000. He thereby effected a saving of military expenditure on the colonies of £1,600,000, and at the same time increased the strength of our army at home by 3000 men. By the War Office Act of 1870 the dual control of the army was terminated, and the subordination of the office of Commander-in-Chief to the Secretary of State finally established. This change was naturally distasteful to the queen, but the practice from which she never throughout her reign departed of acting on the advice of her constitutional advisers caused her reluctantly to give effect to it by the necessary Orders in Council. *Concentration of force.* *Termination of dual control.*

The strain of the South African War, during which a far larger force of British soldiers left the country on foreign service than at any other period of our history, was on the whole well sustained by our existing military machinery. But the Commission on the war, presided over by Lord Elgin, dis- *Constitution of the Army Council and the Defence Committee, 1904.*

[1] 8th March, 1901.

closed defects in organisation and management which seemed to account for the miscalculations and failures which had marked its commencement, and convinced the nation that some measure of reconstruction was essential to the security of the Empire. In 1904 the office of Commander-in-Chief was abolished, and an Inspector-General of the Forces created. The control of the army thus vacated was entrusted to an Army Council on the model of the Board of Admiralty, consisting of the Chief of the General Staff, the Adjutant-General, the Quartermaster-General, the Master General of the Ordnance, a civil member of the Army Council, and a finance member, under the presidency of the Secretary of State for War. The general organisation of defence was placed under the supervision of a committee of the Cabinet, presided over by the Prime Minister, and known as the Defence Committee.

Reconstruction schemes of Mr. Brodrick and Mr. Arnold-Forster.

These changes concerned the War Office. Their object was to locate responsibility and to simplify military administration. Large schemes for the reconstruction of the army itself were also brought forward by Mr. Brodrick, Secretary for War, in 1902, and by his successor, Mr. Arnold-Forster, in 1904. But the Unionist Government in the last years of its long term of office had fallen into great unpopularity, there was a general disposition to regard with disfavour all its proposals, and it had lost the driving power to carry them through. Mr. Brodrick's scheme, of which the chief feature was the creation of six army corps, cost the country £2,000,000, and was abandoned by his successor, to whom time was not given to bring into operation equally extensive, though less expensive, projects. When, on the resignation of Mr. Balfour's Ministry in December, 1905, Mr. Haldane was appointed Secretary of State for War, his reputation for thoroughness and efficiency made the appointment a popular one in the army, little disposed, as a rule, though it be to greet with favour the advent to power of a Liberal Minister, while his tact and accessibility to advice secured to him the ready assistance of the army chiefs.

Mr. Haldane's reforms.

Mr. Haldane did not act in haste as his predecessors had been accused of doing, and it was not until 1907 that his reforms, involving changes almost as extensive as those introduced by Mr. Cardwell, were brought into operation. The main object of military organisation in time of peace should be, he said, preparedness for war. The test of this preparedness is readiness for mobilisation, and Mr. Haldane's investigations led him to the conclusion that with the existing organisation of reserves and auxiliary forces this readiness could not be secured. He therefore divided the forces into two lines in lieu of the existing three lines. The first line consists of a highly qualified field force consisting of four cavalry brigades and six infantry divisions ready for rapid mobilisation, and for operations beyond seas. This is our striking force. The second line, which took the place of the militia and volunteers, is a territorial army with an establishment aimed at of 300,000 men derived from the nation, intended to be capable of defending the British shores, and in times of great stress of reinforcing the troops abroad. In this force recruits undertake to serve for four years with an option of further service, but may withdraw before that time after three months notice. The men are required, if they can do so, to go into camp each year for fifteen days. On the outbreak of war they would mobilise for training at home for six months, and then serve abroad if they consented. The force was organised on a county basis. The most original feature in Mr. Haldane's scheme was the formation of county associations, presided over in each county by the lord-lieutenant, and responsible, under the control of the Army Council, for the recruiting, administration, and finance of the territorial units in their respective districts during peace. These military associations are chiefly composed of the commanding officers of the auxiliary forces, and are said to do excellent work. Thus the powers over the militia, transferred by Mr. Cardwell from the lord-lieutenant to the Crown, have been by Mr. Haldane in some small measure restored.

Alone among the great countries of Europe Great Britain still relies upon an army raised by voluntary enlistment. Her peculiar position in this respect is of ancient date, and its origin closely linked to her constitutional history. In the Middle Ages armies were raised when needed for a war and disbanded as soon as peace was made. For home defence there was the militia, in which every man was legally bound to serve; but this obligation was disregarded and became obsolete. The right to maintain a standing army under martial law claimed by the Stuart kings, was denied by their Parlia- *The system of voluntary enlistment.*

ments, and the practice was finally declared illegal by the Bill of Rights. But the compromise of the Mutiny Act, first passed in 1689, which, while declaring that standing armies and courts martial were unknown to the law of England, authorised their existence for the current year, and has since been annually in various forms re-enacted, placed the army on a regular footing under the sanction of Parliament. To have proceeded further and to have decreed that every Englishman must serve in that army would have seemed to our ancestors a surrender of their liberties. But these historic considerations have long since lost their force. The army is no longer a danger, but a necessary protection to the subject. The king no longer threatens the liberties of his people, but is recognised as their august representative. And there is a growing opinion that universal military service is essential to the security of the realm.

Report of the Norfolk Commission. In May, 1904, a Royal Commission, presided over by the Duke of Norfolk, which had been appointed to investigate the conditions affecting the internal defence of the United Kingdom from invasion, made its report. The Commissioners, after declaring that reliance could not be safely placed upon the auxiliary forces as then constituted, made proposals indeed for their better organisation, but expressed the opinion that the only manner in which security could be really ensured was by the acceptance of the principle of universal military service involving a definite and continuous period of systematic military training. The country was not prepared for this solution, and Mr. Arnold-Forster, on behalf of the Government, at once disclaimed any intention to adopt it, but the report of the Commission gave an impetus to the movement, in furtherance of which the National Service League was founded under the presidency of Lord Roberts. Mr. Haldane's territorial army has been represented as a last attempt to maintain the voluntary system, but if it were to fail through lack of the necessary support the experiment might have a contrary effect.

Arguments for and against compulsory military service. The movement is in harmony with the general tendencies of the age, and it is not surprising that certain socialists have been numbered among its supporters. It is significant that to the common argument that universal military service would improve the national physique and generate certain desirable moral qualities, the old answer that with these matters the State, as such, has no concern is no longer returned. The change would no doubt involve the imposition by the State of a fresh restriction on the liberty of the individual, a new attempt to mould his character after a uniform pattern, but to admit this is not of necessity to condemn the scheme. The same objection might be raised to compulsory education, and to other State activities of unquestionable utility. The question really at issue is whether a large and powerful army is or is not necessary for home defence. If it is, then the elimination of the element of uncertainty in recruiting; the maintenance of establishments at their full strength; the cessation of dependence on external conditions, such as the state of trade and the labour market, involved in the present system of voluntary enlistment; the substitution of a territorial army composed of men who have served their full time in the active forces for one which, ready as it might be to mobilise for training at home, would not, according to the programme, for six months after the outbreak of a war be ready for active service; and, lastly, the obligation by which in equity every citizen is bound to make some personal contribution towards securing for himself that immunity from foreign invasion which, on this hypothesis, only the presence of an effective army at home can preserve, together form an almost unanswerable case for a system of universal service. But, if there is no such necessity; if we can safely rely upon the navy for protection against a sudden raid, while, if the navy were destroyed, no army could avail to protect us against a blockade which would starve us into submission; if our wars in the future are likely to last as long as our wars in the past, and, therefore, to give time to the territorials for their six months' systematic training after the outbreak of hostilities, at the end of which they would be able to reinforce our field army and effectively to provide for security at home; then, the great expense which universal service would necessitate, the diminution in the wage-earning capacity of the nation its adoption would involve, and the break in the national tradition are formidable objections to the proposal.

The work of co-ordination which simplified administration and reconciled conflicting elements in army and local government was found equally necessary during the same period to

The Courts of Law.

effect the same objects in the judicature. In the thirteenth century the king's judicial functions had been divided between the Court of Exchequer for cases touching the king's revenue, the Court of Common Pleas for the private suits of subjects, and the Court of King's Bench for all other matters. As time went on, and new conditions evolved new wrongs for which the common law, administered by the three ancient courts on rigid principles, provided no remedy, recourse was had to the original authority of the king, which remained unaffected by his delegation of judicial functions to the courts. The king entrusted to his Chancellor the management of these matters "of grace and favour," and thus grew up the separate and independent jurisdiction of the Court of Chancery. The Chancellor was generally a Churchman, well versed in the canon law, and his methods and the principles on which he acted were—unlike those of the common law—largely derived from the Roman jurists and the moral rules of their Law of Nature. Not only did the Court of Chancery give redress for wrongs unknown to the common law, but it could forestall the commission of wrong, which that law could punish but could not prevent, by the issue of injunctions commanding or forbidding an act to be done. The Chancellors, down to the time of Lord Eldon, continued, by the practical modifications involved in their decisions, to adapt the law to new social requirements; but at last the principles of equity became as rigid as those of common law and as incapable of further development. Thereafter, this office of adaptation and correction of anomalies was discharged by direct legislation; and the distinction between law and equity, with their separate courts, separate methods of procedure, and distinct principles of action, which had played so useful a part in the past, became an inconvenience and a source of delay and expense.

Sir Roundell Palmer's motion, 1867.
In 1867 Sir Roundell Palmer, afterwards Lord Chancellor Selborne, called the attention of the House of Commons to the waste of judicial power caused by the separation of the courts. The division of jurisdiction between the three Courts of Common Law had become purely technical, except that the Court of Queen's Bench had exclusive jurisdiction in criminal informations and in certain poor law cases. The theoretic distinctions between the jurisdictions had from early

times been evaded in practice by means of fictitious pleadings. The plaintiff, by stating that he was the king's debtor, might bring his suit before the Court of Exchequer; or if he wished to have it tried in the Court of King's Bench he might issue a process for the arrest of the defendant, and allege that he was in the custody of the marshal of the Marshalsea. His opponent was not permitted to deny these allegations and thus the ordinary civil suits were tried in whichever court the plaintiff preferred. But while the judges of the three courts were selected from the same bar, had the same qualifications, and tried the same kinds of cases, there was no power of transferring cases from one court to another, with the result that one court was often over-crowded and heavily in arrear while another was comparatively unoccupied. The consequence of Sir Roundell Palmer's speech was the appointment of a Royal Commission to inquire into the subject, and to report by what measures of reform the delays and waste involved in the existing system might best be avoided.

The Judicature Commissioners, who reported in 1869, made six principal recommendations.[1] They advised (1) that all the Courts of Law and Equity, and the Court of Admiralty, and the Court of Probate should be consolidated into one Supreme Court, which should possess the authority and power of all those courts, and should sit in several divisions; (2) that a uniform system of pleading and procedure should be adopted in the courts constituting the Supreme Court; (3) that uniformity should be adopted as to the sittings of the court and as to the vacations; (4) that there should be a rearrangement of the circuits and assizes of the country, and that arrangement should be made for continuous sittings for jury trials in London and Middlesex; (5) that, as to the administrative department of the law there should be consolidation and simplification of the offices with a view to economy of time and money; and (6) that an intermediate Court of Appeal should be constituted to take the place of the Court of Appeal in Chancery and of the Exchequer Chamber, which, sitting constantly and easy of access, should be common to all the divisions of the Supreme Court.

Recommendations of the Judicature Commissioners, 1869.

Effect was given to the first five of these recommendations

[1] See Lord Cairns' speech in 1875, Hansard, vol. ccxxiii. p. 574.

by Lord Selborne's Judicature Act of 1873. Lord Selborne, who had been an active member of the Judicature Commission, had succeeded Lord Hatherley as Chancellor in 1872; and the first year of his Chancellorship was distinguished by the passage of this valuable measure. The only important respect in which it departed from the proposals of the report was with regard to the Court of Appeal. Lord Selborne's aim, as he himself has described it, was,[1] "to bring together in one Supreme Court divided into two branches, the one of original and the other of appellate jurisdiction, all the judicial powers of the previously existing Superior Courts in England which had, until then, exercised separate and sometimes conflicting jurisdiction". He desired to constitute as good a Court of Appeal as was possible and then to invest it with full authority by making it final. This policy involved the abolition of the appellate jurisdiction of the House of Lords and of the system of double appeals. For these purposes, so far as regarded England, provision was accordingly made in the Judicature Act.

The Courts of Appeal were in 1873 four in number. There was, in the first place, the Exchequer Chamber; in which judges belonging to two out of the three ancient Courts of Common Law sat together to hear appeals from the civil decisions of the third. There was, in the next place, the Court of Appeal in Chancery. From these two courts there was a further appeal to the House of Lords sitting as a court; but whereas all cases in the Superior Courts of Common Law had to come first before the Exchequer Chamber, Chancery cases might, if the appellants so pleased, go direct from the court of first instance to the House of Lords. There was, besides these three courts, the Judicial Committee of the Privy Council which heard ecclesiastical appeals, appeals from the Colonies and from India, and appeals from the Courts of Admiralty and of Probate. The Judicial Committee, to which four salaried members had been added by an Act of 1871, was a court of final appeal.

The bill of 1873 substituted for these four courts one Supreme Court of final appeal consisting of the Lord Chancellor, the Chief Justices, the Chief Baron of the Exchequer,

[1] Memorials Personal and Political, vol. i. p. 298.

the Master of the Rolls, the Lords Justices, peers who had held judicial office, and the permanent members of the Judicial Committee. But Ireland and Scotland having separate judicatures of their own untouched by the bill, Lord Selborne thought it right for constitutional reasons to exclude these countries from its scope, and to preserve the appellate jurisdiction of the House of Lords in Scotch and Irish cases until evidence should be forthcoming that Scotland and Ireland desired to avail themselves of the new court. Ecclesiastical appeals were also still to be decided by the Judicial Committee.

When, however, the bill came down to the House of Commons it was found that the Scotch and Irish lawyers in that House were dissatisfied by the exclusion of Scotch and Irish appeals; and consequently, in order to avoid the loss of the bill, they were included by an amendment among the subjects of the new appellate jurisdiction. An amendment, moved by Mr. Gathorne Hardy, to include ecclesiastical appeals, was also accepted by the Government. But the House of Lords declined to agree to the amendment relating to Scotch and Irish appeals. Lord Cairns claimed, as a matter of privilege, that any measure affecting the jurisdiction of the House of Lords should originate there and not be altered elsewhere. The existence of this privilege was not admitted by the Government; but there were obvious objections to bringing Scotland and Ireland under an appellate jurisdiction framed without reference to their distinct juridical arrangements, and the amendment was not pressed. As the Act was not to come into operation until November, 1875, time was given to settle this matter in another session. *Scotch and Irish appeals.*

The difficulties connected with Scotch and Irish appeals had the unexpected effect of saving the appellate jurisdiction of the House of Lords in its integrity. The general election of 1874 brought the Conservatives into power, and Lord Cairns succeeded Lord Selborne as Chancellor. Lord Cairns had presided over the Judicature Commission, and was in general agreement with his predecessor on the subject of law reform. But on one point he differed from him. Lord Selborne wished to abolish altogether the system of double appeals, and to establish for all causes one supreme court of final appeal. Lord Cairns would have preferred, while constituting a Court *Judicature Acts of 1875 and 1876.*

of Appeal so strong that its decisions would habitually have been accepted as final, to preserve as an ultimate resource the appellate jurisdiction of the House of Lords. He had, however, in 1873, persuaded his party in the Upper House to accept Lord Selborne's original proposal, and, when he became Chancellor in 1874, the law as it stood provided that in November, 1875, the jurisdiction of the new Court of Appeal, so far as regarded England and Wales, should be final. In 1874 Lord Cairns introduced a bill for including Scotch and Irish appeals in the jurisdiction of the new court. This passed the Lords, but was lost in the Commons owing to the preoccupation of that House with the Public Worship Regulation Bill, to which, though introduced by a private member, the Prime Minister thought fit to give a preference. But now the Lords repented them of the sacrifice they had made in the preceding year of their ancient jurisdiction, and, gaining confidence from the conservative indications of the political barometer, resolved to retrace their footsteps. Lord Cairns, somewhat reluctantly, found himself obliged to satisfy them, and in 1875 passed a bill to suspend until November, 1876, the sections of the Act of 1873, which abolished the appellate jurisdiction of the Lords, and to provide that until that date appeals might be brought before their court from any judgment of the Court of Appeal. This was followed in 1876 by an Act which repealed these sections. The constitution of the court thus restored was for the first time defined. The constitutional convention, which precluded lay peers from taking part in the legal proceedings of the House, was still considered a sufficient security against their intervention, but provision was made that no appeal should be heard unless three Lords of Appeal were present, and a statutory description of Lords of Appeal was added. They were to be the Lord Chancellor, the Lords of Appeal in Ordinary, and any other peers who held or had held high judicial office. Under this Act four life peers sit as Lords of Appeal in Ordinary, of whom one is generally appointed from the Scotch and one from the Irish bar. Another distinction was also made. Before 1876, the House of Lords could not sit for any purpose when Parliament had been prorogued or dissolved. But power was now given to the Lords of Appeal to hear causes in the name of the House during a prorogation or a dissolution.

Thus, if the lay peers are excluded at some times from the legal proceedings of the House only by their submission to convention, at other times their exclusion is now prescribed by law.

The provisions of the Act of 1873 relating to the High Court—as that part of the judicature which exercises original jurisdiction is called—were left almost unaltered by subsequent legislation. Their effect, in the words of Lord Selborne, was to subdivide the High Court " into Divisions, or Chambers, for the more convenient distribution of business; giving to all the judges, in every Division, equal jurisdiction in Equity as well as Law; enabling them all to give assistance, when needed, in Divisions not their own; providing for a procedure, in all Divisions, as far as possible uniform; making all times throughout the legal year available for all London business; and excluding all unnecessary circuity or multiplicity of proceedings, with reference to the same disputes, or between the same contending parties ".[1] At first the duties of the Courts of Queen's Bench, Common Pleas, and Exchequer were transferred to divisions of the High Court bearing the same name. But an Order in Council was issued in 1880 under the authority of the Judicature Act to consolidate the three Divisions into one— thenceforth known as the Queen's Bench Division. And later, the Probate Division was amalgamated with the Divorce and Admiralty Division into a single Division under a President. The intermediate Court of Appeal, as constituted by the Judicature Acts, now consists for working purposes of the Master of the Rolls and five Lords Justices. The Lord Chancellor and the Presidents of the three Divisions of the High Court are *ex-officio* members, but are not accustomed to take part in the proceedings.

A reform in the administration of justice—long overdue— was at last, in the year 1898, effected at the instance of the Conservative Chancellor, Lord Halsbury. This was the admission of prisoners on criminal charges to give evidence at their trials on their own behalf. For many years before the Act of 1898 was passed whenever a new offence had been created by statute provision had invariably at the same time been made that persons charged with it might be examined as

[1] Memorials, Personal and Political, vol. i. p. 299.

witnesses. Thus the distinction between the class of prisoners who were permitted to give evidence on their own behalf and the class of prisoners who were denied that privilege was based on no principle, but depended merely on the date at which the Act with which they were charged had been made an offence. A distinction so irrational could not be permitted to endure. The highest legal authorities had long been agreed that the ends of justice would best be secured by allowing prisoners to answer with their own mouths, if they chose to do so, the accusations brought against them, and to submit themselves to examination and cross-examination. It was felt that the latter ordeal, however formidable to the guilty, would have no terrors for the innocent; who would, on the contrary, regard it as a privilege, and an opportunity of proving their innocence. The bill passed easily through both Houses, and its effects have corresponded with the anticipations of its authors.

The Beck case.
Had this valuable privilege been conceded to innocent prisoners two years earlier a miscarriage of justice, which was one of the proximate causes of a still more important reform in the law, might perhaps have been averted. For in 1896 a Swede, named Adolf Beck, was sentenced in London to seven years' penal servitude for frauds on women of low reputation, which had in reality been committed by a Jew called Smith, to whom he bore a remarkable resemblance. Beck was arrested on a similar charge in 1904, and again tried and convicted; but, shortly after his conviction, Smith was himself arrested and confessed his guilt. The police theory had been that Smith and Beck were identical, and a previous conviction of Smith's in 1877 had been alleged against Beck. But at the trial in 1896 the court had ruled that the question whether Beck was Smith could not be raised, so that Beck was not allowed to establish his defence of mistaken identity. It is possible, however, that had he been allowed to present himself for examination and cross-examination in 1896 he would have succeeded in convincing the jury of his innocence, and it is extremely probable that the judgment would have been reversed by a Court of Criminal Appeal, had such a tribunal been then in existence, on the ground that the ruling of the common serjeant that the question of his identity with Smith could not be raised was erroneous.

The Beck case resulted in the appointment of a Royal Commission, under the chairmanship of the Master of the Rolls, to inquire into the matter, and to report whether any amendment of the law was desirable. Among their other conclusions the Commissioners expressed the opinion that the law should be amended so as to make it possible to compel a judge to state a case for the High Court; and they thought that if this were done it would not be necessary to constitute a Court of Criminal Appeal. The preponderance of legal opinion, however, favoured the establishment of such a court with which England, alone among European countries, had hitherto thought it expedient to dispense; and one of the bills introduced in their first session by the Liberal Ministry of 1906 was framed with this object. The bill miscarried in that crowded session, but was re-introduced in a somewhat altered form in the following year; when it became law. It provided for a Court of Criminal Appeal consisting of eight judges presided over by the Lord Chief Justice and appointed by him, from among the judges of the High Court, with the consent of the Chancellor. An unqualified right of appeal was given on points of law; but on matters of fact appeals were only to take place with the sanction of the court. The court was given power to call for fresh evidence; and might affirm, modify, or quash the conviction; or alter the sentence. The jurisdiction of the Court of Crown Cases Reserved was transferred to the new court. The royal prerogative of mercy remained untouched; but the Secretary of State might take the opinion of the court as to its exercise. Some critics of the bill maintained that the power of appeal ought to be limited to questions of law—questions of fact being the special province of the jury—but the Government rightly considered that, unless the new court was able to review questions of fact, it would not be able to take into account all the circumstances that might have led to a miscarriage of justice. In spite of some opposition on this account, the bill was not made a party question; and passed through both Houses without much difficulty or material alteration. The fact that convictions have been frequently set aside by the new court sufficiently justifies its institution; and would seem clearly to indicate that many miscarriages of justice might have been avoided in the

Institution of a Court of Criminal Appeal, 1907.

past had it been sooner established. It has tended also to lessen the very undesirable retrial by newspaper agitation, which prevailed with increasing frequency while the sole power of revising sentences in criminal cases lay with the Home Secretary.

CHAPTER VII.

THE SELF-GOVERNING COLONIES AFTER 1860.

IN the middle of the nineteenth century, at a time when responsible self-government was being introduced into colony after colony, the opinion prevailed in England that the connection of the self-governing dominions with the Mother Country was unlikely long to endure. England, it was thought, had educated and sent forth into the world her hardy sons, she had trained them for liberty, and if and when they considered that the time was come for them to claim a complete independence she was absolved from further responsibility. It was perceived that when the colonies had attained maturity their governments might fairly claim to cease to be subordinate to the Ministry in Downing Street; and the idea of co-ordinate governments, among which the home Cabinet would only be the first among equals, independent of one another in their local affairs, but mutually related by their common allegiance to the Crown, had as yet entered the imaginations of only a few among statesmen and political thinkers. Mr. Disraeli, in 1872, discovered, or pretended to discover, in these tendencies a conscious and deliberate plot of Liberalism to disintegrate the Empire. There had been, he said, "no effort so continuous, so subtle, supported by so much energy, and carried on with so much ability and acumen as the attempts of Liberalism to effect the disintegration of the Empire of England". "Self-government," he added, in a remarkable passage in the same speech, "when it was conceded ought to have been conceded as part of a great policy of Imperial consolidation. It ought to have been accompanied by an Imperial tariff, by securities for the people of England for the enjoyment of the unappropriated lands which belonged to the sovereign as their trustee, and by a military code which should have precisely defined the means

Public opinion and the colonies in the mid-Victorian period.

and the responsibilities by which the colonies should be defended, and by which, if necessary, this country should call for aid from the colonies themselves. It ought, further, to have been accompanied by some representative council in the metropolis, which would have brought the colonies into constant and continuous relations with the home Government."[1] In reality, however, the widely spread and openly avowed expectation that the Imperial connection was not likely to be permanent was neither confined to, nor even especially connected with, Liberalism. Mr. Disraeli, as his custom often was, by an appeal to a largely imaginary past, was shaping the policy of his party for the future. He had himself, when first in office, desired a severance of the colonial connection.[2] It was Sir John Pakington, Colonial Secretary in the short-lived Conservative administration of 1852, who by a dispatch circulated through all the Australian colonies, made the first offer on the part of the Crown to abandon, by the repeal of the Land Sales Act, all control over the branch of colonial revenue derived from the sale of unoccupied land on the condition that the colonists should establish for themselves, under powers given by an Act of 1850, constitutions on the Canadian basis. It was the Conservative Ministry of that year which, in granting a constitution to New Zealand, gave to the colonists control over Crown Lands—a concession refused two years before by the Liberal Government to New South Wales; and it was the Conservative Ministry of 1858 which, somewhat reluctantly, sanctioned a Canadian tariff imposing for the first time duties on British manufactures; while the complete fiscal independence of Canada was finally recognised by Lord Beaconsfield's own Government when they submitted without protest to the protective tariff of 1879. On the other hand, Lord Durham, whose famous report led to the union of upper and lower Canada, Lord Elgin, to whom the united colony owed responsible government, Sir William Molesworth, the third Lord Grey and others were at once Whigs or Radicals and strong Imperialists. When Lord Elgin, carrying out the instructions given to him by Lord Grey, the Colonial Secretary, steadily supported his Ministers in carrying their bills because they represented a

[1] Speech at Crystal Palace, 24 June, 1872.
[2] Lord Malmesbury's Memoirs, p. 260.

majority in the Canadian Parliament, he was indeed violently attacked by Conservatives at home; but his action is now admitted to have been the first important step in converting the disaffection of the French Canadians into loyalty to the Crown. The opposite policy pursued by his predecessor, Lord Metcalfe, had had the effect of directing the Parliamentary Opposition, no longer merely against the Ministers, but, in the words of Lord Grey, "against the Governor personally and the British Government of which he was the organ". Both Whig principles and Tory principles involved in their application their own peculiar dangers to imperial integrity, but neither Whigs nor Tories of that generation appear for the most part to have attached much value to that integrity; and the American precedent of the eighteenth century would seem to show that the greater danger of the two lay in the Tory theory of the government of dependencies. If there were Liberals who, in loosening the ties that bound the colonies to the Mother Country, contemplated without regret a complete severance at no distant date, there were Conservatives who held that unless the imperial control was effective and complete the connection was not worth preserving.

The almost complete self-government enjoyed by the American colonies from the time of Elizabeth down to the War of Independence, modified only by the commercial regulations imposed in the interest of the Mother Country, was followed in the half-century after the American revolt by the adoption with regard to the colonies that remained to us of the contrary policy, namely, that of abstention from fiscal interference combined with direct administrative control and full military protection. During this period, in Mr. Herman Merivale's phrase, we taxed ourselves for the pleasure of governing the colonies. "Since the close of the American War," wrote Sir George Cornewall Lewis, "it has not been the policy of England to vest any portion of the legislative power of the subordinate government of a dependency in a body elected by the inhabitants. The only partial exception is in the Canadian provinces".[1] In the third period—that of the mid-nineteenth century—the self-government of the first colonial period was conceded to the new colonies which had replaced the old; and

The three successive policies.

---

[1] Sir G. Lewis's Government of Dependencies, p. 160.

with greater completeness. The fiscal restrictions on colonial trade for the benefit of the Mother Country, which had seemed to our ancestors the chief advantage derivable from the possession of colonies, disappeared, while the burden of colonial defence, which before the American war had been mainly borne by the colonists, was undertaken by the Mother Country. While there were Conservatives who were dissatisfied by what they thought too ample and unconditional a concession of self-government, there were Liberals who were inclined to grumble at the continued cost, and who argued that the colonies, having reached maturity, might fairly be expected to provide for their own defence.

Growth of the Imperial idea.

When the Reform Act of 1867 had to a large extent diverted the activities of party leaders from the House of Commons to the platform and had made the profession of a striking policy a condition essential to political success, Mr. Disraeli, fully alive to the consequences of the Act of which he was the author, proclaimed the upholding of the Empire to be, together with the maintenance of the constitution and the elevation of the condition of the people, the distinctive aim of the Conservative party. It was true that the Whigs had been in power for a generation, and had left the colonies much more loyal and contented than they had found them. But it was also true that this happy result of the grant of self-government had been the effect rather of accident than of design, and that this grant had been regarded by many as preliminary to separation. This fact, together with their long tenure of power during the period in which those ideas prevailed, gave ample material to Mr. Disraeli for building up on imperial ground a case against his opponents; and the indifference to the connection felt and displayed by his rival, Mr. Gladstone, enabled him to illustrate his theme by a living example. The idea of a confederation of powerful states united in allegiance to the Crown, equal among themselves, each self-governing, yet invincible in their union, had occurred to others before Mr. Disraeli, and Lord Elgin, for instance, had warmly protested against Lord John Russell's notion that the colonial relation was incompatible with maturity and full development; but it was reserved for Mr. Disraeli, while leading the Opposition to Mr. Gladstone's Government of 1868, to inspire with this conception the slow-moving imagination of the British people. Since that time the imperial idea then sown has taken root and become manifest in many ways. The very lack of interest felt by mid-Victorian statesmen in the colonies, and their scepticism as to the permanence of the imperial tie, led them to grant self-government in the fullest possible manner; and thus, by removing all those restrictions on freedom that might have seemed to qualify the unquestionable advantage of being members corporate of a powerful nation bound to protect them against all attack, they attached the colonies to the connection. There is, perhaps, some risk that the desire for closer union which has replaced in England the earlier indifference may produce through the activities to which it leads the opposite result.

The Legislative Union of Upper and Lower Canada in 1840, and the concession some years later of responsible government to the united colony, by harmonising the relations between the representatives of the people and the Executive, removed those causes of discontent which had led to the disturbances of 1837. Lord Durham believed that the union would bring about the gradual absorption of the French race and religion into the English, and he entertained "no doubt as to the national character which must be given to Lower Canada—that of the British Empire, that of the majority of the population of British America". Had this anticipation been realised, the union, followed as it was by the introduction of responsible government under Lord Elgin, would have proved the unqualified success which he expected it to be. It was owing to the non-fusibility of the two races that a new change had to be effected in 1867. *French and English in Canada.*

The constitution of 1841 had provided that each of the two provinces of United Canada should return an equal number of members elected by popular suffrage to the Assembly. At the time of the union this arrangement was favourable to the English of Upper Canada, who were largely outnumbered by the French of Lower Canada. But, as time went on, it was found that the English population increased more rapidly than the French, until in 1861 that of Upper Canada was 1,396,000, while that of the Lower Province was only 1,111,000. The Upper Canadians, enterprising and energetic, considered that *Friction under the union of 1841.*

the prosperity of the country was due to their exertions; they paid the larger proportion of the revenue; and they resented the expenditure of a great part of it on public works in French Canada. They demanded a larger representation, and their demand was resisted by the French, who thought, like the Irish of a later generation in similar circumstances, that an anomaly which had been tolerated so long as they were in a minority ought not to be deemed intolerable when the conditions were reversed. The result of these dissensions was that no strong or stable government could be formed. The view began to prevail that the provinces were "so far akin that they could be united, and yet so far dissimilar that they could not be fused into a single body politic".[1]

Canadian Federation. Federalism was seen to be the remedy for the existing inconveniences; and in the establishment of a federal system the United States served at once as an encouragement and a warning—an encouragement, from a view of the prosperity and power which the States had achieved since their union, and a warning from the spectacle of the tremendous civil war in which at that time they were involved, fairly attributable as it was to the insufficient powers of controlling the separate States given by the constitution to the central Government. When, therefore, in 1864, the Governments of the maritime provinces of Nova Scotia, New Brunswick, and Prince Edward's Island appointed delegates to discuss the terms of a legislative union among themselves, the Canadian Ministry asked and obtained permission to join the conference. The Canadian delegates proposed the confederation of all the British North American Colonies; and the conference adjourned to Quebec. The resolutions there adopted were accepted in the Canadian Parliament, by Nova Scotia, and by New Brunswick; but the legislatures of Prince Edward Island and of Newfoundland refused to accept the scheme.[2] The Home Government, awakened by the Alabama affair to the possibility of war with the United States, and impressed with the importance of the presence on the frontier of a strong and consolidated people, capable of sharing efficiently in their own defence, had encouraged the proposals for federation and welcomed their

[1] Lord Carnarvon, Hansard, clxxxv. p. 576.
[2] Prince Edward Island was admitted to the Dominion in 1873.

acceptance. The Quebec resolutions to which the four colonies had agreed were embodied in an Act which was passed without alteration by the Imperial Parliament in February, 1867, and has proved in its working a signal success.

The Act established a Dominion Parliament for the whole of Canada and local legislatures for the several provinces. Under its provisions the Dominion Parliament is composed of a Senate of seventy-two members nominated for life by the Crown;[1] and of a House of Commons, elected for five years, in which the provinces are separately represented—provision being made that the number of representatives of each province should be decennially readjusted to its comparative population. To the subordinate legislatures certain specified and exclusive powers relating to local affairs and direct taxation within their respective provinces are given; and these specified powers they do not derive from, or hold subject to, the pleasure of the Dominion Parliament. But all subjects of legislation not expressly reserved to the Provincial Legislatures belong exclusively to the Dominion Parliament; whereas in the United States all legislative power not given by the constitution to Congress rests with the separate States. Disputes have arisen as to the scope under the constitution of the legislative powers of the Dominion Parliament and of the Provincial Legislatures respectively, and the exact boundary line between them has been found difficult to determine. *The Dominion of Canada Constitution Act, 1867.*

To deal with these questions of "constitutionality," as they were called, and to act generally speaking as a final court in civil and criminal cases, a Supreme Court of Appeal was established in Canada in 1875. Its decisions were subjected to an appeal to the Sovereign in Council whenever the Crown should think fit to grant special leave to make such appeal. The Judicial Committee of the Council has, in a succession of cases, formulated the grounds on which they will advise the Crown to grant this leave. Such are the public interest attaching to a case—the importance of a question in respect of constitutional law—or the circumstance that property of considerable amount is involved. The general principles on which the division of *Manner in which constitutional questions arising under the Act are decided.*

---

[1] The experiment of an elected Senate, tried in 1854, was abandoned for the reason that, so constituted, it was thought not to have sufficient weight for the work of revision.

power between the Dominion Parliament and the Provincial Legislatures is based have been defined and their application regulated by successive decisions of the Judicial Committee. Thus they have pronounced that, although all legislative power not expressly given by the Federation Act to the Provincial Legislatures rests with the Dominion Parliament, the former enjoy within their own sphere "an authority as plenary and as ample within the limits prescribed as the Imperial Parliament in the plenitude of its power possessed and could bestow".[1] Nevertheless the Dominion Government possesses a veto under the Federation Act on the Acts of the Provincial Legislatures; but to exercise this would be contrary to the spirit of the constitution "unless they contain provisions which are open to objection upon grounds of public policy, as being calculated to affect injuriously the interests of the Dominion or of any particular portion thereof".[2] It was further enacted, with a view to strengthening the Central Government, that the Lieutenant-Governors of the provinces composing the Federation should be nominated by the Governor-General on the advice of his Ministers, instead of by the Crown. Thus the provinces ceased to have any direct communication with the Home Government; and lost their independent existence as colonies. The Governor-General is empowered to assent to, reject, or reserve for the sovereign's pleasure, bills passed by the Dominion Parliament. When bills are reserved it is provided that the assent of the Sovereign in Council must be announced within two years from their presentation to the Governor-General. Bills assented to may be disallowed within two years after they have been received by the Secretary of State.

Movement in Nova Scotia against the Federation Act.

The Federation Constitution came into operation on the 1st of July, an anniversary known as Dominion Day, and kept as a public holiday. Nova Scotia had been brought into the system by a vote of the legislature without any previous consultation of the people, and the change was at first very unpopular in that colony. A formidable agitation for repeal was at once started there. Of nineteen members elected to the Dominion Parliament eighteen were pledged to repeal; while, in the Local Assembly, thirty-six out of thirty-eight members

[1] Judicial Committee in Hodge *v.* the Queen, 9 App. Ca. p. 117.
[2] Todd, Parliamentary Government in the British Colonies, p. 343.

were elected with the same object. The Assembly, in an Address to the Queen, prayed for repeal, and deprecated an arrangement which would place Nova Scotia under the power of Canada. Mr. Joseph Howe, the leader of the movement, crossed the Atlantic with a deputation to present this address. But the English Government declined to break up a constitutional settlement which had been welcomed with general applause, and refused its consent to the withdrawal of Nova Scotia from the Dominion. Mr. Howe, on his return, alarmed at the separatist tendencies of certain among his followers, entered into negotiations with the Government, which were brought to a successful conclusion. Better financial terms in the federal system than were originally arranged were granted to Nova Scotia; and Mr. Howe, thereupon, proved his readiness to acquiesce in the new order of things by accepting a seat as Secretary of State in the Dominion Cabinet.

Provision was made in the Federation Act for the admission of new provinces into the Dominion. Manitoba joined in 1870; British Columbia, tempted by the promise that a railway should be constructed to connect the seaboard with the Canadian railway system, acceded in 1871;[1] in 1873 Prince Edward's Island came in. Finally, in 1878, in response to an address from the Canadian Parliament, an Imperial Order in Council was issued annexing to the Dominion all British possessions in North America except Newfoundland. *Later accessions to the Dominion.*

Self-government had been granted to Canada in a different spirit from that in which it was afterwards conceded to the other colonies, and in different circumstances. Neither the authors of the three great constitutional settlements of 1791, 1840, and 1867, nor the statesmen under whose auspices responsible government was established between 1847 and 1854, had any thought of ultimate separation. Their action, on the contrary, was chiefly prompted by the desire to maintain and to strengthen the Imperial connection. During the critical period for the Empire between 1846 and 1874, when the doctrines of *laissez-faire* and of the Manchester School were in the ascendant, the rulers of Canada, from Lord Elgin *Contrast between British policy with regard to Canada and to the other colonies.*

[1] The engagement was that the railway should be begun by the summer of 1873 and completed within ten years. But unforeseen difficulties delayed the fulfilment of this undertaking, and the new railway was not begun until 1879 or finished until 1886.

to Lord Dufferin, were men of ability and sympathetic imagination who combined most happily Liberal principles with high notions of the destiny of the Empire and of Imperial responsibility. In the hands of such men there was little fear that the Imperial tie would be loosened.

On the other hand, when self-government was granted to the Australasian colonies there was little desire, either on the part of the Mother Country or on the part of the colonies, to avert, or indefinitely to postpone, a separation supposed to be inevitable. "It is a great pity," wrote Sir Frederick Rogers in 1858, "that, give as much as you will, you can't please the colonists with anything short of absolute independence, so that it is not easy to say how you are to accomplish what we are, I suppose, all looking to, the eventual parting company on good terms." And, many years later, in 1885, the same distinguished public servant, then Lord Blachford, who had been in the interval Under Secretary of State for the Colonies, from 1860 to 1871, and in that capacity had exercised a paramount influence on colonial policy, wrote in words that may be taken to express the prevailing view of the men of his day: "I had always believed—and the belief has so confirmed and consolidated itself, that I can hardly realise the possibility of any one seriously thinking the contrary—that the destiny of our colonies is independence; and that in this point of view the function of the Colonial Office is to secure that our connection, while it lasts, shall be as profitable to both parties, and our separation, when it comes, as amicable as possible". The very desire, however, that separation should be amicable contributed to avert the separation itself. The colonists might be mortified by the lack of interest in their concerns shown by the Mother Country, but, while they had small reason to complain of vexatious interference, they derived much material advantage from the connection. New Zealand required Imperial troops for protection against the natives, and all the Australian colonies relied on the British navy for the defence of their commerce and their coasts.

The Imperial connection in Australasia, how preserved.
Another consideration rendered the maintenance of the Imperial connection important to the Australasian colonists in the early days when no reasons of sentiment inclined them to preserve it, and gave time for such a sentiment to grow. The

colonists had adopted constitutions framed on the British model. As in England, the Ministry was in reality the executive committee of the majority for the time being of the Lower House to which it was responsible, but, as in England, the formal right of the Second Chamber to reject money bills and bills for the appropriation of supply empowered that Chamber, when under the control of the Opposition, to bring the constitutional machinery to a standstill. The unwritten law of the British constitution assumes the mutual forbearance of the bodies among whom power is distributed, and had gradually shaped itself at Westminster in usages and constitutional conventions, which indicated clearly when and how this forbearance should be exercised. But in the self-governing colonies there was no such unwritten law. Their constitutions were written in Acts of the British Parliament, and the legislative bodies created by those Acts were disposed to exercise all their statutory rights without much regard to British usage. Parties in the colonies were no natural growth as in England; they sprang from the system, rather than the system from them. The party leaders were without training in constitutional government; and recognised no limitations to their action beyond the letter of the law. The practices and forbearances prescribed by long experience, which made the constitution workable in the Mother Country, were unknown to them. Hence the strong need originally felt for Imperial guidance, and the grave dangers that followed when that guidance was unwisely exercised.

This need and this danger received their fullest illustration in the colony of Victoria. There, the Upper House, being elective, was in a stronger position than its congeners in other colonies. In 1865, the Ministry of the day endeavoured to pass a protective tariff, to which the Upper House objected, by "tacking" it on to the Appropriation Bill. The Upper House had been given by the Constitution Act the power to reject, but not to amend money bills—the sanction of law thus being given in Victoria to what was in England a convention of the constitution. The disadvantages incident to the rigidity of the legal sanction now became manifest, for since it was unlawful for the Council to amend the Appropriation Bill by eliminating the foreign matter improperly annexed to it they

The constitutional crisis in Victoria, 1865.

took the extreme course of rejecting the whole bill, on the ground that it was unconstitutional "that any clause of appropriation should be introduced into a Bill of Supply". No money, therefore, being legally available for the public services, the Governor, Sir Charles Darling, met the difficulty in a manner unfamiliar to British communities since the seventeenth century by sanctioning, on the advice of his Ministers, the levy of the new duties, unauthorised by the Legislature though they were, and he did so after the illegality of this levy had been solemnly pronounced by the Supreme Court. For this "irregular act of power" he was censured by the Home Government, and eventually recalled. "I look with extreme apprehension," wrote Mr. Cardwell, the Colonial Secretary, "on a state of things in which the Governor of a British colony is engaged in collecting money by mere force, from persons from whom the Supreme Court has declared that it was not due. . . . It was not for you to give a victory to one or the other party by a proceeding unwarranted by your commission or by the laws of the colony." Mr. Cardwell admitted that continued conflict between two constitutional authorities, each insisting on its extreme rights, might ultimately result in anarchy, but added that "anarchy has come already, when the Executive Governor, entrusted with power for the maintenance of public order and the protection of private rights, uses that power for the purpose of illegally setting aside the authority of one branch of the Legislature, of overruling the decisions of the Supreme Court, and of depriving the subject, even for a time, of that which the court has decided to be his." It was the duty of the queen's representative "to withhold the queen's authority from all or any of those manifestly unlawful proceedings by which one political party, or one member of the body politic, is occasionally tempted to establish preponderance over another".[1]

The crisis of 1878.

Thirteen years later a crisis of a similar nature led in the same colony to developments still more interesting to the student of constitutional history. In 1878 the Council again rejected an Appropriation Bill because clauses had been added to it providing for the payment of members. Thereupon the Governor, Sir George Bowen, accepted the advice of his

[1] Parliamentary Papers, 1866.

Ministers to discharge a number of public officers, judicial and administrative, on the ground that no money for the payment of their salaries was legally available. Sir George defended his action on the plea that the matter was one of purely local concern, but Sir Michael Hicks Beach, who in that year had succeeded Lord Carnarvon as Colonial Secretary, found himself unable to take that view. "You would have done better," he wrote to the Governor, "in the interests of the colony and in the maintenance of Parliamentary and responsible government, if you had informed your advisers that you felt unable to put your name to the documents directing the removal of these officers". In defending his action, Sir George quoted an extract from a despatch which, when Governor of Queensland, he had received from the Duke of Newcastle: "The general principle," wrote the Duke, then Colonial Secretary, "by which the Governor of a colony possessing responsible government is to be guided is this: that when Imperial interests are concerned he is to consider himself the guardian of those interests; but in matters of purely local politics he is bound, except in extreme cases, to follow the advice of a Ministry which appears to possess the confidence of the Legislature". The doctrine contained in this statement appears to be sound, so long as the action advised by Ministers does not transgress the law; but it is not always easy to determine the exact boundary line which separates matters of Imperial from matters of local interest. In the instance under review, "the contention of the Secretary of State was that it is the duty of the British representative, so long as the Imperial connection lasts, to safeguard the legal interests of those who, however indirectly, are in the service of the queen".[1]

The dispute between the Council and the Assembly increased in violence during the first half of 1878 until, when the session opened in July, the Ministry introduced a measure of constitutional reform aiming at a final adjustment of the relations between the Houses with respect to their legislative powers. The bill provided in the first place that money bills not passed within one month of their reception by the Council should become law without their consent; and, secondly, that

The Victorian Parliament Bill, 1878.

[1] Egerton's British Colonial Policy, p. 382.

other bills, when passed by the Legislative Assembly in two consecutive sessions, and rejected on each occasion by the Council should, if not disapproved by the electors of Victoria, be then deemed to have passed the Council. Bills at this stage might be referred to the electors by the vote of the majority of the Council.

Despatch of Sir Michael Hicks Beach, 1879.
The rejection of this drastic measure by the Council was anticipated by the Ministry, who resolved in that event to send, with the sanction of the Assembly, Commissioners to England to lay before the Imperial Government the proposals to which the Council had refused its assent, with the request that these proposals might be embodied in an Imperial enactment. Sir Michael Hicks Beach deprecated this step, pointing out that since the electors of Victoria had not been consulted directly on the proposed changes the question was by no means ripe for settlement; but, the bill having been rejected by the Council, the Ministry determined to persevere with their project, and delegates, chosen from the leading men of the Assembly, were appointed. The despatch in which Sir Michael Hicks Beach communicated to the Governor the refusal of the Home Government to overcome by means of an Imperial enactment the resistance of the Council in Victoria to the bill for restricting their powers is interesting, not only because it treats of the limits and scope of legitimate intervention by the Imperial Parliament in the affairs of a self-governing colony, but because it states, with the precision and the lucidity by which the utterances of the writer have always been distinguished, the practice of the Imperial Parliament in the matter of money bills so far as the mutual relations of the two Houses in regard to them are concerned. "The intervention of the Imperial Parliament," he wrote in May, 1879, "would not, in my opinion, be justifiable except in an extreme emergency. . . . It would involve an admission that the great colony of Victoria was compelled to ask the Imperial Parliament to resume a power which, desiring to promote her welfare, and believing in her capacity for self-government, the Imperial Parliament had voluntarily surrendered, and that this request was made because the leaders of political parties, from a general want of the moderation and sagacity essential to the success of constitutional government, had failed to agree upon any compromise for enabling the

business of the Colonial Government to be carried on". The mutual relations of the two legislative chambers established by the Constitution Act had been, he continued, to a certain extent laid down by that Act, and required definition rather than alteration. "The recent difference . . . like the most serious of those which have preceded it, turned upon the ultimate control of finance. . . . But this difficulty would not arise if the two Houses of Victoria were guided in this matter, as in others, by the practice of the Imperial Parliament. . . . The Assembly, like the House of Commons, would claim and in practice exercise the right of granting aids and supplies to the Crown, of limiting the matter, manner, measure, and time of such grants, and of so framing Bills of Supply that their rights should be maintained inviolate;[1] and, as it would refrain from annexing to a Bill of Supply any clause or clauses of a nature foreign to or different from the matter of such a bill, so the Council would refrain from any steps so injurious to the public service as the rejection of an Appropriation Bill. It would be well if the two Houses of Victoria, accepting the view which I have thus indicated, would maintain it in future by such a general understanding as would be most in harmony with the spirit of constitutional government. But after all that has passed it may be considered necessary to define those relations more closely than has been attempted here, and this might be effected either by adopting a joint standing order . . . or by legislation. Of these, the former would seem to be the preferable course, for there might be no slight difficulty in framing a statute to declare the conditions under which one House of Parliament, in a colony having two Houses, should exercise or refrain from exercising the powers which, though conferred upon it, must not always be asserted. But I must add that the clearest definition of the relative position of the two Houses, however arrived at, would not suffice to prevent collisions, unless interpreted with the discretion and mutual forbearance which have been so often exemplified in the history of the Imperial Parliament. . . . I can hardly anticipate that the Imperial Parliament will consent to disturb, in any way, at the instance of one House of the Colonial Legislature, the settle-

[1] This refers to the practice adopted, or rather restored, in 1861 of comprising the whole financial scheme for each year in a single bill.

ment embodied in the Constitution Act, unless the Council should refuse to concur with the Assembly in some reasonable proposal for regulating the future relations of the two Houses in financial matters . . . and shall persist in such refusal after the proposals of the Assembly have been ratified by the country, and again sent up by the Assembly for the consideration of the Council."

Settlement of the dispute, 1881. This wise advice bore fruit in 1881, when an agreement was arrived at between the two Houses in Victoria which made Imperial legislation unnecessary. In accordance with this compromise an Act was passed to reduce the qualification of members of the Legislative Council, to shorten the tenure of their seats, and to bring them in other respects into closer touch with the general body of the electors. The incident, tactfully and constitutionally handled by the Colonial Secretary, served but to strengthen the loyalty of both parties in the colony to the Imperial connection, whereas action less prudent or language less well-considered might easily have had the opposite effect.

Internal defence of self-governing colonies. It was clearly just that colonies enjoying self-government should provide for their own internal defence, and the Committee of the House of Commons, which considered the matter in 1861, reported their opinion that this charge should be transferred to them, "not merely with a view to diminish Imperial expenditure, but for the still more important purpose of stimulating the spirit of self-reliance in colonial communities".[1] The statesmen of that day, who for the most part regarded the colonial relation as "incompatible with maturity and full development," and who looked forward without much uneasiness to an amicable parting at no distant date, were naturally anxious to complete the education of the colonies by encouraging them to rely for protection on their own energy, while the few who, more far-sighted, had grasped the idea of an Empire composed of free states united in common allegiance to the Crown, desired the same object with a view to the ultimate organisation of the Empire as a belligerent unit. Accordingly Mr. Cardwell and his successors, Lord Carnarvon, Lord Granville, and Lord Kimberley effected the gradual

[1] See History of British Colonial Policy by Mr. H. E. Egerton—a book to which I am greatly indebted for the matter contained in this chapter.

withdrawal of the greater part of the British troops from the self-governing colonies, "until, in 1873, the Under Secretary for the colonies was able to announce that the military expenditure for the colonies was now almost entirely for imperial purposes".[1]

Another question was raised as the opinion that independence was the ultimate destiny of the self-governing colonies died down, and was replaced by the nobler hope of a united Empire confronting the world. This was the question of the manner in which the colonies should contribute to the common defence. That contribution must be voluntary all were agreed. By endeavouring to compel the American colonies to make a contribution towards meeting the financial burden left by a war waged, partly for their protection, against the French, England had lost her colonies in the eighteenth century; and no statesman was likely to repeat that blunder. But when responsible self-government had been given to the colonies, accompanied by a fiscal independence so complete that they were empowered to tax as they pleased imports from the Mother Country, the injustice of a system under which the whole burden of the naval and military defence of the Empire was sustained by the British taxpayer became evident to the colonists themselves. It was contended indeed that the defence of the colonies ought to be a matter for the Imperial Government because any danger that the colonists were likely to run would be the result of an Imperial foreign policy in the direction of which they had no part; but it was answered that the vast increase in modern times in the means of communication, with the simultaneous increase in the naval power of foreign States, exposed the colonies to perils disconnected with British foreign policy, against which the Imperial navy was their only security.

Little was done, however, so long as the notion prevailed that the Imperial connection would be preserved only till such a time as the colonies had reached maturity, and could stand by themselves. Yet a beginning was made. An Act of 1865 empowered the colonial Legislatures to provide vessels of war, seamen, and volunteers for their own defence, and to contribute ships of war and seamen for the Imperial service. Contingents

[1] Todd's Parliamentary Government in the British Colonies, p. 393.

of troops were sent by the self-governing colonies to the Soudan campaign of 1884. And in 1887, when the completion of the fiftieth year of a glorious reign was celebrated in London, and from all the world-wide dominions of the queen representatives were sent to do homage to that throne which was at once the symbol and the bond of Empire, the Government took the opportunity to propose a conference of colonial delegates for the discussion of questions of common Imperial interest, and especially that of Imperial defence. This conference is of high significance in the constitutional history of the Empire, because it registers the new aspect in which the Empire had come to be regarded, and was the first step in the development that followed. The colonies were no longer regarded as dependencies belonging to England, but as dominions owning, in common with England, allegiance to the queen.

Colonial conference proposed, 1886.

The first intimation of the conference of 1887 was contained in a passage in the Queen's Speech on the prorogation of Parliament in the autumn of 1886. " I have observed," so it runs, " with much satisfaction the interest which, in an increasing degree, is evinced by the people of this country in the welfare of their colonial and Indian fellow-subjects ; and I am led to the conviction that there is on all sides a growing desire to draw closer in every practicable way the bonds which unite the various portions of the Empire. I have authorised communications to be entered into with the principal colonial Governments with a view to the fuller consideration of matters of common interest." Accordingly, early in November, Mr. Stanhope, the Colonial Secretary, announced that the queen had been advised to summon a conference to meet in London in the early part of the following year, " at which representatives of the principal colonial Governments will be invited to attend for the discussion of those questions which appear more particularly to demand attention at the present time ". Great interest was felt in this first experiment of joint consultation on Imperial concerns. The colonies responded with readiness to the invitation addressed to them, and sent as their delegates Ministers, ex-Ministers, and other men of distinction, while it was arranged that at meetings in which the Crown colonies were interested, representatives appointed by the local Governments or named by the Colonial Secretary, should be present and take part in the proceedings.

The conference met in May, 1887. Sir Henry Holland, who had succeeded Mr. Stanhope as Colonial Secretary, presided; and the first meeting was attended by the Prime Minister, Lord Salisbury. The significance of the occasion was not lost to the clear vision of that statesman. "We are all sensible," he said, "that this meeting is the beginning of a state of things which is to have great results in the future. It will be the parent of a long progeniture; and distant Councils of the Empire may, in some far-off time, look back to the meeting in this room as the root from which all their greatness and all their beneficence sprang." It was understood on all sides that the delegates had met for discussion and consultation only, and that they had no power to bind the colonies which they represented. The aim of the conference was in the main twofold—first, to find a means of union for purposes of military defence, and, in the second place, to bring into closer touch with one another the widely separated provinces of the Empire by the extension of postal and telegraphic communications within its boundaries. The question of Imperial federation was expressly excluded from discussion as unripe for useful consideration and of too dangerous an import. *Meeting of the first colonial conference, May, 1887.*

The positive results of the conference were not very considerable. The Australian delegates agreed to submit to their Parliaments proposals for the increase of the Australasian squadron engaged in the protection of the floating trade—an increase subsequently carried into effect by agreement among the colonies. With regard to the postal system no satisfactory conclusions were reached. But it was to its character as the first joint deliberation of delegates from all the self-governing dominions, meeting on a footing of equality with the representatives of Great Britain, that the conference of 1887 owes its importance. The very subjects discussed tended to draw attention to the subject excluded from discussion. For contribution to Imperial defence constitutes a claim to a share in control over Imperial policy, while increase in the means of communication renders in some degree less impracticable the establishment of an Imperial Council in whose hands that control might be placed. *Its results.*

Conference at Ottawa, 1894. The next conference of representatives of the self-governing colonies was held at Ottawa in 1894—Lord Jersey, an ex-Governor of New South Wales, attending to represent the Mother Country—when the questions of communications and of trade relations within the Empire formed the chief subjects of discussion. An important resolution was agreed to in favour of a system of preferential trade within the Empire. The conference recommended that the colonies should give preferential terms of entry to British goods and "place each others' products on a more favourable customs basis than is accorded to the like products of foreign countries". In the preamble to this resolution it was declared that "the stability and progress of the British Empire can be best secured by drawing continually closer the bonds that unite the colonies with the Mother Country, and by a continuous growth of a practical sympathy and co-operation in all that pertains to the common welfare." By these words may be measured the gulf that separated the ideas of the day from those of the preceding generation when the ultimate severance of the Imperial tie was generally thought both at home and in the colonies to be inevitable and the chief desire of British statesmen was to secure that the parting when it came should be amicable.

Mr. Chamberlain at the Colonial Office. When the Unionists returned to power in 1895 Mr. Chamberlain, after nine years out of office, became Secretary of State for the Colonies. During the eight years in which he held this post the Colonial Office enjoyed the new experience of finding itself the chief centre of political interest. From the time of the Jameson raid in December, 1895, down to the opening of the agitation for Imperial Preference and Tariff Reform, which preceded Mr. Chamberlain's retirement, colonial and Imperial questions occupied the political attention of Englishmen almost to the exclusion of all else. Mr. Chamberlain, who, in his radical days, had loudly proclaimed the urgency of social and political reform at home and had startled moderate men by the drastic nature of his proposals for dealing with the land and the Church, was now inclined to dismiss such subjects as parochial, and urged his fellow-countrymen to think imperially. That the general effect of his administration was to strengthen and unite the Empire can hardly be doubted, but a certain precipitancy might be observed in his methods, not without peril to the cause he had at heart, and attributable, perhaps, not only to natural impetuosity of temperament, but to a lack of early training in the larger school of diplomacy. There was truth in the criticism that with regard to South Africa the diplomacy of the Government was more warlike than its preparations; and the war which achieved the consolidation of the Empire involved a serious risk of its disruption.

The sixtieth anniversary of Queen Victoria's accession to the throne was celebrated in London as a high Imperial festival. Mr. Chamberlain invited the Prime Ministers of the self-governing colonies to be present on the occasion. "Should this invitation be accepted," he wrote in his circular letter, "by the Premiers of the self-governing colonies, their presence in London would afford a most valuable opportunity for the discussion of many subjects of the greatest interest to the Empire, such as commercial union, colonial defence, representation of the colonies, legislation with regard to emigrants from Asia and elsewhere, and other similar subjects." This invitation was accepted by all the Prime Ministers. *The second Colonial Conference, 1897.*

On the 24th of June, 1897, the conference was opened. Presided over by Mr. Chamberlain, it was attended by the Premiers of Canada, New South Wales, Victoria, New Zealand, Queensland, Cape Colony, South Australia, Newfoundland, Tasmania, Western Australia, and Natal. For the first time the chief rulers of every self-governing province in the Empire met on a footing of equality to hold council together with a view to collective Imperial action.

Subjects for discussion were suggested by Mr. Chamberlain in the eloquent speech in which he opened the conference. Imperial Federation was no longer excluded from among them. On the contrary, although he proposed that the questions of defence, of commercial relations, and of communications within the Empire, should form, as in 1887, subjects of consultation, before all these he placed the question of the political relations between the Mother Country and the Dominions. He urged them "to take advantage of the bond of sentiment and tighten the ties that bind us together," and affirmed that "in this country, at all events . . . the idea of federation is in the air". Towards that goal, he declared, the grouping of the colonies *Speech by Mr. Chamberlain. His suggestion with respect to Imperial Federation.*

was the first step. Canada had shown the way—Australia and South Africa were preparing to follow. "I feel," he said, "that there is a real necessity for some better machinery of consultation between the self-governing colonies and the Mother Country, and it has sometimes struck me . . . that it might be possible to create a great Council of the Empire to which the colonies would send representative plenipotentiaries—not mere delegates who were unable to speak in their name, without further reference to their respective Governments; but persons who by their position in the colonies, by their representative character, and by their close touch with colonial feeling, would be able upon all subjects submitted to them, to give really effective and valuable advice. If such a Council were to be created it would at once assume an immense importance, and it is perfectly evident that it might develop into something greater. It might slowly grow to that Federal Council to which we must always look forward as our ultimate ideal." But he added that when the colonies had their share in the management of the Empire this power would be accompanied by a corresponding obligation which would appear as "some form of contribution towards the expense for objects which we shall have in common".

Resolution agreed to by the conference. The conclusions at which the conference arrived were embodied in resolutions to which the Premiers agreed for the most part with unanimity. They undertook to confer with their colleagues to see whether an improvement in the trade relations between the Mother Country and the colonies could be properly secured by a preference given by the colonies to the products of the Mother Country, and they earnestly recommended the denunciation of any treaties standing in the way of such preference.[1] They resolved, with two dissentients who were in favour of closer union, "that the present political relations between the United Kingdom and the self-governing colonies were generally satisfactory under the existing condition of things". They were also of opinion that it was desirable, whenever and wherever practicable, to group together under a Federal Union those colonies which were geographically con-

---

[1] Accordingly the German and Belgian treaties which prevented differential treatment by the British colonies in favour of the Mother Country were denounced at an early date.

nected. Lastly, they resolved that it was desirable "to hold periodical conferences of representatives of the colonies and of Great Britain for the discussion of matters of common interest".

Before the next conference was held in accordance with the last resolution of 1897, great events had occurred. The South African war had been fought, and the colonies had proved their loyalty by sending contingents of troops to the assistance of the Mother Country. The Transvaal and the Orange State had been annexed to the Empire, and the Federation of Australia had been at last accomplished. This "great and important step towards the organisation of the British Empire," as Mr. Chamberlain called it, was made in 1900. Federation had long been recognised as ultimately certain, but it was slow to come. To Canada the choice had seemed to lie between Federation and annexation to the United States, but no such external pressure drew together the States of the island-continent or gave them reason to believe that the sacrifice of a part of their independence was necessary to secure the whole. It was a form of external pressure, however, embodied in the suspicious activity of foreign powers that in 1883 enabled Sir Henry Parkes—always an advocate of Federation—to bring together representatives of the Australian colonies to confer upon the subject. This conference led to the constitution of a Federal Council by an Imperial Act of Parliament in 1885. This Council, although its establishment was significant as a first practical advance in the Federal direction, disappointed the hopes of its founders. It was merely an advisory body without legislative or executive power. New South Wales refused from the first to take part in it and South Australia subsequently withdrew. Nevertheless the movement continued. A convention held at Sydney in 1891 agreed upon the draft of a Commonwealth Bill which served as the foundation for all subsequent discussion, and a Federal League was formed to propagate the cause among the various colonies, and to overcome the hostility or at least the indifference with which the idea of Federation was generally received. A further advance was made in 1895 when the assembled Premiers of the Australian colonies agreed with one another to bring forward bills in their respective Parliaments to enable a convention to be held at which a federal constitution

The Federation movement in Australia.

should be framed by delegates entrusted with full powers for the purpose. The convention accordingly met in Adelaide in March, 1897. Queensland had declined to pass the enabling bill and was consequently unrepresented; but the delegates of the remaining Australian colonies agreed upon a draft which was sent to their several Parliaments and returned by them with their amendments. This draft was finally passed by the convention at Melbourne, to which city the delegates had adjourned in 1898, and was afterwards submitted by a referendum to the people with the result that 219,000 votes against 108,000 were recorded in its favour. As, however, the majority in New South Wales did not reach the figure of 80,000, which had been fixed as the minimum, that colony proposed fresh amendments some of which were accepted by a new meeting of the Premiers. The delay was fortunate since it allowed Queensland to take part, as she now consented to do, in the new referendum on the amended draft which the inconclusive character of the first verdict had necessitated. The result was a majority of more than 230,000 in favour of the scheme [1] to which the sanction of the Imperial Parliament was given by the Commonwealth of Australia Act, 1900.

The Commonwealth of Australia Act, 1900. This memorable Act, by which was formed, in the words of the preamble, "an indissoluble Federal Commonwealth firmly united for many of the most important functions of government," was not, like the British North America Act, drafted in England by the Home Government in consultation with colonial delegates, but was in the first instance exclusively the work of Australian statesmen. Some amendments were indeed made by the Home Government to the Act as it came from Australia before it left the House of Commons, but they were few, with one exception of no importance, and, moreover, were not inserted until the Australian delegates had given their consent. Mr. Chamberlain, when introducing the bill, expressly disclaimed all intention or desire of compelling the Australians to accept against their will any alteration whatever in the bill they had prepared. "We have got to a point in our relations with the self-governing colonies," he said, "in which, I think, we recognise, once for all, that these relations depend entirely on their free will and absolute consent. The

---

[1] 377,600 against 141,500.

links between them and us at the present time are very slender. Almost a touch might snap them. But, slender as they are, and slight as they are, although we wish . . . that they will become stronger, still if they are felt to be irksome by any one of our great colonies, we shall not attempt to force them to wear them ". Language so deferential would hardly have been used by any of Mr. Chamberlain's predecessors, nor, perhaps, whatever may have been their inward convictions, would so open a confession that the continued existence of the British Empire lay at the mercy of colonial opinion have been thought judicious even by the Whig statesmen who were afterwards accused by Mr. Disraeli of the deliberate design to disintegrate that Empire.

In certain important respects, Australian Federation was modelled on the constitution of the United States, rather than on that of the Dominion of Canada. Impressed by the recent spectacle of the American civil war and anxious to avoid the conditions that brought it about, the authors of Canadian Federation had attached the highest importance to the establishment of a strong central control. In Australia, on the other hand, where the mutual jealousies of the several States had long proved an obstacle to Federation, it was only possible to achieve it by a careful preservation of State rights. Accordingly, whereas in Canada all powers not expressly reserved to the several provinces belong to the Central Parliament, in Australia, as in the United States, "the Central Government has only powers over matters which are expressly stated and defined in the constitution".[1] These powers relate to thirty-nine subjects and include the tariff, post office and telegraph services, defence, currency, marriage, old age pensions, and external affairs. The appointment of the lieutenant-governors of the various States is vested directly in the Crown, and not, as in Canada, in the Governor-General.

Character of Australian Federation.

The Commonwealth Parliament under the constitution is composed of two Houses, both of them elective and both of them chosen by the same electorate, and at the same elections, but in a different manner and for a different term. The Upper House or Senate consists of six members from each of the States, each State returning an equal number whatever its

[1] Mr Chamberlain's statement.

size or population may be. For the purpose of senatorial elections each State votes as a single constituency, adopting the process known in France as the *scrutin de liste*. The Senate sits for six years—one half of it being renewed every three years—the Lower House for three. Members of both Houses receive salaries.

<small>Provision for the settlement of differences between the two Houses.</small>

The representative character of both Houses in the Commonwealth Parliament and the co-equal authority derived from it suggested the necessity of providing for the settlement of differences between them by constitutional machinery. Accordingly it is enacted that when a bill has been twice rejected by the Senate, the Governor may dissolve both Houses. If, after the election, the Senate again rejects the measure, it is submitted to a joint sitting of the Houses, and the question is decided by a simple majority.[1] The interest of these provisions lies in the circumstance that they represent the first attempt in an Anglo-Saxon constitution to settle differences between the two Houses of Parliament otherwise than by agreement.

<small>Right of appeal to Sovereign in Council.</small>

When the Constitution Bill had been agreed to by the Australian colonies, the delegates, who brought it over to England and submitted it to the Home Government, expected that it would be passed without alteration by the Imperial Parliament. While the bill was under consideration in Australia, the British Ministry had abstained from interference or advice; any substantial alteration now made would in equity have involved a fresh reference of the amended measure to the various States. Nevertheless, the British Government, even at that late hour, took exception to a clause in the bill which they conceived might weaken the bonds that held the Empire together. This was the clause which limited the right to appeal from the highest Australian Court to the Sovereign in Council.

<small>Origin of the jurisdiction of the Judicial Committee.</small>

All powers, judicial as well as legislative, were by the ancient theory of the British constitution vested in the sovereign. The conditions, however, under which these powers might be exercised have been from very early times progressively laid down and defined by charter or statute or

---

[1] The constitution provides that the numbers of the Lower House shall be double those of the Senate.

constant practice. In the Middle Ages the king made laws, or rather declared the law, at the request and in response to the petitions of the representatives of his people; and it was not until the middle of the fifteenth century that these petitions took the form of the statutes to be founded upon them to which the king might grant or refuse his consent, but which he might not alter. Just as the king made laws through his Parliament, he administered them through his judges and his courts; but he continued to be, in fact, as well as in theory, the "fountain of justice" when the days of his legislative activity were past. The power that he delegated to his judges was still his: like the sun, he retained the light that he transmitted. The court of final jurisdiction in civil cases within Great Britain was the House of Lords—the heir and representative of the ancient *concilium regis*. Under the Tudors and the first two Stuarts the committee of the Privy Council, known from the room in which it sat as the Star Chamber, was accustomed to deal, by virtue of the original power of royalty, with matters cognisable by the Courts of Common Law, while legislation by ordinance frequently dispensed with the advice and consent of the Houses of Parliament on the same principle. But, in 1641, the Star Chamber was abolished by Act of Parliament, and all exercise of jurisdiction, whether civil or criminal, by the Privy Council within the three kingdoms was abrogated. Though, however, the Council was no longer permitted to deal with matters cognisable by the ordinary courts, the Act of 1641 did not affect the right of every British subject living in any of the dependencies of the Crown outside the three kingdoms to appeal to the sovereign against a decision of the local courts; and that right remains to this day. In 1661 a Standing Committee of the Council was appointed to hear appeals and "doleances" from the Channel Islands and Plantations; and, in 1687, this committee was made an open committee of the whole Council. The committee heard appeals, and made its report to the king, by whom, thereupon, judgment was given, and an Order in Council issued. In 1833, these functions were transferred to a Judicial Committee of the Privy Council constituted by Act of Parliament. It was composed of the President of the Council, the Chancellor, ex-presidents, ex-chancellors, the holders of certain high judicial positions, and their predecessors in the same offices, together with two other persons nominated by the Crown. No report or recommendation was to be made to the Crown by the Judicial Committee unless in the presence of at least four members. Two Privy Councillors, who had held the office of judge in India or in the other dominions of the Crown, were to be appointed members of the committee with an allowance of £400 a year. The body thus formed was strengthened in 1876 by the addition of the four Lords of Appeal—thus being composed of nearly the same persons as those to whom the judicial work of the House of Lords was entrusted.

Work of the Judicial Committee.   The huge growth of the British Empire, and the inventions of science bringing into closer relations the Mother Country and her most distant dependencies, have extended the scope and complexity of the appellate jurisdiction of the Crown in Council to a degree undreamed of at the time when that jurisdiction was first organised. In his speech on the second reading of the Commonwealth Bill, Mr. Asquith gave a striking description of the operations of the Committee in modern times. "Go into the Judicial Committee of the Privy Council," he said, "for a single week and watch its operations. You will see it deciding on one day a question according to the Roman Dutch law; on another day, the same question according to the French law as it prevailed before the Revolution modified by subsequent Canadian statutes; and on another day according to the common law of England as modified by Australian or New Zealand legislation; and at the end of the week according to the custom of the Hindu or Mohammedan law." This was heavy work for an English tribunal most of the members of which were also occupied with the judicial work of the House of Lords.

Difference of opinion with regard to appeals.   In 1895, an Act of Parliament authorised the appointment to the Judicial Committee of Privy Councillors not exceeding five in number who had held high judicial office in the colonies; and, in 1896, the Chief Justices of Canada, of Cape Colony, and of South Australia were accordingly made Privy Councillors and members of the Judicial Committee. But as no salaries were attached to these appointments the colonial members of the Judicial Committee were unable to reside permanently in

England, while cases might be brought before them on appeal with which they had already dealt in the colonial courts. Hence this attempt to increase the authority of "the great Judicial Court of Appeal of the Empire" met with but a qualified success.

Nevertheless, the supreme appellate jurisdiction of the Crown in Council is perhaps the most substantial link in the chain that binds the Empire together, and all attempts to weaken it are justly regarded with jealousy, not only by the Imperial Government, but by a large section of opinion in the colonies themselves. When the question was raised in 1875 the Privy Council pointed out that " this power had existed for centuries over all the dependencies of the Empire by the sovereign of the Mother Country sitting in Council. By this institution, common to all parts of the Empire beyond the seas, all matters whatever requiring a judicial solution may be brought to the cognisance of one court in which all have a voice. To abolish this controlling power and abandon each colony and dependency to a separate Court of Appeal of its own, would obviously be to destroy one of the most important ties connecting all parts of the Empire in common obedience to the courts of law, and to renounce the last and most essential mode of exercising the authority of the Crown over its possessions abroad." In the case of Canada the respective rights under the Federation Act of the Dominion Parliament and of the Provincial Legislatures had occupied much of the attention of the Judicial Committee in cases brought before them on appeal, and the freedom from local prepossessions of the judges sitting in Downing Street had been recognised as giving a peculiar authority to their decisions. It was precisely this class of questions that the seventy-fourth clause of the Australian Commonwealth bill as originally drawn proposed to withdraw from their arbitrament. The clause as submitted allowed no appeal to the Queen in Council on any matter involving the interpretation of the Federal constitution, or the constitution of a State, unless the " public interests " of some other part of her Majesty's Dominions were involved; and it further provided that the Federal Parliament might in the future make laws further limiting the matters on which appeal might lie. To persuade the Australian delegates to consent to the excision of this clause from the bill was now the earnest endeavour of Mr. Chamberlain. In a Colonial Office Memorandum of the 29th March he urged that the retention of the prerogative intact would strengthen the bonds of union "and, by insuring uniform interpretation of the law throughout the Empire, facilitate that unity of action which will lead to a real Federation of the Empire". But the delegates remained unconvinced. They pointed out in their reply that there was no connection between unity of action and uniform interpretation of the law; and that, while consciousness of kinship and a common sense of duty were the true links of Empire, "no patriotism was ever inspired or sustained by the thought of the Privy Council". If their statesmen were thought capable of framing a constitution and amending it in the future without assistance from the Mother Country why, they asked, should they refer questions concerning its interpretation " to what is practically an English tribunal?" Public opinion in Australia, however, was divided on the subject—the Governments of two out of the six colonies desired to preserve the appeal—and the matter was settled by a compromise. The right to give leave to appeal to the Judicial Committee upon questions as to the limits *inter se* of the constitutional powers of the Commonwealth and those of any State, or as to the limits *inter se* of the constitutional powers of any two or more States, was preserved; but it was transferred from the Judicial Committee itself to the High Court of Australia. And bills for further limitations of this power to appeal were to be reserved by the Governor General for the signification of the sovereign's pleasure.

Settlement by compromise.

The compromise thus effected was regarded by Mr. Chamberlain as provisional and temporary. He saw that the main objection of the Australians to the unlimited appellate jurisdiction of the Privy Council in cases relating to the interpretation of the Commonwealth Act was that the Judicial Committee was "practically an English tribunal," and he thought that if he could strengthen that committee by the addition of colonial judges residing in England and enjoying the salaries and status of Lords of Appeal this objection would be removed. He proposed, therefore, that a representative from each of the three great colonial groups—one from Canada and Newfoundland,

Proposed appellate tribunal for the Empire.

one from Australia and one from South Africa, together with a representative of India—should be appointed for a term of seven years members of the Privy Council, Lords of Appeal, and life peers. This proposal was, however, withdrawn in July, at the suggestion of the Australian delegates, who thought that instead of reforming the constitution of the Judicial Committee the Government might, in consultation with the colonies, consider the question of a single appellate tribunal for the whole of the queen's dominions, including the Mother Country. Mr. Chamberlain adopted this suggestion, and delegates from the self-governing colonies were invited to London to confer upon the subject. They met in 1901 but could come to no agreement. The majority of the delegates wished to preserve the appeal to the King in Council, and to strengthen the Judicial Committee on the lines originally proposed by Mr. Chamberlain; while the representative of Australia recommended the establishment of a single Supreme Court of Appeal for the Empire, into which should be merged the appellate jurisdiction of the House of Lords. In the face of these disagreements Mr. Chamberlain, who held that it would be wrong to force any self-governing colony to accept a change of system against its will, laid aside for the time being his projects for remodelling the Judicial Committee.

The next colonial conference was held in 1902, on the occasion of the Coronation of King Edward VII. In his invitation to the Premiers, Mr. Chamberlain asked them to furnish a statement of any subjects which they thought might usefully be discussed; and, with a view to giving a definite direction to discussion, to formulate the text of any resolutions which their Governments might desire to submit. This suggestion, containing within itself a germ of procedure from which collective action might some day spring, was adopted by the Premiers, and the precedent has been subsequently followed.

The conference of 1902.

The conference met in July. The essential importance to Great Britain of colonial contributions to the sustenance of her ever-increasing armaments had been brought home to the minds of most people by the spectacle of the South African war, and Mr. Chamberlain insisted strongly upon it in his opening speech.[1] He declared that the Mother Country was prepared to give in return to the Dominions a voice in the policy of the Empire corresponding to their contributions. He expressed once more the opinion that the political Federation of the Empire was within the limits of possibility, and he hoped that with the help of steam and electricity difficulties in the way of such a scheme connected with the great distances which separate the different members of the Empire, with the lack of sufficient communication, with the variety of interests concerned, and with the immense disproportion in wealth and population, might eventually be overcome. The demand, he thought, must come, if it come, from the colonies. But if the Dominions were prepared to take a proportionate share in the burdens of the Empire, his opinion was that it might be possible to establish some real Council of the Empire—at first perhaps only an advisory council—to which all questions of Imperial interest might be referred. The Canadian preference, however valuable as a proof of goodwill and affection, had been, he said, altogether disappointing in substantial results, while no preference had been granted by the other self-governing colonies to the Mother Country, in consequence of the resolution of 1897. That true Imperial unity could only be achieved if the Dominions contributed more generously to the support and defence of the Empire and were given a corresponding share in the direction of Imperial policy, was the burden of his speech.

Resolutions passed. Substantial progress was made at this conference in the organisation of Imperial relations. A resolution was agreed to that it would be to the advantage of the Empire if conferences of the Premiers and of the Secretary of State were held at stated intervals for the discussion of questions of common interest affecting the relations of the Mother Country and the Dominions. Increased contributions towards naval defence were promised by the representatives of Australasia and the Cape; a general resolution was unanimously passed in favour of the grant by the self-governing colonies of preferential treatment to the products of the United Kingdom; and the Prime

---

[1] He pointed out that the *normal* military and naval expenditure of 1902 cost the United Kingdom 29s. 3d. per head of population, while Canada only paid 2s. per head, New South Wales 3s. 5d., and New Zealand 3s. 4d.

Ministers urged on the home Government the expediency of granting in the United Kingdom a corresponding preference to colonial products, " either by exemption from or reduction of duties now or hereafter imposed ".[1] Other proposals tending in various ways to draw the countries of the Empire closer together were formulated in resolutions and approved. Among these were the preference to be given to the colonies in Government contracts; the mutual protection of patents, with kindred suggestions relating to the coasting trade; and the cheap postage of newspapers between various parts of the Empire. Of all the resolutions, important as they were and followed by practical results, that in which it was agreed that conferences should be held at regular intervals of not more than four years, and not, as heretofore, only on special occasions, was the most significant. It was the outward sign of a new development. Conferences were beginning to shape themselves as constitutional organs for the direction of Imperial affairs—not perhaps without some menace to other institutions in the Mother Country.

The next conference met in April, 1907. In May, 1903, Mr. Chamberlain had, while still in office, without the consent of the Cabinet, and in direct opposition to the convictions of the Chancellor of the Exchequer and of some of the most eminent of his colleagues, publicly formulated a policy of Imperial preference on the lines of the resolution of 1902. Since, however, this policy involved a tax upon foreign corn and other imported food stuffs, he endeavoured to redress the balance by including in his general scheme the grant of old age pensions and the protection by a tariff of home manufactures from foreign competition. This movement resulted in the break up of the Cabinet in the autumn of 1903, and combined with other conditions to bring about the overwhelming defeat of the Unionist party two years later at the general election of 1906.

The conference of 1907.

The conference of 1907 was distinguished from its predecessors in several important particulars. No special occasion brought together the chief rulers of the Empire. They as-

Distinguishing features.

---

[1] A shilling duty on corn had been imposed as a war tax in 1901, and the suggestion was that colonial corn might be allowed to enter free. The duty was repealed in 1903.

sembled from the most widely separated regions of the world for the express purpose of taking counsel together on Imperial concerns. As Sir Henry Campbell-Bannerman said, in his opening address, it was not a meeting between Premiers and the Colonial Secretary; but between the Premiers and the British Government, under the presidency of the Colonial Secretary. A report of the proceedings was published. And a great advance was made in the co-ordination of the government of the Empire by the resolution which transformed the conference into an Imperial constitutional body, with *ex-officio* members, a permanent secretarial staff, and stated times of meeting.

<small>Proposal for an Imperial Council.</small>

The Commonwealth of Australia desired to go further than this. The Australian Government formulated a resolution for the establishment of an Imperial Council, of the kind formerly suggested by Mr. Chamberlain, to consist of representatives of Great Britain and of the self-governing colonies chosen *ex officio* from their existing administrations. They proposed also that a permanent secretarial staff, whose expenses should be borne by the countries represented on the Council in proportion to their populations, should be charged with the duty of obtaining information for the use of the Council, of attending to the execution of its resolutions, and of conducting correspondence on matters relating to its affairs. A similar resolution was moved on behalf of New Zealand, while the Cape Government proposed in addition that a plan of Imperial defence should be organised under which the contribution of each colony should be equitably fixed and paid for. The British Government welcomed these suggestions, but Sir Wilfrid Laurier, on behalf of Canada, was not prepared to go so far. He objected to the substitution of the name of "Imperial Council," with all that it implied, for that of Imperial Conference, and still more strongly to the proposal of the Cape.

<small>Decision of the conference.</small>

The unanimous resolution ultimately agreed to affirmed the expediency of holding a conference to be called the Imperial Conference, every four years, at which questions of common interest might be discussed and considered between the King's Government at home and his Governments of the self-governing Dominions beyond the seas; and it defined the constitution of this conference. The Prime Minister of the

United Kingdom was to be *ex officio* President, and the Prime Ministers of the self-governing Dominions *ex officio* members. The Secretary of State for the Colonies was to be an *ex officio* member of the conference and to preside in the absence of the President. Each Government of a Dominion was to be limited to a single vote and to two representatives. The resolution further affirmed the desirability of constituting a permanent secretarial staff which should, during the periods between the conferences, keep the several Governments represented informed in regard to matters which had been or might be subjects for discussion. This staff would be charged, under the direction of the Colonial Secretary, with the duties of obtaining information for the use of the conference, of attending to the execution of its resolutions, and of conducting correspondence. It was also agreed that upon matters of importance requiring consultation between two or more Governments which could not conveniently be postponed subsidiary conferences might be held between representatives of the Governments concerned specially called for the purpose. With regard to Imperial defence little was done by this conference. "We do not meet you to-day as claimants for money"—so said the Prime Minister in his speech to the Conference—and what was not asked for was not granted. It was resolved that the colonies should be authorised to refer for advice to the Committee of Imperial Defence through the Secretary of State any local question in regard to which expert assistance was deemed desirable; and that a representative of the colony concerned might be summoned to attend as a member of the Committee during the discussion of the question raised. A proposal by the Commonwealth of Australia for the constitution of an Imperial Court of Appeal was fully discussed; but the resolutions agreed to merely recommended the codification of the rules, the reform of the procedure, and in some respects the limitation of the powers, of the Judicial Committee. After a long debate the resolutions agreed to by the Premiers with regard to preferential trade at the conference of 1902 were reaffirmed—the British Government disagreeing in so far as those resolutions implied that it was necessary or expedient to alter the fiscal system of the United Kingdom.

British expansion in South Africa and its causes.

The surrounding presence of powerful and hostile native tribes has been the governing factor in shaping events and bringing about the expansion of the British Empire in South Africa. The Cape, after its cession by the Dutch in 1814, was valued rather as a halting place on the highway to India than as a place to be colonised; and, after the abolition of slavery in 1833, the chief concern of the Colonial Office was to protect the natives from what, on the report of missionaries, was believed to be the harsh treatment they endured at the hands of the Dutch settlers. By Lord Glenelg's instructions treaties were made with the native chiefs the object of which was to establish complete political equality between whites and natives. The Dutch on the frontier, deprived of protection, renounced their obedience, and established themselves in the territories since known as Natal, the Orange River Colony, and the Transvaal. The danger of allowing an independent republic to hold a long coast line with a port, the presence of numerous British settlers attracted by such a situation, and the action of the Boers in driving natives southwards into the British colony compelled the British Government, sorely against its will, to sanction the annexation of Natal in 1843. The Orange Free State was next annexed in 1847 by Sir Harry Smith, the Governor of Natal—the English authorities consenting chiefly on the ground that annexation for the time, at all events, was necessary in order to protect the natives from the Dutch emigrants, for whose actions they conceived themselves to be in some measure responsible. By the Sand River Convention in 1852 the independence of the Boers beyond the Vaal was recognised, and the Government hoped that an end to these "repeated extensions" had at last been found.

Annexation and withdrawal from the Orange State.

The annexation of the Orange River Colony was at first resented by the Boers, and force was necessary to bring it about; but the transition from a state of anarchy to a state of order, the security achieved from the native menace, and the migration of the irreconcilables beyond the Vaal, soon led to a change of view. The spectacle of the prosperity of the Orange Colony might, had the sovereignty been maintained, have affected the minds of the Transvaal Boers, with the result that the union of South Africa might have been anticipated by a generation. Unfortunately, a Basuto war convinced the British

Government that the Orange Colony was a useless and costly possession. Seven years had sufficed to reconcile the Dutch inhabitants of the Orange Colony to British administration, and both Dutch and British, through their representatives in the Assembly, declared for the maintenance of the British sovereignty. Nevertheless, withdrawal was determined upon, and independence forced upon the unwilling colony.

In 1858, the Orange Free State, at the end of its financial resources, weak, and threatened with annexation by the Transvaal, asked permission from Sir George Grey, the Governor of the Cape, to enter into a treaty of alliance with England. The Volksraad passed a resolution in favour of "union or alliance with the Cape Colony whether on the basis of Federation or otherwise". Sir George Grey perceived the great opportunity thus offered, and formed the conclusion that the moment for Federation had arrived. "By a Federal Union alone," he said, "the South African colonies can be made so strong, and so united in policy and action, that they can support themselves against the native tribes," and he urged this policy upon the Colonial Office. The British Government, however, was opposed to the idea; and Sir George Grey, having propounded the policy of confederation to the Cape Parliament without awaiting instructions from home, was reprimanded and recalled.[1]

Sir George Grey's policy of Federation in 1858.

Representative institutions were granted by letters patent to the Cape Colony in 1850, and a new constitution, comprising a Legislative Council and a House of Assembly, both elected by the people, was introduced in 1853, but it was not until 1869 that the system of responsible government was first suggested for the colony by the Imperial Government. The proposal was at first distasteful to the majority of the colonists, who feared that it would involve the withdrawal of the imperial troops and oblige them to provide for their own defence against the natives; and was warmly opposed by the Governor, Sir Philip Wodehouse. "The form of responsible government," he wrote, "is suitable only to communities who

Responsible Government introduced into Cape Colony, 1872.

[1] By Sir E. Bulwer Lytton, Colonial Secretary in the Conservative Government of 1858-9. "You have so far compromised the Government," he wrote, "and endangered the success of that policy which they must deem right and expedient in South Africa, that your continuance in the administration of government can be no longer of service to public interests."

desire or look forward to a severance at no distant date from the Mother Country, whether by transfer to another power or by the establishment of an independent State . . . when such a severance is not coveted or contemplated, party government is inexpedient." It was, indeed, this consideration that distinguished in the minds of the statesmen of that day the case of the Cape from that of the other self-governing colonies. From those they had come to regard ultimate severance as inevitable so soon as their period of nonage should be past; but the retention of the Cape was essential to the rulers of India. The movement, however, gained ground in the colony, and a bill for the establishment of responsible government passed through the Colonial Legislature in 1872.

Lord Carnarvon's Federation scheme and its failure. Sir H. Barkly, who had succeeded Sir Philip Wodehouse in 1870, and under whose auspices this measure was passed, regarded it as paving the way for the confederation in South Africa of all the territories which formed or had formed portions of the British possessions. His views were shared by Lord Kimberley, the Colonial Secretary, and were held even more zealously by that statesman's successor, Lord Carnarvon, who returned to the office in which he had distinguished himself as the chief author of Canadian Federation on the advent to power of the Conservatives in 1874. A permissive Bill "for the union under one form of government of such of the South African Colonies and States as may agree thereto, and for the government of such union," was passed by the Imperial Parliament in 1877, but the events of the succeeding years deprived it of effect.

Annexation of the Transvaal. The annexation of the Transvaal against the public protests, but with the secret encouragement, of the Boer leaders, who found themselves powerless to defend their country against the Zulus without British help, deferred the question indefinitely. The two Dutch Republics had no desire for confederation for its own sake; and when the destruction of the Zulu power by the British had relieved the Transvaal from all anxiety in that quarter, the chief ambition of the Boers was to recover their independence. The grant of self-government to the Transvaal was unwisely delayed, in spite of the strongly urged advice of Sir Bartle Frere, the Governor of the Cape; and, after four years of sullen discontent, the Boers revolted in December, 1880. Mr. Gladstone had denounced the annexation when in Opposition, but on returning to power in the spring of 1880 he resolved to maintain it, chiefly as a means to Federation, which he afterwards declared to have been at that time the pole star of his policy in South Africa. A succession of reverses in the first engagements of the war caused him to alter his opinion; and without any military demonstration of force or other attempt to vindicate the queen's authority, he accepted defeat, and determined on retrocession. *The first Boer war.*

The convention of Pretoria, signed in 1881, two months after the queen had been made to say in her speech from the Throne that the duty of vindicating her authority had set aside for the time all plans for granting local self-government to the colonists of the Transvaal, granted independence almost complete to those colonists. A British suzerainty was constituted under which provision was made for Imperial control over the external relations of the Transvaal and for the protection of natives by the British Resident. This protection of the natives was found to be inoperative, and, in 1884, the convention of London—omitting all mention of suzerainty in the preamble— restored the old title of South African Republic and limited Imperial control to a right to forbid the conclusion of treaties or engagements between the South African Republic and States other than the Orange Free State and native tribes. The Republic agreed freely to admit all white men into its territory for the purposes of residence or trade, and that they should be liable to no higher taxes than were raised from the other inhabitants. Matters had been so contrived that although the demands of the Boers had been conceded to the uttermost, the effect left on their minds, so far from being gratitude, was strong resentment mixed with contempt, while a sense of almost intolerable humiliation, unfamiliar to men of their race, was experienced by the English in South Africa. The unsolved problem of our colonial system remained apparently insoluble, and the pole star of confederation in South Africa ceased to guide the course of our political mariners. *The convention of Pretoria, 1881.*

Empires, like natural bodies, when they cease to grow must, after a stationary period, begin to decay. This is inevitable, since the forces set free from the necessity of defence are set free to take the offensive, and it is especially the case *Imperial developments in South Africa. Mr. Rhodes and his objects.*

where a civilised power is camped in the midst of barbarous tribes. Up to this time the British Empire had grown in South Africa against the inclination and endeavours of British statesmen. It had been found necessary to protect Cape Colony against the tribes by enlarging its frontiers; it had subsequently been found necessary, not only to protect native tribes against our quondam Dutch subjects, but also to save the Dutch settlements from extinction at the hands of the natives. But a new spirit was beginning to display itself, and the expansion which had been the result of circumstance was continued as the fruit of design. Mr. Cecil Rhodes, who entered the Cape Assembly in 1881, was in no doubt as to the objects at which he aimed. He believed in the Empire, and he believed in self-government. He would have echoed the words of Sir Bartle Frere that "the thing wanted was unity of purpose and action in all matters which concern more than one province, and the utmost possible freedom for self-action with regard to matters which concern only one province or part of it". The existence of the Dutch South African Republics and the "Imperial factor"—as he called government from Downing Street—were alike objectionable to him; since both were inconsistent with the federation of free states at which he aimed. To attain Imperial unity was the object of his endeavour; and he was successful in checking the development of conditions which would have made its attainment for long impracticable.

Boer policy.   The Boers also felt the need of expansion and were troubled with few scruples in its pursuit. Their policy of gradual absorption of native territories was traversed by the Convention of London, which had defined the boundaries of the Transvaal; but they paid little attention to the provisions of that treaty, and by setting the native chiefs against one another, and taking the part of one against the other they pursued, in unconscious imitation, the policy whereby the Romans of old had made themselves masters of the world. A raid into Bechuanaland was foiled by Mr. Rhodes, who had been appointed Deputy Commissioner there by the Cape Government, and at whose instance the British Government sent an expedition under Sir Charles Warren which compelled them to retire. Swaziland they succeeded in annexing, but from Zululand they were turned back by the British, who were resolved that at least they should not reach the sea. Their activity resulted in the extension of British dominion. In September, 1885, Southern Bechuanaland was declared British territory, and a British protectorate was established over the northern regions up to the twenty-second parallel.

Mr. Rhodes, with the goal of Federation always before his eyes, was opposed at the time to the establishment of British protectorates, and upheld the policy of colonial annexation. His genuine belief in complete local self-government gained him the suffrages of the Cape Dutch, and their support brought him into power in 1890 when he became the autocratic Prime Minister of the colony. The discovery of gold in the Transvaal, and the consequent immigration of large numbers of British into that State, changed the conditions of the South African problem, and precipitated its developments. By an alteration in the electoral registration law, the Republic excluded the majority of the new settlers from all share in the direction of policy, while at the same time it raised from them the greater part of its revenue. The discontent of the British "Uitlanders" was secretly fomented by Mr. Rhodes and culminated in the unfortunate raid from across the Rhodesian frontier led by Dr. Jameson; when the attempt was made to overthrow President Kruger's Government by a sudden surprise. Mr. Rhodes was the managing director of the British South Africa Company for which he had obtained a charter in 1889, and it was by his orders that Dr. Jameson, the administrator of the territories of the company, had concentrated the military forces of Rhodesia at Mafeking on the Transvaal frontier. Dr. Jameson's rash action and complete defeat by an overwhelming force of Boers involved the resignation of Mr. Rhodes and gave a welcome pretext to the Boer Government to arm; so that by 1899 they were ready for the war which was to decide once and for all the question whether Dutch or English should be supreme in South Africa. By the treaty of Vereeniging in 1902 that question was decided in favour of the English; but by the same treaty it was agreed that, so soon as circumstances should permit, representative institutions leading up to self-government were to be granted to the new colonies—a condition fulfilled by Sir Henry

The Jameson raid, the second Boer war, and the Peace of Vereeniging.

Campbell Bannerman's Government, by which a constitution with responsible government was granted through the issue of letters patent to the Transvaal in 1906 and to the Orange River Colony in 1907.

Concession of self-government to the Transvaal, 1906, and to the Orange River Colony, 1907.

These concessions were denounced by Lord Milner, who had wished to suspend the Cape Constitution after the war,[1] and who now prophesied disaster to the Empire in South Africa as the certain result of the Ministerial policy; and by the leaders of the Opposition, who, at the time of their resignation in 1905, had been engaged in preparing a provisional constitution for the Transvaal, including in its design representative institutions, but excluding responsible government. That such an experiment would have succeeded is very doubtful, for although it may have been true to say that in nearly every instance the grant to a colony of representative institutions had preceded that of responsible government, it was equally true that the earlier system had seldom if ever worked well. It was argued indeed that responsible institutions implied party government, and that, in a country inhabited by two white races so lately at war with one another, party government would be inexpedient and dangerous. But in Canada the disagreement between the Government and the representative assemblies had accentuated racial animosities and led to armed revolt, while the introduction of responsible government had brought peace and reconciliation. The excellent results attained showed that it was fortunate that in 1907 the Liberal Government were able to carry out their policy by the use of the prerogative, for, had they been obliged to embody it in a bill, it is unlikely that the hostile majority in the House of Lords would have consented to its accomplishment.

Constitutions of the new Colonies.

The constitutions granted to the Transvaal and to the Orange River Colony were framed on the usual British model. As in the case of the Commonwealth of Australia Act, some of the constitutional conventions observed in the British Parliament became a part of the written constitutions of the new colonies. Thus the doctrine that the Second Chamber may reject, but not amend or initiate, money bills was in express words therein embodied, and also the important rule that no

---

[1] This was not done, and in 1904 Dr. Jameson himself was, under the constitution, the Progressive Premier of the Cape.

proposal, direct or indirect, for the imposition of taxation or for the appropriation of revenue may be made except on the recommendation of the Crown—a rule which in the House of Commons rests merely upon a Standing Order of the House, repealable at any time by resolution.

The policy of 1906 was bold, even to rashness, but it has been amply justified by the result. The fatal custom too often observed by English statesmen both in Ireland and in South Africa of refusing to listen to grievances until outrages or armed revolt enforce attention was in this instance happily avoided.[1] *Bis dat qui cito dat.* The gift for once was made at a time when it was impossible to impute it to unworthy motives. This happy event and the reconciliation between the two races which followed was due in no small measure to the loyalty, patriotism, and statesmanship of General Botha, who having served his countrymen gallantly in war did even greater service to them and to the Empire at large in his work of consolidation and reunion.

<small>Their success.</small>

And now the ground was cleared for the union of South Africa. There was less reason in the nature of things for the partition of South Africa into separate colonies than had existed either in the case of Canada or of Australia. This partition had been due less to natural causes—whether geographical or racial—than to the conflict of ideas. There were British and Dutch in each of the South African colonies, though in varying proportions, whereas in Canada the French had been concentrated apart in the single province of Quebec, where their religion and national manner of life presented insuperable obstacles to fusion with the British. But the British Government had felt no wish to form a nation in South Africa. To them Cape Colony was part of the Indian question. They "accepted responsibility for protecting life and property so far as territories already settled were concerned,"[2] but their chief anxiety was to restrict their liabilities. On the other hand the desire of the Dutch emigrants from the Cape was to cut them-

<small>Early obstacles to Union of South Africa. Their disappearance.</small>

---

[1] If in 1879 the advice of Sir Bartle Frere had been followed and the promise of self-government made at the time of the first annexation of the Transvaal in 1877 had been promptly kept, the first Boer war might, perhaps, have been avoided, and the union of South Africa effected twenty years before its actual accomplishment.

[2] Parl. Papers, 1907, lvii. 281; Lord Selborne's Memorandum, p. 15.

selves off from the society they left behind them and "just as the first settlers withdrew to Swellendam and Graaf Reinett beyond the existing frontier of the Dutch East India Company's territory, so did their descendants, in the first half of the nineteenth century, indignantly retire behind the Orange River and even behind the Vaal and Tugela, anxious only to escape a Government whose sympathies were poles asunder from any notions of their own".[1] But, by 1909, these obstacles to union had vanished. The British Government had abandoned the attempt to rule the colonies from London—the Cape was no longer on the highway to India—while South Africa with Canada, Australia, New Zealand, and the United Kingdom itself had become one of the "five principal partners in the confederacy of the British Empire".

Advantages of union. While then the influences which had produced separation had disappeared, the advantages derivable from union were many and manifest. Under the existing system, questions in which two or more colonies were involved could only be disposed of at great expense of time and money by negotiations which were apt to engender friction. Such were questions of high importance relating to railways, to the tariff, to the regulation of the labour supply for the mines, and to the policy to be pursued with regard to natives and Asiatics. Intercolonial disputes on these and kindred subjects could only be settled by reference to the High Commissioner, an official responsible to the Colonial Secretary, who was himself responsible to the Imperial Parliament. Such a tribunal on matters relating for the most part exclusively to their own country could not be satisfactory to the South African subjects of the Crown. There appeared to be no reason why the Parliament of one province of the Empire—for that is what the Imperial Parliament was tending to become—should be the ultimate judge of differences which concerned two other provinces. " Three choices," wrote Lord Selborne, "lie before the people of South Africa, the make-shift régime of the High Commissioner, the jarring separation of the States of South America, the noble union of the States of North America".[2] The choice was easy to make.

Union of South Africa effected, 1909. The lead was taken by the Cape. In November 1906, the Ministers of that colony requested Lord Selborne as High

---

[1] Lord Selborne's Memorandum, p. 14.
[2] Lord Selborne's Despatch, 7th January, 1907.

Commissioner to place in a reasoned statement the circumstances of the case before the people of South Africa in order to give them an opportunity of expressing their opinion as to whether it was desirable to establish a Central National Government embracing all the British South African colonies and protectorates ; and, if so, how best to bring it about. Lord Selborne complied with their request. An able memorandum drawn up by his instructions, and under his supervision, was forwarded home, and to the Governments of the Cape, of Natal, of the Transvaal, of the Orange River Colony, and of Southern Rhodesia. In 1908, a convention of delegates from the colonies met first at Durban, next at Cape Town, and afterwards at Bloemfontein, and a scheme was agreed to. After this scheme had been submitted in the form of a bill to the various South African Parliaments and agreed to by them, it was brought to London by a delegation and, in the summer of 1909, passed into law by the Imperial Parliament.

The new constitution provided for a legislative union—to be called the Union of South Africa—under one Government. It followed the Canadian rather than the Australian model ; but even more power was given to the Central Government and even less to the Provincial Governments than in the case of Canada. The preamble indeed affirmed the expediency of providing for the establishment of provinces with powers of legislation and administration in local matters ; but those powers were confined by the Act to certain reserved and specified subjects. The chief officer in the province is the "Administrator" appointed by the Governor-General in Council, who acts on the advice of an Executive Committee chosen at the first meeting of the Provincial Council. This Council is elected every three years, and is not subject to dissolution save by effluxion of time. It has power to make ordinances on specified subjects of a local nature, and to direct taxation within the province in order to raise a revenue for provincial purposes. In fact its functions resemble those of an English County Council rather than those of an Australian State. *The Provincial Governments.*

On the other hand, the supreme power in South Africa rests with the Governor-General acting on the advice of Ministers responsible to the South African Parliament. This *The Central Government and Legislature.*

Parliament is formed on the customary British model of two Houses, the Senate and the House of Assembly. The Senate, in the first instance, was composed of eight members from each of the four colonies chosen by the respective assemblies of those colonies sitting in joint session. To these thirty-two senators were added eight nominated by the Crown, of whom four were chosen under the statute with especial reference to their knowledge of native affairs. The House of Assembly was formed of 121 representatives of the people, with provisions for the redistribution of seats after each successive census.

The native question. Since the first establishment of the British in South Africa the native question has been a perennial source of difficulty and disagreement, and it was now the only topic on which divergence of opinion manifested itself in the discussions on the South Africa Act in the House of Commons. The bill provided that no one, not of European descent, should be qualified to sit in the new Parliament. This disqualification excluded not only natives, but all Asiatic or coloured subjects of the king, and, so far as the Cape was concerned, it was a novelty, because no such restriction had hitherto existed in that colony, although no one not of European descent had in fact been elected to its House of Assembly. But the arrangement was the outcome of a carefully worked-out compromise including the appointment of the four senators especially qualified to protect the interests of the natives, and the Government were informed that to interfere with it might imperil the whole settlement. They, therefore, somewhat reluctantly, consented to retain this provision in the bill, and carried its retention after a long debate in the House of Commons. The seat of Government was placed at Pretoria;

Other provisions. the seat of the Legislature at Cape Town. The original intention had been to include the Protectorates within the Union, but they were unwilling to pass from under the direct administration of the Crown. Their interests were safeguarded by the Schedule to the Act under which Protectorates taken over by the Union are to be administered and legislated for by the Government.

Thus was accomplished the third great constitutional step in the consolidation and organisation of the Empire. So successful has been the reconciliation within the British

Empire of national freedom with an effective Imperial unity, that men from all parties have come to ask themselves whether, in order to obtain more harmony and more efficiency in the working of the constitutional machine, a readjustment in the relations *inter se* of the group of countries forming the United Kingdom has not become desirable; and, if so, in what manner such readjustment could be effected. Moreover, there are some who hold with Mr. Rhodes that only by conceding to the various parts of the United Kingdom the fullest right to manage their own local affairs can the conditions be produced under which a closer union of the Empire can be brought about, and they believe that closer union is necessary if the Empire is to endure. They point out that the chief link in the chain which binds the Empire together is the Crown. But the powers formerly exercised by the king in person have passed to Ministers who are responsible to a House of Commons elected by the British people. Here lies the difficulty. For the colonies might fairly ask, "What have we to do with the will of our fellow subjects who reside in a certain province of the Empire?" Their allegiance is due to the Crown, not to the electorate of the United Kingdom. "If," said Sir Wilfrid Laurier in 1900, "our future military contribution were to be considered compulsory—a condition which does not exist—I would say to Great Britain, 'If you want us to help you, call us to your councils'."

Empire and liberty.

In what way can the Dominions be called to our councils? By what new constitutional machinery can they be brought to contribute in equitable proportions to the expenses of an Imperial policy, in the control of which they have a corresponding share? At first sight the simplest plan would seem to be that they should be represented in the existing Imperial Parliament, and this is the project that found an advocate in Mr. Rhodes. He was interested in the Home Rule movement, to the furtherance of which he subscribed a sum of £10,000 in 1888, because he believed that Home Rule, with the Irish members in the Imperial Parliament, would be the beginning of Imperial Federation,[1] and he asked Mr. Parnell to use his influence for the inclusion in the next Home Rule Bill of a permissive clause providing that any colony which

Proposals for Imperial Federation.

[1] Life of Parnell, vol. ii. p. 186.

contributed to Imperial defence should be allowed to send representatives to the Imperial Parliament in proportion to its contributions to the Imperial revenue. But all the objections brought to bear against the ninth clause of the Home Rule Bill of 1893 tell with redoubled force against this scheme. The whole balance of our domestic constitution would be upset. Ministries would be formed which did not represent the will of the majority of the people of the United Kingdom; measures might be passed into law on purely domestic subjects by the prevailing help of members whose constituents had no concern in their results and who only supported Ministers from considerations quite foreign to the business in hand. If, on the other hand, the representatives of the colonies were so few in number that these effects would not be likely to follow, they would probably cease to represent colonial opinion, and become, like the colonial members in the French Chamber, party men without distinctive influence or character. [1]

Parliament of the Empire. Objections to its constitution. Another suggestion is that there should be a Parliament for the whole Empire distinct from and co-existing with the local legislatures—of which that of the United Kingdom would be one. These local legislatures would each of them be the centre of smaller bodies, and so a system might be established resembling as to its framework that of Feudalism under the Holy Roman Empire with nations instead of men for its units and a common Imperial Parliament instead of the Emperor for its centre. The main objection to such a scheme was most eloquently expressed by Burke in the eighteenth century when discussing the possibility of colonial representation in the British Parliament. "Perhaps," he said, "I might be inclined to entertain some such thought; but a great flood stops me in my course, *opposuit natura*. I cannot remove the eternal barriers of the creation. The thing in that mode I do not know to be possible." We cannot indeed well conceive the working of such a Parliament of the Empire with binding legislative and taxing powers; nor, without such powers, would it be a Parliament. The difference in character and amount of the goods imported from foreign countries by

---

[1] The whole of this question is explained and discussed in Mr. Bernard Holland's "Imperium et Libertas"—a work from which I have derived great assistance in writing this chapter.

the United Kingdom and the colonies respectively would make it difficult to raise a common revenue for Imperial purposes through customs duties on an equitable basis; while it is impracticable for the United Kingdom to take part in a general scheme of Imperial preference without the imposition of duties on foreign corn and raw material which would, in the opinion of many, throw the burden of supporting the Empire on the section of the population of all others the least able to bear it. Even if the fiscal difficulty could be surmounted, it is doubtful whether a self-governing Dominion would long submit to be taxed for the purposes of an Imperial policy of which it disapproved, but to which it was committed by the votes of the majority in the central assembly. And, if it would not so submit, the break up of the Empire might result from the very system inaugurated to give it cohesion.

There remains the plan of an Advisory Council armed with no binding authority; but, like the Indian Council, possessing the constitutional right to be consulted on questions of foreign and colonial policy, together with the function of suggesting the manner and the proportions in which the several provinces of the Empire should make voluntary contributions to the common expenditure. It is contended that in practice the resolutions of such a council would have irresistible force, and that no single colony or group of colonies would be able to disregard them. But this seems doubtful. The Empire is too large—its provinces are too far distant from one another—to allow of much moral weight being attached by a section of it to the opinion, with whatever formality expressed, of an Imperial Council. The dissenting colony might refuse to contribute to the cost of a policy which it disapproved, and the dispute might shake its loyalty to the Empire. Whereas, under the existing system, a colony, having neither a voice in determining Imperial policy nor being obliged to contribute toward Imperial defence, may be opposed to the foreign policy of the British Government and yet feel no wish to break the Imperial connection. In a country made one by nature the interests of its people in respect of foreign policy must always be really one. But in a vast Empire, held together chiefly by a bond of sentiment, the interests of different parts may be in reality different. And although it is quite true that the

Mother Country has to pay heavily for her monopoly in the direction of the common Imperial policy, yet it may fairly be argued that the gain is worth the cost. Whether, too, the distribution of control over foreign Imperial policy among the representatives of States so distant from one another might not lead to a dissipation of energy and a lack of continuous purpose which would more than counterbalance the gain derivable from the organisation of the Empire as a fighting unit is perhaps also open to question. There are, moreover, formidable difficulties connected with the government of India and the Crown colonies. Still, the evolution of the conference as an instrument of common Imperial action is a tendency to be welcomed. In British constitutional history, as indeed in the growth of the Empire itself, formal recognition of accomplished facts has generally followed their undesigned development. Since 1907 the composition of the Imperial Conference has been determined; it has a permanent secretarial staff; it meets at stated intervals. But hitherto Canada, the greatest of the Dominions, with the longest history, the fullest development, and the largest possibilities, has shown reluctance to transform the Imperial Conference into an Imperial Council with effective power, or to change the existing relations between the Mother Country and the colonies.

CHAPTER VIII.

THE PARLIAMENT BILL.

AT the General Election of 1906 the Unionists suffered the heaviest defeat sustained by either political party at the polls for more than seventy years. But the great Liberal majority in the House of Commons, exasperated by long exclusion from power and eager to use the long-deferred opportunity for legislation, found itself confronted by a still larger majority of Unionists in the other House. The Unionist peers regarded themselves as trustees of national interests, now seriously menaced, until such time as the electorate, returning to its senses, should reverse the overwhelming verdict of 1906. Nor were they alone in this opinion. Mr. Balfour, the late Prime Minister, in a speech at Nottingham which excited much attention both at the time and afterwards, proclaimed that the Unionist party, whether in or out of office, still controlled the destinies of the country; and although the presumption that his declaration contained a reference to the balance of parties in the House of Lords proved to be erroneous,[1] it was through the action of that House that his view was in some measure justified. During the four years of the Parliament of 1906 no Government measure against the third reading of which the official Opposition voted in the House of Commons passed into law. The Second Chamber acted, or was charged with acting, as an integral part of the Opposition, and the fate of Government bills—even when, as in the case of the Education Bill of 1906, the Licensing Bill of 1908, or the Budget of 1909, they had occupied the greater part of the attention of the House of Commons throughout

Action of the House of Lords during the Parliament of 1906.

---

[1] See his statement in the House of Commons, Official Report, XV., 1578. Mr. Balfour at Nottingham was presumably referring to the moral influence of the Unionist party. But if by this alone they can control the destinies of the country what need is there of other checks?

long sessions—was decided beforehand by consultation among their leading opponents.[1] For this state of things—however intolerable it might naturally appear to a Liberal Government —it would be unjust to blame the Lords. They had found, not made, the existing system; and in voting in the same sense as the men who shared their opinions in the House of Commons they were merely acting on sincerely held political convictions—with the difference that, being in the majority, their votes prevailed. The constitution made their assent necessary to the enactment of what they considered to be unjust proposals for changing the law, and they held it their duty to withhold that assent. The Opposition was permanently entrenched in one of the two chambers, the consent of both of which was necessary to every act of legislation: it followed that no controversial Act of Liberal legislation could become law. In every contest between two chambers it is obvious that the will of the one or of the other must ultimately prevail; and, the subjects of controversy in the Parliament of 1906 being those proposed by a Liberal Government, the will of the Lords who had a negative voice invariably prevailed. It became the object of the Government to reverse this order of things, and, when irreconcilable differences appeared, to secure, within the life-time of a single Parliament, victory for the Commons.

Difficulties of the Government.

At the end of the session of 1906, the Government found themselves in a position of great difficulty. They had been unable to accept the amendments made to the Education Bill by the House of Lords; although with a view to agreement they had offered concessions which had sufficed to remove the opposition not only of the Irish Nationalists but also of the Duke of Devonshire—and the bill was consequently lost. The Plural Voting Bill had also been rejected on second reading by the Upper House. The omnipotence claimed by Bagehot for a House of Commons, fresh from the constituencies and engaged in the work to which it was pledged, was clearly a thing of the past; and the Government had now to consider what to do. Five courses from which to choose were open to them. They might appeal to the country by a dissolution;

[1] Thus the rejection of the Licensing Bill was determined on at a meeting of Unionists held in the drawing-room of Lansdowne House.

they might resign ; they might submit ; they might propose a reconstitution of the House of Lords ; or lastly they might by a resolution of the House of Commons pledge themselves and their party to restrict at some future date those powers of the House of Lords which in their judgment had been abused. With respect to the first of these alternatives the reflection presented itself that in the whole course of our political history no Government had ever advised a dissolution of Parliament—a dissolution, that is, of the House of Commons—on account of the action of the House of Lords. In 1884, Mr. Gladstone had declared that if the action of the House of Lords in rejecting the Franchise Bill was to be met by a dissolution it must be a dissolution upon organic change in that House; and to this principle his successors had steadfastly adhered. It is true that in 1894, after the rejection of the Home Rule Bill had been followed in the autumn by disputes between the two Houses on the Parish Councils Bill and the Employers' Liability Bill, Mr. Gladstone wished to dissolve ; but the dissolution, had it then taken place, would have turned upon the question of the relations between the two Houses. In the spring of 1907 the country was as yet unprepared for the determination of so momentous a question—an immediate dissolution would have been understood as a reference to the electors of the Education Bill—and the Government might have been justly blamed for putting the country to the trouble and expense of a fresh election so soon after the decisive verdict of 1906, when as yet there was no sign that the confidence of the electors had been withdrawn, and when much work to which the new Parliament was pledged remained to be done. For resignation the only precedent at all to the purpose was that of 1832. But the occasion of Lord Grey's resignation was the refusal of King William IV. to coerce the peers by new creations rather than the action of the peers themselves. To admit the power of the House of Lords to compel the resignation of the Ministry would be a constitutional innovation even more startling than to admit their power to force a dissolution. On the other hand, the confession of impotence involved in the silent submission to defeat of a Ministry commanding an immense majority in the House of Commons would have brought that Ministry into contempt;

while to propose the reconstitution of the House of Lords would be to invite a fresh defeat. The only course, therefore, that remained to the Government was temporary acquiescence, combined with a declaration of the policy they proposed at a convenient time thereafter to pursue.

Sir Henry Campbell-Bannerman's resolution, 1907.

This was the strategy adopted by the Government. In the King's Speech, at the opening of the session of 1907, allusion was made to the "serious questions affecting the working of our Parliamentary system" which had arisen from the "unfortunate differences between the two Houses"; and Parliament was informed that His Majesty's Ministers were considering the subject with a view to a solution of the difficulty. On the 24th June, Sir Henry Campbell-Bannerman, the Prime Minister, following the precedents of 1678 and of 1860, moved a general resolution; and, in moving it, explained his plan for restricting the powers of the House of Lords. The resolution stated: "That, in order to give effect to the will of the people as expressed by their elected representatives, it is necessary that the power of the other House to alter or reject bills passed by this House should be so restricted by law as to secure that within the limits of a single Parliament the final decision of the Commons shall prevail". This resolution was carried after a three days' debate by a majority of 285.[1] It was distinguished from the resolutions of 1678 and 1860 by the circumstance that, whereas those resolutions merely declared the privileges claimed by the House of Commons, this admitted and asserted the necessity of legislation to effect its object.

His scheme.

In the discussions that ensued the House of Lords was no longer defended as a check on democracy—a form of government until the Reform Act of 1867 generally condemned by both the great parties—but, on the contrary, its function was proclaimed by Mr. Balfour to be to secure that the Government of the country should be a popular Government, and that the considered and settled will of the people, as contrasted with its temporary aberrations, should prevail. The rejection of Liberal bills was justified on the ground that changes in the law of such importance ought not to be made until the democracy had passed separate judgment upon each one of them. Such a position might more plausibly have been held by the

[1] 385 to 100.

Unionist party in the generation which preceded the retirement of Lord Salisbury, at a time when the two parties were moving, if at different rates of progress, yet, on the whole, in the same direction ; and when legislation proposed by Conservative Ministers, though regarded as inadequate, was generally approved, so far as it went, by Liberal Oppositions. But the legislation of the Unionist Government, in their last three years of office, and still more the fiscal changes to which Unionist statesmen were committed, wore a different character. Whatever the merits of the opposite policies, the contest was no longer between positive and negative but between two positives. Each party now appeared to its opponents to require a check. " Startling and unannounced innovations in a reactionary direction," said Sir Henry Campbell-Bannerman in his speech introducing the resolution, " in respect of licensing, of education, and of fiscal policy, need surely to be watched quite as closely as innovations, or, as we should think, reforms in the other direction." He proceeded to comment on the singularity of the circumstance " that the representative system should only hold good when one party is in office, and should break down to such an extent as that the non-elective House must be called in to express the mind of the country whenever the country lapses into Liberalism ". Coming to the details of the plan by which the Government proposed at some future time to give effect to the resolution, Sir Henry thus explained it. When the two Houses found agreement in a bill impossible, a conference of small dimensions, and sitting in private, would be held between members appointed in equal numbers by the two Houses, in order to arrive at a common agreement which the Government might be able to adopt. Should the conference be unproductive, and the same bill, with or without modifications, or a similar bill, be introduced after a substantial interval, it would be passed in the Commons under limitations as to time, discussion being restricted as far as possible to new matter, and returned to the Lords. Should the two Houses still differ there might be another conference, but should they again disagree the bill would be re-introduced and passed swiftly through the House of Commons in the form last agreed to, and sent to the Lords with an intimation that unless carried in that form it would be passed without their consent.

A last conference might then be held and a last effort made at agreement, but if this failed the bill would receive the royal assent and become law. To bring the House of Commons into closer touch with and more under the influence of the electorate the duration of Parliament was to be shortened to five years.

Reception of the scheme. These proposals, while scornfully repudiated by the Opposition, excited small enthusiasm at the time on the Ministerial benches. The Labour party and the advanced Radicals would have preferred the simple abolition of the Second Chamber, while to the moderate Liberals, who perhaps formed the majority of the party, the re-constitution of the House of Lords on a democratic basis combined with a system of joint sittings or some such expedient for the settlement of differences between the two Houses seemed a more reasonable solution of the problem. Under the Government scheme there would be a temptation to Ministers to re-introduce bills, on which the Lords had exercised their suspensory veto, unaltered in the succeeding session; and it was therefore open to the objection, made by Mr. Gladstone in 1890 to the proposal to carry over bills from one session to another, that the great advantage would be lost of altering in a new session the frame and scope of a measure.[1] That a reform in the constitution of the House of Lords was in any event desirable was admitted by the Government, and it was a fair contention that the composition of the Second Chamber should be settled before the extent of its powers was determined. The long delay in introducing the resolution suggested that there were differences of opinion in the Cabinet upon the subject, while the country appeared to be indifferent.

The resolution passed, nothing further was done; and the Lords continued to show an activity in Opposition unparalleled since the days of Lord Lyndhurst. Two Scotch Land Bills were thrown out in 1907, and in 1908 they rejected the Licensing Bill to which the session had been mainly devoted. Ministers were forced to submit; amid the taunts of their

[1] It is true that the Prime Minister in his speech contemplated the introduction of modifications into a bill when introduced a second time under his scheme, but it would have been difficult to define the extent to which these modifications should be allowed and to constitute a tribunal which should pronounce on the question whether the boundaries assigned had been overpassed.

opponents on their inability to pass their measures into law, and on their reluctance to appeal to the country. The Unionist Education and Licensing Bills of 1902 and 1904 were neither more popular nor more unpopular than the Liberal Education and Licensing Bills of 1906 and 1908. They were passed by much smaller majorities in the House of Commons; they were, whether for good or for evil, more evident departures from the principles which had governed in the past legislation on those subjects; but whereas the House of Commons, which had passed them, met with a signal defeat from the electorate in 1906, the House of Lords, which had agreed to their passage, remained unaltered to defeat all attempts at their reversal. While the country was not unequally divided between the two parties the position of the House of Lords entrenched behind the ancient constitution appeared to be almost impregnable. The result of their bold action in the very year of the greatest Liberal victory since 1833 was of a nature to give them confidence. In the succeeding years by-elections, following their usual course, went against the Government with increasing frequency; and the rejection of every Ministerial bill distasteful to the Opposition appeared not even to retard the normal swing of the pendulum. The attacks on the Unionist education and licensing settlements had been repulsed—there remained the question of fiscal policy in respect of which the Unionists had since 1903 been the attacking party and the advocates of change.

In his answer to the Prime Minister during the debate in June, 1907, on the constitutional question, Mr. Balfour, deriding the notion that the action of the House of Lords had reduced the House of Commons to impotence, dwelt much upon the powers of the Lower House with which the House of Lords could not interfere. He pointed out with justice that Ministries were chosen from the party commanding a majority in the House of Commons, and that a vote of censure of that House or its rejection of a measure of importance would at any moment compel them to resign or to dissolve, whereas their continuance in office was wholly unaffected by any vote of the House of Lords. He added that the power of the House of Lords was "still further limited by the fact that it cannot touch those money bills, which, if it could deal with, no

Mr. Balfour on the relations between the two Houses, 1907.

doubt it could bring the whole executive machinery of the country to a standstill". The conclusion, therefore, which he pressed upon the House was that the existing system comprised two Houses not of equal power nor of equal authority "which cannot come into serious conflict in the whole field of administration, in the whole field of the initiation of legislation, or in the whole field of that legislation which deals with finance". "Of course," he added, "these things being true, it is true that the House of Lords is a subordinate partner to the House of Commons." In these words Mr. Balfour with admirable lucidity expressed the true state of the case. It is indeed ultimately to the power of the purse, to its power to "bring the whole executive machinery of the country to a standstill," that the House of Commons owes its control over the executive. That is the fountain and origin of its historical victories over the other organs of the State; and since that power was recognised and confirmed towards the end of the seventeenth century the House of Commons has remained, whether reformed or unreformed, whether corrupt or uncorrupt, the chief arbiter of the national destinies. Only through influence of whatever nature, whether legitimate or illegitimate, brought to bear on the assembly which controlled the national resources, have Ministers for more than two centuries been enabled to maintain themselves in office. So long as these things were accepted as true, so long as the House of Commons commanded uncontrolled the whole field of legislation dealing with finance, the House of Lords must have remained the subordinate partner. The position was boldly challenged in 1909.

Fall in land values and its consequences. The grant of old age pensions in 1908, together with an extension of the naval programme exacted by the sudden energy displayed by Germany in building ships, produced a large deficit in 1909, and rendered necessary the discovery of new ways and means to meet the supply granted to his Majesty. Both parties were ready with new fiscal expedients for the purpose, and the rival policies were finely contrasted. In the days of high Protection, when the right to supply the community with its means of subsistence was in large measure secured to the landlords and manufacturers by the tariff laws, the price they were able to demand for the goods they sold was practically limited only by the capacity of the consumer to pay, although happily the hereditary owners of land in England being, as a class, kindly, conscientious, and patriotic, refused to take full advantage of a position which they were nevertheless naturally reluctant to relinquish. This monopoly after successive modifications was brought to an end by the adoption of Free Trade; and although the manufacturers, having to supply additional exports to pay for the additional imports, gained largely by the change, the great development of the corn area of the Western States of America after the close of the civil war combined, with the extension of American railways and of the British mercantile marine, to lower the price of corn, and to bring about a period of agricultural depression in England. Rents fell; prices fell; purely agricultural land ceased to be very valuable, while, at the same time, it was saddled with burdens imposed upon it at a time when an almost exclusive control over the food of the people had enabled those burdens easily to be borne by the owners of the soil.

Thus the tariff reform proposals of Mr. Chamberlain were welcomed with enthusiasm by the landlord class, who foresaw in them the recovery in some small measure of their former control over the means of livelihood of the community, and who were easily convinced that the additional employment secured by the partial exclusion of the foreigner would enable the working classes to share in the benefit. The source from which the additional wages, required to pay for the additional work undoubtedly involved by production under more difficult conditions, were to flow, was perhaps not so clearly to be distinguished, but they were inclined to discover it in their own enhanced prosperity, which would enable them to spend more in wages. Thus, by refusing admission to wealth from abroad, all classes were to become wealthier at home—an apparent paradox defended on the ground that the exclusion of part of the foreign supply would clearly make it necessary that more work should be done at home to supplement the loss. There was, however, one form of monopoly that no Free Trade could affect, and that was the possession of building land. One effect of agricultural depression had been to increase the number of the working class dwellers in English towns and urban districts, and to diminish their numbers in

The rival proposals for raising additional revenue.

the country. The inhabitants of towns who make their living there are compelled to live within a narrow radius; and the urban landlords control this necessity of their existence much more completely than in the days of the Corn Laws the agricultural landlords controlled the food of the people; for in their case no sliding scale can operate to admit a competing foreigner should prices become unreasonably high. Building land is at once a necessity of life, and one in the provision of which the foreigner by the nature of things cannot compete. To tax the unearned increment attached to this kind of property, that is to say the enhanced value due to no exertions of its owners, but to the increasing needs of an ever-growing urban population, and to use the funds thus acquired for the social and Imperial objects professed by both parties in the State, was claimed by their author to be the chief object of the land clauses in the Budget of 1909. The Opposition professed their readiness and ability to find a greater revenue for the same objects by the exaction of duty on foreign goods of a kind produced at home. They proposed thereby a double benefit to the working classes. For they argued that, while the revenue thus raised would be devoted to the provision of old age pensions and other social objects, the exclusion of foreign goods would result in better and more constant employment. At the same time they denounced the proposals of the Government as confiscatory, and likely to increase unemployment through the impoverishment of employers. Here then the issue was joined.

Claim of the Lords of the right to force a dissolution.
When the Government of Lord Palmerston, after the rejection of the Paper Duties Bill by the House of Lords in 1860, had in the succeeding session included all the financial arrangements for the year in a single bill, they imagined that they had, in accordance with the third resolution of 1860, so asserted the power to impose and remit taxes " that the right of the Commons as to the matter, manner, measure, and time might be maintained inviolate ". It had not occurred to them that the Lords, when objecting to a single section of the Budget, might, while recognising their constitutional inability to excise the obnoxious clauses by amendment, effect the same object by the rejection of the whole. If the House of Lords had made good their right to reject a Budget by a victory at

the General Election of January, 1910, one of two results must have followed. Liberal Governments in the future must either, when their budgets were rejected by the Lords, have introduced others with the clauses to which objection had been taken omitted, and this in effect would be to allow the Lords to amend a Budget and to force their own system of taxation on the people—or else the power of the House of Lords, themselves indissoluble, to dissolve the House of Commons would have been successfully asserted. This power indeed was in 1909 expressly claimed. Mr. Chamberlain, in a message to a Unionist meeting held at Birmingham in the summer and addressed by Mr. Balfour, expressed the hope that the Lords would reject a Budget which, he said, would, if passed, indefinitely postpone the triumph of Tariff Reform, and that they would thereby force a dissolution; while the very amendment to the second reading by which the Finance Bill was rejected at the instance of Lord Lansdowne declared that the Lords could not assent to the measure until it had been submitted to the judgment of the people. The power to compel a dissolution by bringing, as Mr. Balfour said, the whole executive machinery of the country to a standstill involved a control over the Executive which the House of Lords had never before at any period of English history either exercised or even claimed, and was a far more formidable innovation than the power of amending money bills, a power which—after a certain hesitation—they tacitly admitted that they did not constitutionally possess. Had they indeed been in undisputed possession of this latter power they would not have rejected a Budget to a large part of which they could feel no objection, and they would not therefore have commanded a dissolution. It was the very limitation of their power in this respect that enabled them to use a weapon, employed with memorable results by the House of Commons against the Governments of the seventeenth century.

On the 30th of November, 1909, after a week's debate on the second reading distinguished by a high level of eloquence and ability, the House of Lords, by a majority of 275,[1] declined to assent to the Budget until it had been submitted to the judgment of the people. The Budget had been introduced

Rejection of the Budget of 1909 by the House of Lords.

[1] 350 to 75.

in the House of Commons on the 29th April, and read a third time in that House on the 4th November, by a majority of 230. In order to pass it the Commons had sat continuously throughout the year. The session had not only been the longest but one on record,[1] but had been distinguished by an extraordinary number of late sittings. Closure by compartments had not been employed—the majorities in divisions had been throughout very great. The Lords now rejected the whole financial provision made by the Commons to meet the needs of the year, because they objected to a part of it. Influential members of their chamber warned them of the unwisdom of this course. Lord St. Aldwyn, who as Sir Michael Hicks Beach had during seven years of Unionist government administered the national finances with conspicuous ability under difficult conditions, abstained both from the debate and the division. He afterwards explained his absence by the expression of his conviction that the House of Lords had no constitutional right to reject a Finance Bill except on the ground of " tacking "—that is except when matter bearing no relation to the raising of money is included in the bill—and because he thought that no tacking in this sense was to be found in the Budget under discussion. Lord Balfour of Burleigh, much though he disliked the bill, spoke against its rejection, and himself refrained from voting; while Lord Rosebery, whose denunciations of the Budget had exceeded in vehemence those of all other public men, also absented himself from the division.

Effect on finance.

The Finance Bill having been rejected, an early dissolution became necessary in order that sufficient money might be raised for the service of the year. The Lords indeed were ready to agree to the uncontroversial taxes if the Commons would send up an interim Finance Bill containing them; but the Government perceived that to do this would be in effect to allow the Lords to amend the Budget, and therefore declined to adopt the suggested expedient. The usual supply had been voted in the summer, and appropriated to the various services by the Appropriation Act. To meet this supply there were the permanent taxes; and, if these were insufficient, power was granted by the Appropriation Act to borrow money

[1] The Home Rule session of 1903 was longer, but the House did not sit continuously.

sufficient to cover the deficiency. Thus, although the new taxes imposed by the Budget could not be levied, and the income tax and tea duty, which it is the custom of the House of Commons to vote for a year only in order to preserve their control over the Executive, could no longer in this year be collected on the strength of the resolutions passed by the House, the financial inconvenience resulting from the action of the Lords was less serious than in some quarters had been anticipated. The annual taxes continued to be collected from all who were willing to pay them; and, since it was clearly understood that, whatever the result of the general election might be, retrospective provision would be made for their collection in the new Parliament, and that arrears would be called in, those who declined to pay were few in number.

The reply of the Commons to the action of the Lords was quickly made. Two days after the rejection of the Finance Bill, Mr. Asquith in a brief but impressive speech moved a resolution declaring "that the action of the House of Lords in refusing to pass into law the provision made by the House of Commons for the finances of the year is a breach of the constitution, and a usurpation of the privileges of the House of Commons". He concluded his speech by saying that a controversy had been opened which must go to the constituencies and must decide far more than the fate of the Budget. Mr. Balfour in his reply contended that the Lords had rejected money bills in the past, and that their right so to do had been often admitted by the Commons and never seriously called into question. The scheme proposed by Sir Henry Campbell-Bannerman implied, so he argued, that a House of Commons after three years could no longer claim authority from the people to act as it pleased—and that therefore from this point of view a Budget containing new principles and introduced in the fourth year of a Parliament ought to be endorsed by the electorate before coming into operation. But there was no constitutional machinery for bringing this about except action by the House of Lords. On a division, the resolution was carried by a majority of 215.[1]

The Commons' resolution.

The General Election having been postponed until the new year in order that it might be taken on a new register, the in-

The General Election of January, 1910.

[1] 349 to 134.

terval was employed in an electoral campaign of unparalleled vigour. The issue was of far-reaching importance; and, in the opinion of all the contending parties, vital principles and interests were at stake. The reconciliation of the great Whig houses and of the mercantile plutocracy with the Tory aristocracy, suggested and foreseen amid the alarm excited by Mr. Chamberlain's Radical campaign in 1885, confirmed on the introduction of the Home Rule Bill in 1886, and subsequently shared in by Mr. Chamberlain himself, had largely increased the powers and stimulated the activity of the House of Lords which had come to be regarded by the controlling classes as a kind of insurance against political reverses and a harbour in stormy weather. At the same time it became identified more than ever it had previously been with a single political party. In possession of this citadel the allies had repelled during the last Parliament assaults on their various interests; they had devised a scheme of taxation whereby, as they sincerely believed, all classes in the community would profit in and by the very act of being taxed, while at the same time their own control would be placed on a permanent foundation; they had rejected a Budget which they regarded as "a last effort of Free Trade finance to find a substitute for Tariff Reform".[1] Could they win this election they would prove themselves able whether in or out of office to control the national destinies; since, when in office, they would be able to pass all their own measures, and, when in opposition, to reject those of their opponents. It is not surprising, therefore, that immense efforts were made on both sides at this election. The peers themselves took a leading part in the contest, addressing during the five weeks between the adjournment and the issue of the writs some 250 meetings.[2]

Mr. Asquith's speech at the Albert Hall. Of all the speeches made at this time, the most important was that of Mr. Asquith at the Albert Hall on the 10th December in which he formulated the policy of the Liberal party. The three capital issues which he laid before his audience were

[1] See Mr. Chamberlain's letter to the Birmingham meeting in September, 1909.
[2] After the issue of the writs the peers were silent in deference to the Sessional Order passed by the House of Commons to forbid the interference of peers in elections. But since no means existed of enforcing this order it was negatived by general consent in the first session of the new Parliament.

"the absolute control of the Commons over finance, the maintenance of Free Trade, and the effective limitation and curtailment of the legislative powers of the Lords," and he asked the electorate to give him authority to effect these objects. He pointed out that the Lords by their action had in effect made three claims, each of them a constitutional innovation of high import. They claimed in the first place an effective right to control taxation; in the second place, the right to compel a dissolution of the House of Commons; and in the third place, as a corollary of the other two, the right "to make or unmake the Executive Government". These claims the Government were resolved to withstand, and their power to withstand them was an essential condition to their remaining in office. "Neither I," declared the Prime Minister, "nor any other Liberal Minister supported by a majority of the House of Commons are going to submit again to the rebuffs and humiliations of the last four years. We shall not assume office, and we shall not hold office, unless we can secure the safeguards which experience shows to be necessary for the legislative utility and honour of the party of progress." These words of Mr. Asquith were generally understood to imply that it was the intention of the Government, in the event of victory at the election, to ask from the Crown for guarantees that further resistance by the Lords to their proposals would be overcome by a creation of peers. But the declaration may equally well be interpreted in the sense that the Government would only hold office in order to secure the statutory safeguards required and that if they failed to secure them they would retire. The pledge, so understood, would preclude them from other controversial legislation until the constitutional question was settled, but it would not bind them to retire until their attempt at settlement had failed nor would it dictate the manner in which that attempt should be made.

The result of the general election of January, 1910, was satisfactory to no party in the State. The Liberals returned numbered 274, the Labour party 41, the Irish Nationalists 82, and the Unionists 272. The Unionists gained 127 seats, the Liberals and their allies 22. The Government lost heavily in the counties, but maintained their position in the industrial districts of England, in Scotland, and in Wales. The resi- *[margin: Result of the General Election. Questions at issue.]*

dential districts of the south, the cathedral cities, and the agricultural counties returned to their Unionist allegiance, but in Lancashire and Yorkshire the Budget was popular, and Free Trade principles still in the ascendant. The election was fought on three distinct issues not directly connected with each other, and on which it was quite possible and reasonable to hold divergent views. In the first place, there was the constitutional question turning mainly on the claim of the Lords to reject a Budget with all that that claim implied; secondly, the merits of the Budget itself; and, thirdly, the question of Tariff Reform. On the first issue, constitutional authorities, like Sir Frederick Pollock, considered the rejection of the Budget "the most audacious attempt to subvert the foundations of Parliamentary government made since the revolution of 1688,"[1] while other authorities of equal distinction, such as Professor Dicey and Sir William Anson, held that rejection to be perfectly legitimate. When doctors such as these disagreed, how could the ordinary British elector, at work all day long, ignorant of history, and with an inherited distaste for questions of general principle, be expected to form a right judgment, or any judgment, on the subject? And, in fact, except in Scotland, where abstract questions are popular, the matter moved him very little. The second issue, that of the Budget itself, interested him more in every sense. In the northern industrial districts, where the great urban landlords draw large profits from tenants, with whom their relations are for the most part of a purely business nature, and in London, where the same conditions prevail, the Budget was certainly popular; in the country districts, on the other hand, it alarmed the farmers; left the labourers, who failed to see its connection with their old age pensions, indifferent; and was bitterly resented by the landlords. The fiscal question seemed hardly to have moved since the last election. A return of good trade, after a period of depression, was doubtless of service to the free traders, and the beginnings of a Free Trade movement in the United States, in Canada, and even in Germany, also helped them. If any one stood to gain by a return to Protection it was surely, in England, the dwellers in certain of the manufacturing districts, yet these at the election were for the most part faithful to Free Trade; while the agricultural interests,

[1] See his letter to the *Spectator* of December 11th.

which could hardly be expected to profit by the adoption of
Mr. Chamberlain's proposals, voted on the other side. A large
electorate may be flattered by the assumption that it controls
the Government or governs itself, but it can in reality only
answer " yes " or " no " to the questions, singly or collectively,
propounded to it. Its answer will only be intelligible if the
question is single and disentangled from other issues. So long
as the question put relates to a choice of representatives whose
general principles are known, and to whom, as worthy of a
general confidence, administration and legislation are to be entrusted, a rational system is possible ; but if, while representative government is retained, sufficient authority to legislate is
supposed to be wanting unless each act of legislation has been
separately sanctioned by the electorate, great confusion must
follow. The spread of this idea, with the confusion involved
in it, was made manifest by the varying conclusions drawn by
the different political sections from the results of the January
election. The democratic tariff reformer attributed the Unionist
defeat to the unpopularity of the House of Lords and the failure
of the Unionist party to move with the times ; while many an
old-fashioned Conservative, on the other hand, less openly, but
with equal conviction, ascribed the reverses of his party to the
gradual supersession of Conservatism in the Unionist programme and councils. Ministerialists, in like manner, differed
from one another as to the meaning of their victory and the
mandate of the electorate. All were agreed that the will of
the people, provided it could be ascertained, must be carried
out ; but the truth that the people, except on rare occasions,
has no definite will and little interest in, or knowledge of, large
political questions, appears to have escaped attention.

The new Parliament met for business on the 21st February, *Dissension among ministerialists in the new Parliament.* and the indecisive character of the electoral verdict became at once apparent. There had been a fresh split among the Irish Nationalists on the question of land purchase. Ten of the dissentients had been returned as followers of Mr. William O'Brien, and were detached from the main body led by Mr. Redmond. This small party of Independent Nationalists was hostile to the Government: they professed themselves sceptical as to the desire or the capacity of Ministers to fulfil their promises with regard to Home Rule, and accused the followers

of Mr. Redmond of betraying the interests of the new small proprietors in Ireland by their acceptance of the Budget at the close of the last Parliament. The Budget itself appeared by no means safe. It was unpopular in Ireland, and might be rejected at any moment if the Irish party chose to ally themselves with the Unionists for that purpose. Mr. Redmond openly declared that he would support it only when assured that the Government would, by destroying the veto of the Lords, pave the way to Home Rule; and he joined a section of the advanced Radicals in insisting that the abolition of the veto should precede all other business. To take the Budget before the Lords' veto, he said at Dublin on the 10th of February, "would be to disgust every real democrat in Great Britain, and to break the pledge which had acquired the support of Ireland for the Government". In vain was it pointed out that the rejection of the Budget by the Lords had been the immediate cause of the General Election, and that its rejection by a new House of Commons would be claimed as a triumphant vindication of their action. The Irish and a few of their Radical and Labour allies remained obdurate, and Ministers found themselves in a position of great difficulty.

Debate on the Address. The King's Speech was unusually short, and was concerned almost exclusively with the constitutional question. After stating the necessity of making statutory arrangements to deal at the earliest possible moment with the financial situation created by the rejection of the Budget, his Majesty proceeded to say: "Recent experience has disclosed serious difficulties, due to recurring differences of strong opinion between the two branches of the Legislature. Proposals will be laid before you, with all convenient speed, to define the relations between the two Houses of Parliament, so as to secure the undivided authority of the House of Commons over finance, and its predominance in legislation. These measures, in the opinion of my advisers, should provide that this House should be so constituted and empowered as to exercise impartially, in regard to proposed legislation, the functions of initiation, revision, and, subject to proper safeguards, of delay." The moderate terms in which the speech was couched, and the expression "constituted and empowered" which might be interpreted as implying that a reconstitution of the Upper

House would accompany, if not precede, the limitations of its powers, increased the suspicions of the Irish, the Labour party, and certain of the advanced Radicals with regard to the intentions of the Government. Nor did the Prime Minister's announcement in his speech on the Address that he had neither asked for nor received any guarantees for the contingent exercise of the royal prerogative tend to reassure them. No statesman, he observed with justice, could ask in advance for assurances regarding a measure not yet presented to the House of Commons. The guarantees he desired to secure for the discontinuance of the state of things obtaining during the previous four years were statutory guarantees, and the Government were remaining in office in order to obtain them. The opening session of this Parliament was to be devoted exclusively to the subject of the veto after the necessary financial business had been completed. Mr. Redmond, unappeased, declared that the Irish would not vote for the Budget until they had reasonable assurances that the Veto Bill would be carried in the current year. A few days later, in the first division of this Parliament on a fiscal amendment to the Address moved from the front Opposition bench, the Government majority was only thirty-one. Clearly, the Government could not safely proceed with the Budget until they had arrived at some better understanding with their allies.

On the 28th February, Mr. Asquith, when moving that the time of the House should be devoted to Government business up to the Easter adjournment on the 24th March, made a further statement regarding the intentions of the Government, to the following effect. When the House reassembled on the 29th March, the Government would bring forward their proposals on the relations between the two Houses. There would be no proposal in the present session for the reform of the House of Lords, but it would be made clear that the proposed limitation of powers contemplated in a subsequent year a bill substituting a democratic for a hereditary Second Chamber. The Ministerial proposals would be embodied, in the first instance, in resolutions affirming the necessity of totally excluding the Lords from financial control; and of so restricting their veto on legislation as to secure the predominance of the deliberate and considered will of the Commons within the lifetime of a single

Mr. Asquith's statement of 28th February.

Parliament. These resolutions, when passed, would be submitted to the House of Lords; but, whether that House agreed to them or not, the Government regarded the legal limitation of the veto not only as the first condition of the legislative dignity and ability of the Commons, but as their own primary duty, on the performance of which they staked their official existence. Though the Irish, and the Ministerialist malcontents were relieved to hear that no proposals for the reconstitution of the Second Chamber were to be made this session, they were still not altogether satisfied; for the Prime Minister was silent as to the action the Government would take in the practically certain contingency of the refusal of the House of Lords to assent to the resolutions.

Lord Rosebery's resolutions. On the 14th March the peers, at the instance of Lord Rosebery, made their first counter-move. Just as in 1884 they had insisted that redistribution of seats should accompany the reform of the House of Commons, so now it was their contention that reconstitution should precede, or at least accompany, a revision of the powers of the House of Lords. The three declaratory resolutions moved by Lord Rosebery have been set out in another chapter.[1] The first two declared that the strong and efficient Second Chamber necessary to the well-being of the State could best be obtained by the reform and reconstitution of the House of Lords. They were agreed to unanimously. The third resolution, which affirmed the principle that a peerage should no longer of itself give the right to sit and vote in the House of Lords, was accepted with natural reluctance; and, although only seventeen peers recorded their votes against it, abstainers were many, including the small body of Ministerialists.[2] Lord Rosebery followed up these resolutions by placing on the notice paper others, describing in very general terms the methods of reconstruction he proposed, and he announced his intention of moving them at an early date. Unforeseen events frustrated this intention.

Resolutions with regard to the relations between the two Houses passed by the House of Commons. When the House reassembled after Easter on the 29th March, Mr. Asquith, in accordance with his pledge, moved that the House should resolve itself into a committee to consider

[1] See *supra*, p. 54.
[2] The numbers were 175 to 17. In November, 1909, 350 peers had voted for the rejection of the Budget.

the relations between the two Houses of Parliament, and the question of the duration of Parliament. Three landmarks, he said, were now visible marking the stage reached in the solution of the constitutional problem. In the first place, the House of Lords, for the first time in our Parliamentary history, had ventured to reject the whole financial provision of the year; secondly, a general election had been held in which the relations between the two Houses, having regard both to finance and to general legislation, were a leading issue; and thirdly, the action spontaneously taken by the House of Lords constituted an admission of imperfection. The Prime Minister, having then described the functions of consultation, revision, and delay allotted to the Second Chamber under his proposals, and having dwelt upon their importance, declared that the resolutions did not contain a final solution, but must be followed by a re-constitution of that Chamber on an elective basis. He further explained that the resolutions to be moved by the Government differed in certain respects from the proposals of Sir Henry Campbell-Bannerman in 1907. The machinery of conferences proposed by Sir Henry was omitted; and bills introduced into one Parliament were to remain within the operation of the act in the next. On this subject the Government could command the support of each section of their adherents, so that in spite of an effective attack by Mr. Balfour, who pointed out that "alone among the great countries of the world we had no written constitution and no safeguards against violent changes," the motion was carried by a majority of 107. In the following week a limit of time was fixed for the discussion by a closure resolution under which the debate was terminated on the 14th April.

The three resolutions agreed to by the House by large majorities [1] were in the following terms:—

1.—That it is expedient that the House of Lords be disabled by law from rejecting or amending a money bill, but that any such limitation by law shall not be taken to diminish or qualify the existing rights and privileges of the House of Commons.

For the purpose of this resolution a bill shall be considered

---

[1] The first resolution was carried by 339 to 237; the second by 351 to 246; and the third by 334 to 236.

a money bill if, in the opinion of the Speaker, it contains only provisions dealing with all or any of the following subjects, namely, the imposition, repeal, remission, alteration, or regulation of taxation; charges on the Consolidated Fund or the provision of money by Parliament; supply; the appropriation, control, or regulation of public money; the raising or guarantee of any loan or the repayment thereof; or matters incidental to those subjects or any of them.

2.—That it is expedient that the powers of the House of Lords as respects bills, other than money bills, be restricted by law; so that any such bill which has passed the House of Commons in three successive sessions, and, having been sent up to the House of Lords at least one month before the end of the session, has been rejected by that House in each of those sessions, shall become law without the consent of the House of Lords on the royal assent being declared, provided that at least two years shall have elapsed between the date of the first introduction of the bill into the House of Commons and the date on which it passes the House of Commons for the third time.

For the purposes of this resolution a bill shall be treated as rejected by the House of Lords if it has not been passed by the House of Lords either without amendment or with such amendments only as may be agreed upon by both Houses.

3.—That it is expedient to limit the duration of Parliament to five years.

The Preamble of the Parliament Bill. Reference had been made in the speech from the Throne to the necessity of dealing with the constitution as well as with the powers of the House of Lords, and Mr. Asquith in moving the House into committee had re-affirmed this necessity. A proof of the sincerity of Ministerial intentions in this respect was given by the preamble of the bill, introduced to give effect to the resolutions agreed to by the House, and based on those resolutions. "Whereas," so it ran, "it is expedient that provision should be made for regulating the relations between the two Houses of Parliament: and whereas it is intended to substitute for the House of Lords as it at present exists a Second Chamber constituted on a popular instead of hereditary basis, but such substitution cannot be immediately brought into operation: and whereas provision will require hereafter to be made by Parliament in a measure effecting such substitution for limiting and defining the powers of the new Second Chamber, but it is expedient to make such provision as in this Act appears for restricting the existing powers of the House of Lords : Be it therefore enacted, etc." Thus, not only did Ministers pledge themselves to introduce a measure for the reconstitution of the Second Chamber, but a new allocation of powers differing from and probably superior to those entrusted under the bill to the existing House of Lords appeared to be contemplated.

After the resolutions had been passed and the bill intro-duced, Mr. Asquith, in moving the adjournment, made a statement of high import. To meet the exigencies of the political situation and to comply with the urgent demands of the Irish Nationalists and the left wing of his own party, he took the unusual course of announcing to the House of Commons the general sense of the advice that he proposed to tender to the sovereign with regard to the Parliament Bill. Mr. Redmond had declared at Tipperary, a few days previously, that the Budget of 1909-10 ought not to be allowed to pass until it was known what the Lords proposed to do about the veto; and how, in the event of their resistance, the Government proposed to overcome that obstacle. But the Budget could no longer be delayed ; the real intentions of the Government were such as would, if known to them, satisfy the Irish ; and the Prime Minister was therefore perhaps justified in not allowing a pure question of form to endanger the first through a misunderstanding as to the second. The statement of Mr. Asquith was to the following effect. The resolutions passed by the Commons would be presented to the Lords. If the Lords rejected or refused to consider them the Government would tender advice to the king respecting the steps which would have to be taken if the Government policy was to receive statutory effect in the existing Parliament. "If," he added, "we do not find ourselves in a position to secure that statutory effect shall be given to that policy in this Parliament, we shall then either resign our offices or recommend the dissolution of Parliament. Let me add this, that in no case will we recommend a dissolution except under such conditions as will secure that in the new Parliament the judgment of the people as expressed at the elections will be carried into law."

Mr. Asquith's statement of the action contemplated by the Ministry.

The Budget of 1909 agreed to by the Lords.

The Irish were now satisfied, and the famous Budget of 1909, reintroduced on the 19th April, passed in a few days through the House of Commons under a stringent closure resolution, and, being now agreed to by the Lords, received the royal assent on the 29th—only ten days after its introduction in this session—but exactly a year after its first presentation by Mr. Lloyd George in 1909. On the same day the House rose for a spring recess.

Death of King Edward VII. 6th May.

The crisis now appeared to be at hand, and the resignation of Ministers or a dissolution of Parliament was confidently anticipated shortly after the Houses should reassemble. But all these calculations were overthrown by the sudden death of King Edward VII. on the 6th May. So popular a king had not reigned in England for many centuries, and his influence on public opinion might at a time of crisis have proved equal to his popularity. There was a general feeling that a truce must be called, and that the new sovereign must not be confronted at the very commencement of his reign with a crisis in which the honour and the interests of the Crown might be involved. The outcome of these sentiments was a new development in the history of parties destined, it may be hoped, to serve as a precedent of importance. The suggestion was made and adopted that certain of the leaders from both sides should meet together in secret conference and endeavour to draw up a scheme under which the constitutional question might be settled by agreement. On the 14th of June, the Prime Minister and Mr. Balfour met to discuss the conditions of a conference; and on the 17th June, an official announcement appeared from Downing Street to the following effect: "A meeting took place this afternoon in the Prime Minister's room in the House of Commons between members of the Government and some of the leaders of the Opposition. There were present the Prime Minister, Mr. Balfour, Lord Crewe, Lord Lansdowne, Lord Cawdor, Mr Lloyd George, Mr. Birrell, and Mr. Austen Chamberlain. The subject of discussion was the constitutional question. It is understood that the deliberations are to be entirely untrammelled by any limitation or conditions, and that the proceedings will be throughout regarded as confidential."

Conference of party leaders.

The eight statesmen held twelve conferences before the

adjournment in August. An autumn session was announced, and on the 29th July, shortly before the summer adjournment, Mr. Asquith raised the hopes of those who hoped for the success of the experiment by announcing that their discussions had made such progress that, although an agreement had not so far been reached, it was their unanimous opinion that it was not only desirable but necessary that those discussions should continue. " There is no question," he added, " of their indefinite continuance, and if we find, as the result of further deliberations during the recess, that there is no prospect of an agreement that can be announced to Parliament in the course of the present session, we shall have to bring the conference to a close."

Nine more meetings of the conference were held during the recess. Their proceedings have not been revealed, but that some measure of agreement was reached appears to be certain. It was rumoured—and subsequent events gave credit to the rumour—that the eight statesmen agreed that subsequent differences between the Houses should be settled by a system of joint sittings, and that the conference broke down on the question as to the proportion in which the two Houses should be represented in these joint sessions. However that may be, at the end of the twenty-first meeting, on the 10th November, an announcement was made through the press that the conference which had been sitting to consider the constitutional question had come to an end without arriving at an agreement. The conditions under which the conference had been held precluded, in the opinion of all the members, " any disclosure as to the course of the negotiations or the causes which led to their termination ". *Failure of the Conference to reach agreement.*

Thus ended, to the general regret, though to the unconcealed satisfaction of the Irish Nationalists and of the left wing of the Radical party, an interesting constitutional experiment. It is a grave defect in the party system that in times of crisis the first statesmen of the country should be found in conflict with one another instead of labouring together for the common good, and this is especially to be regretted when the question at issue concerns the constitution, since the constitution depends for its smooth working on a general acceptance. One cause for satisfaction remained. The failure of the conference was followed by no mutual recriminations among the statesmen who composed it. It was, declared Mr. Asquith, and his view was emphatically endorsed by Mr. Balfour, " an honest and sustained attempt on the part of men of strong and conflicting convictions to understand one another's point of view, and to build up a structure having at least a promise of stability and endurance ".

It was now evident that a fresh dissolution could not be long delayed. When the members of the Conference, in spite of endeavours, the honesty and sincerity of which were admitted on all hands, had failed to reach an agreement, it was unlikely that their respective followers, amid the heat and confused partisanship engendered by public discussion in Parliament, on the platform, and in the Press, should prove more successful. To have passed a Parliament Bill through the House of Commons and to have sent it to its certain rejection by the House of Lords would have been, so it appeared to the Government, an absolute waste of time, while to have proceeded with other legislation would have been contrary to their pledges.

Ministers advise a dissolution on the understanding that their success shall import the passage of the Parliament Bill.
The Government, however, were pledged by Mr. Asquith's statement of the 14th April, in no case to recommend a dissolution of this Parliament except under such conditions as would secure that in the new Parliament their policy with regard to the relations between the two Houses should, if approved by the electorate, be carried into law. Therefore, when on the 15th of November they advised the king to dissolve Parliament, they accompanied this advice with the following statement which nine months later was, by his Majesty's desire, communicated to the House of Commons by Mr. Asquith :—

" His Majesty's Ministers cannot take the responsibility of advising a dissolution unless they may understand that, in the event of the policy of the Government being approved by an adequate majority in the new House of Commons, his Majesty will be ready to exercise his constitutional powers, which may involve the prerogative of creating peers, if needed, to secure that effect shall be given to the decision of the country. His Majesty's Ministers are fully alive to the importance of keeping the name of the king out of the sphere of party and electoral controversy. They take upon themselves, as is their duty, the entire and exclusive responsibility for the policy which they will place before the electorate. His Majesty will doubtless agree that it would be inadvisable in the interests of the State that any communication of the intention of the Crown should be made public unless and until the actual occasion should arise."

The king, after discussing the matter in all its bearings with Mr. Asquith and with Lord Crewe, assented to the advice of his Cabinet.

Thus, when Parliament reassembled on the 15th November, all were agreed that its life would be short. On the 16th November, the king came to London and received Mr. Asquith and Lord Crewe. On the same day Lord Lansdowne in the House of Lords suggested that Lord Rosebery might be allowed to proceed with his resolutions and that the Government should proceed in both Houses with the Parliament Bill. There were, he pointed out, two distinct but inter-connected questions to be dealt with—that of the powers and that of the constitution of the Second Chamber. Both parties were agreed that a change was necessary in each of those respects, but whereas the Liberals were more concerned with the limitation of powers, the Unionists were more interested by proposals for reform. Could not, he seemed to suggest, those questions be dealt with simultaneously, using the Parliament Bill as a basis for the consideration of the first, while Lord Rosebery's resolutions served the same purpose with regard to the second? Lord Crewe agreed to introduce the Parliament Bill into the House of Lords, but intimated at the same time that no amendments of substance could be accepted. *Lord Lansdowne's appeal.*

On the 17th November, Lord Rosebery moved the following resolution as a corollary to those accepted at his instance by the House of Lords in the spring:— *Lord Rosebery's resolution.*

"That in future the House of Lords shall consist of lords of Parliament—

"A. Chosen by the whole body of hereditary peers from among themselves and by nomination by the Crown.

"B. Sitting by virtue of offices and of qualifications held by them.

"C. Chosen from outside."

The absence of the essential details in the terms of this resolution saved it from serious opposition, and, the Government remaining neutral, it was carried without a division.

Parliament Bill presented to the House of Lords and postponed.

On the following day, in this eventful week, the Prime Minister announced to the House of Commons that, immediately after the essential parts of the Finance Bill had been passed, Parliament would be dissolved, so that the elections might be over before Christmas. On Monday, the 21st November, Lord Crewe presented the Parliament Bill to the House of Lords. In doing so he held out no hope of compromise, unless his declaration of the readiness of the Government to accept the transference of the decision on "tacking" from the Speaker to some other authority may be so considered. Consequently, the Unionist lords, in view of the shortness of the time left to them, perceived that if they wished to produce their alternative policy before the elections it must be in the form of independent resolutions and not of amendments to the Government bill. Lord Lansdowne, therefore, on the second day of the discussion on the second reading, moved the adjournment of the debate; and, on the next day,

Lord Lansdowne's resolutions.

moved the following resolutions with regard to the relations between the two Houses of Parliament :—

> "That, in the opinion of this House, it is desirable that provision should be made for settling differences which may arise between the House of Commons and this House, reconstituted and reduced in numbers in accordance with the recent resolutions of this House."
>
> "That, as to bills other than money bills, such provision should be upon the following lines :—
>
>> "If a difference arises between the two Houses with regard to any bill other than a money bill in two successive sessions, and with an interval of not less than one year, and such difference cannot be adjusted by any other means, it shall be settled in a joint sitting composed of members of the two Houses ;
>>
>> "Provided that if the difference relates to a matter

which is of great gravity, and has not been adequately submitted for the judgment of the people, it shall not be referred to the joint sitting, but shall be submitted for decision to the electors by referendum."

" That, as to money bills, such provision should be upon the following lines :—

" The Lords are prepared to forego their constitutional right to reject or amend money bills which are purely financial in character ;

" Provided that effectual provision is made against tacking ; and

" Provided that, if any question arises as to whether a bill or any provisions thereof are purely financial in character, that question be referred to a Joint Committee of both Houses, with the Speaker of the House of Commons as Chairman, who shall have a casting vote only ;

" If the Committee hold that the bill or provisions in question are not purely financial in character, they shall be dealt with forthwith in a joint sitting of the two Houses."

These resolutions, drastic as they were, and although in operation they would destroy the absolute veto of the House of Lords as completely as the Government scheme, were nevertheless agreed to without a division, and, together with the resolutions accepted on the motion of Lord Rosebery, formally communicated to the House of Commons on the 25th November. Thus an Opposition policy almost equally subversive of the ancient constitution with that of the Government was placed before the electorate ; and, the existing form being by both sides implicitly condemned, the electors were asked to choose between the rival proposals as a substitute. But more was still to come. Although, according to Lord Lansdowne's resolution, questions " of great gravity " were to be submitted to the judgment of the people by referendum, they were only so to be submitted in case of differences between the two Houses arising in regard to them. Since, however, such differences only arose when the Liberals were in power, the inequitable

The policy of Referendum adopted by the Unionist party.

372 THE CONSTITUTIONAL HISTORY OF ENGLAND

nature of this arrangement was much dwelt upon by Liberal speakers, and was indeed too evident to be seriously contested. This grave defect in their scheme the Unionist leaders, with a suddenness which to some of their followers bore the appearance of recklessness, resolved by a new proposal to remove. Speaking at the Albert Hall on the 29th November, a few days before the first polls were taken, Mr. Balfour, in answer to an interruption and amid the enthusiastic cheers of his audience, declared that he had not "the slightest objection to submit the principles of Tariff Reform to a referendum," and subsequently explained on a later day that these principles when so submitted must be embodied in a bill. This declaration naturally gave great satisfaction to the Unionist Free Traders, and is said to have won for the Opposition a few seats in Lancashire; but it was received with dismay by the more advanced Tariff Reformers. It was clear, however, that its application could not be confined to Tariff Reform, and that if the referendum were adopted at all some machinery would have to be devised through which all controversial bills of importance, whether the two Houses agreed upon them or not, should be submitted directly to the people—a change, whether desirable or undesirable, which seemed to threaten the very existence of representative government and to render a Second Chamber superfluous.

Results of the General Election of December, 1910. No change of importance in the relative strength of parties resulted from the General Election of December, 1910. The Liberals returned were 272 as against 274 in January, the Labour members forty-two as against forty-one, the Irish Nationalists eighty-four instead of eighty-two including only eight instead of eleven independents, and the Unionists 271 instead of 272. Thus there was a Ministerial majority of 127, and in this Parliament the Ministerialists, unlike their predecessors of January, were agreed and eager with regard to the work immediately before them. Parliament met for business on the 6th February, 1911.

The Parliament Bill passed by the Commons. As soon as the Address had been voted on the 21st February, the Prime Minister introduced the Parliament Bill. It was, he explained, identical in every respect with that introduced in April, 1910. He claimed that it had been submitted to the electorate definitely and specifically and that a majority had been returned in its favour of more than 120 in the United Kingdom and of not less than forty in Great Britain. The bill was read a second time on the 2nd March, by a majority of 125, and when the division on the third reading was taken on the 15th May, this majority was nearly maintained.[1] The Government resisted all substantial amendments in Committee, where the debates turned to a large extent on points of minor importance, and were lacking in interest and animation. When the main principles of the bill—the complete abolition of the Lords' veto as regards money bills and its limitation to a power of suspension as regards other bills—had been once accepted by the House, little room was left for effective opposition on points of detail. The Opposition endeavoured to except from the operation of the bill certain constitutional changes of importance, but the Government resisted all amendments moved with this object. All men felt that in a House of Commons, a large majority of which had been returned to pass this very bill, the issue of these debates was a foregone conclusion. It was not there, but in another place, that the contest, if contest there were to be, must go forward to an issue.

In the meantime the Lords were not idle. By a bill introduced by Lord Balfour of Burleigh, it was proposed to provide that every bill upon which the two Houses of Parliament failed to come to an agreement should be submitted to the people by a referendum, and that bills upon which both Houses were agreed should, none the less, on the demand of 200 members of the House of Commons, be subjected to the same test. This proposal, although its honesty of intention and fairness as between the two parties were manifest,[2] involved a change in the principles of representative government of too radical a character to be liked by either party. The bill was, however, given a second reading and then dropped. *Lord Balfour's bill for a Referendum.*

Early in May, Lord Lansdowne embodied his proposals for the reconstitution of the House of Lords in a bill which he presented to the House. They were indeed comprehensive; and, considered in connection with the provisions for settling *Lord Lansdowne's bill for the reconstitution of the House of Lords.*

---

[1] The final division was 362 to 241—a majority of 121.

[2] The number 200 may perhaps be thought too high when it is remembered that the Liberal minorities in the Parliaments of 1895 and 1900 did not reach that figure, but Lord Balfour expressly stated that he attached no special importance to the number he suggested.

differences between the two Houses by joint sittings or a referendum contained in Lord Lansdowne's resolutions of the preceding December, constituted a scheme with which it might be thought the Liberal party had no reason to be dissatisfied. The numbers of the Second Chamber were to be reduced to 350, and it was to be composed of three main elements. There were in the first place to be 100 peers elected by their fellow-peers. But these peers were eligible only when possessed of certain statutory qualifications such as the tenure, or former tenure, of political office or appointments at home or abroad, ex-membership of the House of Commons, high rank in the army or navy, and so forth. The chosen peers were to sit for twelve years—twenty-five of them retiring triennially. A large number of the existing peers—perhaps a majority—were ineligible on this basis as Lords of Parliament. In the second place there were to be 120 Lords of Parliament elected from outside. For the purpose of this election the country was to be divided by commissioners into electoral districts. In each electoral district there was to be an electoral college composed of the members of the House of Commons representing the constituencies comprised within the limits of the electoral district, and each college was to return its quota consisting of not less than three nor more than twelve Lords of Parliament. These were also to sit for twelve years. The third category was to consist of 100 members appointed by the Crown on the advice of the Minister "in the same manner as the Select Committees of the House of Commons are now chosen—that is with regard to the strength of parties in the House". The only Lords of Parliament who were to sit by qualification alone were Princes of the Blood, the two Archbishops, and the existing Law Lords. Peers who were not Lords of Parliament were to be allowed to sit in the House of Commons, and, except with regard to Cabinet or ex-Cabinet Ministers, hereditary peerages were not to be conferred on more than five persons in any one year.

The House of Lords had resolved in November, at the instance of Lord Rosebery, that one of the three elements in the reconstituted Second Chamber should be that of Lords sitting by virtue of offices or of qualifications held by them; and the abandonment of this principle in Lord Lansdowne's bill was a fresh concession to democratic opinion. Under the provisions of the bill it appeared to be certain that any Government in command of a majority in the House of Commons such as that of 1906, would also be supported by a majority in the Second Chamber, and that, even when their influence in the House of Commons was much smaller than in that extraordinary Parliament, the system of joint sessions on disputed questions would enable them to pass their bills in the same session in which they were introduced. Thus, in some respects, these proposals might be thought to constitute a more adequate remedy for the grievances complained of by the Liberal party than was contained in the Parliament Bill; and, had they been brought forward in the preceding year, might well have formed at least a basis for compromise. But the conference of 1910 had broken down, and the Government had submitted the Parliament Bill to the judgment of the country. This bill had thereafter been passed by a large majority of the members then returned; and it would probably have been impossible for the Government, even if they had wished so to do, to retrace their footsteps. Lord Lansdowne's bill, sadly described by him as the "deathblow to the House of Lords, as many of us have known it for so long," came too late. It was naturally distasteful to the majority of the peers; but was, nevertheless, read a second time without opposition.

On the 29th of May the House of Lords read the Parliament Bill a second time, and deferred its further consideration until after the coronation. However odious the measure appeared to the Unionist majority in that House, they recognised that its principle had been sanctioned by the electors at the election of December, and that there was no sign that any change of feeling on the subject had since occurred. But they believed that the electoral verdict had been given without a full appreciation of its consequences; and, therefore, while assenting under protest to the principle, the Opposition leaders gave notice that the bill would be so amended in committee as to render it comparatively innocuous. They pointed to the distinction drawn by the founders of the American constitution between organic change and ordinary legislation, and to the provisions whereby alterations of that constitution were made impossible except under conditions which ensured that *Second reading of Parliament Bill agreed to by the Lords.*

they represented the considered will of the large majority of the people, and they asked whether it was reasonable that power to effect constitutional changes of magnitude such as the repeal of the Union should be entrusted to an ordinary Parliamentary majority in the House of Commons without further reference to the electorate. To the answer that this was already the case whenever the Unionists were in office, they replied, first, that no proposals for organic change were likely to proceed from a party opposed to it on principle, and, secondly, that in their proposals for a referendum they had shown no desire to subject their opponents to disabilities to which they themselves were not willing to submit. Perhaps the best answer to an objection most formidable from the standpoint of democracy might be found in the inadequacy as tested by history of the claims made by the Lords to a right judgment of the will of the people, or to any real desire to give effect to that will; and in the repugnancy of the referendum to representative Government and the character of our institutions. It was indeed the contention of Liberals that the system proposed by their opponents, whatever its abstract merits might be, involved a change in our unwritten constitution more far-reaching than that contained in the Parliament Bill itself.

Their amendments. The position of the Lords would have been stronger had they confined their amendments to the exclusion of constitutional changes from the operation of the bill. But, the constitution being unwritten, it became necessary to create a tribunal which should decide what were and what were not organic changes, and they resolved to make use of the body thus created still further to limit the scope of the bill. They proposed to constitute a joint committee of both Houses, to consist of the Lord Chancellor, the Speaker, the Chairmen of Committees in both Houses, a Lord of Appeal to be chosen by and from peers who had held high judicial office, and a member of the House of Commons to be appointed by the Speaker. The Speaker was to preside and to have a casting vote. To this body was entrusted the decision of the question whether a bill was or was not a money bill within the meaning of the Act; and it was further provided that if, in the opinion of the joint committee, the main governing purpose of a bill imposing taxation, or of any portion of such a bill, was not purely financial in character, the bill, or such portions thereof, should cease to be subject to the restriction of the powers of the House of Lords in respect of money bills. This amendment was adopted by the Lords at the instance of Lord Cromer—a statesman to whose mind the financial powers of the House of Commons were precisely those powers most in need of external control. But the definition of a money bill which it contained would have been accepted by no House of Commons since the seventeenth century. The proposal in itself was open to serious objection. The main governing purpose of a bill, or of portions of a bill, is often rather a matter of opinion than of ascertainable fact; and to require a body of men to look into the minds of Ministers and to decide what their governing purpose may have been in each part of their Budgets was to introduce a new principle into constitutional law. It is unlikely that the Lords would have insisted on this amendment, if by its abandonment they could have carried their other proposals.

The chief amendment made by the Lords to the bill was the exclusion from its operation of certain great issues; and, since it was impossible in the absence of a written constitution to determine with precision what was and what was not a great issue, they left the determination of this important question of opinion, except as regarded the Protestant succession to the Crown and the establishment of provincial assemblies, to the sole arbitrament of the joint committee which they had set up. The terms of the amendment were as follows:—

"Any bill

"(*a*) which affects the existence of the Crown or the Protestant succession thereto; or

"(*b*) which establishes a National Parliament or Assembly or a National Council in Ireland, Scotland, Wales, or England, with legislative powers therein; or

"(*c*) which has been referred to the joint committee, and which in their opinion raises an issue of great gravity upon which the judgment of the country has not been sufficiently ascertained shall not be presented to his Majesty nor receive the royal assent under the provisions of this section unless and until it has been submitted to and approved by the electors in manner to be hereafter provided by Act of Parliament.

"(2) Any question whether a bill comes within the meaning of paragraphs (a) (b) of sub-section (1) of this section shall be decided by the joint committee."

It will be observed that the proposals submitted to the country as an alternative to the Government scheme in the resolutions passed by the House of Lords just before the election of December were nearly reproduced in this amendment, with the important variation that the Lords now accepted the substitution of the machinery of the Parliament Bill for their own proposal of joint sittings in ordinary cases of differences between the two Houses, while retaining their plan of a referendum when the difference related to a matter of great gravity which had not been adequately submitted to the judgment of the people. Liberals argued that this alternative scheme had already been submitted to the electors in December, and rejected by them in favour of the Government proposal.

Ministers and the Opposition. Fortified by the consciousness of the understanding with the sovereign into which they had entered in the previous November, Ministers regarded the proceedings in the Upper House with small apprehension, and foretold with the tranquillity of confidence the approaching passage of the Parliament Bill into law. No attempt was made to rouse the country against the bill by a popular agitation, for indeed after the turmoil of the last general election, when the subject had been discussed on every platform in the country, nothing new was left to say. But there were fiery spirits among the Opposition who declared that it was the duty of the Lords to resist to the last this attack upon the constitution; and, even if in so doing they might appear to superficial observers to be resisting the will of the people upon a constitutional issue, to insist that upon such issues the will of the people should prevail. Even Lord Lansdowne declared that so long as they were free agents the peers who were guided by him would deem it their duty to insist upon these amendments.

Ministers were now obliged to choose one of two courses.

Either they must agree to a slightly modified version of Lord Lansdowne's original scheme which in their view had been proposed to, and rejected by, the electors in December, or they must resort to what has been described by a distinguished historian as "the only means which the constitution provides for overcoming, in extreme cases, the opposition of the Lords".[1] No one desired a fresh dissolution, or claimed that it was likely substantially to alter the balance of parties in the House of Commons. Mr. Asquith had declared in April, 1910, that in no case would he advise a dissolution except under such conditions as would secure that in the new Parliament the judgment of the people, as expressed at the elections, should be carried into law. In December, 1910, he had under these conditions advised the dissolution of Parliament; his advice had been accepted, and he now considered himself bound to fulfil his pledge.

When the bill on the 20th July was sent back to the Commons with the amendments inserted it was clear that it could only be saved by immediate action. Accordingly, on the following day, the Prime Minister communicated to Mr. Balfour in a published letter the resolution to which the Government had come to advise the king to create a number of peers sufficient to overcome, if need be, the resistance of the House of Lords to the bill, and the acceptance by his Majesty of that advice. "When the Parliament Bill," he wrote, "in the form which it has now assumed returns to the House of Commons we shall be compelled to ask that House to disagree with the Lords' amendments. In the circumstances, should the necessity arise, the Government will advise the king to exercise his prerogative to secure the passing into law of the bill in substantially the same form in which it left the House of Commons, and his Majesty has been pleased to signify that he will consider it his duty to accept and act on that advice." Great was the indignation excited among Unionists by the publication of this letter. In the House of Commons the Prime Minister, when he rose to make a statement to the House, was refused a hearing by an angry group of members, and the Speaker was ultimately obliged to close the sitting under the

Mr. Asquith's letter to Mr. Balfour.

[1] Lecky's History of England, vol. i. p. 185.

standing order.[1] But the country remained apathetic, and seemed to pay little attention to the stir and strife at Westminster; while it was manifest that whether with or without a creation of peers the Parliament Bill was destined speedily to pass into law.

<small>Lord Lansdowne's advice to his followers.</small>

The last consideration determined Lord Lansdowne and a large majority of Unionist peers to bow to the inevitable and, by abstention from further resistance, to save their order from destruction. Had they continued to insist on their amendment, a creation of at least 400 peers would have been necessary to secure the safe passage of the bill; and from such a blow recovery seemed impossible. They therefore resolved to follow the example set by the Duke of Wellington with respect to the Reform Bill of 1832 and to refrain from further opposition.[2] But there was a minority in the party, influential,

<small>Continued resistance of a section.</small>

powerful in the press, and led by ex-Ministers of the Crown to whom such a course appeared not only pusillanimous but unwise. Regarding the creation of peers in order to force a decision on one branch of the legislature as a daring violation of constitutional right, they wished to make the nature of the action of Ministers visible to all, and to compel them to commit the outrage they had threatened. It was agreed, so they argued, among Unionists that the bill practically abolished the House of Lords and established single-chamber Government; why then for a poor pretence of life, abandon all reasons for living? The hope, it was true, was a forlorn one, but what could be more demoralising than surrender? The party that held these views and resolved to translate them into action rallied round Lord Halsbury, the ex-Chancellor, whose unbending Toryism appealed to the admirers of resolution and consistency. Among its leaders were Lord Selborne, Lord Milner, and Mr. Austen Chamberlain; and its organisation was mainly the work of Lord Willoughby de Broke, in whose expressed view no number of General Elections would justify

---

[1] Lord Hugh Cecil, a leader of this group, had in a letter to *The Times*, written shortly before this incident, hinted at the probability of an attempt on the part of the Government to coerce the House of Lords being met by organised disorder in the House of Commons.

[2] "An argument fit for great princes, that neither by overmeasuring their forces, they lose themselves in vain enterprises; nor, by undervaluing them, descend to fearful and pusillanimous counsels."—Bacon.

the peers in refraining from voting against a policy which they held to be wrong.

During the week which followed the return of the bill from the Lords to the Commons, the matter was fiercely disputed in the Unionist press, especially in letters addressed to *The Times*, by the protagonists on either side; and, until the last moment, it was doubtful what the result of the division in the Lords would be. Lord Lansdowne published a list of some 330 Unionist peers who had agreed to follow his advice and to refrain from voting, but the number of irreconcilables was not known. Lord Halsbury was entertained at a great banquet by his admirers where fiery speeches were made, and where a policy of resistance to the end was proclaimed. A message from Mr. Joseph Chamberlain was read at this banquet in which the veteran statesman commended in strong language the policy of "No Surrender"—just as by a former message in 1909 to the Birmingham meeting he had urged the rejection of the Budget. There were also a few peers, whose numbers were unknown, but on whom all was ultimately to depend, who resolved that if no other means were left to avert the creation of peers, they would themselves avert that creation by voting with the Government.

On Monday the 8th of August, Mr. Balfour moved a vote of censure on the Government in the following terms: "That the advice given to his Majesty by his Majesty's Ministers, whereby they obtained from his Majesty a pledge that a sufficient number of peers would be created to pass the Parliament Bill in the shape in which it left this House, is a gross violation of constitutional liberty, whereby, among many other evil consequences, the people will be precluded from again pronouncing upon the policy of Home Rule". In his reply to Mr. Balfour's energetic attack, Mr. Asquith narrated with characteristic directness and lucidity the steps which had led up to the actual crisis, and disclosed, as has been seen, by the king's permission certain of the communications which had passed between the Ministry and the Crown. He challenged the Opposition to say, on the assumption that the Parliament Bill had been approved by the electors[1] and the alternative solution of the referendum rejected, what constitutional course

Vote of censure.

[1] In an interjected reply Lord Hugh Cecil denied this assumption.

other than that which they had adopted was left to the Government if the Lords persisted in substituting the referendum for the proposals of the Parliament Bill. The resolution was rejected by a majority of 119, and on the next day an identical one moved by Lord Curzon in the House of Lords was there passed by a large majority.

The Commons disagree to amendments.
The Government, having first taken steps to ascertain what support they could rely on from the Liberal lords, now resolved to take the risk of losing the bill and to send it back to the Lords without advising an immediate creation of peers. Accordingly, on Tuesday, the 8th of August, the Lords' amendments were considered in the House of Commons. To the more important of these the Commons disagreed by large majorities; to one, however, whereby bills for extending the duration of Parliament were excluded from the operation of the Act, they agreed. They also provided that the Speaker, in deciding whether a bill was a money bill, should consult with two members of the Chairmen's panel chosen by the Committee of Selection.

The Bill passed.
The bill was sent back to the Lords, and on Thursday, the 10th of August, after a two days' debate not unworthy of the great traditions of the House, the decisive division was taken, with the result that the Lords resolved by 131 votes to 114 not to insist on their amendments. Until the last moment the issue had been doubtful. Hopes had been entertained that the creation of peers, if carried into effect, would be but a small one, and merely sufficient to overcome the resistance of the irreconcilables, so that the Unionists would still be left with an overwhelming majority in the House of Lords until such time as the return of a Unionist majority to the House of Commons at a fresh election might enable them to settle the constitutional question in their own manner. But this calculation was overthrown by an authoritative declaration from Lord Morley, the Minister in charge of the bill, who, reading from a paper, announced that if the bill were defeated that night "his Majesty would assent to a creation of peers sufficient in number to guard against any possible combination of the different parties in opposition by which the Parliament Bill might again be exposed a second time to defeat". This statement decided certain wavering Unionists to cast their votes

with the Government; and, although the Duke of Norfolk, with several other peers, who had reluctantly agreed to follow Lord Lansdowne in his course of abstention, announced that in that case they would record their votes on the other side; they persisted in their purpose. Their votes, together with those of the two Archbishops and of eleven other Bishops, carried the day, and the threatened creation was averted. On one previous occasion the Lords Spiritual had held the balance in a momentous division in the House of Lords. In 1831, disregarding the warning of Lord Grey, they had voted against the second Reform Bill, when, by voting in its favour, they might have carried the second reading; they now interposed with results even more decisive, and, at a time when it was in their power to defeat a bill which they disliked, they saved the peerage from destruction by subordinating their inclinations to considerations of public policy.

Thus fell before the united forces of Crown, Commons, and electorate, the independent power of the oldest assembly in the world. By their action in rejecting the financial provision made by the Commons for 1909, and so forcing the dissolution of the Parliament of 1906, their critics asserted that they had usurped one of the prerogatives of the Crown; they fell by what they declared to be the unconstitutional misuse on the advice of the Cabinet of another prerogative. Had the Unionist party made use of the long period which began with the election of 1886, and, interrupted only by the short Parliament of 1892, continued down to the end of 1905, during which they controlled all the forces of the State, to make some serious attempt to reform the constitution of that branch of the legislature which had never known reform, the powers of the Upper House might have long been preserved inviolate, or even, had that been thought desirable, have been increased. Or had they taken warning by the great reverse of 1906 and perceived that something more was implied by that election than the ordinary movement of the political pendulum, the issue might have been different. But in the Parliament of 1906 they elected to reject the normal legislation of a Liberal Government, while passing without amendment bills to which they were even more strongly opposed, in which the Labour members—their irreconcilable opponents—were chiefly in-

Retrospect.

terested. And they did so without concealing their detestation of those bills. By these tactics they forced the unwilling hand of moderate Liberals whom they drove into an alliance with the extremists—an alliance which was sealed by the rejection of the Budget in 1909. A last opportunity of settlement by consent was given by the conference of 1910. The failure of this conference is deeply to be regretted ; but, both because it may serve as a precedent and because it has enabled the leading statesmen on either side to recognise that their differences on the constitutional question are not insuperable, it is well that these meetings were held.

Conclusion. The Parliament Act is but the first step in the constitutional settlement. Both parties are pledged to a complete reform of the constitution of the House of Lords—the Unionists by Lord Lansdowne's bill, the Liberals by the preamble to the Parliament Act. Schemes for the federation of the United Kingdom are in the air; and the promised concession of self-government to Ireland may prove the first step in their accomplishment. Who can say how the question of the powers and constitution of a Second Chamber may be affected by changes such as these? The constitution is now at the disposal of a vast and mobile electorate, to whom tradition and history mean very little. To this electorate, as to all the successive depositaries of power, the flatteries of ambitious men are addressed. A modern theory, resting on no historic basis, seeks to show that the main function of the House of Lords has always been to give effect to the permanent and considered will of the people, whereas in fact it is as a check to democracy that a Second Chamber is really useful, and was always justified as such in former times not only by Tories but by Whigs. It is consoling to remember that every great constitutional or legislative innovation in our history has been attended by confident prophecies of ruin, hitherto unfulfilled. That the constitution may once again emerge from the clash of contending parties in renewed strength and vitality must be the strong desire of every patriotic Englishman.

INDEX TO VOLUME III.

ABERDEEN Ministry, reference to, 19.
Affirmation Act (1888) passed, 227.
Agitators, political, agricultural labourers affected by, 30. *See also* Home Rule question.
Agrarian distress in Ireland, 99, 122, 154; evictions and outrages, 159-161, 177, 191, 197.
Agriculture, Council of, 188.
Alabama, the, claim by United States concerning the escape of, 79, 298.
American Colonies, position of practical self-government from Elizabethan era, 295; severance from the Mother Country by the American War, 295, 309.
American Fenians. *See* Fenian Conspiracy.
Amnesty Association (1868), for release of Fenian prisoners, 143.
Anne, Queen, Act of 1708 affecting offices of profit held by members of the House of Commons, 85; Law Lords' ruling, 85; authorisation of army purchase (1711), 273.
Appeal, Courts of, reform of, 285-289; position of the Supreme Court, 286, 289; Criminal Court of, appointed 1907, 291. *See also* Judicature Reform.
Arch, Joseph, and agricultural agitations, 30.
Archbishops and Bishops. *See* Lords Spiritual.
Army, reform in the, 77, 273-283; abolition of corporal punishment, 95; army purchase, officially recognised since 1683, 273; prohibited by William III., 273; authorised again by Queen Anne, 273; army regulation bill of 1871, abolition of purchase, by royal warrant, 276, 277; short service system and reserve forces, 277-279; reconstruction and reorganisation, 279-283; territorial army, establishment of, 280-283; universal military service, question of, 282, 283.

Arnold Forster, Mr., references to, 92, 215, 280, 282.
Asquith, Rt. Hon. H. H., Albert Hall speeches, on Home Rule, 199, 200; on the reform of the Lords, 356.
Bill for disestablishment and disendowment of the Welsh Church, by, (1909) 241, 242.
Reform of the House of Lords: composition of the Second Chamber, 53, 54; resolution charging the Lords with usurpation of privileges, 355; policy formulated before the election of 1910, 356, 357; resolutions as to reform carried by the Commons, 363-364; preamble to the Parliament Bill, 364; advice tendered to the King, (George V.), as to the creation of peers, 365, 368-69, 379, 381, 382; Unionist indignation at the action of the Government, 379; votes of censure moved by Mr. Balfour, and Lord Curzon, 381, 382.
Women's suffrage, speech against, 65. *See also* the Parliament Bill.
Associations. *See* Political.
Atheists and the Parliamentary Oath, 222-223; passing of the Affirmation Bill, 227. *See also* case of Mr. Bradlaugh.
Australasian Colonies, 294, 302-326; their relations to the Home Government, 302; the Imperial connection, 302, 303; crises in Victoria, 1865 and 1878, 303, 304; Victorian Parliament Bill, 305; financial aspects of the Imperial connection, 303-10; Imperial defence, 309-312, 323-27; Australian federation, 315-318; Australian Commonwealth Act (1900), 316, 322; right of appeal to the Sovereign in Council, 318-323; Imperial Preference and Tariff Reform, 312, 324, 325. *See also* Colonies and Colonial Conferences.
Ayrton, Mr., and the question of unauthorised expenditure by the Government (1869-72), 85.

VOL. III. 385 25

BAINES, Mr., proposed reduction of borough franchise, 2.
Balfour, Arthur J., minor references, 104-105, 343.
Administration, Premier, (1902), 131; resigns, (1905), 136; Character and policy, 133-136, 343, 349, 350.
Chief Secretary of State for Ireland, 177, 181.
Education Bill of 1902, 131; " Fourth Party " and, 104-5.
Free Trade and Tariff Reform, 133-136.
Leadership of the House of Commons, 127, 182.
Reform of the Lords, 349, 350, 353; view as to the relation of the two Houses (1907), 349, 350; letter to Mr. Asquith, 379; vote of censure on the Government moved by, 381.
Women's suffrage, academic attitude towards, 65, 66.
See also Parliament Bill.
Balfour, Gerald, Chief Secretary of State for Ireland, his policy, 186, 190.
Balfour of Burleigh, Lord, his Bill for a Referendum, 373.
Ballot, election by, 24, 25; passing of the Act of 1872, 26; results of, 26, 27, 87.
Beach, Sir Michael Hicks, Chief Secretary of State for Ireland, 119, 120, 177; Chancellor of the Exchequer, 127; retires, 131; policy as Colonial Secretary, 305-308.
Beaconsfield, Earl of. *See* Disraeli, Benjamin.
Beck, Adolf, false imprisonment of, 290.
Begg, W. Faithful, his Bill for women's suffrage (1897), 63.
Bentham, Jeremy, axiom of, 160 *n.*
Birmingham, political school of, 90, 91, 103-104, 106. *See also* Chamberlain, J.
Birrell, A., Irish Councils Bill of, 197; the Irish Universities Act of 1908, 244.
Bishops. *See* Lords, Spiritual.
Board Schools, instituted under the Act of 1870, 229, 230; abolished 1902, 232. *See also* Education.
Boer revolt. *See* South African War.
Boroughs and counties, changes in the franchise of, 9-11, 28-31, 34-35, 40-42.
Bowen, Sir George, Governor of Victoria, references to, 304-308.
Bradlaugh, Charles, his character and views, 222-223; made member for Northampton (1880), 222; claims the right of affirmation, 223; litigation concerning, 223-227; imprisoned in the Clock Tower, 225; takes the oath (1886), 226, 227; his death in 1891; resolutions against him expunged from the Journals of the House of Commons, 227.
Bribery at elections, 22, 26; penalties for, 32, 33.
Bright, Jacob, Bill for the enfranchisement of women, 61, 62.
Bright, John, Radical views of, 4, 11, 21, 23, 24, 33, 73, 75, 76, 78, 116, 175; vote against Home Rule, 175.
Broderick, Mr., scheme of army reform, 280.
Brunswick, An Impeachment of the House of, by Ch. Bradlaugh, reference to, 223, 224.
Budget of 1909, rejection of, by the House of Lords, 53, 353, 358-360, 384; agreed to, 1910, 366.
Burials Act, passing of (1880), 228.
Burke, Edmund, on Colonial representation, 340.
Burke, Thos., Under Secretary of State for Ireland; murder of, in Phœnix Park, 161.
Butt, Isaac, as leader of the Moderate Party for Home Rule, 92-95, 143-150, 159, 174; breach with Parnell, 150; his death in 1879, 95, 157.

CAMPBELL-BANNERMAN, Sir H., Administration, 48, 326, 327, 346, 347; proposals for the reform of the House of Lords, 346-47, 355.
Canada, its early constitution, 294-95, 301; absorption of the French element, 297; federation of British North America, 298; Dominion of Canada Constitution Act (1867), 299, 300, 321; Canadian preference, 324; her present position as regards the Home Government and other Colonies, 342.
Cape Colony. *See* South Africa Colonies.
Cardwell, Mr., and Army reform, 274-279; his policy as Colonial Secretary, 304.
Carnarvon, Lord, Viceroy of Ireland, his federal policy, 165-170, 174; his Canadian and South African schemes of federation, 165, 174, 330.
Catholic Emancipation Act (1869), 134, 206-208; completion of, under the Reform Act of 1884, 168.

INDEX TO VOLUME III

Caucus, the. *See* Chamberlain, J.
Cavendish, Lord Frederick, Chief Secretary of State for Ireland, murdered in Phœnix Park, 110, 161.
Cavendish, Lord Richard, President of the Royal Commission on Parliamentary reform, 58, 59.
Cecil, Lord Hugh, references to, 239, 380-381 *n.*; action as regards the Parliament Bill, 380-381 *n.*
Censure. *See* Vote of Censure.
Chamberlain, Austen, references to, 65, 380.
Chamberlain, Joseph, minor references, 33-4, 131, 251, 381; the caucus introduced by, 12, 90, 91, 103, 106, 107.
 Home Rule policy, 117, 164-173, 180; opposition to Mr. Gladstone, 117, 171-172.
 Imperial federation (Colonial), and, 312-315, 323-325.
 Tariff Reform, 132-134, 136, 141, 351-352, 356.
Chancery, Court of. *See* Judicature Reform.
Chandos Clause, and the franchise, 31, 35.
Children, legislation affecting the welfare of, 81, 137, 141.
Chinese labour in South Africa, introduction of, 135; unpopularity of, 135.
Churchill, Lord Randolph, and the Tory-Democratic party, 104-109; policy for Ireland, 119, 120, 176.
Church Rates Act (1868), 76, 203.
Church of England, the, Education and, 213, 214, 219-220, 234-237, 239; demand for denominational teaching in Church Schools, 233-239; the State and, change in the relations of, 201-203; disestablishment and disendowment, question of, 240; Public Worship Regulation Act, its failure, 221, 222; legalisation of marriage with deceased wife's sister (1907), 242; clergy free to refuse to solemnise such marriages, 242-243. *See also* the Church in Ireland and Wales, the Roman Catholic Church, and Church of Scotland.
Civil Service, reforms in, changes in the system of appointments, 271; evils of the patronage system, 271; open competitive examinations for the Indian Civil Service (1853), 272; for the Home Service (1870), 272; importance of the reform, 272-273.

Clan-na-gael, American Fenian organisation, 150, 152.
Clarke, Sir Edward, on vested interests and Licensing Bills, 253.
Closure, the, 102, 103; closure by compartments, its effects, 123, 178, 179, 233.
Coercion Acts (Irish), 160, 161.
Coke, Lord, formal condemnation of the practice of allowing women to vote, 59.
Collings, Jesse, amendment on the allotments question, 115.
Colonial Conferences in England, 310, 311, 313, 323, 325, 342.
Colonies, the self-governing, after 1860, 293-342; mid-Victorian opinion, 80, 293; first step towards self-government, 294, 302; the three successive policies, 295; Imperial consolidation, its growth and development, 80, 293, 295, 296, 302, 306, 307-309, 311-326, 336, 339-342; Imperial defence, Colonial contributions towards, 309, 310, 315, 323, 324; proposals for Imperial federation, 339; Parliament of the Empire, objections to, 340-342; Imperial Preference and Tariff Reform, 312-314, 325; right of appeal to the Sovereign in Council, 318-322; Women's suffrage in the Colonies, 63. *See also* American Colonies and the War of Independence, and the Colonies of Australasia, Canada, Newfoundland and South Africa.
Common Pleas, Court of. *See* Judicature Reform.
Commons, House of, Ballot Bill, passing of, 24, 27, 87; closure introduced, 102-103; by compartments, its hampering effect, 123, 178-179, 233; controversy over the Bradlaugh case, 222-227; its issue in the Affirmation Act (1888), 227; financial questions and the Upper House, 363-64, 376-377; opposition policy of the House of Lords, 1906-1911; *see* the Parliament Bill; growing subordination of the Commons to the electorate and Ministers of the Crown since 1867, 17, 20, 83-88, 178-179, 233, *see also* Franchise, extension of; obstruction, policy of, by the Irish party, 93-95, 148-152, 157-158, 190; by the Tory-Democratic Party, 104-109; Mr. Asquith refused a hearing over the the Parliament Bill in 1911, 379, 380. *See also* Lords, House of,

25 *

Party, and Reform in Parliament.
Compensation for Disturbances Bill (1880), 158.
Competitive examinations for the Civil Service instituted, 76, 272.
Compulsory Church Rates abolished, 76, 203.
Compulsory Education (1880), 229.
Compulsory military service, arguments for, and against, 282.
Conciliation Bill for the extension of the franchise to women, 65, 66.
Concurrent endowment. *See* Ireland, Church in.
Conferences of party leaders on the question of the reform of the House of Lords (1910), 366-368, 375. *See also* Colonial Conferences.
Conservative party in the Government. *See* Party.
Corn Laws, repeal of, references to, 19, 135.
Coronation Oath, amendment of the Royal Declaration (1910), 244-245.
Corporations Acts, municipal franchise extended to women, 61, 262.
Corrupt and Illegal Practices Acts (1868), 14; (1883), 31-33.
Councils, County, appointed, 1888, 252; London County Council, 253-55, 260-61; Provincial County Councils, 252, 256; District and Parish, 256-59.
Counties and boroughs, changes in the Franchise, 9-11, 28-31, 34-35, 40-42.
County Councils. *See* above.
County rates and Quarter Sessions, 250-51.
Cowper-Temple Clause in the Education Act of 1870, 216; retained in succeeding Acts, 234, 238-39; dissatisfaction of advanced Churchmen and Roman Catholics with the compromise, 239.
Crewe, Lord, and the Parliament Bill, his interview with the King, 369; introduces the Bill into the House of Lords, 369.
Crimes Act (Ireland), 111, 113, 122, 161, 162, 165, 166, 177-178, 181, 191; made perpetual (1887), 177-178.
Criminal Court of Appeal, institution of, (1907), 140, 291.
Cromer, Lord, question of the financial control of the Upper over the Lower House, 376-377.
Crown, the, Colonial right of appeal to, 318-23, 326.

Constitutional position of, since 1688, 17; changes following the Reform Act of 1832, 17, 270.
Hereditary right of royalty to representation in the House of Lords, 52, 374.
Orders in Council, reforms effected by, 272, 273.
Power to prevent meetings in a royal park, 6, 11.
Royal prerogative, of mercy, 291; to create peers, 360, 365, 369, 374, 379, 381-382. *See also* Ministers of the Crown, the Parliament Bill, and Royal Commissions.
Curzon, Lord, vote of censure on the Government moved by, 382.

DARLING, Sir Charles, levy of duties unauthorised by the legislature, 304.
Davitt, Michael, and the Home Rule party, 153, 154, 161; land league founded by, 154, 155.
de Broke, Lord Willoughby, opposition to the Parliament Bill, 380-81.
Deceased wife's sister, marriage with, legalised (1907), 242-243.
Democracy, growth of, with the extension of the Franchise, 74-80, 95, 96, 103, 129, 135-140. *See also* Tory Democracy.
Derby, Earl, his Ministry (1866), 6; his resignation, 13, 67, 69, 72; his Reform Bill (1867), 8, 67.
Devolution, schemes for the federation of the United Kingdom, 384.
Dillon, Mr., and the Home Rule party, 185, 186, 196.
Dillwyn, Mr., and the Irish Church question, 204.
Disestablishment and disendowment. *See* the Church of England, Ireland, and Wales.
Disraeli, Benjamin (afterwards Earl of Beaconsfield), minor references, 221, 249 *n*.
Administrations, 69; resigns, 75; his refusal to accept office (1873), 82, 86; returns as Prime Minister with a majority (1874), 89; his death in 1881, 105.
Character and policy of, 13, 67-69, 70, 80, 97, 106, 293-297.
Franchise extension, views on, 16; opposition to Mr. Trevelyan, 28-30.
Home Rule and Catholic emancipation, his opposition to, 97, 101, 156, 206, 209.
Imperialism, his conception of, 80, 97, 293-297.

Reform Bill of 1867, 7-9, 68-69.
Speeches, at the Crystal Palace, 80; at Edinburgh, 68.
Dissenters. *See* Nonconformists.
Dissolutions of Parliament, questions of procedure concerning, 12, 19, 345, 352, 368; claim of the Lords to force, 352.
Dublin Convention (1896), 186, 187.
Dunkellin, Lord, amendment to the Reform Bill of 1866, 5.
Dunraven, Lord, his Irish policy, 194.
Durham, Lord, report on the Union of Upper and Lower Canada, 294, 297.
Dyke, Sir Hart, Chief Secretary of State for Ireland, resignation of, 170.

ECCLESIASTICAL Titles Act (1871), 212, 213.
Education, Public Elementary, 131, 228-240; Education Acts, 229, 230, 232; Bills, 231, 234, 238.
Board Schools established, 229, 230; abolished in favour of County Council Schools, 232; voluntary and non-provided schools, case of, 131, 230, 232, 235-239; compulsory school attendance, 229; free education instituted, 231; payment by results abolished, 231.
Religious teaching in the schools, 131, 216, 229-239; the Cowper-Temple clause, 234, 238-239; dissatisfaction of Churchmen and Roman Catholics, 229, 235, 238-239; Nonconformist objections, 131, 229, 233-235; compromise proposed by the Bishop of St. Asaph, 238. *See also* Church of England and Nonconformity.
Edward VII., proposals for redistribution in the King's speech (1905), 47; reference to the financial relations of the Upper and Lower House (1910), 360; his death in 1911, 55, 366; his extraordinary popularity and influence, 366.
Egerton, H. E., *History of British Colonial Policy*, reference to, 305 *n*, 308 *n*.
Electoral anomalies, discussion of, 55-59.
Electorate, growing power of. *See* the Franchise, and Corrupt Practices Acts.
Elgin, Lord, and the Government of Canada, 294-296.
Empire. *See* Imperialism.
Employers' Liability Bill, discussions over, 345.

Evidence Amendment Act, 223, 224.
Exchequer, Court of. *See* Judicature Reform.

FACTORY legislation, 77, 81.
Fawsett, Mr., proposals for the abolition of religious tests, 218, 219.
Fenian conspiracy, 94, 142-157, 161; its American origin, 94, 142-3, 153; work of the Clan-na-Gael Association, 150, 152, 153; the Phœnix Park murders, 161.
Forgeries. *See* the Parnell Letters.
"Fourth Party," the. *See* Tory-Democrats.
Fowler, Mr., introduces the Local Government Bill (1893), 256; passing of (1894), 256.
Franchise, extensions of, 2-11, 15-17, 24-25, 28-31, 33-39, 40-42, 56-59, 98, 134, 345; alternative vote, the, 56 *n.*, 59; constitutional changes following Reform Act of 1867, 15, 16; democratic character of the franchise, 24, 87, 98, 136; difficulties introduced by the increase of parties, 55, 59; electoral anomalies, 55, 56; minority rights, 56, 57; proportional representation, 57, 59; schemes of voting, 56; plural voting, 42, 48, 49, 344; vote by ballot, 24-27. *See also* Boroughs and Counties, Redistribution of Seats, and Women's Suffrage.
Free Trade and Tariff Reform. *See* Tariff Reform.
Frere, Sir Bartle, on self-government in South Africa, 332, 335 *n.*

GEORGE V., his accession to the throne (1910), 366; first sovereign to make the royal declaration, 244-45; His position with regard to the reform of the Upper House, 360, 361, 365, 368, 369, 379, 381-383; His address (1911); advice of the Crown Ministers to His Majesty on the creation of peers, 368-369, 379-382.
George, Lloyd, his Budget of 1909 rejected by the Lords, 53, 353, 358-360, 384; agreed to (1910), 366; his attitude towards Women's suffrage, 66.
Gladstone, William Ewart, minor references to, 2, 3, 8, 33, 74-76, 102, 103, 111, 123, 225, 227, 241, 348.
Administrations, his four: *first*, 75, resigns, 82, 83, 88; *second*, 99, resigns, 112; *third*, 116, resigns, 119; *fourth*, 124, retirement from political life (1894), 124, 129, 185.

As Chancellor of the Exchequer, question as to whether he has vacated his seat, 85, 87.
Character and policy, 68-70, 71, 84, 86, 87, 97, 98, 109, 113, 114, 121-122, 124, 125, 129, 167; address at Greenwich, 86, 87; Hawarden manifesto, 113, 114, 167; Midlothian campaign, 98, 167.
Franchise, his policy of extension, 2, 9, 18, 28, 30, 31, 34, 35, 62, 63; Act of 1884, 34-40, 345.
Home Rule, his policy in favour of, 42, 43, 98-102, 105, 116-119, 121, 123, 124, 129, 142-143, 156-157, 163, 167, 169, 170-175, 182, 183, 185, 205; Bills of (1886), 170-175; (1893), 124, 183; the two compared, 183; split with the Parnellites, 182.
Irish Church, disestablishment and disendowment of, 70-71, 76, 93, 143, 159, 168, 204-211; Catholic Emancipation Act passed (1869), 211; completed by the Reform Act of 1884, 168.
Irish Universities, Test Act (1871), 212; Bill of 1873, to establish a new university at Dublin, 218.
Oxford University, rejected by, 3.
Reconstitution of the Upper House, attitude towards, 43, 44, 110, 111, 185, 345.
Women's suffrage, opposition to, 62, 63.
Gordon, General, death of, and the fall of Khartoum, feeling against the Government aroused by, 111.
Gorst, Mr., and the " Fourth Party," 105.
Goschen, Mr., references to, 75, 76, 116, 119-121, 246; Chancellor of the Exchequer, 119-121; conversion of the National Debt, 121, 248; President of the Poor Law Board, 248.
Grey, Earl, his resignation on the refusal of William IV. to create peers, 345.
Grey, Sir George, his policy of South African federation, 329; his recall, 329.
Grosvenor, Earl, amendment to the Reform Bill of 1866, 4, 5.
Guillotine, The. See Closure by Compartments.

HABEAS Corpus Act suspended in Ireland, 101, 159, 206.
Haldane, Mr., and Army reform, 280-282.
Halifax, Viscount, and denominational teaching in Church schools, 239.

Halsbury, Lord, admission of the evidence of prisoners obtained at the instance of, 289; leader of the " No surrender " party against the Parliament Bill, 380-381.
Harcourt, Sir W., and the Round Table Conference, 180.
Hartington, Lord, supports Mr. Trevelyan's Franchise Bills, 1874-1875, and 1876-1879, 29-31; refuses the Premiership (1880), 99; his differences with Mr. Chamberlain, 93, 113-114, 117; again declines the Premiership (1886), 119; opposition to Home Rule, 34, 116, 171, 179-180.
Healy, Mr., and the Home Rule Party, 185, 186, 199.
Hereditary principle of Representation. See Lords, House of.
Herschell, Lord, and the Round Table Conference, 180.
High Courts. See Judicature Reform.
Holland, Bernard, *Imperium et Libertas* by, references to, 340.
Home Government Association (Ireland), 88, 143-145.
Home Office, management of prisons transferred to (1877), 249; responsibility of revising sentences shared with the Court of Criminal Appeal, 291-292.
Home Rule for Ireland, general references, 88-96, 101, 112, 113, 115-16, 121-24, 127, 137, 142-200. See also under names of Leaders—and Mr. Gladstone's policy of Home Rule.
Confederation, 150.
League, its foundation, 145.
Movement, 142-200.
Acts and Bills—Coercion Act, 160, 161; Compensation for Disturbances Bill (1880), 158, 159; Crimes Act, 111, 113, 122, 161, 177-178, 181, 191; Habeas Corpus Act suspended, 101, 159, 206; Home Rule Bill of 1886, 172; the Bill of 1893 compared with that of 1886, 183-184; its defects, 184; shelving of the Bill owing to the retirement of Mr. Gladstone, 185; Land Act of 1881, 159, 160; Land Court and test cases, 160; the three F's, 159; Mr. Wyndham's Land Purhase Bill of 1903, 193, 195; anger of the Orange party, 196; his resignation, 196; Irish Councils Bill, 197.
Conservative attitude towards Home Rule, 165-167; evictions and out-

INDEX TO VOLUME III

rages, 159, 160, 177, 191, 197; the Fenian Conspiracy, 94, 142-157, 161; Mr. Butt's Scheme of Federation, 146-48; the Parnellite group, 148, 149; breach between Mr. Parnell and Mr. Butt, 150-151; Parnell's policy, 151-153; visit to the United States (1879-80), 155; leader of the Home Rule party, 157-158; his arrest, 160; the Phœnix Park murders, 161; Parnellism and crime, the forged letters, 181; split in the Nationalist party and death of Parnell, 182; Irish balance of power in Parliament (1910), 200. *See* Party. *See also* I. Butt, W. O'Brien, C. S. Parnell, the Land League and the Irish policy of Mr. Disraeli and Mr. Gladstone.

Hyde Park riots (1866-67), 6, 11.

IMPERIALISM, development of the Imperial Idea, 80, 97, 293, 295, 296, 302-315, 320-326, 332-336, 339-342, The confederacy of the Empire, 336. *See also* Colonies, the, and Conferences, Imperial.

Independent Labour party. *See* Party.

Ireland, agrarian distress in, 99, 122, 154; evictions and outrages, 160-161, 177, 191, 197.

Arrests and imprisonment of political offenders, 96, 101, 143, 160, 161, 181, 191.

Church in, disestablishment and disendowment of, 70, 71, 76, 93, 134, 143, 204-212; Catholic Emancipation Act of 1869, 211; completed by the Reform Act of 1884, 168; concurrent endowment, principle of, 209-212.

Devolution, policy of, 194-196, 199.

Fenian conspiracy, the, 94, 142-157, 161.

Home Rule Movement in, 142-200; prominence of the Irish question between 1885-1892, 42. *See also* Home Rule.

Imperial Parliament for, objections and difficulties, 173.

Irish Nationalist Party in the House of Commons, rise and growth of, 26, 27, 35, 36, 41, 93-101, 105, 112, 115, 116, 121-124, 127, 137, 147, 149-152, 157, 158, 168, 198, 199, 200, 344, 359, 360; Independent Nationalists, their attitude, 359-360; balance of power in the Parliament of 1910, 200.

Orange Party and Home Rule, 143, 177, 195, 196.

Roman Catholic Church in, its political power, 145-147, 151, 157.

Round Table Conference, 180, 181.

Social and political conditions before the Fenian conspiracy, 142, 148.

University Tests, 211, 212; Act of 1871, 212; Queen's College, Belfast, 217, 218, 243; position of Trinity College, Dublin, 217-219; Act of 1908, 243; founding of two new universities at Dublin and Belfast, 244.

Irish Reform Association, 194, 195.

Irish Republican Brotherhood, 153, 154, 157.

JAMESON'S Raid, its political results, 333.

Jingoism, origin of the expression, 97.

Judicature Reforms, 283-292; the three Ancient Courts, 284; consolidation of existing courts into a supreme court, 285; Judicature Acts (1873, 1875, 1876), 286-287; Courts of Appeal, 286-287. Scotch and Irish Appeals, 287; the High Court, 289; admission of prisoners' evidence, 289; institution of a Criminal Court of Appeal, 290-291.

Judicial Committee, its work and origin, 318-323. *See also* Colonial right of appeal to the Crown.

KHARTOUM, fall of, and death of General Gordon, its political effects, 111.

Kilmainham, Treaty of, 160, 164.

King, Locke, attempt to lower the county franchise, 2.

King's speech in Parliament, the. *See* Edward VII. and George V.

Kruger, President, and the second Boer War, 333.

LABOUCHERE, Mr., the hereditary principle of representation condemned by, 43, 44; moves that Mr. Bradlaugh be allowed to affirm instead of taking the oath, 225.

Labour Exchanges, formation of, 141.

Labour Party, rise and policy of, 56, 79, 80, 137-140, 348; and the reconstitution of the House of Lords, 348.

Laing, Mr., and the redistribution of seats, 4, 9.

Land Act of 1881, 159, 160.

Land League (Irish) founded by Michael Davitt (1879), 155; Mr. Parnell's work in connection with, 101, 158; its increasing power, 159; sup-

pressed by royal proclamation, 160, 162.
Land Purchase Acts, and Bills (Irish), 111, 175-177, 191, 193, 195, 199.
Land Sales Act, offer by the Colonial Secretary, on behalf of the Crown (1852), to repeal in favour of the Australian Colonies, 294.
Lansdowne, Lord, and the Parliament Bill of 1911, 369, 370, 373, 374, 378, 380; the Lords' amendments, 378; his advice of non-resistance, 380.
Laurier, Sir Wilfred, on the allegiance of the Colonies to the Crown, not to the electorate, 339.
Law and equity, distinction between Courts of, a source of delay and inconvenience, 284. *See also* Judicature Reform.
Laws, expiring, Act to continue (1880), 26; Ballot Act included in, 26.
Lecky, on the *Constitution* between 1832-1867, 18.
Liberal Associations. See National Federations and Unions.
Liberalism, its ascendency in the middle of nineteenth century, 21; its decline at the end of nineteenth century, 128; the doctrine of *laissez-faire*, 76, 77, 216, 270, 301.
Liberal Party. See Party.
Liberty of opinion. See Nonconformity, Religion and the State, and the case of Mr. Bradlaugh.
Liberty of the subject. See Habeas Corpus Acts, and Political Prisoners.
Licensing Laws, legislation concerning, 253, 343, 344 *n.*, 348-349.
Life peerages, proposals for the modification of the Upper House by the creation of, 22, 23, 44, 51; the royal prerogative of creating, 360, 365, 369, 374, 379, 381-382. See *also* the Parliament Bill.
Local Government after 1870, 246-269; chaotic state of Local Government in 1870, 246; Local Government Board appointed (1871), 247; Royal Sanitary Commission and Public Health Acts (1872, 1875), 248-249, 257, 268; transfer of prisons to Home Office, 249; Quarter Sessions and County Rates, 250; Local Government Act (1888), 252; powers and duties of County Councils, 252-256; London County Council, 253-256; Act of 1894, 256; Poor Law and sanitary administration, 257-260, 264, 266; London Government, 260-262; London Government Act of 1899, 261; Central control in Local Government, its historic growth, decline and revival, 262-264; advisory character of the Central authority over local bodies, 265-269; summary of results, 369.
London County Council appointed, 253-256; party spirit among Moderates and Progressives in, 254-256.
London government, its reforms, 260-262; Act of 1899, 261; Bill of 1909 against plural voting, 49-50.
London vestries, anomalous position of, in 1890, 261.
Lords, House of, abolition of voting by proxies, 14, 15; action with regard to measures passed by the Commons, 20, 22-26, 37-39, 50, 83, 131, 132, 158, 185, 235-237, 275-277, 343-349, 352-384.
Hereditary principle, proposed modification of, by election, and creation of life peers, 22, 23, 43, 44, 51-55, 78, 110, 111, 360-361, 363-365, 368, 369, 379, 380-382.
Powers of, their assertion of rights over the Commons, 50, 51, 343-349, 352; relation between the two Houses defined by Mr. Balfour, 349; claim of the Lords to force a dissolution, 352; resolutions to limit the power of, 363-365, 369-370, 383-384.
Rejection of the Budget of 1909, and the passage of the Parliament Bill, 53, 343-384; General Election (1910), 357; advice of the Government to the Crown, 368-369, 379; resolutions by Lord Rosebery and Lord Lansdowne, 369, 370, 371, 373; Lords' amendment to the Parliament Bill, 375-379; Lord Lansdowne's advice to allow the Bill to pass, 380; opposition of Lord Halsbury and his party, 380-381; the Bill passes, 382.
Lords Spiritual, their ancient relation to the State, 203; question of their position in an elective Second Chamber, 51, 52, 374; balance of power held by, in the Upper House, 1831, 383; in 1911, 383.
Lowe, Robert, Chancellor of the Exchequer, 84-85; his opposition to the extension of the franchise, 2, 8, 9, 18, 30, 77.
Lubbock, Sir John, and the question of unauthorised expenditure, 84, 85.
Lyndhurst, Lord, reference to, 348.

INDEX TO VOLUME III

Lytton, Sir E. B., recall of Sir G. Grey from South Africa, 329 *n.*
Lytton, Lord, and the Conciliation Bill, 65.

MACAULAY, on the relations of Religion and the State, 201 *n.*
Macdonnell, Sir Anthony, under Secretary of State for Ireland, 192; his policy, 194-197.
Malmesbury, Lord, opposition to Lord Russell's Life Peerage Bill, 23, 24 *n.*
Manchester School of Politics, references to, 77, 81.
Marlborough, Duke of, Viceroy of Ireland, Lord Beaconsfield's letter to, in defence of the Union, 156.
Marriage with a deceased wife's sister legalised (1907), 242; rights of the clergy to refuse to solemnise, 242, 243.
May, Sir Erskine, reference to previous editions of his *History*, 1 *n.* 211 *n.*
Mayo, Lord, and the Irish Universities, 218.
Members of Parliament, question of payment of, 33, 34, 43, 57 *n.*; political arrest of, *see* Home Rule and the Bradlaugh Case. *See also* Commons and Lords, Parliament, and Party.
Metropolitan Board of Works, establishment of, 254.
Metropolitan Water Board, establishment of, 262.
Middle classes, position of, between 1832-1867, 18.
Militia, reforms affecting the, 279, 281.
Mill, John Stuart, on the enfranchisement of women, 60-61; his Parliamentary oath (1865) cited in defence of the Bradlaugh case, 222.
Milner, Lord, and the introduction of Chinese labour into the Rand, 135.
Ministers of the Crown, increasing power of, and the electorate, since 1867, 17-20, 83-88, 178-179, 233.
Minority representation, importance of, 56, 57.
Miscarriages of justice, Adolf Beck, a case of mistaken identity, 290, 291.
Mitchell John (editor of *The United Irishman*), his imprisonment and escape, question as to his disqualification for a seat in Parliament, 96.
Moderates and Progressives. *See* London County Council.
Monsell, Mr., Postmaster General, and the question of unauthorised expenditure, 84-85.

Morley, Lord, on the position of the Liberal Party in 1886, 116.
Municipal franchise given to women by the Corporation Act of 1869, 61.
Municipal Reform. *See* Local Government.

NATIONAL League (Irish), foundation of (1882), 123, 162.
National Liberal Federation, establishment of, 90, 91, 100, 106, 117, 118.
National Service League, founded by Lord Roberts, 282.
National Society for Women's Suffrage, formation of, 1867, 60.
National Union of Conservative and Constitutional Associations, 106-109, 121.
Nationalist Party (Irish). *See* Home Rule Movement, Ireland, and Party.
Native question in South Africa, 336, the Act of 1909, 338.
Navy, extension of the naval programme, 125, 350.
Newcastle, Duke of, on Imperial interests in the Colonies, 305.
Newcastle Programme, the, 42, 46, 48, 129.
Newfoundland, refusal to join the Canadian Federation, 298, 301.
Newton, Lord, Bill for the re-constitution of the House of Lords (1907), 51.
Nonconformists, disabilities of, removed, 211, 212, 221, 228; religious education and, 131, 228, 229, 233-235, 237-240.
Religious tests abolished under the Act of 1871, 212.
See also Wales, the Church in.
Norfolk, Duke of, and the Parliament Bill, his refusal to follow Lord Lansdowne's policy, 383; President of Royal Commission on the conditions affecting internal defence, 282.
Northcote, Sir Stafford, references to, 107, 225, 271; reforms in the Civil Service, 271.
Nova Scotia, refuses to join the Canadian federation, 298; agitation against, and final acceptance of, the Federation Act, 300, 301.

O'BRIEN, William, and the Home Rule movement, 189, 196, 199, 359; leader of the Independent Nationalists (1910), 359.
Obstruction, policy of. *See* House of Commons, Irish Nationalists, and Tory Democrats.

O'Connell, Daniel, and the repeal of the Union movement, reference to, 142.
Offices of profit under the Crown held by members of the Commons, Act of 1708 concerning, 85; modified, 1867, 85; division of legal opinion in the case of Mr. Gladstone, 85.
Old Age Pensions, establishment of (1908), 141, 350.
Orange River Colony. *See* South Africa.
Orange party in Ireland, and the Home Rule movement, 143, 177, 195, 196.
Ottawa, conference at (1894), 312.
Outlook, the political, in 1911, 383, 384.

PAKINGTON, Dame Dorothy, franchise exercised by, in the reign of Elizabeth, 59.
Pakington, Sir John, and the sale of Crown lands in the Colonies, 294.
Palmer, Sir Roundell. *See* Selborne, Lord.
Palmerston, Viscount, political tranquillity under his second ministry, 1, 2, 19, 20, 67, 81; ministerial position with regard to finance in 1860, 352; his death, 3, 20.
Parish meetings and councils, establishment of, 125, 258-259. *See* Councils.
Parliamentary Oath, the Act of 1866, 222; (1888), 227.
Parliament, Houses of. *See* Commons and Lords. Parliament Bill of 1911, 343-384; Parliamentary reform and its consequences, 1-66; *see also* Reform; Parliaments of the Empire, suggestions for, 163, 164, 339-342; Party in, 67-141; *see also* Party; Power, balance of, in, 88, 98, 119, 129, 131, 147, 168, 200, 357-360; predominance of the Irish party in 1910, 200, 357-360; self-governing Colonies, their relation to the Home Government, 293-342.
Parliament Bill, the, 343-384.
Action of the House of Lords during the Parliament of 1906, 343; their opposition of Government measures, 343-344, 348-349; Government difficulties, 344-346; Sir Henry Campbell-Bannerman's resolution (1907), 346-349, 355, 363; Mr. Balfour on the relation between the two Houses (1907), 349-350; questions of finance, 350-352; the Budget of 1909, 352; Lords' claim of the right to force a dissolution, 352-353; their rejection of the Budget and its financial consequences, 353-355; their action regarded as a breach of privilege by the Commons, 355; the general election of Jan., 1910, 355; its results, 357-59; dissensions in the new Parliament, 359-361; debate on the King's speech, 360; Mr. Asquith's resolutions with regard to the relation of the two Houses, 363-65. The Budget passed by the Lords in 1910, 366; death of King Edward VII., 366; conference of party leaders, 366-368; advice of the Ministers of the Crown to King George V., 368-369, 379, 381, 382; proposals of reconstitution moved in the Upper House, Lord Rosebery's 362, 369-370; Lord Lansdowne's 370, 373, 374; the Referendum, 371, 373; General Election, Dec., 1910, 372; the Parliament Bill passed by the Commons (1911), 372; the Lords' amendments, 376-378; Lord Lansdowne's advice of non-resistance, 380; active opposition by Lord Halsbury's party, 380-381; votes of censure on the Government moved by Mr. Balfour, and Lord Curzon, 381-82; the Bill passes (Aug. 10, 1911), 382; retrospect and political outlook, 383-384.

Parnell, Charles Stewart, 27, 93-99, 143-182, 339-340; character and policy, 27, 93-99, 143, 148-153, 161, 163, 165, 181; visit to America, 155; imprisonment, 101, 160; leader of the Irish party (1880), 93, 157; the Phœnix Park murders, accused of condoning, the forged letters, 122-124, 181; his acquittal, 181; his retirement from leadership, 182; his death (1891), 182.
Parnellism and crime, the forged letters, 122-124, 181, 182.
Party (1865-1909), 67-141.
Close of an era, 67; influence of the great Whig families ended, 67; the new leaders, 67-68; dangers to party government, 95; new tendencies of parties (1909), 141.
Conservatives, under Mr. Disraeli and Lord Salisbury, 69-118, 127-131; Unionist coalition and its effects, 115, 118-120; the South African War and its effects, 130-131; Mr. Balfour Premier, 131; the modern Conservative party, 132; Mr. Balfour resigns, 136.

INDEX TO VOLUME III

Irish Nationalist (Home Rule) party under Mr. Parnell and Mr. Redmond, 88-104, 122-124.
Labour party, rise of, 137-140.
Liberals, under Mr. Gladstone, 67-124; Lord Rosebery Premier, 125, 129; depressed condition of Liberalism, 128, 129; Sir H. Campbell-Bannerman Premier, 136-137; the trend of legislation at the close of 1909, 140-141; rejection of the Budget (1909), 141.
Radical party, 74-75, 77-78, 81, 90-92, 109, 114, 117.
Tory Democrats and Lord Randolph Churchill, 104-109, 119.
Unionist party, its rise and development, 106-111, 115, 118-120; Tariff Reform and, 132, 134, 141. *See also* Parliament, balance of power in, and the Parliament Bill of 1911.
Passive Resisters, and the Education Act of 1902, 233.
Patronage system, evils of, 270; its gradual abolition, 270, 271. *See also* Scottish Church.
Payment of members of Parliament, 33, 34, 43, 57 *n.*
Pearson, C., *National Life and Character*, by, reference to, 129 *n.*
Peel, Mr. Speaker, allows Mr. Bradlaugh to take the oath, 226.
Peel, Sir R., repeal of the Corn Laws, 19, 20 *n.*
Peers, the Royal prerogative to create, 345, 360, 365, 368-369, 374, 379, 380, 382. *See also* Life Peerages.
Perceval, Mr., his acceptance of office in the Treasury in 1809, cited as a precedent, 85.
Phœnix Park murders, and the Parnell letters, 122-123, 161, 181.
Plural voting, question of, 42, 48, 344. *See also* Redistribution of seats.
Political Associations: *Conservative*, 63 *n.*, 106-109, 121; *Irish*, 88, 115, 123, 143-145, 150, 153, 157, 159, 160, 162, 189-191, 194, 195; *Liberal*, 63 *n.*, 90, 91, 100, 106, 117, 118; *National Service*, 282; *Socialist*, 282; *Women's Suffrage*, 60, 63 *n.*
Poor Law Reform, 247, 253, 257-258, 264-266; out-door relief order, 264 *n.*
Premiers. *See* Asquith, H. H.; Balfour, A. J.; Campbell-Bannerman, Sir H.; Derby, Lord; Disraeli, B.; Gladstone, W. E.; Palmerston, Viscount; Rosebery, Lord; Russell, Lord; Salisbury, Lord.

Pretoria, Convention of (1881), 331.
Prison Reform, 249.
Prisoners' Evidence Amendment Act (1898), 289-90; Criminal Court of Appeal instituted (1907), 291.
Privy Council, origin and work of, the Judicial Committee of, 203, 263, 318-323.
Probate, Court of. *See* Judicature Reform.
Progressives and Moderates. *See* London County Council.
Proportional representation, importance of, 57, 59.
Protection of Life and Properties' Bill, 101, 102.
Public Health Acts, 246-249, 257, 268.
Purchase of Commissions. *See* Army reform.

QUARTER Sessions and county rates, legislation affecting, 250.
Queen's University (Belfast), unsectarian character of, 217, 218, 243, 244; effect of University Act on (1908), 243-244.

RABIES, extinction of, through the muzzling order brought in by Mr. Long, 267.
Redistribution of seats, 5, 9, 10, 13, 29, 30, 34, 35, 38-42, 46-48, 110, 111.
Acts of 1867 and 1868, 9, 10.
Act of 1885, 40; Queen's intervention concerning the Bill of 1884, 38.
Mr. Trevelyan's Bill, 1876-1879, 29, 30, 31.
Scotch and Irish Bills, 13.
Unionist movement for fresh redistribution, 46-48. *See also* Franchise.
Redmond, John, his Home Rule policy, 184, 186, 193, 197, 360-361, 365; leader of the Nationalist party in 1900, 190.
Referendum, the, proposals for, by the Unionist party, 371, 373.
Reform Acts and Bills. *See* Reform, Parliamentary.
Reform, Parliamentary, and its consequences, 1-66.
Political tranquillity during Lord Palmerston's last administration, 1-2; attempts to disturb the franchises of 1832, 2; revival of reform, 3; Earl Russell's Bill (1866), 4-6; Earl Derby's Bill (1867), 8-12; Scotch and Irish Reform Acts, 13, 14; Election Petitions and Corrupt Practices Act (1868), 14; abolition of voting by proxies, 14; constitu-

tional changes resulting from the Reform Act of 1867, 15-22; the Reform Act of 1832, its effect, 17-19, 27; Lord Russell's Life Peerage Bill (1869), 22, 24; the Ballot, 24, 25; the Ballot Act (1872) and its results, 26, 27; Mr. Trevelyan's County and Rural Franchise Bills (1873-75), 28, 29; his resolutions in favour of redistribution (1876-1879), 29-31; Corrupt and Illegal Practices Act (1883), 31-33; Reform movement (1883), 33-34; Franchise Bill (1884), 34-39; secured by the intervention of the Queen, 38; Conservative character of the Act, 39; Redistribution of Seats' Act (1885), 40-42; Registration Bill (1894), 43; proposals for the reform of the House of Lords, 43-45, 51-55; Reform in abeyance (1895-1905), 45; Unionist movement for redistribution, 46-48; Plural Voting Bill, 48; London Government Bill (1909), 49, 50; electoral anomalies, 55; proportional representation, 57-59; Women's Suffrage movement, 59-66; militant methods, 63, 64; the Conciliation Bill, 65, 66. *See also* the Parliament Bill of 1911 and under titles of Acts and Bills.

Reform of the House of Lords. *See* Lords, and the Parliament Bill. *See also* Army, Civil Service and Judicature Reform, and Local Government.

Registration Act of 1894, its effect on the franchise, 43.

Religion and the State, 201-245.

Relations of the State to Religion, 201; the National Church, 202-203; Act of 1868, 203; the Irish Church disestablished and disendowed, (1869), 204-212; University tests, 212-213; Education, in its relation to religion and the State, 213-221, 228-239; the Public Worship Regulation Act (1874), 221; the Parliamentary oath and the Bradlaugh case, 222-227; the Burials Act, (1880), 228; religious neutrality of the State, 228; the question of disestablishment, 240; movement for Welsh disestablishment, 240-242; legalisation of marriage with a deceased wife's sister (1907), 242; Religious Disabilities Removal Bill (1891), 243; Irish University Act (1908), 243-244; amendment of the Royal Declaration (1910), 244-245.

See also the Church of England, the Irish, Scotch and Welsh Church, and under Education.

Religious Disabilities still extant, 243.

Religious Tests, abolition of, 77, 84, 212. *See also* Nonconformists, and Irish Universities.

Representation, constitutional changes in, following the Reform Act of 1867, 15, 16. *See also* the Franchise.

Rhodes, Cecil, his South African policy, 331-333, 339, 340.

Riots. *See* Hyde Park riots.

Ritualists and the Public Worship Regulation Act of 1874, its injustice and ineffectiveness, 221, 222.

Rogers, Sir F., on self-government in the Australian colonies, 302.

Roman Catholic Church in England, demand for denominational teaching in the schools, 235, 239; Ecclesiastical Titles Act, 212; Religious Disabilities Bill (1891), 243; University tests abolished, 212. *See also*, Ireland, and the Coronation oath.

Rosebery, Lord, Administration (1894-1895), 43, 46, 125, 129; character and policy, 125, 126, 185, 354; reform of the House of Lords, resolutions and proposals for, 44, 45, 51, 54, 55, 362, 369, 374.

Round Table Conference (1887), the, 179, 180; policy suggested by, rejected by Mr. Parnell, 180.

Royal Commissions, 58, 59, 131, 176, 247, 248, 285, 291.

Royal Declaration. *See* Coronation Oath.

Royal prerogative of mercy, 291.

Ruskin, John, and social reform, 77.

Russell, Earl, Prime Minister (1865), 3, 19, 20; his Life Peerage Bill, 22-24; his Reform Bill (1866), 4-6.

St. Asaph, Bishop of, compromise proposed by, with regard to religious teaching in schools (Education Bill of 1908), 238.

Salisbury, Lord, Administrations, *first*, 112, 113; *second*, 119, 120, 124; *third*, 127; resigns 1902, 131.

Character and policy, 38, 39, 115, 118-119, 127, 128, 131, 311.

Colonial Conference of 1887, speech at, 311.

Home Rule, his attitude towards, 36, 113, 167-168, 170.

Schnadhorst, Mr. and the Liberal Association, 90, 104, 117.

INDEX TO VOLUME III

Scotland, Appeals and the Supreme Court, 287.
Church of, transference of patronage, 222.
Land Bills and Laws, 140, 348.
Reform Act (1868), 13, 72.
Scudamore, Mr., and unauthorised expenditure (1872), 84.
Second Chamber, reconstitution of. *See* Reform of the House of Lords and the Parliament Bill.
Selborne, Lord (Roundell Palmer), Judicature reform initiated by, 284, 285, 287, 288.
Shackleton, Mr., and the Conciliation Bill for Women's suffrage, 65.
Shaftesbury, Lord, on party politics, 80, 81, 87.
Shaw, Mr., and Home Rule, 98-99.
Shawe-Taylor, Captain, proposed conference between landlords and tenants (Irish), 191, 192.
Short Service. *See* Army reform.
Small Holdings Act, 140-141.
Social Reform, movement towards, 78, 80, 81, 89, 131, 137-141. *See also* Local Government Reform.
Socialism, rise and development of, 137-141; Congress of Trades Unions and Socialist Associations, 138. *See also* Democracy, and the Labour Party.
South Africa, British expansion in, 328-337; Orange River Colony, 328-329, 334; Cape Colony, 329; the Transvaal, 330-331, 334; first Boer War, 331; convention of Pretoria, 331; Imperial developments, 331; Jameson's Raid, 333; second Boer War, 333; concessions of self-government and constitution of the New Colonies, 334-335; Union of South Africa (1909), 336; the Native question, 338.
South African Wars, and their political effects, 46, 130, 131, 190, 231, 315, 331, 333.
Stanley, Lord, and the Reform Bill of 1866, 5; amendment on the Irish Church question, 207.
Star Chamber, legislative powers of, 263, 319.
State, the. *See* Education and the State, and Religion and the State.
State aid to voluntary schools, 131, 230-237, 239.
Survival of offices and institutions in name only, 202, 203.

Taff Vale case, decision of the Lords against the Trades Unions, 135, 140.

Tariff Reform and Free Trade, Mr. Balfour's policy, 133-136.
Mr. Chamberlain's policy, 132-134, 136, 141, 351-352, 356.
The Budget of 1909, as an alternative to Tariff Reform, 356. *See also* the Colonies, Imperial Preference.
Tenants' Relief Bill (Irish), 176; Royal Commission in favour of, 177.
Territorial Army. *See* Army reform.
Times, the, and the alleged "Parnell Letters". *See* Parnell, C. S.
Toleration Acts (1689), 221; (1779), 221. *See also* Religion and the State.
Tory Democratic Party. *See* Lord Randolph Churchill, and Party.
Trade, Board of, its establishment, 269.
Trade Disputes Act, 140.
Trades Unions, 135, 136, 138, 140; the Taff Vale decision, 135, 140; Congress of Socialist Associations, 138.
Transvaal. *See* South Africa.
Trevelyan, Sir Charles, and Civil Service reform, 271.
Trevelyan, Mr. (afterwards Sir George), County Franchise Bill of, 28-29; Resolutions in favour of redistribution, 29-31; retires from the Cabinet over the question of Home Rule, 117, 171-172; Round Table Conference, 180.
Trinity College (Dublin). *See* Ireland, Universities.

Ulster Protestant Party in Ireland. *See* Orange party.
Unauthorised expenditure (1869-1872), inquiry into, 84-86.
Union, the, danger in a preponderance of Irish members recognised by Pitt, 41. *See also* Home Rule movement.
Unionist Party, in the House of Commons. *See* Party.
United Irish League, founded (1897) by Wm. O'Brien, 189-191.
United States, and the *Alabama* claim, 79, 298.
University Test Acts, passing of, 77, 212.
Universities, Irish. *See* Ireland.

Vereeniging, the Peace of, 333.
Victoria, colony of. *See* Australasian colonies.
Victoria, Queen, references to, 38, 39, 111, 211, 276; intervention of, on behalf of the Franchise Bill of 1884, 38, 39; royal warrant for

the abolition of Army purchase, 276.
Voluntary schools. *See* the Church and Education.
Vote of censure on the Government, moved by Mr. Balfour in the Commons, 381; by Lord Curzon in the Upper House, 382.

WALES, disestablishment of the Church in, movement towards, 122, 129, 240, 241; Bill of 1909 withdrawn, 241.
Walpole, Mr., and the Hyde Park riots, 11.
History of Twenty-five Years, references to, 6 *n.*, 11 *n.*, 97 *n.*
Wellington, Duke of, attitude towards the Reform Bill of 1832, cited as a precedent, 380.
Wilkes, Mr., refusal of the House of Commons to allow him to take his seat (1769), 228.
William III., prohibition of purchase of commissions in the army by, 273.
William IV., his refusal to create peers, 345.

Wodehouse, Sir Philip, and the question of Imperial Government in Cape Colony, 329.
Women's Liberal Federation, and the suffrage, 63 *n.*
Women's Liberal Unionist Association and the suffrage, 63 *n.*
Women's Suffrage, question of, 50, 59-66; franchise exercised by women in the Middle Ages, 59; beginnings of the movement (1867), John Stuart Mill and, 60; deputation to Mr. Asquith in 1908, 50; municipal franchise given to women, 61, 262; women's suffrage in the colonies, 63; the Conciliation Bill, 65-66; militant methods, 63-64; non-party character of, an obstacle, 64.
Woolff, Sir H. D., and the "Fourth Party," 104, 105; his objection to allow Mr. Bradlaugh to take the oath, 224.
Workmen's Compensation Act, 140.
Wyndham, Mr., Irish policy of, 186, 190, 191, 193, 196, 197; Land Purchase Bill (1903), 193.

STANDARD HISTORICAL WORKS.

Works by LORD MACAULAY.

COMPLETE WORKS OF LORD MACAULAY.
Cabinet Edition. 16 vols. Post 8vo, £4 16s.
"Albany" Edition. 12 vols. With 12 Portraits. Large crown 8vo, 3s. 6d. each.
"Edinburgh" Edition. 8 vols. 8vo, 6s. each.

HISTORY OF ENGLAND FROM THE ACCESSION OF JAMES THE SECOND.
Popular Edition. 2 vols. Crown 8vo, 5s. | Cabinet Edition. 8 vols. Post 8vo, 48s.
Student's Edition. 2 vols. Crown 8vo, | "Albany" Edition. 6 vols. Large crown
12s. | 8vo, 3s. 6d. each.
People's Edition. 4 vols. Crown 8vo, 16s. | "Edinburgh" Edition. 4 vols. 8vo, 6s. each.

CRITICAL AND HISTORICAL ESSAYS, with LAYS OF ANCIENT ROME. In 1 volume.
Popular Edition. Crown 8vo, 2s. 6d. | "Silver Library" Edition. Cr. 8vo, 3s. 6d.

CRITICAL AND HISTORICAL ESSAYS.
Student's Edition. 1 vol. Crown 8vo, 6s. | "Edinburgh" Edition. 3 vols. 8vo, 6s. each.
"Trevelyan" Edition. 2 vols. Cr. 8vo, 9s. | Cabinet Edition. 4 vols. Post 8vo, 24s.
Library Edition. 3 vols. 8vo, 36s.

MISCELLANEOUS WRITINGS AND SPEECHES.
Popular Edition. Crown 8vo, 2s. 6d. | Student's Edition. Crown 8vo, 6s.
Cabinet Edition. Including Indian Penal Code, Lays of Ancient Rome, and Miscellaneous Poems. 4 vols. Post 8vo, 24s.

Works by WILLIAM EDWARD HARTPOLE LECKY.

HISTORY OF ENGLAND IN THE EIGHTEENTH CENTURY.
Library Edition. 8 vols. 8vo. Vols. I. and II., 36s. Vols. III. and IV., 36s. Vols. V. and VI., 36s. Vols. VII. and VIII., 36s.
Cabinet Edition. ENGLAND. 7 vols. Crown 8vo, 5s. net each. IRELAND. 5 vols. Crown 8vo, 5s. net each.

LEADERS OF PUBLIC OPINION IN IRELAND: FLOOD, GRATTAN, O'CONNELL. 2 vols. 8vo, 25s. net.

HISTORY OF EUROPEAN MORALS FROM AUGUSTUS TO CHARLEMAGNE. 2 vols. Crown 8vo, 10s. net.
POPULAR EDITION. 1 vol. Crown 8vo, 2s. 6d. net.

HISTORY OF THE RISE AND INFLUENCE OF THE SPIRIT OF RATIONALISM IN EUROPE. 2 vols. Crown 8vo, 10s. net.
POPULAR EDITION. 1 vol. Crown 8vo, 2s. 6d. net.

DEMOCRACY AND LIBERTY.
Library Edition. 2 vols. 8vo, 36s. | Cabinet Edition. 2 vols. Crown 8vo, 10s. net.

HISTORICAL AND POLITICAL ESSAYS. 8vo, 5s. net.

Works by SAMUEL RAWSON GARDINER, D.C.L.

HISTORY OF ENGLAND, from the Accession of James I. to the Outbreak of the Civil War, 1603-1642. 10 vols. Crown 8vo, 5s. net each.

HISTORY OF THE GREAT CIVIL WAR, 1642-1649. 4 vols. Crown 8vo, 5s. net each.

HISTORY OF THE COMMONWEALTH AND PROTECTORATE, 1649-1656. 4 vols. Crown 8vo, 5s. net each.

THE STUDENT'S HISTORY OF ENGLAND. 378 Illustrations. Crown 8vo, 12s.

CROMWELL'S PLACE IN HISTORY. Crown 8vo, 3s. 6d.

OLIVER CROMWELL. With Frontispiece. Crown 8vo, 5s. net.

LONGMANS, GREEN AND CO., 39 Paternoster Row, London;
New York, Bombay and Calcutta.

STANDARD HISTORICAL WORKS.

A HISTORY OF BRITISH INDIA. By Sir WILLIAM WILSON HUNTER, K.C.S.I., M.A., LL.D.
  Vol. I., Introductory to the Overthrow of the English in the Spice Archipelago, 1623. With 4 Maps. 8vo, 18s. Vol. II., To the Union of the Old and New Companies under the Earl of Godolphin's Award, 1708. 8vo, 16s.

A CRITICAL EXAMINATION OF IRISH HISTORY: being a Replacement of the False by the True. From the Elizabethan Conquest to the Legislative Union of 1800. By T. DUNBAR INGRAM, LL.D. 2 vols. 8vo, 6s. net.

HISTORY OF THE INDIAN MUTINY, 1857-1858. By Sir JOHN W. KAYE and Col. G. B. MALLESON. 6 vols. Crown 8vo, 3s. 6d. each.

THE CONSTITUTIONAL HISTORY OF ENGLAND SINCE THE ACCESSION OF GEORGE III. By Sir THOMAS ERSKINE MAY, K.C.B. (Lord Farnborough). 8vo. Vols. I. and II. 1760-1860. 15s. net. Vol. III. By FRANCIS HOLLAND. 1860-1910. 12s. 6d. net.

HISTORY OF THE ROMANS UNDER THE EMPIRE. By the Very Rev. CHARLES MERIVALE, late Dean of Ely. 8 vols. Crown 8vo, 3s. 6d. each.

WORKS BY FREDERIC SEEBOHM, LL.D., F.S.A.

THE ENGLISH VILLAGE COMMUNITY. With 13 Maps and Plates. 8vo, 12s. 6d.

THE TRIBAL SYSTEM IN WALES: being Part of an Inquiry into the Structure and Methods of Tribal Society. With an Introductory Note on the Unit of Family Holding under Early Tribal Custom. With 3 Maps. 8vo, 12s. 6d.

TRIBAL CUSTOM IN ANGLO-SAXON LAW: being an Essay supplemental to (1) "The English Village Community"; (2) "The Tribal System in Wales". 8vo, 12s. 6d.

CARTHAGE AND THE CARTHAGINIANS. By R. BOSWORTH SMITH, M.A. With Maps, Plans, etc. Crown 8vo, 3s. 6d.

WORKS BY W. STUBBS, D.D., LATE BISHOP OF OXFORD.

HISTORICAL INTRODUCTIONS TO THE ROLLS SERIES. 8vo, 12s. 6d. net.

LECTURES ON EUROPEAN HISTORY. 8vo, 12s. 6d. net.

LECTURES ON EARLY ENGLISH HISTORY. 8vo, 12s. 6d. net.

GERMANY IN THE EARLY MIDDLE AGES, 476-1250. With 2 Maps. 8vo, 6s. net.

GERMANY IN THE LATER MIDDLE AGES, 1200-1500. With 2 Maps. 8vo, 7s. 6d. net.

THE AMERICAN REVOLUTION. By the Right Hon. Sir G. O. TREVELYAN, Bart. Vols. I., II., III., IV. Crown 8vo, 5s. net each.

ENGLAND IN THE AGE OF WYCLIFFE. By GEORGE MACAULAY TREVELYAN. 8vo, 6s. net.

ESSAYS INTRODUCTORY TO THE STUDY OF CONSTITUTIONAL HISTORY. Edited by HENRY OFFLEY WAKEMAN, M.A., and ARTHUR HASSALL, M.A. Crown 8vo, 6s.

WORKS BY SIR SPENCER WALPOLE, K.C.B.

HISTORY OF ENGLAND FROM THE CONCLUSION OF THE GREAT WAR IN 1815 TO 1858. 6 vols. Crown 8vo, 6s. each.

THE HISTORY OF TWENTY-FIVE YEARS (1856-1880). Vols. I. and II. 1856-1870. 8vo, 24s. net. Vols. III. and IV. 1870-1880. 8vo, 21s. net.

LONGMANS, GREEN AND CO., 39 Paternoster Row, London;
New York, Bombay and Calcutta.